DRAGON TAELS

DRAGON TAELS

MEMORIES OF THE GOLDEN AGE

AT

HONG KONG INTERNATIONAL SCHOOL

EDITED BY
DAVID GRANT KOHL

WISDOM HALL
PORTLAND, OREGON
2007

Spirit Press/Wisdom Hall Publishing
PO Box 12346
Portland Oregon 97212
www.wisdomhall.org

Dedicated to

Bill Mahlke

Christian Fontaine Myers

✔

Golden Tales From the Dragon's Tail

Taels -- I remember the moment as if it were yesterday, instead of 1973.

It was my first semester teaching high school art and ceramics at Hong Kong International School, set above the idyllic Repulse Bay on the south face of Hong Kong Island. Since the students had learned all the basic hand-building methods of working with clay, I had given them an assignment to construct a model of something lying around their house -- a sculpture of an appliance, or furniture piece, or artwork -- an object that was ordinary or common. They had two days to do the studio work.

We assembled around a large table for the critique session after the pieces were made, but not completely dry. Reproductions of cameras, irons, sofas, and kitchen appliances, even toys were displayed for the discussion. I had made a model of an electric toaster. One student, a very likable Eurasian freshman with a positive attitude, set down four small flattened rectangles about 1" by 2" about 1/8 " thick. They had some scratchings and drawings on each side. Disappointed at the lack of complexity in his piece, and thinking that he had turned lazy on me, or done these at the last minute, I chided him about the tile-like objects:

"OK, Patrick, tell me about these. They don't seem to represent much work"
"So, Patrick, what are they?"
"Oh, Mr. Kohl, I think I did a lot of detail work on the surfaces"
"So, Patrick, what are they?"
"But they are taels!"
"Tails?"
"No! You know, taels"
"Sorry, Mr. Hotung, maybe you should explain to me what a tale is"
"Oh, you know, taels of gold."
"OK, I'm new here, just what is a tael of gold"
"Come on, Mr., Kohl, you know, they're like ingots of gold, about an ounce"
"You've got ingots of gold laying around your house?"
"Yeah, my grandma gave me some for my birthday. They're paperweights."

That was the real beginning of my journey to understand the wide variety of students I would have in my classes for the next seven years. Adolescents from so many different walks of life –wealthy long-established Chinese and Eurasian families, kids from the US, and other Consulates and Embassies, missionary kids, children of businessmen from more than 30 countries, youngsters whose dads were war correspondents covering the Vietnam conflict, families of "China Watchers," some displaced and unhappy juniors and seniors who had been yanked from the comfort of their mid-western US schools to follow dad's career - leaving Peoria, Midland, Tulsa, Dallas, Washington DC, and just about every major European, African, and Asian metropolis.

Me? I was a greenhorn high school teacher from Chicago, with four years' experience, a new MA in Art Ed, and a lovely wife of less than a year. We'd accepted an appointment to serve through the Board of Missions for the Missouri Synod Lutheran church. It was a time of great changes as the USA was in turmoil over Watergate, a worldwide petroleum crisis was growing, and neighboring China was embroiled in the Cultural Revolution.

I was embarking on the most excellent teaching experience of my life.

HKIS was just six years old. We had a sleek air conditioned seven-floor building with one elevator that was off-limits to students, 1200 students in a structure built for 800 and classes from Kindergarten through 12th grade using an American curriculum. The students all wore light blue uniforms (all students in Hong Kong wore school uniforms) with the HKIS patch sewn or stuck on the chest. They arrived at school via walking, private cars, pak pais, light bus, China Motor Bus # 6 or # 73, or by school busses operated by the Kwoon Chueng Bus Company. Initially the school mascot was a medieval European Crusader but was changed in time to the Dragon, the ancient and contemporary symbol for China and oriental culture.

HKIS is 40 years old with the graduating class of 2007. It's time to look foreword and backwards. I came to the realization that the students and staff at HKIS had experienced many wonderful and unique adventures in those early years in Repulse Bay. Kindergartners were being fed lunch by their amahs in the school cafeteria side-by-side with the high school students. Mrs. Chan ran a tight ship in the cafeteria selling drinks and ice cream treats like Nutty Nibbles to students of all ages, while offering (behind the counter) quality jade pieces to interested staff. The delicious ice cream came in metal cans from Dairy farm. Many families had several students at the school, and they saw each other and worked with each other throughout the campus. Seniors helped the elementary teachers. Sometimes small groups met in the hallways or stairwells. Three principals had offices while the founding Headmaster was content to operate from a converted closet.

Before and after school, students functioned in Hong Kong with amazing ease. They sailed, swam, rode horses, hiked, camped, partied, took Cotillion dance lessons, practiced their singing and instrumental skills, played squash, joined Rugby teams, had school sports, modeled clothing for advertisements, made short movie appearances and voice-overs, hob-knobbed with consular representatives, learned their father's businesses, walked the dog on the beach, shopped for their parents in the open air markets or at pseudo supermarkets, flew off to Bangkok or Singapore for weekends, traveled to European and Asian countries over week-long Interims, and socialized with their teachers at church, the American club, and at the Proms. They participated in fund-raising drives such as the annual Walk for a Million which benefited the Hong Kong community.

Social life revolved around several grand hotels on both sides of Hong Kong Harbour, several night spots in WanChai and Tsim Sha Tsui viewing Hollywood movies in local theatres even though they were six months old and had Chinese subtitles, picnicking at Repulse Bay and Deep Water Bay beaches, sailing in the South China Sea and camping in the Sai Kung Peninsula and Tai Long Wan beach.

Teachers were dedicated to presenting quality material at the highest American standards so students would be competitive in college entrance procedures. They also coached, directed plays and musicals, organized art fairs, attended classes at Hong Kong University, and got involved in Hong Kong society. Several acted in plays presented by the Garrison players. They spent many hours with students on independent projects, weekend hikes, photo expeditions, church and scout activities. We were family away from family. We shared the celebrations of births, baptisms, confirmations and graduations, the sadness of death, spontaneous meals at Wah Fu and The American restaurants, holidays together in the absence of our families "back home;" and several years of camping and feasting over the four-day Thanksgiving break at Tong Fuk beach on Lantau island.

Parents provided not only emotional and financial support to the school, they organized a Mothers Club that promoted extra-curricular events with the highlight being the annual World's Fair. It was truly a miniature representation of the United Nations. Nearly everyone felt included, respected for their nationality and religious backgrounds, and their own home customs. Students were encouraged to present aspects of their family's culture in class activities. The school was an island in the world, free of international tensions.

It wasn't all easy sailing. The calamities that could befall any community hit this one particularly hard because almost everybody knew everyone else. Several tragic deaths of students forced the community to face mortality, sorrow, and eventual healing. A number of parents had died or been killed while their students attended HKIS and those losses affected the atmosphere but built camaraderie through the healing. There were crisis's over the usual "drugs, sex, and rock n' roll." They were not to be dismissed lightly but were issues for concern, dialogue and resolution. HKIS was not a good fit for all the staff so some left earlier than contracted. And some family situations forced unplanned departures from the Colony.
Students and adults experienced a concentrated adventure with life.

This book is a compilation of their own views and memories of Golden Days in Hong Kong and HKIS. The Dragon Taels and the way I've chosen to present the writings is modeled on the Roshomon Effect (individuals experience a common event differently.) Some items were written with this book in mind, many snippets were gleaned from the alumni list-serv, DragonTrain. Other writings were penned in the '60s and '70s as parts of letters home or informational reports. The exchange rate at the times referred to in this book was approximately HK$ 5 = US $ 1.

Through the miracle of e-mail, this book was compiled in about two months. It is not exhaustive, many individuals of great importance are not mentioned, but the ones who are represent the friendship and mutual enjoyment of those who have written.

Welcome to the Golden Age of HKIS. Happy 40th Anniversary!!!

David G Kohl
HKIS Art Teacher 1973-1980
Portland, Oregon
June 2007

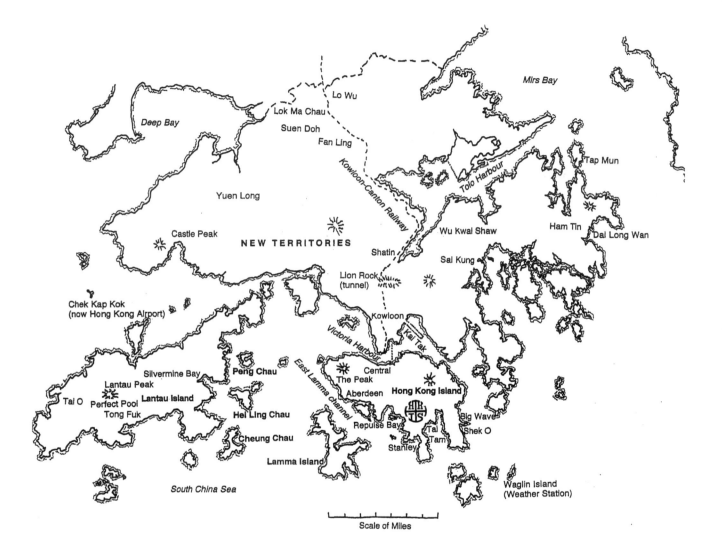

Lo Wu

Mirs Bay

Lok Ma Chau

Deep Bay

Suen Doh

Fan Ling

Tap Mun

Tolo Harbour

Kowloon-Canton Railway

Yuen Long

Castle Peak

Wu Kwai Shaw

Ham Tin

Dai Long Wan

NEW TERRITORIES

Shatin

Sai Kung

Lion Rock
(tunnel)

Chek Kap Kok
(now Hong Kong Airport)

Kowloon

Kai Tak

Victoria Harbour

Silvermine Bay

Peng Chau

Central
The Peak

Lantau Peak

Aberdeen

Hong Kong Island

Tai O

Perfect Pool Lantau Island

Tong Fuk

East Lamma channel

Hei Ling Chau

Repulse Bay

Tai
Tam

Big Wave
Shek O

Cheung Chau

Stanley

Lamma Island

Waglin Island
(Weather Station)

South China Sea

Scale of Miles

HONG KONG TERRITORY

These three maps show the major locations referred to in various writings in this
book by the alumni and former staff of Hong Kong International School. These are
many of the places that were most important in our social life, as well as weekend
hiking, camping, and sailing adventures. A few of them are our own unique names
for places, and may not appear on standard maps as Perfect Pool, Daimler Falls, or
Nubian Pool.....but we know where they are.   Ed.

HONG KONG ISLAND

xiv

DRAGON tAELS

Chapter One -
History - How HKIs came to be

In presenting a brief historical summary of Hong Kong International School, the question of where to start this "golden" tale is philosophic. Martin Luther could be creditied with the origins of strong Christian education for all. Or, one could start in the mid-19th century when Christian missionaries first came to China from England and America. Jesuits had established a presence in the 16th century, but the new wave of the 1800's were mostly Protestants, among them Lutherans of various synods. Lutherans were active in central China, in costal cities (known as the Treaty Ports after the 1860s), and in the British Crown Colony of Hong Kong by the time of the Japanese occupation. At least three HKIS faculty were born of missionary parents, some spending the war years in POW camps.

Christian missionaries were forced out of China in 1949, many fleeing to Hong Kong to continue their work in exile. Missouri Synod Lutheran missionaries formed a Conference, and from that group, their education director Mel Kieschnick became instrumental in establishing a system of Lutheran schools, some on the roof tops of re-settlement estates. Because of their work, the HK Education Department was receptive to a private school for expatriates on Hong Kong Island, propopsed by a Lutheran congregation.

That congregation, Repulse Bay Lutheran Church, was pastored by Rev Leonard Galster. Under leadership of businessman Joseph Mache, and guidance from Mr. C. S. Hung of Hong Kong University, they formed the first Board of Directors for a potential American International School in 1963. Permission to proceed from the HK government came that year. An architect was engaged after a site was found and leased from Government in 1965. That building was under construction when Robert Christian and his family accepted the call as Headmaster, or 'head of school," and arrived in the summer of 1966.

Enthusiasm to open a school in the American tradition excellerated when Pan Am Airways made HK the base of their Asian operations in 1966. This was a result of the escalating Vietnam conflict, 1000 miles to the south. Within a month of his arrival, Bob was supervising a provisional school in a rented 6-flat apartment building on Chung Hom Kok Road. Over 150 students filled that Provisional school to over capacity in '66-'67 while construction on the permanent school in Repulse Bay concluded. On Sept 14, 1967, Hong Kong International School officially opened its doors with 650 students, 45 teachers, and a full K-12 curriculum.

While the original school was built to hold about 700 students, it was already overcrowded by 1969, and plans to build a second building across South Bay Close began. that building, an elementary school complete with a swimming pool and 14 residential apartments, was dedicated in 1975.

Continued student enrollment brought about study groups and plans for an entire second campus. A site was procured overlooking Tai Tam Bay, once a pirate's cove 6 miles to the east on HK island. The new high school was dedicated there in 1988, and the new middle school was added adjacent to that in 1993. Hence the current school, at age 40, is comprised of two geographic campuses, a student body of 2700, and a teaching staff of over 300. Over 4000 alumni have attended. Of these, about 800 reside in Hong Kong at the time of this writing.

- Ed.

1. A Chronology of Church of All Nations and HKIS:

1956 - Mel Kieschnick accepted position with Lutheran Missionary Conference of HK

1960 - The Mache´ family arrived in the British Crown Colony of Hong Kong. We attended Lutheran English Church Services at Concordia School in Kowloon.

There were no Churches on the HK side - especially around Repulse Bay, so Dorothy (Mrs. Mache´) and I decided to try and start a congregation in the Repulse Bay area.

Sept. 1961 - I wrote the HK conference. They replied that they were "too busy", because they were sent to do missionary work amongst the poor Chinese.

Nov. 1961 - When in the USA on a business trip, I stopped in St. Louis and explained my thoughts to Dr. H.H. Koppelmann - Ex Sec. of Board of World Missions. He was interested.

Early 1962 - Dr. Koppelmann visited Hong Kong. He and I and Dottie (Mrs. Mache´) sat in the reading room of the Repulse Bay Hotel where we proposed renting space to start a congregation. We asked for a 6 week trial and he said, "why not 6 months? I have two men here in HK studying Cantonese. I'll give you one and you can start." Since Rev. Leonard Galster was then already involved in the survey work he was assigned. It was made official by a HK conference resolution in Feb. 1962. We asked Mr. Ostroumoff if we could rent space at the Repulse Bay Hotel and he gave it for free. First worship services were held where the cake shop now is. ater we moved to the Reading Room.

March 4, 1962 – We held our first service (26 in Sunday School, 18 in worship service).

Total Sunday School and worship service attendances:

March '62 = 189
Nov. '62 = 399
April '63 = 538.

Sunday School was very successful with an average attendance of 100 (120 enrolled) in late '62 and early '63.

Jan. 1963 - A meeting of the male members of the congregation. It was agreed to work toward a permanent church building. Of this original group we still have with us Mr. Hung (Faye's father), Mr. Yamashita, Mr. Paul Li, Dottie and myself.

Feb. 1963 - A second meeting was held. The high cost of land almost ruled out a church building on its own. The idea was proposed to consider a school/church combination in hopes of obtaining a land grant from the HK government. It was proposed that we consider an "American School in Hong Kong" and everyone agreed!

The HK Conference was approached and they asked their Christian Education Committee to study the matter. Mr. Mel Kieschnick was then head of the committee and he really did a fine job for us. It was finally agreed that a school/church combination in Repulse Bay was feasible – with a 12 grade American curriculum.

11 April 1963 – I wrote the new Director of Education in HK proposing the school. Mel Kieschnick became principal of Concordia, Kowloon, That year Concordia had the highest number of students pass their GCE out of all the schools in HK. The Director of Education said, "If we must have an American type school in HK, then I'm glad that the Lutherans will be running it. They've got an excellent record. You will not, however, refer to it as an American school." Hence the International School label.

The school board from 1963 to 1965 was Mel Kieschnick, Joseph Mache´, Mr. C. S. Hung, and Rev. Leonard Galster.

28 April 1966 – The official ground breaking for the HK International School. William Wong was hired as architect.

Summer 1966 – Bob Christian arrives. Two female teachers also sent from the US.

Sept. 1966 – Provisional Primary School opened in an apartment building near Stanley.

Sept. 1967 – HKIS started in the new building. Growth was much faster than anticipated and the school was full within 3 years. We had predicted 5 years.

1969/70 – Work started on planning of new facilities.

1971 – Land was granted and architect Tao Ho was assigned.

I think that the Church of All Nations and HKIS were clearly an excellent example of the hand of the Lord at work. It was His doing and no one else's. Events occurred and things happened that were beyond what even the most optimistic could have hoped for.

Joseph H. Mache´, Board of Managers, 1971

2. Founding Repulse Bay Lutheran Church

• Beginnings

The initiative for beginning work in Repulse Bay, Hong Kong, came as a result of one family, the Joseph Mache' family, formerly members of Trinity Lutheran Church, Scarsdale, New York, moving to Repulse Bay from Tokyo, Japan in 1960. The Mache´s found that there were other Christians who also sought worship services, fellowship, and especially Sunday School for their children in the Repulse Bay area. It was only logical to raise the question, "Why not here?" Others in the area, although not Lutheran, asked the same question, "Why not at least a Sunday School?"

In September of 1961, the Hong Kong Lutheran Conference authorized me to work together with Mr. Mache' in making a survey of the Repulse Bay area and bring a report to conference. Since there were no other large rooms in the area, such as school auditoriums or the like, we decided to ask the manager of the Repulse Bay Hotel if they had any facilities in the hotel which we could use or rent. Mr. Ostroumoff, the manager, willingly consented to let us use the TV room on the ground floor for worship services and the reading room on the first floor for Sunday School. There was to be no rent or no other financial obligations, except that we were to tip the hotel boys who would bring up enough chairs from the dining room for our use each week.

With nothing more than that verbal agreement, we sent out invitation cards. They were delivered to about 400 homes in the immediate Repulse Bay area. Cards came back indicating that 23 children would come to the Sunday School and 16 adults checked that they would be interested in attending worship services. Since we had covered only about one fourth of the homes in the area, the results of these statistics gave us the indication that the potential of the entire Repulse Bay area would be at least 100 children in Sunday School, and enough for Worship Services to make work in Repulse Bay possible.

Dr. H. H. Koppelmann, Executive Secretary of the Board for World Missions of The Lutheran Church-Missouri Synod was in Hong Kong and saw the hotel facilities. His encouragement to give this work a good try was much appreciated at this time, and warranted our thinking in terms of a permanent church in Repulse Bay.

At the first Sunday gathering in the Hotel's TV room on March 4, 1962, the attendance was 26 in Sunday School and 18 in the Worship Service. Sunday School classes were taught by Mrs. D. Mache', Miss J. Mache', Mrs. L. Galster, and myself. Mrs. Galster played the portable organ which the Mache´s loaned to the congregation. Joseph Mache' supervised the coming and goings of the children. Since we had no hymnals, we used Sunday Bulletins from CPH by airmail, and made arrangements to have the entire Order of Service, including the hymns printed at the South China Morning Post.

From the beginning, the growth, especially of the Sunday School, was gradual, but steady, usually about 2 or 3 new children being added each Sunday. Our opinion is that the area now warrants intensive efforts and bold steps forward in the most immediate future. With the area growing as it is, there will be an increasing demand for a school, and it is taken for granted that if we do not continue to work towards a school someone else will. The same holds true of a church

• Factors involved in establishing permanency:

In a meeting on January 4, 1963, attended by male members of the congregation and others who had been attending the services regularly these problems were discussed. Some preliminary discussions had been held with the Crown Lands Dept. of the Hong Kong Government as to whether or not they would have any good sites available for a church in the Repulse Bay area. During this same meeting, the matter of operating a school was discussed, especially since there is neither church nor a school in the entire Repulse Bay area, High school students now travel over an hour to attend school in Kowloon at King George V School. This trip involves a seven mile bus ride, a ferry ride across the harbor, and another 3 mile bus ride. Primary pupils require almost a half hour drive to their schools.

Mr. Mel Kieschnick, Lutheran Coordinator of Education in Hong Kong, was asked if he would take the leadership in working with the congregation towards seeing through a school in Repulse Bay. In the meantime, there has been a great amount of agitation from various people, especially the American community, to build a school with an American-type curriculum.

The problem of staffing a primary school and high school with American teachers would be a large one. We talked about a primary school only, but this would make it difficult if not impossible for primary graduates to get into the British Middle Schools in Hong Kong. In the final analysis, it seemed best to think of all 12 grades, which would prepare students from America for college, as well as prepare a number of Chinese whose English-speaking ability was high enough for them to get in and through the school. The tuition does not seem to be a problem, since most people in the area receive educational allowances commensurate with the demands of the school.

3. Proposal for a school:

Mr. Kieschnick has suggested that the most desirable size or school would be one of about 1000 students, and the executive committee of the congregation has agreed that the church should seat no fewer than 250. This leaves us with the hope that the Hong Kong government will grant us a suitable site for a school, a partial grant and/or loan, plus a grant from the Board for World Missions for the rest of the cost of bringing the school building into reality.

What seems very necessary is that at this time not only the Hong Kong Conference, but also the Board for World Missions and other leaders in Synod express a desire to see this venture through. With coordinated efforts the challenge can be met. The Lord has given us the opportunity to extend our Faith Forward vision. With His continued blessing we shall see the fruits of the Holy Spirit's call to rise up and build.

Rev. Leonard Galster, edited report to the Lutheran Church-Missouri Synod, 1963

3. Lutheran Origins of Hong Kong International School

• Before the seed was planted

Beginning in late 1956 I had responsibility for planning a "colony-wide" system of Lutheran schools for Hong Kong. Our vision was audacious. We wanted preschools, elementary and high schools. We wanted to reach the poorest of the poor through special afternoon schools or even rooftop schools. We anticipated serving the emerging middle class. We hoped to appeal to a small segment of the wealthy. Our goal was for schools taught in both Chinese and English,

It wasn't until 1961 that our vision included an American or International School.

Our original Lutheran Church-Missouri Synod (LCMS) Missionary Conference was composed of missionaries forced out of China. These included 3 most remarkable women (2 deaconesses and one educator) and three pastors (two of whom had spouses.) They had all been evacuated (some on the very last flight out of ChungKing by a plane piloted by two Germans which was sent there by Lutheran World Federation to bring out the last of the fleeing missionaries. By the time my wife Jane and I got there there had been added 2 new missionary pastors (and their spouses) and another teacher/nurse.

I was 29 years old when I blindly accepted the call to be the Coordinator of Education for the mission. When I got the call to Hong Kong, I had to dig out a map to even see where HK was.

It is to the everlasting credit of my Chinese colleagues that they accepted me. They were all veteran educators from China I was the young non-Cantonese speaking upstart when I was named principal of Concordia Kowloon. Incidentally, had those teachers not done such a fabulous job of teaching there would not have been a HKIS. We had decided to send all of our Senior III students to the all important school leaving exams. We had a 100% pass rate-which I was told was unprecedented in the history of HK. Thus when we applied for HKIS from the Education Department, they knew that we Lutherans knew something about how to run good schools (by that time we must have had about half a dozen of them.)

The roof-top schools were under my responsibility. I had little to do with getting the first one going but did manage the process for the remaining three. The schools were literally on he roof-tops of Resettlement Estates. We had them in Wong Tai Sin, Hung Hom, and in Shek Kip Mei following the devastating fire there. An American business man called me one day and asked to see what the Lutherans were doing, because he had been refereed to us by some HK Government official. I showed him a our first roof-top school. He took me out to dinner, said he represented a Private Foundation, and promised to fund the opening of as many new roof-top schools as we could manage in the next fiscal year-and so we did!

•Planting the seed

Once we decided to seriously explore an "American School" we needed to find a potential site. I was very accustomed to inspecting piles of maps, plots, projected new towns and plans for land reclamation. Virtually every month I was once again at Crown Lands offices looking for potential school sites. It surprised both the British officials and me to find an as yet unallocated tiny spot in Repulse Bay. It was small, hilly, not completely accessible and occupied only by a kindly squatter farmer. We picked that site, figuring we would never need space to accommodate more than 500 students. That's where the first HKIS and Church of All Nations were born.

Amazingly, Government offered us not only the site but even an interest-free loan to assist with construction costs. Then this news hit the public. The red (Communist) press picked it up immediately and headlined: "FOUL, Unconscionable!" How could Government allocate limited space for a school for wealthy expatriates when there were still thousands upon thousands of Chinese children for whom there was no school space?

We, and Government, held our ground and the project continued.

In the midst of the negotiations an interesting development with the American Consulate developed. The question was asked whether salary stipends for USA Consulate employees could be allocated for their children to attend a church affiliated school. Was this "mixing Church and State"?

A representative from the State Department in Washington came to meet with me. I'll never forget that encounter in the lobby of the Peninsula Hotel. Turned out that I knew the man! He was

Paul Leubke, a graduate of my alma mater, Concordia Teachers College, River Forest, Illinois. We had earlier attempted to recruit his brother, Fritz Leubke, as an educational missionary to Hong Kong. We felt it best to keep those connections to ourselves. He agreed to declare the proposed school as one that might be helpful in attracting USA citizens to come live and work in Hong Kong and a good option for consulate-related families.

Among the many building issues to resolve was the issue of air-conditioned classrooms. Hong Kong Government had never before allowed that as an expenditure in schools receiving an interest-free construction loan from Government. We worked it out. We got air conditioning.

In late 1965 my family faced a medical emergency. Before leaving, I had been requested to stop at the Education Office for a personal confidential meeting with the Director of Education. He expressed personal concern for our family health issue. Then he stepped from behind his desk. He held up a sealed envelope. He told me, "I am putting this confidential memo into your official file. It states my conviction that you and your colleagues will make every honorable effort to live up to the conditions of your land grant and interest-free loan. I state that it is my recommendation that should unforeseen circumstances make it impossible for you to repay the loan, I recommend the loan be forgiven. I believe that strongly in the strength and wisdom of your dream."

He was right. The loan was, of course, fully repaid. *Mel Kieschnick, LCMS missionary, '56-'66*

Mel Kieschnick was replaced by Harold "Blackie" Schmidt. The two of them suggested to the Mission Board in 1966 that I be considered for the Headmaster role. They knew of me because I was currently the headmaster of Our Saviour in the Bronx, a New York Lutheran K-12 school supported by a single congregation.
Bob Christian, first headmaster '66 - '77

I briefly chatted with Dr. Mel Keischnick in 2003. He was the founding Chairman of the HKIS Board. I told him that I had started 1st grade the year the Provisional school opened in '66 out on Chung Hom Kok. He said that there were enough students that year that HKIS opened a year early. Does that mean we all most went to Island School? He remembered most of the families as being Pan

Am families and the dads flew US R&R troups in and out of Vietnam.

He reminisced about how he convinced the HK Government that the plot of land in Repulse Bay could not fit the local school that government had planned for to handle 1000+ students. His argument was than an international school for 500 students would fit better. After he won that argument, he then went back and had to convince the government that they could also build a church on the same site.   *Clayton Cole '77 written in 2003*

The way I remember the story is that 'things were GO for the school to be built' (government approvals, etc) so Mel was down at a government office going through plat books with officials, looking for a suitable site. At the 'same time', Rev Galster was at South Bay Close area and praying that this would be the site chosen. Apparently there were some flats off South Bay Road but the back part by the mountain where a farmer had squatted a claim was available. It was all kind of a miraculous coincidence.   *Lois Voeltz, teacher '96 - '03*

4. The Birth of HKIS...

The Hong Kong International School initially grew out of a need for a Lutheran Church in the Repulse Bay area.

When my husband, Joseph Maché, and I arrived in Hong Kong in 1960 with our 4 children after living 3 years in Japan, we looked for a Lutheran church to attend, but found nothing in the Repulse Bay area. We went to the Lutheran group in Kowloon and asked them for their help.

Joe went to the Hong Kong government and asked them what the provisions were for building a church. They advised him that churches were usually attached to schools. Taking this into consideration, Joe arranged for a series of conferences at our apartment on Headland Road with interested parties. Mel Keischnick, who was in charge of education for the Lutheran Church in Kowloon and Hong Kong helped to guide us.

We invited many people from the American community to our home to see what the consensus would be for starting a school with a church attached through the Lutheran educational system. The results ended in overwhelming support.

A board was formed which included Mr C. S. Hung, who was a Chinese professor at the University of Hong Kong, who gave us the Chinese view of the problems we would face. Other members of the board included businessman Tom Yamashita, Dr. Eugene Seltz, Paul Li, and Pastor Leonard Galster. My husband was made chairman of the board, and as chairman he traveled to St. Louis and Australia to seek funding for the school from the Lutheran communities.

We got funding from St. Louis and called in Walt Oestman who was a volunteer construction engineer from the US, and work officially began. While we were in the construction stage, we called Bob Christian as headmaster, and he began the Provisional School prior to the completion of construction of the large school building in Repulse Bay. In the meantime, the board hired locals and people from the Synod as teachers.

By 1967, the new school was initially only going to be open through the 7th grade. However, there was such a large influx of people who wanted their children to have a US curriculum that the school opened fully operative through the 12th grade. I supervised the art department on the 7th floor, teaching all grades.

We finally had our Lutheran church as part of the school building! Happy 40th Anniversary!!
Dorothy(Dottie) Maché
Art Department Chairman, 1967-'75

5. Reflections on eleven years as the first Headmaster

• Prologue

Following World War II, Hong Kong, a British Crown Colony, emerged as a center for business, banking, manufacturing and trade in the Far East. As Hong Kong continued to grow in the 1960's, it was heavily impacted by a flow of refugees from China, and by the war in Vietnam.

Meanwhile, Christianity was slowly making an impact in the dense population of the Colony, with missionaries from the United States and all over the world sharing the Gospel message through schools, churches, and social services. The government also did its best to provide primary level schooling for all, and even constructed school buildings and offered subsidy to legitimate bodies, including church groups, that could provide administration, supervision, and teachers to operate the schools. Hong Kong gradually became the Far East Center for worldwide business firms, including many American businesses, banks, and manufacturers.

The Lutheran Church-Missouri Synod, with its strong background in education, stepped into this picture, operating schools, primary and secondary, with the support both of the Hong Kong/British Government and of its national church body in the United States. Mel Kieschnick, Harold Schmidt, and Bob Dickhudt were among those who came to Hong Kong from the US as educational missionaries to spearhead these efforts.

There were no reservations within the Hong Kong Education Department in regard to schools that were operated by church groups with a religious/spiritual focus. Along with this, the Chinese Lutheran Schools in Hong Kong were held in high regard, since they were filling a tremendous need for the "exploding Chinese population" in the colony. In fact, in a novel idea to provide education with limited facilities, the Lutheran educational leaders headed by Mel Kieschnick and Harold Schmidt, had even opened rooftop schools in re-settlement estates.

Mel Kieschnick, had developed excellent relationships with the HK Education Department, and was able to secure authorization, a grant of land in Repulse Bay on Hong Kong Island, and a loan for the development of an American type school, kindergarten through grade 12. Assisted by American business leaders Joseph Maché and LCMS missionary Pastor Lenard Galster, plans moved forward, with strong support, financial and otherwise, from the LCMS Board for Missions

Building plans were designed by William Wong for a K-12 school of 1000, I was called as an LCMS educational missionary, to arrive in Hong Kong in the summer of 1966. I had served for 17 years at a multicultural elementary and high school program at Our Saviour Lutheran School in the Bronx, New York. My wife Arleen and I had four children. My task was to work with the supervision of construction and the development of the program for opening Hong Kong International School in 1967.

However, the American population in Hong Kong continued to rapidly increase, and as Hong Kong became a center for "R and R" American military during the war in Vietnam, Pan American Airways, quickly brought many pilots and their families, to Hong Kong. The provisional school, marking the beginning of the International School

a full year earlier than originally planned, grew out of the urgent requests of the growing American Community in Hong Kong. Consequently, I was notified in the spring of 1966 that my first task would be to open a provisional grades 1-6 school, shortly after our arrival in August. Along with this, Dow Chemical Corporation agreed to sponsor a limited program, especially for grades 7 & 8 of its company's families, utilizing the leadership services of Mr. P. S. Remington, a retired United States public school administrator.

•Opening the Provisional School - 1966-67

A month after our arrival on August 10, over 150 boys and girls from the USA, Hong Kong, and other parts of the world, would be on the scene - to live and learn together in a new school, in a new and very different setting.

An apartment building with six three bedroom apartments on Chung Hom Kok Road, between Repulse Bay and Stanley, was rented as the facility for the provisional school. This overlooked a beautiful beach and the South China Sea. Occasionally, American destroyers and aircraft carriers would be seen in the distance, giving rise to spontaneous cheers from the students gathered on the verandahs of their apartment classrooms.

I ordered textbooks, estimating quantities and curricular areas by guess while still in New York City, and had them sent to Hong Kong. Student desks were constructed by Chinese carpenters. Drinking water and coolers were placed into the classrooms, providing water later consumed in huge quantities by thirsty children coming in from the tropical sun.

Two young American women, Elizabeth Duval and Sue Witt, had been called by the LCMS Board for Missions to serve in the school, and arrived in Hong Kong before school opened, Sue actually coming on the scene only the day before classes began in her fifth grade classroom.

At least four more teachers were needed, an apartment building had to be converted into a school, a program developed, students registered, and preparations made for the opening scheduled for September 19. In addition to Liz and Sue, the good Lord led us Shirley Reedy an American whose husband was in Hong Kong on business, Mrs. Carr whose husband was in Hong Kong with the Canadian Government, Mrs. Button from Australia whose husband worked for an American firm in Hong Kong, Mrs. Cutler, wife of a British army officer, and Mrs. Ivy Vasey, whose husband worked with the British army as a civilian employee. Fortunately, these were all experienced teachers who could understand the Christian atmosphere and approach to be developed in the school, and they quickly became a team that carried out a very special ministry for that first year.

Mrs. Chan Fuen, whose husband worked at the Repulse Bay Hotel, became our staff person who helped us in various ways during the schoolday. Her son began work as our janitor after school hours, but he stayed only a few days, leaving a note, saying that he "enjoyed working for us, but had to leave, because later at night when he had to walk from the school to the main road to catch a bus, he was deeply afraid of robbers and wild beasts that might attack him."

Faye Hung, daughter of C.S. Hung, member of the Repulse Bay Lutheran Church and professor at Hong Kong University, assisted with clerical work for the school. Being bi-lingual, she was a helpful resource for communication with the Chinese population. Mr Walt Oestmann and Dolores Milke, came from the US as volunteers to serve in the Lutheran Church in Hong Kong. Walt gave tremendous assistance in supervision, working with the architect, William Wong and the contractors for the permanent school facilities being built in Repulse Bay, and Dolores did secretarial work .

I went to stores in Hong Kong to shop for basic suppliess – light bulbs, brooms, dustpans, drinking water, and toilet paper. I'll never forget going into the Wing On Department Store to purchase some of the necessities, attempting to get a school discount for a school that was unknown and not yet in existence. Interestingly enough, I received the discount, and even got free delivery, all of this in conversation about seven eighths in Chinese by the clerks, and one eighth in English by myself. Eleven years later, they still recognized me and gave me discounts on personal items, even as I was leaving the Colony.

Tuition for the provisional school was HK $ 2600.

The school was to be an American-type school with an international flavor. With the American population in Hong Kong growing rapidly, many families found that the adjustment to British Schools was difficult for their children, sometimes creating major tensions, adding to the difficulty of leaving home and moving overseas.

This presented a unique opportunity for Christian ministry. Here would be the only "American type school" in Hong Kong. It would serve a community oriented to United States public school education, but within a Christian School setting. And this is where the exciting tension began, with the question as to how this could be realized among families with huge differences in their cultures, their experiences, their expectations, and their religious or non-religious preferences.

During the first weeks of the provisional school, a number of parents opposed to religious instruction in the school, called a parent meeting to protest this instruction. Fortunately, with positive discussion, the intervention of some parents, and some good listening on the part of the school, this crisis was met through positive interaction, setting the stage for the school to continue with a Christian approach, offering a "gentle" exposure to an understanding of God's love through Jesus Christ. However, it became very clear that undue pressure for acceptance of what the school stood for as a Christian program would have negative results.

The provisional school was a helpful reality test for the future of the school. It also provided experience on a smaller scale for future study and understandings of what the mission and the approaches of the school would be. Since I was serving as a missionary in Hong Kong, I was also part of the General Conference of the Lutheran Church in Hong Kong, and was involved with the Chinese Lutheran Churches and Schools. This was helpful for me in seeing the bigger picture of the International School in relation to the worldwide mission of the church.

Meanwhile, back in Repulse Bay, there was the supervision of construction, and the decisions for "decorating" and equipping the new facility - an eight-story building on the side of a mountain. All of this was in preparation for opening a K-12 program, with an exact number of students not known, but estimated to be in the neighborhood of 400 to 450.

• The Repulse Bay Campus opens 1967

When the school did open in its new facilities in Repulse Bay in 1967, Walt Oestmann continued on a volunteer basis as the school's business manager. Dolores Milke assisted with the secretarial work. Four teachers from the Provisional school continued at the new HKIS.

To carry out the school's Christian philosophy and approach, Pastors Paul Heerboth and Paul Strege of the LCMS Board for Missions Asia staff issued several appointments on our behalf, but the first six were declined,. This was a discouraging trend. Many declined because the Cultural Revolution in China had reached Hong Kong, and the riots in HK were making headlines in US newspapers. With devaluation of the US dollar, and China cutting off Hong Kong's water supply - resulting in a severe water shortage - the spring and summer of 1967 seemed to be a time of instability in the colony.

Then, Werner and Marie Von Behren from Chicago, former fellow students of mine at Concordia College in Illinois, accepted the call to come to Hong Kong, And by the grace of God, a nucleus of 15 teachers from the US, who had the important spiritual background to understand the Christian philosophy and approach of the school, were hired. This group, because of its background and experience, was able to do the vital work for opening the school, basically in the last two weeks before school opened… registering students, making schedules, developing a handbook for faculty, students, and parents, and doing hundreds of other tasks.

The 15 "Lutherans" included were Pastor Karl Boehmke who had accepted the call to replace Rev. Galster as pastor of the Lutheran Church which now had its chapel at the school. Others were Ed Brackmann; Mel Schroeder; Liz Duval; Sue Witt; Dorothea Feil; Mariellen Lense; Bill Mahlke; Anne and Bob Rupprecht, new graduates from Concordia; Werner and Marie Von Behren; and Les and Lil Zimmerman; and myself.

Other teachers, hired locally, were from the US, Hong Kong, Canada, the UK, and Australia. Special mention should be made of Dorothy Maché, an art teacher with a rich background, who set up the art program for the entire school, and who was the wife of Joe Maché, the American businessman who was so very instrumental in working for opening both the school and Church of All Nations.

My wife Arleen and some friends from the Provisional school were able to arrange for the design and manufacture of classy summer and winter school uniforms. Textbooks arrived almost on time from the US, and an international school faculty of 44 individuals was assembled. All new to the school , Hong Kong, and each other, except four who had served in the provisional school program.

The new facilities were only a little behind schedule in construction. Over 600 students were enrolled in kindergarten through grade 12 for the opening day on September 14, 1967.

Tuition the first year was HK$ 3200 (Elementary); $ 3500 (Junior High); and $ 3800 (High School).

The school was named the International School rather than the American School, both because it would serve an international community, adding an international flavor to an American curriculum, and because of the political situation in the Far East at that time. Where possible, the attempt was made to downplay the American presence in the region and to at least reduce its visibility to a great extent.

The boys and girls in the school that first year were typically American, but they were a long way from home, and their fathers were often traveling all over Asia as part of their responsibilities as representatives of American business firms. These factors presented some special challenges to families, and sometimes these circumstances led to the acting out of negative behaviors in the classroom and playground. Fortunately, the faculty was able to meet these with understanding and care, and with appropriate educational practices.

I will always remember the last day of school before the Christmas holidays, when the entire school gathered together in front of the building and sang Christmas carols under the broiling sun. Following this, the students distributed gifts to Chinese children in a convalescent hospital and in a resettlement club in a nearby village. Unknowingly, this was the beginning of the "Day of Giving", which later became a permanent school tradition for the day before the Christmas holidays.

6. Growing Pains

The school continued to grow. In the mid 1970's, with the facilities stretched to their utmost, and every bit of space being utilized, including offices in storage areas and classrooms in hallways, a second construction program took place when Crown Lands again provided an adjacent site with a no cost lease. The side of the mountain was further excavated, and a six story colorful elementary school building allowing for flexible use of classroom space, was constructed with design by a young Chinese architect, Tao Ho, and Hsin Chong as contractor.

The entire two building campus then included traditional and flexible open space classroom facilities for up to 1500 students, two well furnished libraries, two gymnasiums, rooftop playgrounds, a large outdoor swimming pool, and all the special classrooms and other facilities needed for a high quality American School program serving the needs of a diverse international community. The second structure also had an eight story residential tower, with 14 apartments rising over one end of the classroom building , housing almost half of the 30 overseas-hire teacher families as part of the faculty of 100.

The student body in the 1970's, although about 65% American, included students from more than 35 nationalities all over the world, with about 10% being Hong Kong Chinese. The Christian setting of the school may well have not been the primary motivation for all students to attend the school, although families were usually willing to accept this feature, and many did appreciate the values and the spiritual focus of the experiences offered there.

Robert E. Christian, first headmaster, '66-'77, 2003

• A student perspective

I am fixated on the early memoirs of Bob Christian and others and realize how much this reflected on my own family's life. My father, when we first moved to HK from Virginia in 1966, was from one of the school's early company sponsors, Dow Chemical, and his family was from the Wing On lineage where Bob purchased the first school supplies. It is very much a double connection for my family.

I'm also intrigued about the 1960's Church inception by the Mache' family and how government ordinances in HK required churches be tied to schools in order to get land grants. I admire Bob Christian's determination of completing the school by going to the PRC to buy contraband bricks....these are important stories that must be preserved.   *Kevin Kwok, '79*

• Coming and Going

It is approaching that bittersweet time of year again. Schools will soon close, the summer holiday draws near, and it is time for yet another round of leave-taking. We expatriates call it "Exodus", although the biblical implications are dubious at best.

Why we leave and why we stay, however, can be seen as a barometer of how Hong Kong is regarded by the rest of the world.

If I count friends, colleagues and neighbours, not to mention all the secondary-school students I have taught who were bound for universities overseas, I have said an average of 150 goodbyes a year, for a total of more than 2,000 Hong Kong farewells during my 15 years here.

I have seen people leave our city under all manner of circumstances and moods. Some could not wait to get out; others were loathe to depart. Almost always, though, their reasons for going were entirely personal and had nothing to do with the perceived foibles of Hong Kong.

Sure, there are always a few who appear "stricken by a cryptic condition I can only call the Hong Kong syndrome." It seems the humid clamour and bustle simply depress them, and they must leave or suffer dire psychological consequences.

But my years of informal exit interviews also tell me that, for most people, Hong Kong is a place of tremendous energy and character where they feel more fully alive than they ever did in their home countries.

So, while they depart for their own reasons - a corporate transfer, an ailing parent or something else - they also leave a piece of their heart and soul behind.

I will never forget one 1997 pre-handover farewell party I attended for English friends. It was a posh, catered affair held at an exclusive club, but the atmosphere struck me as something approaching a funereal. It took me a while to understand how, amid such privilege and abundance, anyone could appear so dour.

Then I got it: as life would never be this good

again, the occasion was one for mourning rather than celebration. At a farewell for colleagues last week, the mood was also melancholic. This was pre-handover, of course, and they were saying goodbye to a different Hong Kong. But I found myself wondering: will life ever be this good for them again?

In the end, however, what is most interesting about this time of year for expatriates is not what prompts the departure of a relative few, but, rather, what compels the rest of us to stay. The city has proved its resiliency time and again over the course of its history. The Hong Kong story is as compelling as it is unique.

I, for one, want to be around for the next chapter.

Kent Ewing, teacher. article in the SCMP

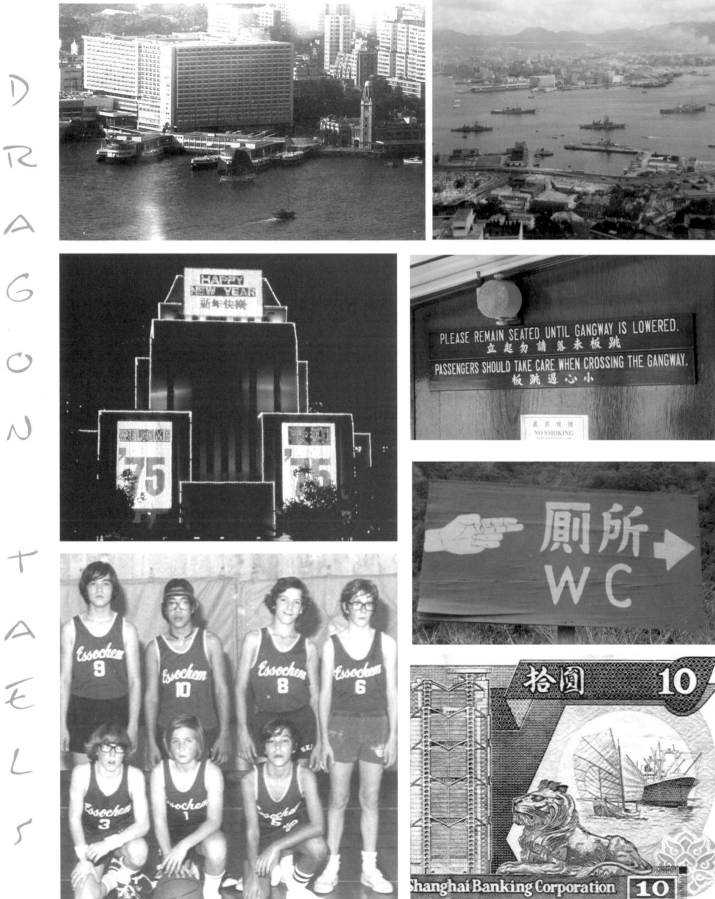

DRAGON tAELS

Chapter 2
First Impressions

Anthony Lawrence, in his 1993 book *The Fragrant Chinese* notes that newcomers to Hong Kong often spend their first months and years making great efforts to find out everything about the local traditions and mannerisms. This includes the Cantonese population, the European community, and the ubiquitous fast food spots, both Asian and American. But after a year or so, the curiosity diminishes and the learning curve slows into daily life. It's easy to feel like we know all about Hong Kong after a bit.

Therefore, when one recollects their first impressions, they are sometimes taken aback at how unusual their first observations and experiences were and how much those actually shaped future attitudes. It's good to re-awaken those experiences.

- Ed.

Hong Kong 62-67 68-71 We left Dallas TX by by train in 1962. In San Francisco we boarded an APL liner, I believe it was the *President Wilson*. West to Honolulu, then to Yokohama then to Hong Kong. The entire trip took about three weeks - I was seven. Ships were still the major means of international transport at this time.

Our first apartment was within walking distance of Quarry Bay School. The school was two stories, very old, four ceiling fans in each class room and huge windows. The playground was concrete with the exception of one area which was divided into four foot square plots. One could rent one of these plots from the school and grow things. This was probably a remnant of WW II victory gardens. We built roads in those plots and played with our Dinky Toy cars.

The student body was primarily English, a few Americans, a few Dutch, a few Eurasians, a few 'others'. My mother once asked a girl from school where she was from, all the girl knew was that her family belonged to the American Club. The dot at the end of this sentence is called a period, in American. In English it is a full stop. Mrs. McDonald, my teacher used to say "Don't make bloody great footballs like Mr. McIntosh". My favorite teacher was Mrs. Taylor, she had grown up in British Kenya. A lot of the English Government people were refugees from colonies that had shut down.

As we came down the steps we would all be met by our Amahs who would walk us home, a few kids were picked up by drivers. When they picked us up at the end of the day the Dairy Farm guy would be there on his bike and we would by ice cream.

All of the teachers were female, married and English. The janitorial staff was a Chinese family whom lived in the back of the building.

Occasionally we would have Sports Days. I can't recall where we went for that but it had a running track. After the kids ran the parents would compete. Occasionally a male PE teacher would show up at school and we would have to do bizarre exercises - his favorite was the 'Duck Walk.' I dislike duck to this day.

Weekly we would have an assembly where announcements were read and hymns sung. Then they would sing *God Save the Queen*. I remember asking my father what should I do when they did this – I knew She wasn't my Queen. My father gave me valuable advice, "Stand at attention - to show respect - and keep your mouth shut." Which I did.

On Saturdays my parents would take us to the Library which was down by the Star Ferry. By combining my family's cards I could get a lot of books. After a while I was allowed to go by myself. Very few people had a TV at this time. The TV came on at 5 pm and went off at 10 pm. I did not watch TV for five years. Going to the Peak and to Victoria Park were 'big things.' We did not have a car for the first two years so everything was by tram or bus or cab. My parents thought rickshaws were exploitive and in over forty years of living in Asia I have never been in one.

Our dentist was an American educated Chinese, his office was in the Shanghai bank building and I remember after a filling we would walk to Dairy Farm for a warm Ovaltine. Our Doctors were Lik Yue and Lillian Ding – Chinese refugees from Burma, educated in the US.

In the early sixties we had severe water shortages. Everyone's schedule revolved around when the water was on. These created a boom market for tin smiths as every body had large tin water barrels through out the house.

In the mid-sixties the war in Vietnam started picking up which directly led to the establishment of HKIS. Hotels sprang up over night to accommodate the GI's on R&R. The rumor was that were owned by Lady Bird Johnson. One of the planes taking GI's back to the war went off the runway at Kai Tak - no survivors.

Also there was the Cultural Revolution going on next door in China. It was '67 when due to a five cent fare increase for the Star Ferry, a demonstration turned into riots. Hong Kong's Chinese population were virtually all refugees from the mainland. Some of them had loyalty to Taipei, some to Beijing. Many of the Chinese schools were financed by Beijing. One of these schools was virtually across the street from where we lived on Kowloon and I remember walking past the British armored cars and armed Gurkhas on my way to school.

There was an American family living in our building and for reasons unknown, one of their sons, a kid about 16, went over to that school. I watched from our balcony as they beat him to a pulp, I was eleven. My dad and the Gurkhas got him out. Some time late while boarding a bus, my dad received a minor stab wound. Many years later I discovered that the embassy had set up an emergency evacuation plan for all of us. Things were pretty bad for a short period of time.

We moved from apartment on Kings road to a garden flat in Jardines Lookout. It was owned by the Southern Baptists and the family assigned to it had gone home for a years furlough. We had a grass lawn and a Peugeot. We had to car pool.

Then we moved to Kowloon, close by Kowloon Junior School and King George V. Kowloon was less British. KJS was still exclusively staffed by English women and most of the kids were English but there were also more Americans, Indians and others. *Mark Mcintosh' 73*

In the spring of 1966 my dad was called by the Mission Board of the Lutheran Church Missouri-Synod to head up a new American type school in Hong Kong. … and so began a family adventure. We had been living in New York City and so were accustomed to living amidst tall buildings, a diverse population, and an active harbor, but the move to Hong Kong provided all sorts of surprises.

Shortly after my fifteenth birthday, we began our journey to Asia on a passenger train. After the chaos that is part of any move, we welcomed the calm of rail travel as we took the well-known *Twentieth Century Limited* between New York and Chicago. In the Midwest, we visited both sets of grandparents and took our time with goodbye visits because, as was the case with other "missionaries," dad's call was originally for a five-year term, followed by a one-year furlough. This practice was intended and made sense for a missionary setting out to a remote mission field, but given the character of the HKIS position, the policy was changed a couple of years later to include a summer return to the US every three years.

In early August we boarded a plane for Los Angeles where we joined Liz Duvall, an elementary teacher ready to join the HKIS staff. Travel was a different sort of thing in the '60's as we "dressed" for the trip. I recall wearing a tie and a madras sport coat and I'm sure my younger sisters wore dresses. Because this was well before airline deregulation, the planes were not at all full, and we got to spread out across three seats and nap as we crossed the Pacific on "Pan Am." The one way airfare for that trip was $555 per adult … quite a steep price in 1966 dollars … and certainly a factor in the number of empty seats.

With a brief overnight stop in Tokyo, we continued to Hong Kong where we had our first encounter with Kai Tak airport. It was night, we were tired, and my excitement was colored by apprehension as I looked down at the city lights … and then the lights on boats close below us ... and then the lights were not very far at all below us … and then the water seemed to be getting awfully close … and then, suddenly, bang, we were down on the ground.

We were greeted in Hong Kong by a host of missionaries, and by several representatives from local newspapers. For a fifteen year old in a madras sport coat, it was an exciting evening.

Dave Christian '69

16

• Riots and Water Rationing

1967 was a difficult year for Hong Kong. We began to experience the fall-out from the Cultural Revolution sweeping across China. Posters started appearing around Hong Kong condemning the British colonial administration as "capitalist running dogs" and other derogatory, but colourful, terms. Peaceful demonstrations became noisy demonstrations until one day, they finally became riots. What had been perceived as the safest and most stable place in Asia suddenly became a hotbed of civil unrest and police took to the streets in riot gear.

At the time, I was still a student at King George 5th(KGV) School in Kowloon. There was no English language secondary school on the Hong Kong side so all of us crossed the Star Ferry every day to get to school. During May and June of 1967, school abruptly ended early on several occasions as riots broke out on the streets of Hong Kong and it was decided to send kids home from school rather than risk getting stranded on the Kowloon side. Several home-made bombs went off in different parts of Hong Kong. Loud speakers placed out of the windows of the Bank of China Building in Central (next door to the Hong Kong Bank and across the street from the Hilton Hotel) broadcast communist revolutionary music and cultural revolution propaganda. As unpleasant as it was, it did not seem to interfere with the British colonialists playing cricket at the Hong Kong Cricket Club across the street.

We knew things had taken a turn for the worst when a bomb went off in one of the elevators in the Hilton Hotel. No one was hurt but it sent a clear message that personal safety was no longer guaranteed. I remember being on Pedder Street in Central on a Saturday afternoon with my father waiting for our car to pick us up. We watched what must have been 1,000 communist sympathisers (read "unionists") march down Wyndham Street, dressed in white short-sleeve shirts and dark grey pants, shouting communist slogans and waving little red Mao books. I recall thinking to myself that something about the Hong Kong I knew had definitely changed.

In later years, it occured to me what a sheltered existence we all had and that the unrest that was so common in many parts of Asia had truly taken us by surprise. Government House, home to the British colonial governor (Sir David Trench), was under seige for most of that summer, with slogans stuck on the walls and gates praising Chairman Mao and condemning the British "running dogs." Little did we know that millions on the Mainland were being slaughtered or "re-educated" in what was probably the biggest purge in history.

We were also unaware of the fact that the British actually had a contingency plan to abandon Hong Kong in the event that the Red Guards came across the border at Lowu. The worst of the unrest was over just after the October 1st National Day celebrations of 1967. Things started to quiet down and life got back to normal. The stock market slowly recovered and property prices gradually made a comeback.

When I look at the Hong Kong that I live in today, it's hard to imagine the summer of 1967 and the upheaval that we all witnessed. It was a stark reminder to us that China features in every aspect of Hong Kong life and, despite the heavily guarded border that existed in 1967, we could not completely escape the effects of the Cultural Revolution that was destroying China.

The Hong Kong of 2007 is a very different place. It is Asia's world city and one of the world's leading financial centres. However, nothing has changed as much as China itself. Next year, 2008, we celebrate the 30th anniversary of Deng Xiaoping's "open door policy." I believe history will record Deng's decision to "open" China as the most significant event of the late 20th Century as it has had international political and economic ramifications like nothing else.

The HKIS of today is home to 2,500 students, many of whose families live and work in Hong Kong in order to reap the benefits of this "open door policy". All of us living in Hong Kong witness daily the emergence of the "Sleeping Giant" and the impact that China will have on the 21st century. We are privileged to have front row seats.

Robert Dorfman '72

During these years, the Cultural Revolution was in full swing in China, and we felt its impact in Hong Kong, even in athletic competition. The interschool track and field meet (called "Athletics" in Hong Kong) was a three-day event at Government Stadium. In the spring of 1967, one of the unheralded but dominant teams was from Pui Kiu, a school clearly shaped by communist values. Their athletes performed very well, and they diligently studied their *Quotations from Chairman Mao* between events. The atmosphere was hardly tense, but it definitely brought a new perspective to high school athletics.

Unrest from the Cultural Revolution eventually spilled more into Hong Kong and came to a head when the Star Ferry increased its fares. On one occasion, the disturbances concerned the KGV administration enough that school was let out early and all students were whisked away from campus on chartered buses. An evening curfew was enforced throughout the colony, and while it all seemed like an adventure to me, I'm sure my parents were wondering what on earth they had taken on.

At time of uneasy relationships with China, Hong Kong also experienced a severe drought. The Plover Cove Reservoir in the New Territories had not yet been completed, and Hong Kong depended on a contracted amount of water piped in from China. The colony's own small reservoirs did not provide nearly enough storage for a growing population, and drought conditions meant we had used the contracted volume water much more quickly than had been anticipated. Water rationing started early in the summer. It began with a limit of 8 hours of water per day, but as the rains continued to stay away, rationing became more extreme until we were limited to 4 hours of water every fourth day. (Flushing water, which runs through a separate non-potable pipeline, was not affected.)

During those four hours, we all scurried and focused on water related activities … washing clothes and dishes, taking showers, filling containers, etc. And then, for the next 92 hours, we made do with what had been collected. We could always, of course, rinse off our August sweat by swimming at Repulse Bay, but then we might have to wait a couple of days before showering off the salt. It was an inconvenient but tolerable adventure.   *Dave Christian '69*

I remember Mom bought these huge (must had been 50 gal.) tin drums for water and put them in the middle of the living room. They leaked.
Patrick Pang '79

The bombs put a quick end to firework sales on the streets. To this day I still drive around bags or whatever in the road. And Mom loved when someone came to visit us during the water rations

and stayed in a hotel. She would go down to shower in their room before going out to dinner. And I remember throwing paper wads at the pool... I remember my brother dropping water balloons on Garden Road!   *Debbie Smiley '72*

The summer of the 67 riots was a trip, leaving HK but not sure if we were comming back. 15+ pieces of luggage at KaiTak. Dad had a pretty close call with the rioters on his way from the office in Union House to the old parking lot where the Bull & Bear now sits. Our poodle Bianco and he went to a quiet office on Saturday morning only to leave by the side entrance and be locked out of the building in the middle of the riots, "Gweiloh/ White Poodle, YUM YUM!". Close call between that and having your children being escorted by armed Gurkas to KGV... we left for the summer, parents unsure of whether it was going to fall or not.
Rich Vaughn '72

In a way, I have to "thank" the 1967 upheavals in HK. One of the reasons why we moved from HK to Tokyo was the sight of a PRC gunboat at the HK Yaumati vehicular ferry terminal. My father decided to send us to Japan where we stayed from '67 till end of '68. I had gone to St. Joan of Arc for my compulsory 2 years of kindergarten. When we left HK, it was in such a hurry that my mom forgot to reserve places for us for the following school year (ultimately, though, I ended going to St. Mary's and my sisters to Sacred Heart). That's when my mom heard about a new school called HKIS. She's a graduate from ASIJ and really wanted us to continue the American style education we were getting in Japan (in my case, Canadian/Jesuit, I guess). So mom went to see Bob Christian...I was enrolled in HKIS in the Fall of '69 and 38 years later, I'm still involved with the school and will be seeing my 2nd child graduate from HKIS in 2007. And now, we're doing the 40th Reunion ! Like they say, "the rest is history..........."
Ken Koo '79; alumni association president

I can remember 4 hours of water every third day! (Or was it three hours every 4th? I was so young) and having to fill every bathtub and plastic bucket in the house when the water ran..... it sure is hot in HK in the summer!!! (And how the water then always looked so brown.)
Tami Whitrock '77

Being only 6 years old, 1967 wasn't a particular scary time for me. The water rations, to my delight, simply meant I didn't have to take many baths. I remember my mom and amah collecting the water in buckets whenever it was our building's turn for water.   *Liz Calouri '79*

I'm always amazed at the history that we lived in HK..it all sounds so very exciting, but to me at the time it was just rather a nuisance. All we could ever focus on as children was not being able to get a hamburger every time we went out to eat! Gosh darn it, all we ever got was gourmet Chinese.
                                        Tami Whitrock '77

I remember the summer of 1967 when we had very few monsoons and typhoons and the three reservoirs were almost empty. Chairman Mao Tse-tung decided this would be a good time to show off more of his power and he had the water supply, that the island usually purchased from China, shut off. To conserve on what little water was available in the reservoirs, the island was divided into four sections - A, B, C, and D. Each section would receive water on their given day from 4:00pm to 8:00pm. Since we were section A, we were very grateful when the fifth day came, and we could brush our teeth under running water, take a warm shower or bath, etc., etc.

There was never any hot water but the cold water would run through a small copper pipe in a geyser and would heat as it went over the flame. The heat was supplied by gas, and the flame was similar to a pilot light. The really good part of this type of water heating was that we never ran out of hot water and could shower as long as we wanted, except during the water shortage. The downside was the gas fumes could be very dangerous.

The riots (often called the disturbances) were a time we will not forget. One afternoon which was our water day, we felt so good after warm baths and showers, we wanted to celebrate. That evening we decided to risk going to a movie to see "A Man and a Woman." That was after the price of a movie ticket had risen from $2.50 HK$ to $3.00 HK$. During the show, a bomb exploded outside. Our question was did we panic, get up and leave, or continue watching the movie until we smelled smoke. We stayed and when we went outside much of the area was cordoned off. We got home safely, but did not attend a movie for some time.

I also remember the newspaper-wrapped packages left on the steps of the Star ferry, along the tram tracks, etc. Norman (Bomber) Hill was one of the best Police Ballistics Officers to safely detonate the bombs. He was not injured during the riots. Some time after the riots were over, I read a newspaper article showing how he had dismantled a bomb planted outside the Central Government Office and it exploded, causing him to lose his right hand and forearm. The queen awarded him the M.B.E. in 1968 for his numerous "bomb disposals" during the 1967 disturbances.
                      Jacquelyn Smiley, mother '66-'71

I remember the riots and bomb scares and wondering why the communists would hate us and also learning what communism stood for. What I remember most about the Provisional School that first year was the horrible lunches they made us eat! Cows tongue! And trying to walk up to the 2nd floor w/crutches-I had gotten hit by a car waiting for the bus in front of South Bay Villa Apts where we lived. I remember Miss Witt. When she came to HK her luggage got lost and she wore the same dress to school forever-I always felt sorry for her. And there was Mr Von Behren, whose son died from some kind of gas fumes in their apt. That was really sad.   *Debbie Salter Jackson '74*

When we first moved to HK, the communists were coming and we had all the riots and bomb scares. To a seven year old that was VERY scarey. I also remember being in a taxi in the middle of an anti-American riot in Japan at some point. The hate on the protesters faces left a very strong impression. I can also remember a vacation that we took to Cambodia just before the end of the 60's - seeing soldiers with machine guns and my parents telling me that the tour group got "kicked out" and we all left very quickly. (What WERE they thinking to take two children under 10 through there?
                                        Tami Whitrock '77

We arrived in the Colony on New Year's Day, 1967, and I remember that first harbour crossing on the HYF vehicular ferry - waves splashing over the bow, and that unique "fragrant" harbour smell. A surreal feeling - your're kind of wiped out from the long flight (we came frum Zurich), so everything's kind of hazy. A group of Dow families that I didn't know had just met us at Kai Tak and, boom, your surrounded by lots of people speaking a very singsong language. it was all pretty confusing and amazing to a 9 year old at the time.

Kerry Prielipp '75

We arrived in HK in late summer of '69 having followed the Trepanier clan from California who arrived a little earlier in the year (Both Dads worked for Fairchild Semiconductor.)

I remember all the shots needed for the trip (13) and wondering what HK would look like. My thoughts were more along the line of Pagodas and huts. A little naive I must say!

My first impressions were walking out of the cabin of the plane was like hitting a solid wall of air. Hot, humid and oh so fragrant. Everyone seemed to hanging their laundry off the side of the buildings. Wow look at all of the people.

Gavin Birnie '75

I can remember a bus taking all of us over to the "first" school in Chung Hom Kok in the apartment building. (Boy - I hated that - I got sick on it once I was only 7). I can still remember the "big kids" having a sit-in at the first school and all of us little ones runnng over to join in- even though we didn't have a clue... *Tami Whitrock '77*

•Entering HKIS

My story is about the awe I felt walking into the Church of All Nations as a First Grader, and how chapel is still the single biggest influence on the adult and parent I have become today. I have a story to tell of a young school, an American/international school in Hong Kong, the first of its kind, of how this school struggled against negative vibes and criticisms from a very traditional Chinese society, how this school stood up on (at first) spindly legs, grew strong, took its first steps and then first bounds forward into a proud history. I have a story to tell of graduating, coming back, watching my children repeat my history at HKIS. I have a story to tell of hello's and goodbyes to countless HKIS administrators, faculty, classmates, alumni, parents and my children's classmates and teachers. How these hello's and goodbyes are so happy, so sad, and when all have come and gone, I'm still here with my school, my HKIS. *Ken Koo '79*

My first memory was the fear of going to a "religious" school. We had zero church background and I couldn't imagine what these people would make us do...the first person I met was Christian Stevens - I seriously thought everyone at school was going to be called Christian! Hey – I was only 10 years old and from PEORIA, Illinois!! How many kids were at that school? Jonathan and I are trying to figure out how it was possible that we didn't know each other at such a small school.

Barbara Stone '74

I arrived at the Provisional school in the apartment building in September, 1966. My family had spent the past five years in Geneva, which has a climate similar to the U.S. Pacific Northwest (i.e., cloudy and rainy winters). One of my first memories was sitting in the classroom (with 13 students, we had one of the bigger classes, so we got one of the master bedrooms) looking out the window and wondering if I was in a dream. I saw tropical trees and a beach, and farther out, junks sailing. The weather was perfect, and we didn't yet have to wear uniforms.

There are so many marvelous memories: dim sum at the Aberdeen resettlement estates, picking out wild patterns in cloth alley and having shirts tailor-made, watching the water churn when the Star Ferry docked, being squeezed on a tram with amahs returning from the market, body surfing at Big Wave Bay, climbing the hillside above the school and watching the boats out on the ocean, and taking the train out to the New Territories. What could be finer? *Scott Lazenby '72*

•Typhoon time!

My first memories were of HK was taking the car ferry across the harbour and arriving just in time for Typhoon Rose while staying at the Repulse Bay Hotel. Watching the water streaming down the hills in thousands of waterfalls, the beach covered with huge waves, and the water running down the hallways in the hotel. What an awesome place to live – we had the run of the place, and met other kids who would be going to school with us.

Then we stayed in a flat on Headland Road with Mr. and Mrs. Mache´ and Debbie Burroughs and family. Truly magic. Our final spot was incredibly at 17 Magazine Gap Road with spectacular views of the harbour. We had this whole glass wall of 2 huge windows in the living room where we had to put up typhoon boards when the signal went up to 7. We could watch the submarines come in, check out the typhoon flags at Tamar, watch the planes at Kai Tak, check out which cruise ship was in at Ocean Terminal, and sit for hours watching all the ferries and boats come and go. What a life.

Barb Schwerdtmann '77

Typhoons: I remember going out with Mary Jo during a typhoon and trying to see how far we could lean into the wind without falling over. We were trying to get the same angle as if were on the tram to the Peak. It worked! We only gave up when we heard glass breaking above us and figured it was time to go inside. I also remember Mary Jo and me each holding Laurie (youngest sister) under the arms and the wind was so strong, her legs were actually flapping in the wind.

Rebecca Leudtke, '66-'72

We stayed in one of the apartments of one of the teachers who was on home-leave in the high-rise apartment building next to HK. We had to put up the storm shutters on the windows and then kept towels along the floor by the windows to soak up the rain being blown into every little opening.

Bill Mahlke's brother Richard

I had to dig through the mud near HK University after the big landslide in the dark with my dad in tow to find "my back way" to Poshan Mansions. My dad refused to believe we could not make it to our Apartment since my little brother was at home with the amah.

What a harrowing night that was. Cold, wet, pitch dark and not knowing if the building was still standing. Luckily it was (the actual building that fell was 2 buildings over from ours.) The next few months were very strange as we had to travel past all of the debris and the high rise that had toppled. The stench from rotting bodies was not very pleasant.

Gavin Birnie '75

We arrived one week after our marriage, Aug 12, 1967. We skidded on our landing at Kai Tak because we were on the lead edge of our first typhoon. I thought that the Lord couldn't let us get this far and kill on our landing at Hong Kong? Our first two weeks were spent at the old Repulse Bay Hotel. What a honeymoon! We were served some awesome meals, but we also wanted to be conservative because the school was paying the bill. Our first apartment was on the 16th floor of Cape Mansions, overlooking the South China Sea.

Our apartment was 3,200 square feet for us two newly weds, and we had $300 US dollars to our names. Our furniture consisted of a card table, four folding chairs, and four Japanese pillows. There was an rash of break-ins at our buildings. The thieves climbed down the pipes of the building and entered windows. We always said that if one broke into our place they would leave something behind for us rather than steal anything. In those first years our income was US $ 3,500 per year. We still don't know how we made it.

All four of our children were born in Hong Kong during our six years stay. Ed Dollase was such a wizard at finances, we figured out that you could actually have some funds left over from the maternity health plan. It was actually Ed who said we had to leave after six years, because we were breaking the school's health program's bank. Ha! Ha!

The most memorable birth was that of our third child, John. The round Adventist Hospital had just been completed no more than one week before Ann entered the hospital. The maternity ward was totally vacant, because the first two maternity cases resulted in girl infants. Absolutely no one was going there because of a "curse." Our John was the first boy baby to be born at Adventist Hospital. Boy was he spoiled by the nurses! Within hours the oriental mothers were flocking to the hospital. By the time we left two days later, the maternity ward was packed!

When we first arrived, I taught 6th grade elementary during the morning and Earth Science for the 9th Grade in the afternoon. The school was not ready when we arrived. Up to the day before the school opened, there were workers that had their cooking utensils and sleeping mats in many of the rooms. The day before school opened, we were finally able to get into our classrooms to bring in the desks and the books. The real highlight of the first day was actually after the end of the day. A small group of ninth grade boys carried a baby cobra into my classroom. They never considered the potency of the venom of a cobra that perhaps had not yet killed its food. They did remove the snake with haste!

Bob Ruprecht, teacher '67-'73

Even before I got to Hong Kong, I had heard about the Repulse Bay Hotel, and was disappointed that HKIS put us up at the Caravella Hotel in Happy Valley. We arrived in August '73, in the midst of a typhoon. Those first three days were such a blurr, getting to the Magistracy, dealing with HK electric, getting the drivers' license, dealing with "the shipment" and all sorts of other odds and ends. Dale and Carolynn Elmshauser were our sponsors, and were very patient, considering she had just had a baby 2 days earlier. The third day was Sunday, our first at Church of All Nations. I remember looking across the congregation and seeing what I assumed were a high school age brother and sister. Then we were introduced to them - Fritz and Lois Voeltz - two other new teachers!

All the new teachers (7 families) went out for Dim Sum at Wah Fu afterwards, treated by Bob Christian to our first resettlement estate lunch. That's when I learned the basics of dim sum from Arleen Christian. And I still use them today – *ha gow, sui mai, dong tok, and chassio bau.* Also bo lay tea. The place was slimy, noisy with the clacking of mah jong tiles behind screens, and the tile floor must have been inch-deep in tea water. But the food was great, and we didn't see any rats...that time.   *Dave Kohl, art teacher, '73-'80*

You know what I remembered the best?– our coming to Hong Kong on the plane. We came out through the door at Kai Tak onto a ramp, where everyone was waiting for their friends. We came through and a great cheer went up. I remember asking Jay if he saw any one important. We got to the bottom of the ramp and there was a crowd of people – there to meet us!!!!! I was so impressed and for the next five days, we went and welcomed other newcomers, and kept doing it till they were all there. Wonderful welcome!!!!!
Dusty Knisley, high school librarian, '74-'79

My first year '73 I remember the *Haka* ladies banging on gongs in the 4th floor courtyard area warning of blasting for the new elementary school across the street. I remember rocks landing in the courtyard.   *Wally Tuchardt '81*

•Local Customs & Festivals *from a letter in 1973*

"After just two days of school, we had a holiday!!! It was the mid-autumn festival. People go to the highest place around or to the beach at night and burn candles in the sand or carry fantasy-shaped silk lanterns with candles burning inside

them. It's really impressive late at night at Repulse Bay Beach where we went to watch. People go till well after midnight burning their lanterns, barbequing chicken wings, and watching the moon, while eating mooncakes. We bought some of the lanterns and have them in our living room. They are shaped like fish, and are really little works of art. Katy and I hosted "the family" for a dinner before we hiked down Shouson Hill to the beach. there were 8 of us, and since we didn't have a table big enough, I took off one of the bedroom doors and we laid it on some cinder blocks for a dinning table, and everyone sat cross-legged on the floor. After the meal, I set the door on the back porch, then forgot to bring it back in. The groundskeeper threw it away!!!

The next day was a day off from school, so the"family" went on a hike up in the hills behind Stanley. We hoofed it for three hours along a rocky stream. It wasn't a trail and was rough walking. We finally ended at a 30-foot falls, which Dennis Bartz dubbed Daimler Falls (I think in honor of Pat Hotung's dad's Daimler, where he is house sitting) The deep pool beneath the falls was christened Nubian Pool. We went swimming (wading, really), ate our NZ cheddar cheese and drank the South African Wine we had been carrying. At the end of the weekend, Bill Mahlke took us to the Hong Kong Hilton for an all-you-can-eat buffet, featuring all the prime rib you could want (and we wanted a lot!) and about 45 other dishes. I'm afraid we really "pigged" it, but the cost was only HK $ 21 each (plus 10% - the ubiquitous service charge added to every food bill)."

Dave Kohl, art teacher '73-'80

The first night I arrived in HK, we moved into the Hilton for 4 months and I still remember being totally amazed at the lights; swimming in the Hilton swimming pool; and someone yelling from a window that the Vietnam conflict was over.
John Morris '76

"But I have said nothing yet about Hong Kong present. I am still making the many adjustments necessary to fitting in with a new culture and its methods of organization. The feeling is still much like "camping out." You just don't run down to the local supermarket to buy a few items. The process is a longer one of discovering who sells the freshest fruit at the open-air stalls, how to catch busses, taxis, trams, from here to there. It does seems that more time must be spent on just accomplishing daily necessities that can be done back home in just a matter of minutes.

Hong Kong, if one should even attempt to combine impressions into words, is like combining Chinatown with Las Vegas size neon signs crammed closely together written in Chinese and English. Add to that New York traffic or cars, taxis, people and old double decker London-type busses. On top of that, mix in dogs in the gutters; people sweeping those gutters with bamboo and straw brooms; others carrying heavy loads balanced on their shoulders with a bamboo pole; men in undershirts and shorts or pajamas lounging on chairs in the doors, smoking a slow cigarette; people and kids squatting on the sidewalk playing games; outdoor butcher shops with meat hanging all over the place; outdoor fruit and vegetable markets; the noise of busses; wash hanging out over the steet on poles...and maybe you will come up with a slight image of all that is happening to the senses here continually."
Bev Larson, teacher, '73-'74
from a letter in 1974

My first memory should be a lesson to all greenhorns as they arrive to HKIS. Be careful what you say. For the first few weeks of school in '67 as a fresh graduate, I tried to impress upon the local folks my interest in learning the culture. Every morning I would address the young ladies at the office window with a cheerful "Jo San, Nay Ho Ma?" All I got was this quaint little giggle every morning. Now you must realize that we have a tonal inflection when we ask a question; we raise the tone at the end of the question. Finally I could take it no longer and asked what was so funny. I believe it was Faye who finally informed me that when I was trying to ask: "Good Morning! How are you?" I was actually asking "Good Morning! Are you a good horse!" So much for my Chinese language study!
Bob Ruprecht, teacher '67-'73

We moved to Beijing from Germany in December 2006 and have been experiencing China as I never imaged. I thought HGK was a mad house but the masses here beat anything I've seen. The first few years in Germany I used to get apprehensive just walking through the pedestrian zone of downtown Munich on a Saturday. Here it feels like the 13 million inhabitants of this city are all out

at the same time, in their cars. I remember old photos of the masses on bicycles. Now the bike lanes are a side lane of the main 3 and 4 laned streets to accomodate the traffic. Most times of the day it takes really long to get anywhere. I think the main thing we've all had to learn is to be patient with everything you do or want.
Helen Hoenig '77

Hiking the beautiful green hillsides. Shopping in the alleys in Central. Double decker buses. Fake polo shirts. Body surfing at Tai Long Beach. Noodles on the ferry to Lantau. Trams so crowded you wonder how even one more person could squeeze on, let alone the 30 that do. Sailing on a Junk. Hydroplane trip to Macau. The Peak tram. The Star Ferry.

Interim trips to the Philippines to learn how to windsurf, to the beautiful white sand beaches of the Malaysian coast, to China, to HK outward bound. How many Stateside schools do that sort of thing?!!

Hong Kong, for me anyway, was a City of many contrasts. Everywhere you looked, everything you participated in, contrasted. The crowded, jostling city to the green spacious hillsides with hiking trails and no people in site. The beautiful sandy beaches where you wouldn't think to go swimming because of all the refuse in the water. The very rich with their mansions and Rolls Royce's to the squatters living in shacks on the hillsides. Lane Crawford vs. the bargain deals in the alleyways. What a wonderful, amazing place.
Crystal Ostheller '84

•Lasting Impressions

Learning about real *Feng Shui* took time - like putting a pool on the top of the Hopewell Centre to make sure the candle shaped building never had its wick lit causing a fire, or leaving a hole in an apartment building to allow a dragon spirit to freely exit and enter a hillside behind the building.

I also learned to use a real Asian 'toilet' for the first time (don't lose your balance while squatting!)
Wally Tuchardt, '81

•Chinglish

Having long, dark, straight hair, high cheekbones, and olive tone skin, the locals spoke to me frequently in Chinese and became angry when I did not respond. They must have thought I was part Chinese. Anyway, I learned very quickly to say Ngaw hai May qwok yen, mhai Jung qwok yen (I am American, not Chinese.) This happened primarily on the long bus rides from North Point to HKIS. I also remember the shock of discovering that my skin color was the exact same color as the skin color of the Chinese. I was holding on in the bus and noticed it with amazement, since I always thought the Chinese had "yellow" skin

Rebecca Leudtke,'72

I impressed my American friends with Kung-hey-fat-choy-lice-eee-dow-joy. We loved to answer the phone, "way-nay-wah-been-doh-ah. Ok, ok, I can see some of you wetting your pants now over my pronunciations, but is amazing how we can really fake them out.   *Debbie Smiley '72*

I got the shock of my life once, when someone asked me to speak Chinese. I was sick of rattling out Yat-Ye-Sam-Say-Ng-Lok-Chat-Baht-Gau-Sahp, so I let loose with a few infamous Chinese curse words   *Deborah Smith '80*

South Bay Villas = Nam Wan Sun Chun
South Bay Close = Nam Wan Fung
Repulse Bay = Chin Soy Wan

Wan is bay and Nam is south.

The new secondary school is located in Tai Tam on the Red Hill Peninsula (Hung Shan Boon Dough)
Hung is Red.
Shan is Hill
Boon Dough is peninsula.
Tsim Sha Tsui is on the Kowloon
BoonDough.

Hong Kong International School - Gwak Jai Hock How
American School - Mai Gwa Hock How
Ken Rohrs, jr hi teacher, '73-current

mei guo xue xiao = American school
nam wan sun chuen = South Bay Close

sang daan fai loh = merry Christmas
gung hei fat daaaaiii choi = happy new year to you   *Gabe Lau '77*

Ngo Dei Juk Nei Sing Daan Fai Lok Bing San Neen Yu Fai.
= we wish you a merry christmas...and a

happy new year
("Kung Hei" = congratulate "Juk" = wish "Nei" = you.)   *Ken Koo '79*

gung hei fat choy = happy new year
lai cee dow loy = where's the red packet (for lycee)
dow ling mn oi = 5 cents I don't want
umn nmun dow loi = 5 dolla OK
Richard Vaughn '72

wei, bin sui ah? = hello, who is this
jiu gu lik san = chocolate milk
gwei pak = a white female, and supposedly, very insulting
gwei lo = foreigner
Jill Liddiard, '77 (one time li li, now tai tai)

yat gau bei jau um goi = one beer please
Ian Goepfert '80

way, neigh wa bin doah = hello, who do you want?   *Debbie Smiley '72*

yau moh gau cho, ah = what, are you kidding/are you out of your mind?
Kelvin Limm '79

neh yau moh gau chaa = have you not made a mistake?   *Rich Vaughn '72*

lei ho yea = I am speechless   *Gabe Lau '77*

ho pang yau = a real friend, i.e. San Miguel beer
lap sap chuen = garbage worm = litterbug
Dave Kohl '73-'80

nb: I take no responsibility for the romanization of Hong Kong Cantonese as heard and pronounced by these people -ed.

Mandarin uses Pinyin romanization, whereas Cantonese uses Yale (or Wade-Giles) romanization. Thre are two good books by Rita Mei Wah Choy on pronunciation, *Read and Write Chinese* and *Understanding Chinese,* which cover both dialects. Plus she devotes 8 pages to food terms, which I know will go over well with anyone from HKIS.   *Mark Shostrom '74*

•Chinese names

When we first arrived, everyone seemed to want to assign us a Chinese name, especially Mrs. Chan and the Chinese staff in the lilbrary. the procedure is usually to select a good fortune Chinese name that sounds similar to your western name. So they wanted me to be Goh (sounds like Kohl?). but having a name that in German means 'cabbage', I wanted a ploy on that name, so I selected 'choi' as in the Chinese vegetable. They gave me some pretty strange looks at first, but it has stuck. When my godparents visited 3 years later, his last name is Reitz, so we played with Rice as a sound, which translates to 'fan'. He and my dad are business partners, hence we now joke with them as being 'cabbage and rice.'

Dave Christian was Got Dai Wai = Christian = God = Gott in German

Dave Kohl, art teacher '73-'80

Because my dad occasionally spoke, with an interpreter, to Chinese audiences, he was given a Chinese name … that sounds something like "Got Lo Baht." Literally translated, the characters meant "Lucky Happy Knowledge" and the "Lo Baht" was intended to have some aural similarity to "Robert."

When I later decided I wanted a Chinese name, Mrs. Chan helped me out, suggesting I should have the same "Got" surname as my dad, and then use "Dai Wai," a common Chinese equivalent for David. *Dave Christian '69*

Faye Hung and my secretary Eve Yau gave me my Chinese name - C. Y. Duk. I thought it no big deal, but they spent 3 or 4 days coming up with just the right name. C sounds like Schmidt (?) the other letters or sounds are those of another person in history that has similar qualities as I. I don't remember what they were, but they said they were flattering. *Walt Schmidt, PE teacher '70-'81*

nb: When Barry Kolb came on staff in 1973 in the PE program, he was dubbed C. Y. Goose - ed.

•Aiya

A great commentary Aiya!!!I always use such language and even in Hawaii with it's multiple Ethnic background still get strange looks. Sai lay, jun hai ho teng nei, Sing Dan Fai Loh one and all. and of course Gung Hei Fat Choy!!!

Rich Vaughn 72

I've lived in New York and now in Taiwan, so along the way I've tried to assimilate by using *oy* and *wa sai*. But alas, there is nothing so irrepressible, so gratifying, and so comprehensively suitable for all occasions as *aiya*. Ever notice also that this expression, which begins and ends in vowels, is utterly therapeutic. No so for those expletives we use too often in desperation when trying to relieve tension: i.e., those words which begin with a consonant like "sh" or "f" or "d" and end respectively in "t", "k" and "n" or in many cases, double consonants like "ck" and "mn". These dead end sounds tend to drive up blood pressure, and often cause embarrassment and regret. Three cheers for *aiya*!

Marcus Woo '75

I had a craving for a sweet taste of childhood the other day; so I went shopping for some *moy*. I was putting said treat into my cart and looking for my Ranch 99 VIP card, when a woman with three kids in tow ran into my cart. At that moment, both of us said, *aiya*.

The children giggled, she apologized, and I quickly replied, "M'si...No apology needed." Although it was a minor exchange, I later realized that aiya is more than just two characters; it is part of the spirit of being Chinese...in a moment of surprise I could've said just about anything — my reaction was to say *aiya*.

I was surprised that I would instinctively use my mother's tongue because I've always known that I don't speak Cantonese well. No matter how far removed I've become as an American, there is something at my core that is Chinese.

I decided to conduct informal research about *aiya*. First, I went to a national bookstore chain to review its Chinese language materials. I thumbed through all the Chinese language materials, but couldn't find any vocabulary drill including *aiya*. Seeing that the publishers of tourist books were not going to be helpful, I decided to observe its use in the community. I clipped my cell phone to my belt, grabbed a couple of pink bakery boxes and sat around San Francisco's Portsmouth Square drinking 7-Up and eating dim sum. Lo and behold, I heard *aiya* used in a variety of ways. Based on my personal experience and this observation, I've developed a personal understanding of *aiya*.

Aiya is 24-carat Chinese gold. Aiya is more than just two characters; it is part of the spirit of being Chinese and may even go back to antiquity. It is used wherever the Chinese have been in the diaspora of the last sesquicentennial.

How you say *aiya* can say volumes about your state of mind. For example,when the problem is minor, I can say *aiya* in a short/curt manner. However when I am extremely stressed, I can draw it out to nearly five seconds. (I'm planning an experiment where I get a room full of people to meditate using it as a mantra. With practice, I might get them to draw out *aiya* even longer.)

To explain more deeply how to use *aiya*, imagine a worker slaving on the Great Wall when he accidentally drops a brick (a quickie *aiya*)...on the work foreman (*aiya!!*) —getting him thrown into the wall to die an agonizing death (*AIYA!!!*)

As you read the following ways aiya can be used, the mental image to solicit is to picture any of the mothers from Amy Tan's The Joy Luck Club. For those who have met anyone in my family, you can picture one of my relatives instead:

•Surprise: *"aiya*! A surprise party for me?"

•Joy: *"aiya*! You got 5 out of 6 in Lotto!"

•Distaste: "You expect me to drink that herbal medicine concoction of yours? *aiya!"*

•Doubt: "Do I have to wear that lemon yellow/lime green sweater my mother made? I wonder if she would notice if I 'accidentally' donated it to Goodwill? *aiya."*

•Awe: "Your son got accepted into Harvard Law School!?! *aiya!"*

•Irritation: "Clean your room. *aiya!* Why do you live like a pig?"

•Great astonishment: *"aiya!* She switched majors from Business to Art History!"

•Disapproval: "Report Card — 5 As, 1 B? Always a B in Math. *aiya."* (Actual quote from my mother when I was a sophomore in high school.)

•Shock: "What? Ketchup on Yang Chow Fried Rice...*aiya!"*

•Lamentation: "aiya...why me...ungrateful child... aiya." (Probably what my mother is thinking when she reads this.

•Outrage: "Never clean your rice cooker with that steel scouring pad! aiya!"

•Verge of internal combustion: "I can't deal with the family asking when and if I'm getting married! ai-yaaa!"

Aiya is an all-purpose phrase that comes from deep in the soul. aiya is both simple and complex: on one hand it is a couple of Chinese characters; on the other hand it can be a whole speech describing the state you are in. aiya says "I'm afraid", "I'm in pain", "I don't believe it." It is an exclamation of exuberance, a shout of hurt, a cry of fear, and the reflex of being startled, and the embrace of joy.

It is unfortunate that English has no equivalent to aiya. It saddens me that American English doesn't afford me a fun phrase to emote. "Shucks," "Darn" and the plethora of swear words cannot convey what aiya can. So, I'm going to propose that we start an initiative. American English should grab on *aiya* or the Yiddish *oy* for our use.

So the next time you go to a teahouse for dim sum or decide to go shopping at an Asian market, listen to the lively banter as friends and families meet. It's a wonderfully vibrant, alive community out there. Who knows, you just might get caught up the lyrical rhythm of the people. *Aiya*, what fun!
anonymous, submitted by Gabe Lau '77

aiiiYahhh!! I hope you folks didn't mistaken I have written the article. The credit should go to whoever wrote it, twice *ho yieh* to her!! *Chun hei mmm ho yee see*! A lady friend of mine sent the article to me. When I checked back with her, she said it was from her friend. But I'm sure somebody she knows has written that article here in Southern California. *Gabe Lau '77*

Merry Christmas, Sing Dan Fai Loh to all of you!! Gung Hei, Gung Hei, Fat DAAAIII Choy to you too!!! *Gabe Lau '77*

Check out www.engrish.com

5. Britlish

26

British Wit: I directed a production of The Music Man for the American Community Theatre. One fellow with a reputation as a pillar of the expatriate performing community was Bernard (last name forgotten), accent of course on the first syllable. He was short, thickset, with red skin and thinning blonde hair. He was perfect for the part of Marcus, played in the film by Buddy Hackett.

Early in rehearsal, when the cast was sitting around reading through the script, there was a pause and I had a sudden impulse to tease Bernard. "Do you know, Bernard," I said, "I've always wondered why you British cousins have a schedule but you don't go to school?"

"Ah, but we do, lad," he fired back without a moment's pause. "Every bloody Shhaturday." I never tried wordplay with Bernard again.
Andrew Grzeskowiak, teacher, '78-'80

My favorite sign in English was: Mind your head. It was on the bus, going upstairs so you wouldn't hit your head. I wonder if they still use it.
Rebecca Leudtke, '66-'72

Aha — their IS a difference in the English language!!! Spotted in a toilet of an office building: *Toilet out of order. Please use floor below*

In a Laundromat: Automatic washing machines: *Please remove all your clothes when the light goes out.*

In a department store: Bargain basement upstairs.

In an office: *Would the person who took the step ladder yesterday please bring it back or further steps will be taken*

In an office: *After tea break staff should empty the teapot and stand upside down on the draining board*

Outside a secondhand shop: We exchange anything - bicycles, washing machines, etc. Why not bring your wife along and get a wonderful bargain?

Seen during a conference: *For anyone who has children and doesn't know it, there is a day care on the first floor.*

I discovered early-on when everyone kept leaving, there are many different levels of friends. Time marches on, but the long term friends are always still a part of my life. I sometimes think we spoke more Chinglish with each other than English. It is really a second language, and I can switch it on at any time! I used to forget and use it when on vacation, like with the hotel cleaning ladies. A real riot was to watch Mark Ketterer asking everyone if they were English, with an invisible monocle of course
Barb Schwerdtman '77

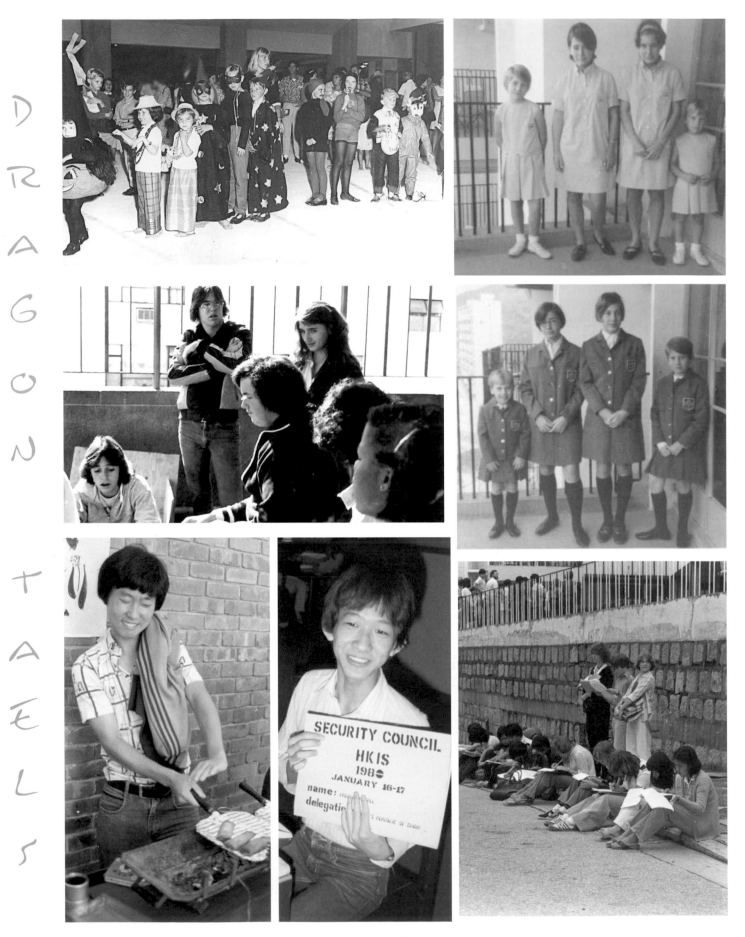

DRAGON taels

28

Chapter 3

Traditions

Like every major institution, HKIS has developed many long standing tradition over its history. Some were intended – a logo, several programs of service, the expectation of academic excellence. Other traditions evolved through practice, happy accident, or just the daily solving of repetitious situations. Most are delightful, a few are questionable. And I don't think anyone would question including Mrs. Chan in this chapter – she was a tradition!!!   -Ed.

1. Planned Traditions

• The Logo

The HKIS cross logo was in use when I arrived in September 1968. I never once heard any mention of the origins or meaning of the design. I always assumed that is was a religious reference -- in those early days, the role of the Lutheran church was quite strong at HKIS -- daily hymn singing and prayer services in the adjacent Lutheran Chapel were mandatory, and the athletic teams were called the Crusaders. I vaguely recall seeing a graphic of some sort depicting an armored knight on a horse with the HKIS cross logo on his shield.   *Peter Wang '71*

The symbol was a Crusader on his prancing steed. The cross was the cross used by soldiers of the Crusades. I dug up my old handbook and PE uniform.   *Bob Auman '71*

I was at HKIS from '66 thru '72, class of '73. The first year was in the apartment building, while the school was built. The original crest/emblem, was designed, I think, by an art student, either in '66 or '67. He was a junior or senior. But whenever it was that it became politically incorrect to use the religious symbol, the emblem was changed. We were known as the HKIS Crusaders. services in the adjacent Lutheran chapel were mandatory, and the athletic teams were called the Crusaders. I vaguely recall seeing a graphic of some sort depicting an armored knight on a horse with the HKIS cross logo on his shield.   *Peter Wang '71*

My understanding was that Leonard Galster, the LCMS missionary who started the Lutheran gathering/worship/Sunday School at the Repulse Bay hotel was the person that suggested the Jerusalem cross be used for HKIS. I understand he

thought this would be a cross that would be less offensive and misunderstood by local people. The Latin cross, the traditional one, carried some baggage with it. And the four little crosses showed the universality of the cross of Christ.

In 1973, Dave Kohl was asked by Bob Christian to 'play around' with the design' (my words, not Bob's) because he wanted something on the gym floor center circle in the gymnasium. The termites had eaten up much of the floor – Bob said the floor boards were like ice cream to the termites! – and the flooring needed to be fixed and refinished. Dave created the design, using the Jerusalem cross and then put the HKIS letters around it.
                                Lois Voeltz, teacher, '73-'80; '95-'03

I can take perhaps two-thirds credit for designing the round HKIS logo. Here is the true story, as I remember it. During the first week of meetings before school, Bob Christian came up to me during a break and told me that workmen were re-finishing the gymnasiun floor, and wouldn't it be nice to put some sort of design into the center circle on the newly painted floor. Would I work on something?

Hey, I was the new kid on the block, anxious to please the boss, and the meetings were quite dreary (sorry Bob!) and this gave me an excuse to doodle legitimately while listening to rules and policies being explained. There was a minor typhoon outside washing waterfalls over the hillside outside the cafeteria. Glancing thru the pile of papers in front of me, I noticed the Crusader cross on several pieces of letterhead. Some were the simple Greek Cross design with the four smaller crosses in the quadrants; some another design had the letters of the school in the quadrants. But they were really small and hard to see. I started doodling and playing around with enlarging the letters, then realized that all the letters could be connected to the center cross if I put serif endings on the letters.

By lunchtime, I had a pencil sketch on a paper napkin and thought I'd run it by Bob. He liked it, and basically grabbed it from me and gave it to the painters. That was the last I thought of it until the day school started when the gym was first re-opened. Low and behold, the Chinese painter had refined my sketches into a very nice graphic, well balanced, in red and blue colors. OK, end of story...I thought.

Fast forward two years to 1975...I don't ever remember seeing that design anywhere but on the gym floor. So the the new elementary building is dedicated, and there on the front wall next to the main doors is my HKIS logo in stainless steel! Five-feet in diameter and the most prominent part of the entrance. And they had thickened up the proportions, which improved it. Lois Voeltz was next to me at the ceremony and said "David, you should get a commission" Yeah, right.

Suddenly, the design was on the new school letterhead, in nice red to contrast the blue type, and the thing took on a life of its own. I'm glad to see it still in use 30 years later, and still portraying Christ as the center of our school. For a time, there was even thought of using a similar design for the CISS school in Shanghai, but they thought better of making the cross too prominent. I have recently found a copy of a very early Repulse Bay Lutheran Church paper from Leonard Galster, and there is a very similar modified Jerusalem Cross design on it that he may have used as a symbol for the church. Deja vu!!!   *Dave Kohl, art teacher '73 - '80*

•HKISCHOOL

Many folks may wonder about the cable address that the school has. I was having to send many cables to the US for various business items related to the school and to other parts of the world. However, when you called Cable & Wireless to send one the first thing they would ask is "do you have account and what's your cable address." I had to say we didn't have one. So I went down to the cable office to set up an account and get a cable address. I really wanted it to be just HKIS but the manager said no it has to be at least six letters. So after much thought I decided well let's just go with HKISchool. The man said that would work. So I assume this is still the cable address but that's the story on how it came to be.

Ed Dollase, Business Manager, '67-'74

•Uniforms, 1966-1977

My wife Arleen and some friends from the Provisional school were able to arrange for the design and manufacture of classy summer and winter school uniforms.

Bob Christian, first headmaster '66 - '77

"All material for winter uniforms must be purchased at United Tailor, No 3 G/F Hang Chong Bldg, # 5 Queens Rd. Central. Mr. William Woo, proprieter, will also make the boys' blazer. If you desire to use your own tailor, the official style and fabric must be followed."

Susan Chan, 2 Pak Sha Rd, 1st Fl, Causeway Bay, is the supplier for girls uniforms. Girls jackets, jumpers, and winter skirts are factory-made after measurement at school. Girls slacks are to be tailored at their own choice, but must follow the official style and fabric.

One day automatic cleaners (as Westinghouse) are recommended for winter uniforms, so that uniforms can be cleaned on Saturday. Winter uniforms can also be washed with care. Parents are asked to label all uniforms parts to avoid mix-up from an HKIS mailing, 1974.

When we first went over to HKIS, we went to register, me for 4th grade and David for 6th. Then we went to get our summer uniforms from the bookstore that was located outside of the main glass doors of the old school building in 1968. They held them up until we found one that sort of fit. It seemed like they moved the bookstore almost every year. For our winter uniforms, we went to some tailor who measured us and got our made to measure suit! My Dad ended up going there for years to get his suits done. Miraculously one year, pants were added to our uniform options. I had a cartilage problem in my knee and was in a cast from my hip to ankle for 6 months, my Mom said I had to wear my uniform every day, but I changed in the car into other pants so no one knew I had a cast. Go figure.

Elementary school kids had to wear knee socks that never stayed up, so we had to use rubber bands.

With uniforms, everyone checked out to see what shoes people got over the summer to start the year with. A couple of times my Dad went back to the States on business and got me new shoes! That was totally cool! Mid year US shoes! One pair unfortunately were brogues, which I hated, so I switched with someone everyday at school.

Ah, then there were free dress days, with rules of course. All those clothes bought over the summer could finally be worn to school. Bells, hip huggers, my natty wooden peace symbol, go go watches, mood rings, patches, etc...I used to have hot uniform debates with Michelle! I used to pin up my hem after I left the house every day in the pak-pai.

Barb Schwerdtmann '77

The first day of our HKIS adventure began with the Star Ferry ride in the morning to catch the bus to Repulse Bay. Dressed in our spiffy new uniform bought at the 4th floor (I think) store.

We had a little HKIS patch to sew on the short sleeve white shirt. Dark blue Levi dress slacks, white gym shirt with Crusader emblem and blue shorts. Later would come the Winter uniform fitting.

I know this was a bit odd for a lot of folks coming from the States (uniforms that is) but being only 3 years removed from the UK I still remembered my uniformed schoolboy days in Northern England.

Gavin Birnie '75

Douglas refused to wear a "boing-boing," but he was so short that a regular tie hung somewhere around his knees. Our amah would stand behind him and work some kind of looping magic to raise the tie to a more normal length. For those unfamiliar with "boing-boing" ties, this was a tie, already knotted and attached to an elastic strip that slipped over the head. Unfortunately, it could be grabbed and snapped, hence the term "boing-boing."

Gloria Lannom, mother 66-'72

I hid a plaid shirt in my backpack, and sec-

onds before the school picture was take, I put it on over the uniform shirt. I also remember having longer hair than the girls I dated.

I also remember having a group of Christians invite me to a meeting and changing my life!

Dave Porter '73

I dated Bryan Anderson most of the two years I attended. We could usually be found playing poker in the cafeteria. Remember the uniforms? Micro Mini was our form of rebellion.

Cindi Webb '78

One memory is the girls in those crazy light blue dresses. What were they anyway? Dresses is too kind a description. What fascinated me were the complete outfits the girls wore under the dresses. Some dress code! Some creativity!!

Bev Larson, teacher '73-'75

The first week of school has passed, quietly, at HKIS. I've got some very good kids, many nationalities- American (about 60%), Chinese, Japanese, Indian, Pakistrani, Swiss, Nepalese, Thai, etc. I have three basic art classes with a total enrolment of 70; one intermediate art class of 3, and a ceramics class with about 12 kids. And a nice kid named Cal Golay who is doing independent study mechanical drawing – he does great detail work and I grunt in approval. I also work with the junior high teachers for their art lessons. All the kids wear uniforms...I feel like I'm in a hospital ward.

from a letter in 1977, Dave Kohl, art teacher '73-'80

It sure was nice having uniforms (I know I am in a minority here) but I really enjoyed not having to decide each morning what to wear.

Gregg Saunders '75

When I was in the 7th or 8th grade midis, (skirts below the knee), first came into style. If my memory serves me right I was the first one to have my winter school uniform skirt made into a midi. Prior to that we had all been in the shortest of minis. I remember hiding in the school bathroom for a while before mustering up the courage to come out with my new midi skirt and platform shoes. Quite a few girls subsequently followed suit.

Liz Calouri '79

Dave Landdeck found Rob Reiner and one

of the Luedtke girls making out at the top of the 7th floor stairwell one day. He came to them, and once he got their attention, told her that he was going to write her up for being out of uniform. She protested that she was not out of uniform. Mr. Landdeck replied that if they kept up the way they were going, she and he would both be, real soon!

Lois Voeltz, teacher '73-'80

There were pink slips you'd get if you were out of uniform. *Mike McCormick '80*

There was a petition to allow the girls to have trousers made for the winter uniforms. I think Moira Gaveghen was in charge of that.

Eileen Keenan '80

Trousers were part of my winter uniform during the '74-'75 school year. I remember how exciting it was to get into high school where you could wear ANY colour blouse and/or socks with your winter uniform...not just blue or white. that led to many interesting fashion choices...like those multicolored striped toe socks...with sandals. My last day of school, I had everybody sign my uniform. The funniest thing was that my sisters and I realized that all three of us had worn that same uniform. It even had Karen's name sewn into the neck. The hardest thing for me about uniforms was moving to the States and having to figure out what to wear EVERY DAY. *Deborah Smith '80*

The uniforms were abolished in '77. Celebration! Joan Rice and Jonica Hassa and I lugged all of ours down to Repulse Bay Beach where we dug a pit and burned them in a huge bonfire. The wonderful polyester fabric more or less just melted into one sizzling, plasticized lump (which, ironically, was how we felt wearing them). I'm sure the fossilized remains were uncovered years later by some unsuspecting beachcomber, who probably determined it, quite correctly, to be ancient toxic sludge. *Melissa Miller '79*

Then, after all those years of uniforms, once WE left, they went to free dress all the time.

Barb Schwerdtmann, '68-77

• Proms

Along with that familiar role, I also remember a lot of "firsts" associated with those first two years at HKIS.

The first Junior/Senior prom was held in the school cafeteria. We got dressed up, and the cafeteria was decorated ... but it was still the cafeteria. We danced to live music by one of Hong Kong's well-established cover bands, and then, following the prom, we scattered to different locations ... including The Scene, a dance club behind and below the Peninsula Hotel. (The second prom was held at the Mandarin Hotel.)

A professional photographer often showed up to cover the prom or other school social events, and then, several days later, we could visit the studio (on Nathan Road in Kowloon?), view the proofs, and order our own copies. I still have a small but amusing collection of those black and white photos. *Dave Christian '69*

Al Jimmerson & I on prom night took the bus back to Repulse Bay (after the post-prom party) in the morning. With all the vendors headed out to set up shop for the coming day, we stood out just a bit! *Kris Brannigan '69*

The 1977 Prom was held at the Grand Ballroom of the Hong Kong Hilton which was a special evening for me since I wrote the official Prom Song called *Remember Me*. We performed it that night. I played piano and vocals and my brother John Cashman (6th grader at the time) played drums along with Gilbert Lo on string synthesizer, Paul Westrick on guitar and vocals, Cathy Clasper vocal and violin.

I was a junior in 76-77 school year and I dated a senior Julia Obayashi. Everyone knew Julia as she dominated a conversation. Always friendly, cheerful, smiling, she was a lot of fun to be around. She lived above me of May Rd.

Jerry Cashman '78

• Serendipity

I took a serendipity class where we learned to make pizza from scratch and poached pears, when you cook the pears in liquid. I believe we used wine, do you think they'd let you do that in a U.S. High School? I still have that pizza recipe and I still make it on occasion. My Mom loved that I knew how to make something for dinner, now that I'm a mom I realize she also liked taking a night off from cooking! *Wendy Liddiard '73*

Serendipity was a marvelous idea. I took

sailing and waterskiing. I think each lasted for 6 weeks. One of the Serendipity activities I signed up for was "Meditation Hikes." Mr. Westrick walked with us through temples, graveyards, villages and in the hills. He shared himself and encouraged my Christian faith to grow.   *Debbie Noren '73*

We didn't have to wear uniforms on Serendipity Day, and got to do something other than classes for the afternoon. The only thing I remember is sailing.   *Robin Conserva '75*

• Mock United Nations

The Mock UN was always great. But the one where we had a mock terrorist attack with hostages taken was quite something. To think that our fellow students staged this in the early 70's. It makes me wonder why people in the US were so slow to realize that this is not a new phenomenon that started with 9/11 that this has been going on for decades around the world.   *Gavin Birnie '75*

•Science fairs

David Hockett made a real hovercraft for Science fair! In 7th grade Gwen Juneau and I made apple fritters and had a coin collection, how scientific was that! Dropping our egg rockets – in milk cartons off the 6th floor, everyone's broke! One year we gave everyone toothbrushes, had them brush their teeth and then chew those pink tablets to see where they missed, everyone ran around with red mouths! The one that you couldn't do today, was when we blood typed everyone. We got to prick their finger, and use their blood to type them. For some reason, some kids had to get poked more than once, hmmm, imagine that.
          Barb Schwerdtmann '77

• Senior Slave Day

Lisa Pearce, Janna Dieckhoff and I once bought Kevin Kwok at Senior Slave Day (that oh-so-P.C.-fund raiser). We had him wear Lisa's bikini top and sarong. And he looked good in it!!
          Sheila Baker '82

• Dance Marathon

Cherri Libby helped me, or I would never have completed that 52-hour Dance Marathon
          Robin Conserva '75
In 9th grade, I did the dance marathon (all 52

hours!). I remember late one night, or early one morning, Karen Koch and Mark Kunsman lip-synced Meatloaf's *Paradise by the Dashboard Light* from the DJ stand. It was the first time I heard it and I still think of them whenever I hear it. Better than thinking of Meatloaf, that's for sure….
          Sheila Baker '82

• Walk for a Million

I did the Walk for a Million twice, on foot. Then I found out that a lot of people finished the 16 miles in taxis. No wonder they finished the whole thing in an hour. I think I still have a card from one of those events with the check point stamps on it.
          Patrick Pang '79

I remember the Community Chest charity walk. Going from building to building collecting sponsors for donations per mile, and then back again to collect after the walk. If my memory serves me right I believe the walk was 25 miles or so and covered a big part of the island. Our legs were sore for days after. Apartment living was fabulous at Halloween, let's see…three apartments per floor, twenty stories per building, four buildings visited, the candy bounty was not to be believed!!   *Liz Calouri '79*

We did the 'walk-for-a-million' charity events, a 20 mile hike around the entire island for charity! always a lot of fun, and a way to see everybody who was anybody in HK. Bruce Doolittle and I ran it one year and almost died! first and last attempt at a near-marathon distance!
          Scott Schroth '77

• American Fortnight

I sure do remember the Rangerettes. Them and American Fortnight back in, I think, 1976. I remember Theo Janssen and a couple of other high school kids participated in an exhibition American football game down at the HK Stadium. Anyone have any tales of American Fortnight? I remember it was quite an extraveganza. But unfortunately only a one-off event.   *Ken Koo, '79*

"It's American Fortnight, and there are all kinds of events going on, some of which involve people from the school. So today there was an entertainment in Statue Square, and Bob Christian and some teachers including Art and Corky Himmler were singing in a Barbershop quartet.

Some kids were dressed up as Disney characters and were roaming around the Square like they do at Disneyland. Then there was also the Spanish teacher, Maggie Gordon, dancing with a rose in her mouth!!!
Dave Kohl, art teacher '73-'80
from a letter in 1973

• Visitors at HKIS:

I vividly remember when Jose Greco, the famous flamenco dancer, danced in the gym and we all thought he would go right through the old wooden floor! Bits of dust and grit were jumping when they were stomping. Then there was the world Yo Yo champion, we all got Coke yo yos, I still have mine somewhere, Coca Cola on one side, and Chinese characters for Hola Hola on the back!
Barb Schwerdtmann '77

Bob Christian and the principals frantically tried to secure the plywood floor to the gym floor. Jose needed a specific type of wood and finish in order to do his routine. I think it may have still been wet when the assembly started. I think the administration sweated bullets over this....and the foreign language department was gaa gaa, especiallly the Spanish-speakers like Mrs Maggie Gordon. She may have had Carman Miranda visions, I'm not sure.
Dave Kohl, art teacher '73-'80

The OK City band played nearly every year in the cafeteria. I just remember them as being one of the best bands I've ever heard back then. The U.S.S. Oklahoma City was part of the 7th Fleet. I remember their basketball teams were pretty awesome.
Ken Koo, '79

• World's Fair

HKIS World's Fair Spaghetti Sauce Recipe

Ever since my Mom was in charge of the Spaghetti Dinner, this has been our family's favorite sauce recipe! She had never used the sausage before. We've no idea whose recipe it was to begin with! Those huge pots of spaghetti pasta boiling and the sauce warming! I think we had red & white checkered table cloths with paper placemats. Most of the sauce came in old square Dairy Farm ice cream containers. What fun! We sure had

a great Mother's Club at school!

HKIS WORLD'S FAIR SPAGHETTI RECIPE
Sauce for 10

In a 6 quart Dutch oven saute until yellow:
¼ cup oil (vegatable or olive oil)
clove garlic minced (about ½ tsp
cup chopped onion
½ cup chopped celery
        Add:
pound minced beef
½ pound minced port or Italian sweet
    sausage; cook until meat loses pink color
        Add:
pound – 12oz tin whole tomatoes
(No. 2 tin) – broken up tin tomato soup plus
    1 tin hot water
6-oz tin tomato paste plus 3 tins hot water
bay leaf
tablespoon salt
tablespoon Worcestershire Sauce
teaspoon sugar
teaspoons Italian Seasoning or Oregano
    1/8 teaspoon pepper
Simmer all for 4 hours.

If possible, kindly deliver on the 10th of April, Saturday, before 3 p.m., please, to the Cafeteria. Otherwise, it may be delivered the day before to Mrs. Chan in the Cafeteria between 1 p.m. and 3 p.m. (IN DISPOSABLE CONTAINERS, PLEASE!)
** This sauce may be made any time and frozen. In fact, the flavour improves if it is made the day before use. Thank you again for your cooperation.
Betty Schwerdtmann c 1975

P.S. Please do not bring your sauce frozen as it would be very difficult for us to thaw it all before the dinner time.

• Arts Festival

I remember the fabulous arts festivals the school had when we could attend performances on either side of the street. I would sit down with my class and discuss the options – I loved it when they decided to try out the quartet of singers from high school or other performances from the high school.
Judy Butler, elementary teacher, '76-'83

• Day of Giving

Day of Giving was usually the Wednesday in November before American Thanksgiving, one of the two times per year that the entire student body, full faculty and staff gathered together for an assembly. I was asked to organize the Day of Giving assembly for November of 1982. I enlisted Pastor Paul Tuchardt from Church of All Nations to give the message, and asked high school art teacher, Steven Nesheim, to prepare a project for the entire school that could be constructed or put together during the assembly.

The week before the assembly each elementary classroom, junior high home room, and high school advisee group received a piece of paper, markers, and a small abstract drawing to blow up and colorize. The finished product was to be brought to the Day of Giving assembly. During the assembly there was singing from The Chordbusters and a fine message by Pastor Tuchardt. He spoke with a theme that centered on gifts. He talked about the fact that even though we may feel that our gift or contribution is insignificant, when these gifts are added together with those gifts of others, significant things can happen.

As this message was being given, representatives from each group brought their piece of art to the stage to be placed on a large board. (This was when the entire school could still fit into the gym at 6 South Bay Close!) As more and more pieces were added, it became clear that a picture was being formed. It was an enlargement of Sadao Watanabe's J*esus Washing the Disciples' Feet*. What a wonderful image and message for the day as the students and staff of HKIS prepared to go all over Hong Kong to help where they could – be it at a Vietnamese refugee camp, with mentally handicapped children, or an often-forgotten old folks home, etc. My hope is that each of us, who were touched in some way by HKIS, continue to give to those in need – each of our acts or gifts small, seemingly insignificant pieces of a larger picture of Christ's love. What a grand image that could make for the world!

William Kuhn, music teacher '80-'93

At Christmas time we did "Operation Santa Claus."
Debbie Smiley '72

Someone else can say this more precisely than me but seeing our service program grow over the years has just been amazing. We have a number of academic courses with direct links to service. There is a Service on Saturday program (SOS) with over 10 activities that regularly throughout the year helps organizations in Hong Kong. Around 1/3 of our interims are service oriented. We sponsor trips to orphanages. A number of new service clubs have been established at HKIS. Habitat for Humanity and Heifer International are huge programs at our school. The list goes on and on.
Dave Elliott '82-'07

• Holiday Tournaments

When I started at HKIS the Christmas Basketball Tournament was held from Dec 26-30 and brought together expat families from across Asia. They were held in what is now the Upper Primary Gym with 3-4 rows of bleachers. My son fell in love with basketball watching those teenagers sweat and dive into stands and just play great ball. As our son grew we would help more and more. Video cameras were just coming into vogue and I have way too many hours of video tape of high school basketball. That was one of the major sports events of the year.

In recent years the tournament has become a Thanksgiving weekend tournament but Jim Handrich continues to enjoy announcing the games and the DragonNet broadcasts all the games from the high school gym on the web. Today at HKIS there are tournaments on at least 15 weekends of the year in a huge variety of sports. HKIS participates in multiple leagues of schools across China and in Hong Kong. As long as I can remember HKIS has had a large percentage of the students in high school put on a uniform and play for the school sometime during the year.
Dave Elliott '82 -'07

2. Unintended traditions

• Mrs. Chan

I remember Mrs. Chan, The cafeteria "den mother"... 50 cents nutty nibbles, 30 cents joysticks, wonderbars...popsis for 10 cents..........those were the days !
Steve Chiu '69

Mrs. Chan was the one consistent feature of HKIS we kids got to see every day. I don't think that woman was ever sick, plus she came to almost

35

every other cafeteria related function! She knew everyone's favorite things. Mr. Himmler always got his Pepsi, and Mrs. Chan got my strawberry ice cream cup out every time when she saw me line and then it was Tropical Sundaes. THEN there was the time when she was making fresh doughnuts, and one batch had bugs in them, I saw one crawling out of my doughnut, and that was it for me.

The Cafeteria sure did go through some major transitions. My Mom was lunch monitor, and on those days, I couldn't trade my lunch for a cookie. In 4th grade, Ralph Trueb used to have chocolate sandwiches, and we all thought he was the luckiest kid in the world. I was sort of disappointed to discover Nutella years later, sort of spoiled the magic of his Mom melting chocolate bars for his lunch.

I also enjoyed going to visit Mr. Lam down in his workshop.   *Barb Schwerdtmann '77*

A typical conversation with Mrs. Chan:
   What you wantee?
   Nutty Nibble, please
   Nuddy nibbo??
   Yes, nutty nibble.
   Go boon
   Pardon?
   Solly, dolla fitty cen
   A dollar fifty?
   Hai, Dolla fitty
   Thanks
   You be good boy

Mike McCormick '80

Mrs. Chan served Borsht soup every day before the introduction of McDonald's
Renee Doyle '78

One of my first impressions of HKIS was the cafeteria lunchroom, when all 13 grades were in the same building and often had lunch together. High school kids and 1st graders in an amazing cacaphony. The school let the amahs come and feed some 1st and 2nd graders. And over in the corner taking milk money was Mary Ketterer, with her silver cigarette holder in her mouth (unlit, of course). And Mrs. Chan helping Ping Shan dish up lunch and selling hola hola, peksi hola, joysticks, nutty nibbles, and Mr. Christian's white vita soy in the glass pop bottles.   *Dave Kohl, art teacher '73 - '80*
•The Third Floor Lounge

I do not know whether any other department at the high school had offices. The English department's was at the balcony end of the main building's third floor. Just outside the hallway's double doors was the so-called 3rd floor Lounge, soon to be infamous for its location as the place to smoke, of course only with parental approval (an administrative master-stroke proposed by Werner von Behren, though a requirement more honored in the breach than the observance.)

Especially during pleasant weather, with the office windows open, I often overheard smatterings of student conversation. I soon found irresistibly uninhibited—that is, kids talking as they normally talk in each others' company. This not only included occasional profanity but a level of honesty most adults simply did not hear from adolescent mouths. After burning my ears for some weeks and debating whether or not this tone would vanish as soon as I appeared, I took the plunge.

Like encountering any wild creatures, my first few appearances were met with stunned silence that gradually became scattered murmurs. I anticipated this. But, like the fox's instructions to the prince in *The Little Prince* about how to tame an animal, I gradually was accepted. Like much in Hong Kong, once accepted I was, more or less, wholly (if only figuratively) embraced.

Memory of specific conversations elude me, but what I recall is their pattern. Kids were impressed with a teacher who lit their cigarettes, and many times a student—usually a girl, for whatever reason—would swiftly reflect on what they had just said, widen their eyes and say, "I can't believe I just said that in front of a teacher!", followed by mild laughter all around.

My visits to the third floor Lounge did not make me outstandingly popular, but I deeply enjoyed those interludes. This was, after all, the first time I had taught high school, and the Lounge was part of the process whereby the HKIS kids made teaching high school years later in the States such a difficult transition.

Andrew Grzeskowiak, teacher '78-'80

I have to accept blame, or credit, for the Third Floor Lounge. In 1975, the high school faculty had the opportunity to "re-design" the older school building into a high school, since the new building was set to open across the street. As faculty chairman, it fell to me to make proposals about where departments and classrooms would be re-assigned. We always left the Junior High on the top floor - 7th. I had spotted the nice grassy area outside the second floor, and made sure the art rooms were always proposed to be there. All the other departments got what was left, as we went through at least three proposed arrangements.

But, in surveying all the nooks and crannies of the seven floors, I noticed a triangular rooftop over the gymnasium showerrooms, off the end of the third floor's east end stairwell. It was covered with old classroom furniture dividers, and assorted desks....left over from the first set of furniture made in 1968. The faculty had recently held an all-day planning meeting at Maggie Gordon's, and decided we could meet the needs of our kids better with more places to be comfortable, relax, and work on homework(were we naive?). And I had grown tired of having kids hang out at the end of my hallway from the original art room on 7th floor. They liked to giggle, smoke, and smooch in that small space outside the double doors. I'd always hear them shooshing themselves when I'd come out into the hallway, and see them snuffing out their cigarettes in haste. Busted!!! But I've never been big on policing. There were a few instances where it was too blantant, even for me, so I had filled out some papers that went to the principal's office.

Solution.....clear off the rooftop and set up a nice student lounge outside the English office, and those guys could monitor students there. Bingo, everyone bought the idea. Paul Kan and Josephus Kwan and crews cleared out and demolished the old furniture. I then spent a week over the summer constructing benches and moveable platforms. A couple kids helped, I think Chris Myers was one. It was clean and bright, with fresh air, non-airconditioned, and a pretty nice view of the South China Sea. A nice place to sit out a free period or an extended break.

Guess what I (we?) forgot?.....ash trays...and a system to monitor those students who had permission to smoke and those who did not. It was the loosey-goosey '70s. There was often a haze of bluish smoke that could be seen off this area, even from South Bay Close, three levels down. And the material used for the uniforms those last two years held the smoke smell quite well. Several amorous couples found the 3rd floor lounge the perfect place to be "cozy." Somebody brought a transistor radio and there was always music. The thought that kids would use the place for quiet study proved overwhelmingly naive.

I had fostered a den of iniquity...or umbiquity...or sublimity? It was the '70s.
Dave Kohl, art faculty '73-'80

I recall the smoking policy was rather whacked in high school. You had to have your parent's permission to get on a list to smoke or you weren't supposed to...as if that was going to make a bit of difference. It sounds like something an attorney would come up with to limit liability.
Mike McCormick '80

Dave Kohl is the one to blame for Lisa Feldman running through the boys locker room while I was taking a shower! I told you Fritz's PE classes could be cruel...   *Richard Grayson '78*

I distinctly remember the grafitti on one bench: "If you can't be with the one you love, the one your with" CSNY.   *Chris O'Keefe '80*

When I told my two teenage boys that there was a smoking lounge (the Third Floor) at my high school, they just couldn't believe it. I showed them the pictures to prove it! I don't remember actually studying on the Third Floor, but I do remember listening to music and playing cards, especially with Corinne Abary.   *Linda Reizman '80*

I used to tell my youngest daughter Ellen (who's a 7th grader now in HKIS) about the 3rd Floor Lounge. In the Fall of 2004 on registration day, I took her to see her new 5th grade teacher and homeroom. Lo and behold, her new homeroom was basically the Lounge converted into a spanking new airconditioned classroom. So when asked by her teacher what she thought of the new premises, imagine the surprise of her teacher when Ellen said "Yechh.......this used to be the high school smoking lounge when my dad was in school !"
Ken Koo '79

•Bomb Scares

One day a group of us girls cut school and went to Repulse Bay to soak in the sun. A bomb scare was called in that same day and we were all caught cutting because the school tracked who wasn't in class so we were all questioned. They did catch the caller eventually and it was a student at school who probably just didn't want to take a test that day.   *Linda Reizman '80*

In one particular week of my first year at HKIS we had something like 9 bomb scares in a week and a half. I remember on one occasion the bomb scare happened at lunch time so my 2nd graders and I carried our plates of Ping Shan food in the rain across the street to the apartment complex to wait for the police to check the school and let us return.

Judy Butler, elementary teacher '76-'83

Bomb Scares - totally cool to head down to the beach AGAIN! We learned quickly to make sure we had money to buy snacks. Sad how it all unfolded.   *Barb Schwerdtmann '77*

•Streaking

The streaker incident happened with our family's getaway car. Involved were of course Brad Sandler and Mark Leonard. My brother Sean and sister Megan were partners in the crime. They had our driver Ah Lee bring the car to the Star Ferry and park towards the City Hall. When the dynamic duo came running toward the car, clothes clutched in one hand against their chests, Ah Lee, wide-eyed ...aiya... but reassured by Sean to be cool. Then Go Go!!! They were followed by people and the press, who had been tipped off, taking pictures.

It was on the news that night and in the papers the next day. My father was not too happy that the getaway car was a green station wagon, the only one in HK. My dad questioned Sean and Megan about the streaking incident in the paper, and was very curious that the getaway car was a green station wagon. Maybe a Rolls Royce would have been a little less unusual. Accusations flew that it was HKIS students and Mr. Westrick had to deal with the press.   *Chris O'Keefe '80*

It was me with Brad Sandler at the Star Ferry. Have had to live that up (or down) ever since.
Mark Leonard '74

As long as the streaker story is still alive, I will share my experience. Mark and one of the con-spirators came to me as I was getting ready to leave school that day. They swore me to secrecy and I listened. I did try hard to convince them that there could be serious consequences. They informed me that the "bets" were too high, and they could not pull out. I think Rob McLaren and Mike McCoy were among them. I believe I even mentioned that he might be out of the Colony sooner than he had anticipated. I called my husband at the Consulate and asked him to go over to the Star Ferry to keep an eye on things.

Mark called as soon as he safely landed, and said he thought I had blown the whistle on him, when the car wasn't where they expected. His dad was in Bangkok at the time. The next day, I took the American History students to see the new JFK movie, and when we left the theater, we saw the newspapers on the stands with full front page "coverage."

Sharon Prechtl, history teacher '70 - '74

Sharon called to say that Mark Leonard and Brad Sandler were gong to "streak" at the Star Ferry. She asked me to go and confirm this most intelligent of school pranks! At the Star Ferry, I saw two guys arrive and go directly to the row of plexiglass telephone booths. Once in the booth, they removed clothes and put then in a bag. I saw an old Chinese man in the next booth looking perplexed while clothes were shed, and he watched the boys leave the booths running (his mouth was slightly ajar!). The boys ran past a line of Chinese women, who were chatting while waiting for a bus. They did not stop talking, but checked out the boys running by–some shocked, some with a slight smile on their faces. Following the tableau, I saw the boys stop at the curb and a look of panic came over their faces. NO CAR WAITING! Looking anxiously right and left, they finally spotted the car about a block away. Their white faces broke into nervous smiles and they took off to the car, piling in, reminiscent of a bank robber getaway in Chicago circa 1920s.

I went back to my office, called Sharon to authenticiate the marvelous feat and leaned back, knowing Mr. Hoover would be proud of my time well spent protecting US citizens!!

Rod Prechtl, faculty husband '70-'74

•Mooned!

DRAGON TALES

I was on both the swim team and the volleyball team. I don't know when they started working on building the pool, but for our team training, we had to do laps around the school – out the gym door, straight up the side stairs to the 5th floor, down the sidewalk around the school and up again.

One day doing laps with June Steagall, the rugby team bus was parked on South Bay Close by the ground floor exit. They started "mooning" us through the bus windows, laughing and yelling. Chris Collins, Jim Pendergast, Gavin Birnie and, of course, Mark Feldman were bouncing around the bus, laughing, mooning, and hooting until one of the coaches, who heard us screaming, came out and put a stop to it all.

Karen Simon '77

DRAGON tAELS

40

teachers and staff

Faculty at HKIS have represented much of the United Nations, and almost the entire British Commonwealth. Initially, HKIS staff consisted of a core of Lutheran missionary teachers appointed by the Missouri Synod's Board of Missions. These teachers were recruited from their home city, with travel allowances, regular home leave, and housing provided by the school. Supplementing this core were a larger number of "local hires" - American and British teachers, as well as English-speaking third-country nationals.

Over the years, the teaching base has expanded, with the primary criteria still being philosophic alignment with the school's mission statement: Dedicating our minds to inquiry, our hearts to compassion, and our lives to service and global understanding. HKIS provides an American-style education grounded in the Christian faith and respecting the spiritual lives.

-Ed.

1. Administratively speaking

HKIS…Where does one begin? It's a unique school, a place where lives are touched by God's love, but where the school's very setting, along with the diverse backgrounds and needs of the community it serves, keep the school "living on the edge" through ever present challenges and opportunities.

Arleen and I vividly remember the continuing question that had to be confronted… "With the diversity of the ever changing HKIS community, how can the school be Christ-centered and Gospel-oriented, that lives may be touched by God's love?" Thanks be to God that through the years, this basic question has continued to be addressed, with love and understanding, and with positive results.

Scripture, Ephesians chapter one, tells us that in eternity, God determined to create human life as we know it today, knowing that because of sin, this would cost Him dearly. But He did it out of love for the lives He would bring into the world… and now, HKIS is an extension of His love. HKIS can be a catalyst for more lives throughout the world, to be touched with God's love.

2 Corinthians 3:3 provides some insight into how HKIS fulfills a Christ-centered mission. This happens as all of us, alumni, students, teachers, parents, and leaders in the HKIS community are "living letters" portraying an alive relationship with God through our Savior and our friend, Jesus. This happens at reunions, on Dragon Train, and with contact and conversations among "HKIS people" themselves.

I praise God for the many HKIS persons who have been, and who are "living letters portraying God's love," and Arleen and I thank the Lord that we, and our family, have personally been touched so deeply by the HKIS experience…By God's grace, we carry on.

Bob Christian, founding headmaster '66-'77

I remember the first day that I went to work and Headmaster Bob Christian gave me the checkbook and said "This is the money we have in the bank. Let's see what we can accomplish with it." Even by US dollar standards it was a very small amount. The exchange rate was 6.12 at the time. So I will let others decide if we accomplished our task.

Getting to know what a crossed check stood for was an interesting experience. I had an issue with someone who said they had paid their tuition and I said not according to the records. They sent me a copy of their check and I took it to their bank and asked how this could have cleared the bank when we didn't have a record of depositing it through our bank. The manager explained to me that it was not a crossed check and the words are bearer were not crossed out. So the person had written a check and gone to their bank and cashed it and then tried to state that because the check had been cashed that their bill was paid. It didn't work as their employer made them pay it immediately.

Ed Dollase, business manager '67 - '74

My family and I earned the infamous Ed Dollase "Flying Fickle Finger Award!" of 1970.

We were heading home for our first summer furlow. When you are gone for more than two months, you want to make sure that you have packed properly, especially when you are traveling with two infants. I knew we were in trouble as our plane's wheels made that clunk sound as we lifted off from the old Kai Tak airport. That clunk shook my memory and struck fear to my inner core; we forgot our health books in our apartment! When we arrived at Tokyo's airport, we marched up to the security officer and reported our plight. We rolled up our sleeves; we were ready to repeat all shots necessary, but we were not going back to Hong Kong.

We must not have been the first, for they took us to a motel on the airport grounds for quarantine. We were restricted on the base, so to speak. We called Ed Dollase and informed him where our health booklets were in our filing cabinet. I figure Ed must have figured such emergencies might happen, because he required everyone to give him a copy of our apartment keys. Brilliant man! The following morning our health books were on the flight from Hong Kong to Tokyo. Our flight plans were altered; we could not go to Seattle by way of Anchorage as we had originally planned. To this day we still can not claim Alaska as a state we have visited.

Bob Ruprecht, teacher

• The Second BusinessManager

When I told Bob Christian in Oct. of '73 that I would be leaving in June of '74, he started a search for someone to take the Business Manager position. He was on a recruitment trip back to the US and decided on Richard Johnson from Minnesota. All the arrangements were in place and the man along with his wife and family arrived in Hong Kong in early June so I could try and unload six years of experience and procedures that I felt he would need to carry on the work as Business Manager. He arrived on I believe it was a Thursday and agreed that he would like to get started on knowing all the duties. We took a tour of the first building, talked about the new building under construction across the street. I told him about all the things to do when you arrived in the Colony, like going to get your identification card, registering at the US Consulate, getting a driver's license, and all the other things you needed to do to set up your residence.

He agreed that we would meet part of the day on Saturday. We continued on Monday. On Tuesday morning he came in to my office and said that he had something to tell me. I said what was that. He said that he had decided after the number of hours of training we had done that he felt the job was too big for one man to handle and that he wanted to take his family back to the US as soon as possible. He did resign and it was agreed to put him and his family on a plane back to the US.

Then I was honored that the faculty voted to ask me to stay. However, that was not possible at that point as we had shipped our household items back to the US and sold our car etc. I appreciated that vote very much but it was too late.

Bob Christian and the Board of Managers would have to then struggle with finding another person to take the position. They did find a British man ("Sir" Richard Horwood) who was already in Hong Kong so they didn't bring over another American for the position.

Ed Dollase, Business Manager

In the spring of 1974, my 8th year as an educator, I was offered a one-year gig at Concordia Teachers College, River Forest, near Chicago, Illinois. I was riding high, until a day two months into the school year when the division chairman stopped in my office and started making small talk. Small talk always leads to big talk and the big talk was, "So, what are your plans for next year?" I was still working on what I was doing in the current year and said so. "Well," he said, "I have a friend who's coming through and interviewing for science and math teachers." "Great." I said. "Where's he from?" "Hong Kong," the Chair replied.

My internals said, "Hong Kong. Ri-i-i-i-i-ght, Lord. What's a cubit?"

That evening I relayed the information to my wife and her reaction, no smile, no emotion: "We're not going to Hong Kong." I responded, "Of course not, but we've never interviewed before and this will be a good opportunity to practice." We agreed and an appointment was set to meet this guy named Bob Christian. He was interviewing at his mother's home on the Northwest side of Chicago and as we walked across the vast lawn my wife said," Remember, we are NOT going to Hong Kong."

What followed was not an interview, but a dialogue. Bob presented the opportunity at hand, complete with yearbooks. He regaled us with stories and alluded to the great times we would have in Hong Kong…all the time I'm asking myself, "How do I tell this guy 'there ain't no way we're going to Hong Kong." At the close of the interview, as we were preparing to leave, Bob said, "Dave, just one more question." …"If I were to ask your former principal what he liked least about you, what would he tell me?" I was relieved. I was off the hook. I knew answering that question honestly, there was no way Bob would hire me. I said, "Bob, he would tell you that I'm too close to my students." (And, for any of you reading this who remember Walter Steinberg from Luther South in Chicago, you'll understand.) Bob wagged his finger at me in a way that only Bob can and he said "You're just the guy I'm looking for!"

On the long walk across the lawn to the car, my wife started off with, "When we get to Hong Kong…"

Such are the persuasive powers of Robert Christian.   *Dave Meyer, science teacher, '75-'81*

I owe a big thank you to Bob Christian, who gave me a chance to develop on my own, and Mr. Wallis let me work in the "Interest Center." Earl Westrick made it all come through. They believed in me and my three kids. It was a colorful and growing time....we were all so young.
Margrete Agell, elementary aide '71-'81

•Missionaries   from a letter "home" in 1973

The situation here is interesting. We get letters from churches and youth groups all over the country. Aparently the Lutheran church puts out some kind of listing of missionaries for churches to write to at Christmas time. They are nice thoughts. One even sent us two US dollars, cash. We'll give that to the Timothy Paul Study Center, that our church sponsors. Many times, I don't feel like much of a missionary, but as our principal Werner Von Behren says, 'you live as a type of Christ.' It's a challenging situation, and the problem is to try to acquaint the non-Christians with Christ, for His own beauty and the joy of His salvation, and not as some western cultural tradition that is just like all the other western traditions that Europeans have forced upon the Chinese. So many of our ways of doing things look so stupid over here when the Chinese have time-tried systems that function much better. So in the opportunities I've had to witness Christ, I try to keep that as background.
Dave Kohl, art teacher, '73-'80

•Global understanding

A while back I applied for a position where one of the listed qualifications required experience with diverse cultural environments. I most likely scared them away when I stated that I had first hand experience with employees/students from over 25 nations.

I have fond memories of the high school office during my second stint at HKIS. People from America, Australia, India, and Northern Ireland dutifully reported for work each day. We worked hard, and conversed hard. Politics, religion, sports, were but a few of the topics considered. Regardless of the topic, the give-and-take was robust and informative. Those conversations contributed mightily to my sense of global understanding. Now, repatriated to the United States, I find that I deeply miss those interactions.

Thus, my contribution to capturing the heart of HKIS at its best. Those interactions, and conversations, between students, faculty, and staff from all over the world are remarkable. I trust they will continue, and even get better, in the years to come.
Fritz Voeltz, middle school teacher '73-'80
high school vice principal '96-'03

2. Elementary Staff

I taught half-day kindergarten in the '80s with Ginny Schiefer and Aileen Wallis in the 2B cluster. Each of us had 18 children and no teaching assistant. The day started with a 30 minute religion lesson followed by a morning filled with workbook activities! The children sat quietly at tables. We had a math, language arts , social studies and handwriting workbook. No food was permitted to be eaten in the cluster so we hiked to 3C for snack each day which consisted of 2 cookies and milk.

The morning kindergarten children went home at 11:00 and the afternoon children arrived on the buses that were used to take the morning children home. Since the programs dovetailed, there was no time for the teachers to have a lunch break. After some discussion, Darrel Wallis hired Lucy Wong to watch 52 children play in the classroom while the teachers disappeared to the lunch room for 20 minutes. Lucy did a magnificent job managing 52 children.

Mr. Lam, whose snow-white hair distinguished him from other employees, was hired full time to shuffle mail from building to building. Each of us had large mail boxes that we emptied twice a day. Stacks of brown inter-school envelopes were everywhere to be seen.

In the 80s each floor in the Lower Primary had an open-air space in the rainbow staircase. On rainy days, children played outside their clusters. This space was also used to dry paintings and to play games.

Around 1984 Charlene Schneiter worked at designing a new faculty lounge. She and Darrell went to the Sheraton Hotel in TST and bought furniture they were selling. Green and gold velveteen wicker furniture looked quite stunning. Old pieces can still be spotted in the building today.

Private Music Lessons: In the early 80's Mr Koo taught private music lessons to children during the school day. His music room was in 2B.

• Things that have remained the same for 27 years.

1. Matthew Wong's bus service
2. Sand box on the 2nd floor play ground
3. HKIS badge design
4. Annual year book
5. All school Christmas assembly
6. Rainbow staircase in the Lower Primary
7. Free coffee for teachers all day
8. Cars getting ticketed by the police on South Bay Close

Mary Jane Elliott, elementary teacher '80-'07

The first year the elementary building was opened, kids loved the rainbow colored vertical pipes that lined the central staircase, but I remember early on that a kindergartner got his head caught between the rainbow painted bars.

Mary Kaye Soderlind, counsellor '74-'80

My last year at HKIS – after school was dismissed for the year, I fulfilled my desire and swung on those rainbow bars. HKIS – Thanks for the memories! *Judy Butler, teacher '76 - '83*
• Multiculture

I will always think of HKIS as synonymous with multiculture because of so many varied memories of teaching in the elementary school. While students spoke varieties of English, many spoke another language as well which they would use at recess, lunch and some unlikely times. The varieties of foods eaten at HKIS were always interesting such as curry, fried rice, chicken feet, kimchee. I was there when McDonald's was controversial but won over as the lunch of choice.

I remember the students bringing so much of their cultures to the classroom in the form of stories, art, games, and ways they made friends. The teachers also brought many ideas of how to present lessons and intriguing mini-lessons. Teachers being educated and having taught all over the world brought many stimulating viewpoints of education, some more acceptable than others.

When I was at HKIS there was always an effort to learn the latest in effective methods based on solid research, such as the Individually Guided Education (IGE) program. It was a privilege to be part of a faculty that could learn so much conveniently at the school and receive credit. The "frosting" for me was the opportunity to discuss and apply what we were learning. We were always encouraged to stretch ourselves trying new theories of instruction.

Carole Feddersen, 5th grade '72-'75
& jr hi '78-'90

• Twenty four years

When I started at HKIS it was as a substitute primary teacher in the spring of 1975, when we were all still in one building. Little did I realize that I would continue on for 24 years, - as a teacher, Unit Leader, ESL "expert" who contributed ESL "Pearls" to the faculty newsletters every week, Gesell Developmental Examiner, Learning Center teacher and leader - remaining in the elementary, now primary, school.

Things that come to mind from those years in the elementary school - school closure on the first day of the opening of the new elementary school because of a typhoon, Lippincott Readers, IGE, MAG, FGT, open classrooms, ESL classroom on the 4th floor, Radio Shack "computers", Cantonese lessons to be replaced with Mandarin, specials galore, disappearance of the science lab to make way for the Learning Center, cafeterias on two floors with McDonald's lunches, bomb threats, all-school assemblies, building of first the high school campus at Tai Tam to be followed by the middle school, division of the elementary into upper and lower primary, returning college students who marvel at the smallness of the elementary building.

Most of all I remember the feeling of love, care and concern surrounding the children and faculty. HKIS was the best place to be both a teacher and a parent. How I miss it!

Carol Thomas, elementary teacher '75-'99

•Chicken Fat

Chicken Fat was an exercise warm up that we did periodically that the gradeschool kids really loved. They sang with gusto the the words "GO YOU CHICKEN-FAT GO." The song was commissioned by Pres. John Kennedy for his new Youth Fitness Program, written by Meridith Wilson in '68, and sung by Robert Preston.

Once the new building opened I felt it created a wedge between the Jr.Hi/High School and the elementary school. Prior to the new building, all ate in the fourth floor dining room. Once the new building was built, the two schools ate separately, and did little to continue the relationships that were developed when one building was all that we had. I continued going to the high school for my lunch so I could see my friends in that building. The elementary school didn't have one area to eat lunch: they all ate on the floors in which they taught, making it difficult for the "Special Teachers" to mingle.

Walt Schmidt, PE teacher 71-83

•Unforgettables

There were lots of unforgettable teachers at HKIS. Mrs. Duval, my first grade teacher, with her Mary Tyler Moore hairstyle whom I thought was so pretty and learned so much from. Mrs. Mache with her ever present smile and colorful flower print art smocks.

Mr. Rausch in the 6th grade, encouraged my creative side. He had a corner nook in his classroom with four boxes, two on the top and two on the bottom where we could go to read or just hang out – pretty cool for 6th graders! I think he was one of the forerunners in creating open and more casual classroom spaces.

David Christian was a senior at HKIS when I was in the second grade, than he came back and taught my 7th grade class. I believe it was his first teaching experience. Poor guy, we were not an easy bunch!

Liz Calouri '79

•My first HKIS teacher

I have several different memories of our school – Hong Kong international School. My earliest memory was from 1966 when I was in the 4th grade and we were schooled in what seemed to be an apartment building somewhere in Repulse Bay. Our class was quite small, but the teacher was Mrs. Cutler, who I vividly remember. She had a traditional style, which including giving "gold stars" to good students, and spanking to bad ones. Anyway, I do remember moving to the new facility also in Repulse Bay and having actual classrooms and playing areas.

Kendra Lannom '66-'70

My most embarrassing moment was being called into Mr. Hollar's office and asked to repeat what some kid had said. It was Mr. Hollar! He had a paddle in his office! I was quaking in my saddle shoes - must have been 4th grade. I had to say the f- word and the s- word. I just knew he was going to tell my mom, but he didn't. I think the kid got the paddle. I remember just sitting there quaking looking at the paddle. Then I had to see him on Sundays at church, but he always pretended nothing had happened.

Barb Schwerdtmann '77

• Musical Adventures

Back in the 1970's I remember going to China Products in Central and being overwhelmed by the smells of that store. It was a mix of camphor and moth balls, as I remember it. Never mind the smell, the large number of items for sale, and the bargains, what a deal!

One of the departments on the first floor, second floor to Americans, sold all sorts of exotic musical instruments. They were fascinating. My husband, Alan, is a collector and could not resist buying all sorts of instruments. I could not see just collecting them. I thought they should be played. So, I chose one, basically I closed my eyes and pointed. I chose the pipa, the pear shaped lute.

Whenever we were out in the markets or crowded areas, we heard Chinese music. Most of it sounded like so much off-key wailing but, now I am going to learn to play one of those awful-sounding noise makers. I asked Mario Koo, the music teacher at HKIS, to help me. Mr. Koo played all of the western instruments and gave lessons to legions of children, patiently listening to them squeak their way through lessons. I enjoyed my lessons and I outlasted Mr. Koo. He passed me off to his friend, Mr. Lim. While Mr. Lim played the pipa well he spoke no English and my Cantonese was minimal. I listened to him play and repeated it. Mr. Koo had taught me to read music according to the Eastern style of numbers, characters and lines. I learned quite a lot from Mr. Lim, enough to appreciate the music I was hearing. I learned a number of folk songs and enjoyed playing them.

One time a pipa player, Gloria Ku, was scheduled to play live on Radio HK. I could not resist. I went down and listened to her play. I was enthralled. After the performance I introduced myself and told her that I could play the pipa a little. I asked her if she knew of someone who spoke English and could teach me some more pipa. Gloria said that she would be happy to teach me. Thus began four years of friendship and lessons that I shall never forget.

I went to Gloria's flat in Midlevels for lessons. We always began our lessons with tea. Gloria would tell me things about the tea and its special qualities. Then we would settle down to the lesson. Gloria taught me to read western notation music and many different pieces. I thought they were difficult.

Pipa concerts were now a joy. I remember hearing Gloria play at the new concert hall in Tsim Sha Tsui. I was so proud of her. I also participated in some musical productions at HKIS. It was fun to play. Then there was the time a group of us were eating at the Jumbo Restaurant in Aberdeen and there were pipa players serenading us. When they took a break I was challenged to go up a play. I did. It was fun, but fortunately most people talked loud enough they did not have to be disturbed by my plucking.

Carole Feddersen , teacher, '72-'75, '78-'90

Mr. Koo the music teacher was the best. I remember in 4th grade, him introducing us to the instruments, he was playing the trombone, and he had to throw the slide, we all thought that was the funniest thing we had ever seen and he didn't un-

derstand why we were all laughing so hard! Keith Quong and I got into trouble because we couldn't stop laughing. *Barb Schwerdtman '77*

I remember Mr. Koo playing the bass at any number of musical performances at HKIS. The bass was as tall as he was. He was very faithful to music for kids. One of the memories of I have of Mr. Koo was eating some noodles at a stall. He drowned his bowl of noodles in catsup!
Carol Fedderson. teacher,   '72 - '75; '78 - '90

How can anyone forget the music teacher Mr. Passarella He played the sax and was in a really cool band. He was quite the hippy, even more so than Bob Matthews.   *Mike Roth '79*

No matter how bad you sang, you still got to be in choir, and in those scant boy participation years, I had to be a tenor. It was a wonderful experience to be part of a group and create music. The leadership and teachers are the "make it or break it" of success and deriving joy from anything.
Barb Schwerdtman '77

I am very fond of my participation in various orchestra pits, the piano trio with Marcus Woo and Cathy Clasper, and other music activities.
Katy Kohl, now Anderson, teacher '73-'76

Dale Elmshauser was taking his concert Band to Macau for a performance in '74 and wanted the students to travel quickly on the hydrofoils. This was fine, but they could not take their instruments on the hydrofoils, since there is no space for bulky luggage. He asked Katy and me if we'd go on the trip, but take the Macau Ferry Lo Shan and accompany all the band's instruments. OK - no big deal, a free weekend on the school.

This was fine on the way over, but the next day on return, there had been a drug bust at the Macau Ferry Terminal, so the constabulary were keen to rout out any more illicit activity. Imagine their eyeballs popping from their faces when they saw 40 or so instrument cases piled up at customs!.....and did they have fun! Every case and instrument was thoroughly examined in the finest bureaucratic fashion...white gloves...lots of whispered talk...but no drugs!
Dave Kohl art teacher '73-'80

My name is Victor Guy and I taught music and band with Werner Von Behren from 1970-72.

At that time I was known as Victor Lee but I have changed my last name since 1972. Our concert band won the HK Kiwanis Music Festival in 1972.
Victor Guy(Lee), music teacher 1970-1972

•Paper Mache
'

I'll never forget hearing Mrs. Mache' yelling "FREEZE" in art class as everyone made a mad dash for the door when the bell rang.
Wally Tuchardt '81

Mrs. Mache´ who always encouraged you to try something in a new way along with the required lesson in the early years.
Barb Schwerdtmann '77

•Bombed

Even a series of bomb threats didn't disrupt the process of education. I can remember going with classes to continue their work at the beach and, on at least one occasion, bringing a whole class back to our apartment overlooking Repulse Bay. It was a family kind of place.

There was the most beautiful school library in the world, with cushioned rattan chairs and grasscloth on the walls – a graphic demonstration of someone's theory (was it Earl Westrick?) that if their surroundings were attractive, students would take care of them. From the librarian, Dusty Knisely, I learned the basis of librarianship with its two most important rules: the library is for the service of its users and handle a piece of paper only once.

From my colleague Judy Stringer in the joint 4th-5th grade classroom in which she was the volunteer and I a paraprofessional my first year in Hong Kong, I learned to teach – to pay attention to the students and teach them what they needed, wanted, and were ready to learn. In my subsequent 25 years of teaching and occasional librarianship I have often been grateful for those two women who set me on a very satisfying path.
Kathy Isaacs, teacher, '73-'78

3. Teaching Junior High

In June of 1973 I accepted a teaching job back at my Alma Mater, HKIS. I found myself back in Asia, initially with some new HKIS colleagues at an Individually Guided Education workshop in Singapore. Those days together were formative for the junior high faculty as we wound up being a close group that had a lot of fun with each other and with the students during the next several years.

Ironically, I almost got sent packing before the workshop had begun. Without my dad around to watch my grooming, my hair had gotten quite a bit longer during my four years at Valparaiso, and when I arrived at passport control in Singapore, there was some murmuring among the officials. They let me pass, but only after taking my passport and saying that if I wanted it back, I had to report back to them with a haircut within the next 24 hours. That night Mark Silzer, our Junior High Principal, got out his scissors, and the next day we returned to the airport to reclaim my passport.

The Junior High Faculty developed a collective personality pretty quickly, and much of that began with motorcycles. Mark Silzer, Bob Matthews, Fritz Voeltz, Ken Rohrs, and I each had bikes … although I would guess that the combined displacement of our five bikes was smaller than that of a current Harley Davidson. From time to time we would rise early on a Saturday morning and take off for a ride in the New Territories, stopping for breakfast at some open-air kitchen where we heavily relied on Bob Matthew's language abilities.

The ongoing war in Vietnam and the continual presence of US servicemen on R&R had led the formation of the "China Fleet Club," a purchasing club that enabled military personnel to buy cheaply and safely. The HKIS faculty had shopping privileges at the "Fleet Club," and many of us used it to buy cameras or stereos … and we put those stereos to good use at several junior high dances. We gathered our various speakers and hooked them all up to whose ever amplifier was the largest, and turned the school cafeteria into a rockin' dance site.

On at least one occasion, we substituted live music for the "super stereos." I don't recall if we ever gave ourselves a name, but Mark Wallis (high school student playing drums,) Paul Westrick (high school student playing guitar,) G. Barnes (third grade teacher on guitar and vocals,) and I (bass and vocals) managed a pretty fair approximation of a rock band.

Each spring the junior high spent a week at our Suen Doh outdoor education camp. The teachers slept in the dorms with the students, and so we were all quite tired by the end of the week … but the experience gave us a chance to interact with the kids in new ways, and to learn in a far different environment.

None of us will forget the camp when we slaughtered, butchered, roasted, and then ate a young pig. We had prepared the kids for what would happen, and while some were squeamish and stayed in the distant background, most were attentive as Fritz slaughtered the pig. The Chinese staff at the camp was quite amused by the whole affair, and then asked for the entrails as the butchering progressed. Ken Rohrs organized the open spit roasting … and we all enjoyed samples of fresh roasted pork during our evening meal.

While the junior high faculty had its own particular character, the entire HKIS faculty enjoyed a strong sense of camaraderie. I recall regular "Eat In's," organized social events in which we would share a meal, occasionally with an accompanying program. The Oktoberfest of course included San Miguel, but also brought faculty musicians together in a "sort of" polka band. Without these events, who would have ever known that my dad was a pretty fair clarinet player!

Dave Christian '69, Jr. Hi teacher '73 - '75

• We Had Fun

At 28, I was the oldest teacher in the Junior High School, older than the principal (Mark Silzer). HKIS had around 1,100 students from K-12 at 6 South Bay Close. All Junior High teachers drove motorcycles. Study groups moved into the halls. 33 students were in each of my 6 science classes. When our principal held a confidential meeting, his secretary rolled her typing table into the hall. Crowds packed the HKIS Christmas basketball tournament.

High school students watched out for the kindergartners. K-12 school uniforms were blazers over a white shirt with a school necktie for boys and a dark navy two-piece suit with a white blouse for the girls. HKIS was the only school in Hong Kong with air-conditioning. Students rode the #6 bus (HK$0.60) to school and to the Star Ferry to the Salisbury Road YMCA in Tsimshatsui. The student who came to school in a fancy car was rare.

At Junior High camp students built bamboo bridges over the Indus River, killed, dressed and cooked pigs and chickens for dinner, and back-packed overnight to Tai Long Wan or Lai Chi Wo. High school students participated in the cross harbour swim from Queen's Pier to Star Ferry Kowloon side. HKIS teams were frequently "colony" swim and track champions.

After the K-12 Thanksgiving or Christmas assemblies, all students participated in the Day of Giving. Weekly Junior High chapels filled Church of All Nations with enthusiastic singing. HKIS was full of youth, energy and motivation. In 1976, I and three other teachers became the first non-Lutherans to receive over-seas contracts.

Ken Rohrs, Jr. Hi science teacher, '73-current

In 8th grade, there were 90 of us crammed in one corner of the 7th floor in the (now) upper Primary Building. Ken Rohrs was my homeroom teacher. His first year in HKIS and the only year he taught 8th grade. Our class was crammed amidst the hardware of the first HKIS language lab. Next door (actually partitioned off) were Fritz Voeltz' and Dave Landdeck's classes. We were very experimental in those days. *Ken Koo '79*

• Fritz Voeltz

Mr. Voeltz in the eighth grade, he and the Jr Hi Motorcycle Gang, Mr. Rohrs, Silzer, Matthews, Landdeck et al… on their bikes, came after a group of us who had ditched classes and headed for the Repulse Bay beach one beautiful and sunny day! A brilliant plan…meeting at the shack followed by beach time… all thwarted by the sound of their bikes coming after us! *Liz Calouri '79*

One time Fritz Voeltz was squatting against the wall waiting for the elevator on third floor while my parents and I walked by. After finding out he was a teacher, they wondered why they had sent me HKIS. I heard he was in a movie called *FoxBat*, made in Hong Kong where he was in playing a US Marine. *Patrick Pang '79*

• History teacher and coach

I taught at HKIS from 1972 to 1980. My experience there is somewhat unique as I had been a high school student myself in HK from 1963 to 1967. I went to La Salle, as there were no international schools then. We went to dances every Friday night at St. John's Cathedral and every Saturday night at Christ Church on Waterloo Road.

Two girls I had dated were in the first HKIS class of 1968 - Mindy Gooch and Cheryl Muschett. However I was at the University of Tennessee from 1967 -1971, and ran track there.

I returned to HK in fall of 1971 and worked in business.

New Year's day 1972 was memorable for 2 reasons. As I was walking around the Peak Loop and turned the corner facing the harbor, I saw this plume of smoke rising to several 1000 feet in the air! Only thing big enough to have a fire that big was the Queen Elizabeth, the ocean liner being re-fitted to become a university. Also, that day in the paper the news of Barry Laubach's death hit the press. He was also a talented track athlete and member of the mile relay record at HKIS. I never met him but his death compelled me to write to Mr. Christian and to apply for a job as I felt in my heart that teaching, not business, was more my calling.

I was not yet a Christian, which happened on Feb 17th 1972, 35 years ago. Mr. Christian answered my letter after I had given my heart to the Lord. I interviewed with Werner Von Behren and Earl Westrick at the Imperial Hotel in Kowloon. They were going to start a new junior high with home room teachers. Mr. Landdeck and Mr. Silzer also started that year with me.

Mr. Rohrs was often a passenger behind me on my motorcycle his first year teaching and can attest that we made it to HKIS from Nathan Road in 11 minutes with him on the back - in a 175cc Honda.

I taught the classes of 1978, 1979, and 1980 in 7th grade, and classes of 1980, 1981, and 1982 in 8th grade. Then I taught high school in 1978 to 1980. So the class of 80 had me three times! James Barnett and Kelly Prechtl were in my first class...poor you! I had Rosemary Rarvey in religion in '72, not to be confused with Rosie Garvey, who the Lord sent to torment me my 2nd year of teaching.

I coached every senior class from 1973 to 1980 in track. We always had 80+ kids on the team as we has 6 teams – grades a b c, boys and girls. Some may recall b grade for boys was over age 15, or over 5'7" tall. God help you if you were a 5'7" 7th grader, as you would have to compete with 16 year olds - a problem Mike Kinne or David Brooks never had (vertically challenged).

I was only 5 years older than the seniors in 1972 and I coached Tal Albertson and Mike Sullivan to gold medals that year and Gregg Westrick was a javelin thrower and shot putter. So that makes them 52 years old and my first 7th graders are at least 47 years old. That's why this is written in capital letters.... So you can read it!

Teaching at HKIS was a blast. Some faculty members will never forget the pre-school meeting where we rode our motorcycles to the altar in the chapel (Church Of All Nations). Silzer's idea!

I've never stopped enjoying spending and sharing my life with teenagers and ushering them through those wonderful years. To me it was yesterday. Kelvin Limm is still an 8th grader to me, and maybe still tries to act with the same energy. He was always a handful.

It was a privilege to teach and coach during the 70's, whether they were at the senior prom or Suen Doh camp gutting a pig, or watching Keith Quong in "Guys and Dolls" or watching Michelle Champeau trying to hurdle. Much love in Jesus!
Bob Matthews, teacher and coach '72-'80

Yes, Mark and I were Bob Matthew's two most respected track timers. To this day, my friends are still dazzled by my stopwatch abilities. I guess it's a skill you never loose. The only thing that slowed me down when I ran on the team was that carton of cigarettes in my back pocket.
Patrick Gould '70-'74

I still remember Mr. Matthews tormenting me by pointing out that the Island School uniform was brown!!! My mom (Mrs. Prechtl) had told him that it was a threat made to me if I did not shut up in class, and he had fun with it. *Kelly Prechtl '78*

Mr. Matthews was only person that ever let me babysit their children. When everyone else paid attention to the bad reputation that I managed to cultivate during my short time at HKIS ('78-'80), a true believer in the good that lies within. Of course, I did invite Ian Goepfert over to assist but that was purely innocent. *Lisa Pearce '82*

We had free-for-all paper-fights in Mr. Matthew's 8C (to relieve the tension from that triple-period class, of course). My sister Leslie was in the class that hazed him his first year, as I recall.
Sheila Baker'82

•Devotions with Snoopy

My HKIS devotions invariably used Peanuts cartoons. One favorite speaks about combating evil in a world fraught with evil. Lucy (Lucifer, the devil's advocate) is angry with Snoopy (image of the little Christian). Lucy has Snoopy backing up on his dog house, threatening with her balled fist saying, "I'm gonna pound you! There's no way out! Prepare to meet your doom!" Snoopy retreats as she approaches, nearing the back edge of his doghouse. As Lucy is about to clobber him, Snoopy turns and slobbers a messy dog kiss right on her lips. Lucy falls away, crying out with disgust.

Snoopy ponders her response and says, "One kiss is worth two judo chops any day!"

We don't overcome evil with evil, but by doing good. God didn't defeat Satan with heavenly powers but with love and forgiveness personified in Christ's words and deeds. He calls us and empowers us to do likewise. The love we received and learned at HKIS calls us to do what the Lord requires of us, "to do justice, and to love kindness, and to walk humbly with your God." (Micah 6:8)

Alan Feddersen, teacher,'72-'75 &
Middle School Principal, '78-'90

Alan Feddersen created the Hong Kong International School's Middle School. From 1967 to 1971 grades 7 and 8 were administered by the high school principal as part of the 7 through 12 High School. In 1972 these grades became their own entity as the Junior High School. Alan created the 6, 7 and 8 Middle School.

Alan was a sixth grade teacher when he became the Principal of the Junior High School. He worked hard to educate faculty, parents and administration about the differences between a junior high and a middle school. Alan persistently pushed us forward and included more choices for kids in our program. Alan started life skills (cooking, sewing), health, drama and more music offerings. He started focusing us more on integrating curriculum, teaming and advisor/advisee programs. The sixth grade joined the seventh and eighth grades, first from their location in the Elementary Building. Then, when the High School moved out to Tai Tam, the sixth grade joined us across the street in our renovated Middle School As a 6, 7 and 8 school, evening dances became afternoon activities and ice cream socials.

We outgrew a single junior high camp and a program of separate grade level outdoor education activities started. Sixth grade went to Macau, seventh grade biking in China and eighth grade continued with a focus camp in Sai Kung.

The HKIS Middle School continues expanded and enriched, but pretty much as Alan nurtured it in its beginning. The major differences are that Snoopy and Charlie Brown don't show up at chapels and no administrator approaches the unique standard of Alan's couturier.

Ken Rohrs, MS science teacher, since '73

Another great HKIS teacher was Mr. Fedderson. He used to read C. S. Lewis' *The Lion, The Witch and The Wardrobe* to us aloud in class. The *Chronicles of Narnia* was Christian through and through. Mr. Federson never mentioned that, the dirty sneak! Insensitive and politically incorrect of me to point out that Charles Schulz was also Christian. The secret mission of Charles Schulz's creation Snoopy (Hound of Heaven) and C. S. Lewis' creation Aslan (Christ) was the same. Schulz was a secret agent of goodness. Another HKIS teacher, Mr. Schrock, shared with me *The Gospel According to Peanuts*--where some minister helpfully points out all the Biblical and theological references of Charlie Brown, Lucy, Linus, and the gang. I've got a used copy of that minister's book next to my beat up old Good News Bible, the one that Dr. Herb Meyer made me underline and highlight in the 7th grade.

Those HKIS teachers instilled the love of God in us blockheads. Darn those teachers!!! They saved my soul back there in Hong Kong. I once was a spoiled, sullen, bratty American diplomats' kid, but now...I'm a grateful one

Moira Gavaghen '78

4. High School

• The First High School Principal

The very first year we had students from all over the world and from about that many church affiliations. What a challenge! After 13 years in Lutheran Schools in the U.S and now this! Those six years were a SUPER experience for me and my family under the leadership of Robert Christian. Working with students from all walks of life was an experience that God put me through, which showed the importance of the mission of HKIS. My family experienced the involvement with faculty, students and parents as one big family. Those six years were a real blessing to all of us.

The spiritual uplift for me was working with students from all walks of life. Sharing the gospel in chapel and individual consultations was an experience that I was able to take with me throughout the rest of my 45 year career in Lutheran Education. Graduates coming back from college and coming into my office to tell me they were glad that I insisted they be in chapel every time. They wanted me to know it was a help as they struggled with religion and now they had found their Savior. This was the most satisfying blessing I can think of.

My prayer is that HKIS continue in its Mission statement serving students and families sharing the Christian faith and respecting each one for who they are.

Lester Zimmerman, high school principal '67-'73

• Earl Westrick

Earl…so many names popped into my head for you during those first months in Hong Kong…"Earl the Pearl" lead to "the Pearl of the Orient", the "Earl of the Orient", "the Earl of Westrick", "Duke of Earl"...

And just plain "The Earl."

For me, three things about Earl Westrick are significant…

#1 You and Marg raised seven of the finest young people, ever.

#2 You were an educational administrator who, along with Bob, fully understood that to get the job done, hire the right people, point them in the right direction, provide the right tools, then stand back and stay out of the way. Earl, you unleashed all of the best in me. Thank you.

That was important for my professional life.

#3 Earl also saved my daughter's life! At age 4, I was prepared to put her in a 55 gallon drum, pound on the lid and set her adrift. No 4-year old was ever (or, so I thought) so contentious, so strong-willed, so difficult, so, so-o-o-o...

Earl saw the issues that I had with Annette and one day approached me and said, "I might be able to help. I'm teaching a class (Parent Effectiveness Training) that I think might be worthwhile."

Shirley and I signed up, listened, and participated. I'm thinking it was a nine week course on Wednesday nights.

About the 5th session, lights went on and I said, in the middle of class, "Earl, I get it. I need to go and talk with Annette, now." What followed was an hour-long conversation, with Annette and I sitting in a bean bag chair, discussing our aspirations and differences. It was a near miraculous "conversion" between Annette and me.

Earl...not only did you save Annette's life, you provided all of us with skills that we have used for the past 3 decades that have made us better people, dealing better with other people, helping people be the best that they can be.

Dave Meyer, science teacher '75-'81

• The HS Librarian speaks

Ramblings actually. I ran into Lois Voeltz in the hall one day. She said I heard you kicked someone out of the library – big man on campus, I gathered. She said ' You'll do just fine.'

My own son David played me in a skit in the chapel one day.

And he kungfued people out of the library. Students loved it, I am told by David. I remember that we had a number of students we were responsible for called "advisee groups." I remember I had Virginia (?), she came in one day and said she had skipped Home Ec, I think for one week. (IF that had been one of my kids I would have grabbed them around the neck and yelled, YOU DID WHAT? But with Virginia I was good. I sat her down and said, Okay, let's look at your options? Everything worked out well, she handled it all. Why can't I be objective with my own?. . . . . . She had grown up in Hong Kong and then they moved. Her Dad came back to see me one day and said Virginia said he had to look me up and tell me how much she missed HK. I asked him what he missed most about HK. He replied "having my jockey shorts and jeans ironed." Don't you love it?

Then there was Brent and Beth Broyhill, whose son was president his senior year, his only year at HKIS??? Well, I had never heard of a Chinese firedrill – no clue. They rented a tram for their 25th anniversary, Jay was in the hospital, had had a bypass and we were about to leave. They rented the tram,brought along a long board, and put it over the bottom floor seats on part on one side. Voila! Bar and snacks. We rode up and down through Wanchai all evening. Every time we stopped for a light or traffic, these stupid gweilos would get out and yell and run around the tram, then get back on. Over and over – Chinese firedrill

– where did that come from?

A teacher's son had almost died one year in the tub. Remember you had to have a window open if you had an instant geyser? Well, he didn't and he had slipped down into the water and they found him in time and he lived. One day I heard this kid at the front desk, he was asking Alice, how much he owed for the Time magazine being damaged. I knew right away who he was. I went out and I am not certain I was not very polite. I just wanted him to go away before I cried. said, 'It's okay, you don't owe anything.' That's alright just go away.'

I remember Paul Tuchardt calling it Church of all Notions, cause everybody of all sorts came to it. But we all took communion also.

Dusty Knisely, High School Librarian '74-79

• The beginning of HKIS computing…

When I arrived in HK in August of '75, the computer development was part of my responsibility, in addition to teaching physics, auto shop, computer science, and two other 1-quarter courses. Richard Schrock, Jon Malmin, Carl Schiefer and I (among others who cannot remember) all arrived in '75. The Computing power of the school consisted of an ASR33 teletype machine. This is the rattly, clanky, bang-bang machine that you still see, occasionally, on television shows in a newspaper office. The ASR33 technology was the fore-runner of the IBM Selectric typewriter. Anyone remember a typewriter?

The ASR33 was wired to a large Digital Equipment Corp. (DEC) computer at the Charter Bank in Hong Kong, courtesy of an executive there who wanted his son, Brad Sandler, to have a computer in high school.

Along with the ASR33, there was a breadloaf size box sitting alongside with a mysterious toggle switch on top of that and a curious wire running through the switch from the front to the back of the box. Definitley not standard equipment!

After a bit of experimenting, and some help from Kevin Kinne, we determined that, to communicate with the computer, one hit the "Return" key, waited and prayed an indeterminate period of time, then flipped the toggle switch in the hope that information would come back.

The process was unpredictable, frustrating and unacceptable! I arranged a meeting of all the players: representatives from the bank, from Con Conway who had leased the ASR33 to HKIS, from the phone company and from the Postal Department — wait! Did I say the Postal Department? Yeh. Simple. The use of a modem and transmission of data constituted delivery of information. Who better to be in charge of delivering information over phone lines than the Royal HK Mail.

We then negotiated for a workable solution and a local phone company engineer said that he could show me how things could be made to work satisfactorily. Two days later he showed up and plugged in another box, this one the size and shape of the German chocolate cakes my mother baked. We fired up the terminal and, Lo! Data was sent and received as expected. Life was good. I said, "I'll take one of those." He responded "So sorry. Prototype." At which point I said, "Clear all of this stuff out of here! We gotta start over."

A year later, the Chartered Bank politely suggested that International school should investigate other sources of computing power. This may have been because of an unnamed student experimenting with a little-known activity called "hacking". OK, it was…na-a-a-h.!

On short notice, with few options, I purchased the first Radio Shack TRS-80 (also known as the Trash-80) shipped into Hong Kong. At that time, the only option was a Taiwanese knockoff of something called an "Apple." The creative Taiwanese, named their product the "Pineapple." Really, folks. I'm not creative enough to make up this stuff!

We then started a search for the next generation computer. The final choice: a DEC 1134, widely used in educational institutions in the States.

It had 4K and additional 4k memory cache ($4000); one fixed disc (5 megabytes); one removable disc pack (2.5 megabytes) three terminals. It was the size of a refrigerator, put out the heat of a small furnace, and cost US $85,000.

…and that is how I left it in 1981.

Dave Meyer, science teacher '75-'81

• Joseph Kung and Computers

When I came to HKIS, one of the first people I met was Joseph Kung who was then helping with the computers in 1982. Since I was hired to help with the computer program, he was the computer guy along with Roger Van Andel. This year (2007)

Joseph retired, which marks a huge part of the HKIS history.

The history of technology at HKIS would fill a whole book and it would be an important book to write as technology moved from an on-line terminal for a few people to our situation today where every faculty and staff could not do their job without one and many of the kids in high school bring a laptop to school every day. The first year I started work in 1982 we had 6 Radio-Shack TRS-80 computers in the elementary school and 8 Atari 800 computers in the Middle School. The TRS-80 machines were on large trolleys that were rolled from class to class and stored their programs on cassette tapes.

In the mid 80's we donated the TRS-80 computers to the Hei Ling Chau Vietnamese Refugee Center. They were used by an educational program that within a year was told to quit because the refugees had it too good. When I moved to the high school in 1991 we were already into PC's (286 machines) and continued to grow from there. Shortly after I arrived, we started the HKIS BBS (Bulletin Board System) which changed to the DragonNet in 1998 after a Strategic Planning Session that created our first web site.

The technology changes related to the HKIS technology infrastructure are even more dramatic but may not be remembered by many.

David Elliott, teacher, '82-'07

• Leading High School Chapel

I wish I could remember the young man's name. He was 14 or 15 years of age at the time and a student in one of my French classes. School was difficult for this young man, and my class presented certain difficulties. I administered a learning styles instrument to this young man as I had background in that area. He and I spent perhaps 30 minutes together; he was very willing to see what the instrument might prescribe.

We learned that he was "hands-on" and needed a lot of movement. We looked at the list of strategies together and jointly determined that his trying to read on a stationary bicycle might be a partial solution. The exercise room in his block of flats had such a bike, and he assured me that he would try out this strategy.

Several weeks later, he knocked at my classroom door, interrupting my class, but I did not

care. I was delighted that he would seek me out. Yes, riding the stationary bike had worked. He said he was able to read and focus on his social studies for at least 20 minutes at a time whereas previously he was unable to even read a single page.

We had sporadic contact, and this young man faded from my memory when he left HKIS at the end of the year.

Imagine my shock when I heard of his death the following year. He was in another Asian international school and on the equivalent of our Interim trips. He had slipped from a ledge into the pool below and had died immediately. I was devastated. I had felt he had taken some small strides at HKIS, and his death was such a waste. When we held a memorial chapel, it was the first time I had felt that I wanted to lead a chapel. His death had touched me to the core, and I wanted to share his story and small successes with other teachers and students.

His memory…and that chapel 15 years ago…remain with me until this very day.

Nancy Kroonenberg, French teacher, '77-'96

• A Time of Opportunity

The Ostheller family came to HKIS in August 1979 on a three-year contract to see what overseas teaching would be like. Twenty years later we retired back to the USA after experiencing a lifetime of adventures and the making of unforgettable memories and friends. The power of the HKIS community is in the people, both faculty and students, you continue to connect with even after you are gone.

The highlights for me personally include the areas of Interim, sports, student connections, and the Hong Kong food and countryside with SAG outings and many a visit to Suzannas and the American Restaurant. My three children, Karl W. (class of 1981), Crystal (class of 1984), and Kelly (class of 1986) all graduated from HKIS and my wife, Pauline, taught in third grade, second grade, and pre-school. Pauline and I moved back to Washington State in June of 1999.

I will always remember all my interim experiences. Mine include my first interim where we landed in the wrong Malaysia after planning to do a jungle trip. This was topped by the "boy who swallowed the spoon" on the diving interim to the Maldives. Japan Skiing and the New Zealand Adventure trips with Peter Hardman were definitely my favorite trips. The memories and stories will last forever.

I truly enjoyed my basketball coaching with the highlight of the boys team coming in 1990 with Trevor Wright as the team captain and team standouts Stahi Pappadis, Mike Elliott, Todd Walters, and Danny Tuck. They won the Hong League, Christmas Tournament and took 3rd place in the DOD tournament in Korea. The yearbook quote says, "This is the best team I've ever had - Doc O". In 1992 I begin coaching the girl's varsity team. We had three years of unbelievable success winning the Hong Kong league and Christmas tournament 3 years in a row. Starting with captain Bonnie Pratt and ending with captain Allie Overholt and a great cast of supporting players, i.e. Jen Johnson, Alice Han, Jennifer Chen, Michelle Hoepner, and Faith Fischer. These players set the stage for a very successful girl's basketball program at HKIS.

While I taught mathematics for 20 years, my most memorable experiences came toward the end of my teaching career. Dave Bickel talked me into doing portfolios in math and some truly remarkable work took place because of it. It led to a period of time when the key word was "integrity" and kids took up the challenge of doing the right thing. They started a group called IMAD "Individuals Making A Difference - I'm Making A Difference". This led to me making a talk to the National Honor Society of the importance of people having integrity. Students who inspired me and wrote wonderful pieces for their portfolios and on integrity include Corrie Zacharia, Klair Cristiani, Cheryl Mainland, Angie and Ingrid Chen, Alison Overholt, Achal Kapoor, Michelle Kwok, Paul Langford, Elena Beveridge, Candice Tong, Theresa Cheng, Lance Star, and Todd Wong. I put together a HKIS memory book called "The Joy of Teaching" with all the cards and letters that students sent to me. Then having the high school section of the yearbook dedicated to me in 1989 and again in 1999 definitely put the "icing on the cake."

HKIS is all about people connecting with people! The BEST 20 years of my life happened at HKIS and I thank all of those wonderful students I got to work with, those dedicated faculty friends (too many to name), a wonderful group of teachers in the math department, and to Headmaster David Rittmann who hired and inspired me. God bless all of you at HKIS and I wish you continued success.

Dr. Karl Ostheller (Doc O.), math teacher '79-'99

My very favorite teacher was Mr. David Bickel. In fact, it was because of him that I decided to major in journalism. I ended up working in Hong Kong for a decade as an editor and eventually even wrote and published a cook book...so I have a lot of good memories of enjoying literature class while at HKIS. *Anita Lau '84*

My nightmare was the hundreds of college applications lying all over my office on the day before Christmas vacation. I still fear getting some student's application in the wrong envelope. But then, there was always Mrs. Chan, smiling as she handed us our coffee.

Mary Kaye Soderlind, counsellor, '74-'80

One of the biggest surprises when we returned to teach again at HKIS in 1996 was teaching children of students I taught in 1973-74 as well as the privilege of being on the Alumni Board with students of that era! Years pass and changes occur but the people of HKIS still deeply care and help each other enjoy the international experience. We learned how to respect people of all cultures and religions as well stretch our personal worldviews to include those different from ourselves. We were reminded to deepen our relationship with God and people as well as ways to be responsible compassionate world citizens.

I thank God for each time I think of you and the HKIS community.

Lois Voeltz, PE, religious studies '73-'80 & '96-'03

•Snake hunting

One of the least intelligent activities that I got involved with as a science teacher was letting myself get talked in to being Richard Schrock's photographer on a "Snake Hunt. We drove out to the New Territories following a torrential rainstorm. The heavy rains washed the snakes down into the water catchments (which drained into the reservoirs) and were easy pickings...for those of steel nerves and few smarts. We drove to the "home" of an old timer, a shack somewhere deep in the New Territories, who may have been associated with the faculty of HKU.

The guy was a legend in Hong Kong, known as "The Snake Man" and he accompanied us on our hunt, complete with rice bags for the catch and long poles to actually catch the snakes.

Richard had a permit to send the snakes back to Kansas State University, or wherever he was working on his Doctorate. My job, as official photographer, was to get in close during the lassoing operation and get a good photo (night time shot) of said snake, prior to lassoing. Now, keep in mind, Schrock was after only the deadliest of the species—no garter snakes here: Banded Krait, Many-Banded Krait, Bamboo Pit Viper, etc.

I lasted one night!

Dave Meyer, science teacher   '75-'81

•Sharon Prechtl

I was a student in one of Mrs. Prechtl's American History classes. Kudos for her efforts to teach us how to learn. I remember the day that someone posted a note in an elevated locker window about Aswan Dam having been bombed. She was a very smart teacher and I admire her for that.
Eric Lee '75

"Mrs. Prechtl" was known as a tough teacher but my class (1975) loved her. I remember vividly several debates over the Civil War (or the War Between the States,' as it was known in the South) and our term papers (my first). She inspired learning in all we did and helped my self-confidence immensely. In a survey, I listed her as my favorite teacher at HKIS. Or maybe she was the one who influenced us the most. She is much appreciated.
Cathy Smith '75

The best teacher I ever had was Mrs. Prechtl. Ms. 99 & 44/100's. It was explained that she never gave 100's just like the Ivory soap girl 99 & 44/100's pure. What an amazing teacher though. I still remember most, if not all, of my American History lessons. She had a unique way of teaching that engaged all of us, made us fully aware up front of what was expected of us and how we would be graded. Also added extraordinary class material to challenge our thinking.
Gavin Birnie '75

Mrs. Prechtel energized everyone to learn, and it worked! That and the mystery of which secret government agency did her husband work for? *Barb Schwerdtmann '77*

•Teaching Art

"I've been having the kids evaluate them-

selves, and then I sit down with each one and look at their work and talk with them. It takes a long time, but I think it's working well. The kids hate grading themselves. Not only did I ask them to give a grade, but to justify why they should get that grade. I'm glad I didn't have me for a teacher.

A mother of one of my students invited me to see her impressive collection of Chinese and orientl art objects. She is classic, spoke with a heavy Hungarian Zsa Zsa accent, and had a diamond in her ring the size of a small marble. The house was drippingwith Persian rugs, Ming and Ching China pottery, and European artifiacts of all sorts. These people have their own museums!
Dave Kohl, art teacher '73-'78

Dave Kohl was an integral part of my education. I often reflect back on those wonderful times with fondness. He, obviously, was my most influential teacher. And for that, I will always be grateful. I hear a lot of politicians always pushing "math and science..." but they are short selling the public. Art and music was such a strong presence in my high school learning. In fact, it was because of these subjects, I chose architecture, profession filled with a broad spectrum of learning.
Amat Tadudin '77

•My art teachers

Who could forget Mr. Prout cracking his nose, much to our amazement, boy, were we stupid! I found the arts classes an opportunity to discover my creative side, one that I derive personal pleasure from, nothing recognizable to others.

Mr. Kohl, I still recognize "Buns" Boucher, and it helped my daughter in AP Art History as well! How lucky we were to really get into photography, mess around with the chemicals, develop our own film, and to see the world through different perspectives. My Mom and Dad kept my ceramics and used every dorky thing I made, I now have them myself. I still claim that I purposely made the little wheelbarrow that small so we could serve *After Eight* mints on it. My Mom used it all the time for guests, what a gal! Jewelry making was really special, not only for the cool things I got to make myself, but for the opportunity to watch other kids make some incredible art and the different processes we all were able to use. I wore a ring I made for 20 years before it finally broke.
Barb Schwerdtmann '77

I spent 3 years at HKIS '76-'79. I can honestly say they were 3 of the most exciting years of my life. It totally changed me as a person and my outlook on life and the world. Believe it or not Mr. Kohl was actually an influence in my desire to create. What influenced me most was the photography that we did in his class. I loved being in Hong Kong and photographing people. It was such a great atmosphere to live and learn in. Having a teacher like him that was totally non-threatening, allowing us to create in whatever way we desired, and to grow into ourselves created a confidence in myself as an artist. I did graduate from the University of Denver with my degree in Art History.

Kathy Anderer '79

Mrs. Flynn was my first, and favorite all time art teacher at ASIJ (sorry Mr. Kohl, I spent more time in her class in elementary school than the semester I spent with you), where Mr. Flynn taught drama to my sister.

He then, of course, became my drama teacher in HK. I will never forget Mr. Flynn who was without a doubt my favorite all time teacher, he influenced me to this very day and I will always thank him for giving me a love for live theatre.

"WHEN YOU SEE I GUY REACH FOR STARS IN THE SKY YOU CAN BET THAT HE'S DOING IT FOR SOME DOLL…"

Richard O. Grayson '78

Somebody threw a linoleum cutter knife in art class. I remember the incident very well, somebody was bleeding, and our poor art teacher always had it so rough. Her name was Mrs. Hughes, I think either British or Australian. We had a dear pet name for her, or at least some of us did. She was "Mrs. Huge." I wonder if anyone remembers why we had that nickname for her? Junior high kids can be so cruel and crude, huh, especially us!

Vincent J Chow '84

•My Favorite Teachers

My best HKIS pal was Faye Hung Butcher, I used to go and help Faye in the Library when I was young. We also went to CAN together, and became good friends over the years before I graduated.

Funny & great teacher moments - Tall lean Jon Malmin, calling me squirt gun. Mr. Clark

throwing the chair in Geometry class. Mrs. Salama, French, poking the kids on the side of the head saying "Quiet Choo - Quiet Choo" (quiet you) and her always getting mad at Charles Waters, poor kid, she had it in for him.

Mr. Rausch read us great stories and you could hear a pin drop. He also used to get mad at us for tipping our chairs back, especially when Doug Jahn fell over, that makes me chuckle still! I was one of the worst chair tippers, but didn't get caught!

Mr. Pfaff was totally cool. Plus, we did biology and dissecting with him, the frog thing was so interesting, that I almost didn't mind the spattering of frog stuff when he was helping us dig out the brain. Pithing was totally gross though.

Mssr. LeBrun was so suave, plus he was on the board to rate films in the colony. We had some great discussions! Then there was the time his son subbed for us, we thought the senior Mssr. LeBrun was suave, his son showed up in a velvet coat! Ooo la la!

Mr. Harnish in IPS - EUREKA!!! We spent all year saying Eureka!

Mr. Carlton with his endless patience, when I took the remedial math class with him, I finally got everything and felt so good about myself and math, finally!

Mr. Silzer once chased me down to give me a make up test in the lobby - Thanks!

Who wouldn't want a teacher called Doc Holliday!

Then there was the filmstrip version of sex ed. Enough said.

I felt connected with all my teachers, except one who was downright weird in the early years, but I won't name names. Yes, I was a challenge at times, but then again, if you were a teacher who didn't care, you would have never noticed me. Thanks for noticing me.

Barb Schwerdtman '68-'77

•Traveling.....

I remember when Judy Stringer's husband plane was blown up over Malaysia. We went to the funeral and Judy and her daughter's cheered us up when we were leaving the church, after crying our way through the service. Judy was the one who persuaded our family of four - Jay, me, Alan and Tanya that we could indeed travel for six weeks with just a flight bag each. She and her husband had done it when she was pregnant.

So we did......We four Knisleys and MaryKaye Heisler and Norma Schroeder. Did that for 6-7 weeks. Bought a ticket from HK to Kathmandu and a ticket from Tehran to Hong Kong. The rest of the way we played it by ear - cheap, cheap, cheap, easy to do with just flight bags. A change of clothing and lots of toilet paper.

We went to Nepal, fell in love with the place and thought about retiring there, then on thru India, Pakistan and Afghanistan, saw the two Buddhas that the Taliban later destroyed - 150 and 175 feet tall in the mountain side. They already had their faces cut off, an amazing feat in Genghis Khan's time. Then we went way south of Tehran, where we had friends. Stayed with them for 2 weeks. They were thrilled to see us. Had a Thanksgiving feast and wonderful things we hadn't seen in weeks. BUT we had been living off warm cokes (you could take the cap off and knew it was clean) and fruit that could be peeled – mostly that was what we ate coming thru Afghanistan. Took us three days to get our appetites back, except it was so hot.

We flew back from Iran with a samavar on my lap. I had never seen one, but in Tehran they had stores of them and I knew what they were. That impressed me. One nite in the dark bazaar, a quiet voice said, "Wanna see my carpets?" I grabed Jay's arm and said, "Here we go." We went down I swear three flights into a long, high narrow, hall like and they showed us rugs and rugs and rugs. We said we were poor teachers and really couldn't afford them and had no way to take them home - they kept telling us about each rug, serving us tea and showing us rugs. Never bought any, and we were royally treated. Came home to our Chinese inch-thick rugs and were content.

Thanks, Judy, a wonderful trip. Would probably never have taken it if we had known some of the places we stayed in, and how we traveled. But it was truly a marvelous, unforgettable trip.
Dusty Knisely, librarian, '75-'79

• A PE teacher remembers

We were the "Class of 1973": young, long-haired, thin, idealistic, experienced, enthusiastic teachers - Barnes, Bartz, D. Christian, Kohl, Kolb, Larson, Rittmann, Rohrs, Voeltzes, Windhorst. We all came bounding into the British Crown Colony of Hong Kong, excited to teach at Hong Kong International School. The childless folks soon paired up (Barnes, Bartz, Christian, Kohls, Rohrs, Voeltzes and Windhorst) to become a "family" away from our State-side familes.

Those were days when one waited for a telephone to be placed into the flat, long-distance phone calls had to be booked down in Central at the Cable & Wireless building where you entered a booth to make your call. Richard Nixon and the ping-pong diplomacy had just come to China so the prices in the China Products stores (lovingly called "The Communist Stores") had sharply risen, visas to visit China weren't available for us in Hong Kong. No McDonalds, the cross-harbor tunnel had recently been completed, HKIS faculty families met the in-coming faculty at Kai Tak (enjoying drinks beforehand and Chinese food at a favorite restaurant after the meeting), one shopping centre at Ocean Terminal, grocery shopping was done in the vegetable stalls and small stores, pigs were walked by their owner down Wong Chuk Hang Road, Aberdeen was truly a fishing village where they still built junks and sampans, and Stanley was a fishing village where most homes also housed pigs.

There were 1100 students in one building at the original site on South Bay Close. That meant one elevator, one gymnasium, no pool and no fields. But we could hardly wait to get to class and enjoy the multi-cultural student body.

I taught physical education in the junior high and high school while Fritz was an 8th grade homeroom teacher specializing in language arts and history. Each day in my office was an adventure: Eve Wong, the secretary, with the longest red nails I had ever seen; Bobby Wan who was always reading the newspaper with the latest in horse racing tips from Happy Valley; Diane Hardy from York, England who I thoroughly enjoyed (but Fritz often had to translate her strong English accent for me); Barry Kolb, a friend from my hometown of Seward, Nebraska; and Walt Schmidt, a.k.a. CY Duk, our fearless leader and always our boss - or at least that's what we wanted him to think!

Walt coordinated the gymnasium schedule so all students in school had physical education. It was well-equipped with everything needed for a strong curriculum. The only problem was the plethora of soccer balls I lost while trying to play soccer on South Bay Close above the school next to the church, or the excess of students sent to Mrs. Westrick, the school nurse, because they got hit in the head by the golf clubs. But we had a great time every day.

I also "coached" swimming (with Mark Silzer) and girls cross country. With swim practice in Repulse Bay, the jelly bugs were the challenge when swimming out to the raft. Dogs and pigs, as well as runners losing their way, were the challenges for the cross country teams, but we were always rewarded by Mary Ketterer's oranges at the end of a run. I also got to sponsor several cheerleading squads that year, too. The student body enjoyed a track and field day in Aberdeen (where the sun seared my corneas and my eyes were covered for several days) and a swim gala at Victoria Park as well as regular Rice and Mok Cup intramurals.

Even with all the school activities, the 'family' still had time to eat lots of Chinese food at the American Restaurant and Wah Fu; hike the water catchments to Daimler Falls and Nubian Pool behind Stanley; create Lantern Festival traditions that we practiced each year; worship together at Church of All Nations where Hillard Ranta was the "Voice of CAN" when the service was recorded for RHK radio; explore New Territory villages; watch movies together by using a 16mm film projector from school but I don't know where we got the movies! (the Consulate library?)

As the years passed, several of the family got married, had children, some left that Colony but we all shared the joys and sorrows that families bear, like baby Aaron Kohl dying after only 44 hours of life. I would venture to say that we are still family, caring for each other via e-mail or phone and often recalling those wonderful memories of Hong Kong, HKIS, and our times together from 1973-1980.

Lois Voeltz, teacher, '73-55; '95-03

I remember having some pretty cruel PE experiences, like when we had to run laps around the gym for the entire gym period (or until we dropped, whichever came first!)......I ran until the end but wondered to myself, "why?"

Jill Liddiard '77

•Directing Plays

I had been told by David Rittmann and Ronnie Chern that I was in charge of the senior high drama program. Theater Arts classes were part of my workload. Gary Barnes had been trained at the same undergraduate program as I at Concordia Teachers College in Seward, Nebraska, and only a year behind me, although he arrived in Hong Kong long before I did. He had worked with Vincent Flynn, my predecessor, in producing plays, so I wondered how we would achieve balance on this issue.

That proved to be easy, thanks to Barnes. He came to me after I'd been there a couple of weeks and said, "Listen, I'd like to do one show a year. I'd also prefer to choose it." That was short, simple, and suited me down to the ground. I figured I could do at least two other shows a year, and that would probably be enough.

My first production was a medieval European text, *The Second Shepherd's Play*, which told the story of Jesus' birth from the viewpoint of those working-class peasants, the shepherds. My cast reflected the school's diversity. One of the shepherds was Jewish, another a Protestant American, the third was Korean. An American girl played the innkeeper's wife, the Virgin Mary was a Japanese girl, and the baby Jesus by a forty-watt light bulb.

Having been trained in children's theater, I put one of those shows together each year and toured the colony for a week after the show opened, a process in which Werner von Behren was crucial by getting kids excused from classes and finding substitutes for me. In 1980, we performed in the Church of All Nations for a bunch of students from a Chinese boys' school. One character in *The Land of the Dragon* was Princess Jade Pure, and she was played by Kelly, a classic American blonde girl. Cantonese soap operas and films were often centered on some kind of love story, often tragic and always overly dramatic, and many times this woman was blonde, probably because so many blonde Chinese were alive long ago. So when Kelly made her entrance, there was a gasp from 200 pre-adolescent throats: here was the blonde heroine, just as they had seen a thousand times.

That was of course not my intent in casting Kelly; just another one of those cross-cultural moments that made overseas life so endlessly fascinating. *Andrew Grzeskowiak, teacher '78-'80*

In one of Mr. Barnes' theatre classes, he wished out loud that something out-of-the-ordinary would happen, "Like finding the courtyard filled with ducks." As a goodbye gift, I decided to try to fulfill part of his wish by filling his office with ducks.

Enlisting the help of Mrs. Greenwald, who had a key to his office, we went down to the market in Central early one morning to buy the ducks, but once face-to-face with the beasts, we realized ONE duck was probably all we could deal with. After convincing the vendor that we did NOT want it killed, we put it in a Cathay Pacific flight bag and took a cab to school. The duck was squawking and the driver was confused about what the heck these two weird gweilos were up to.

After unlocking the office, Mrs. Greenwald made me swear I'd never rat her out (sorry), and I was left to fill the office with balloons, to make up for the lack of ducks. I don't know when exactly Mr. Barnes discovered the "surprise", but walking by his office later in the day, I found him sitting at his desk, gently telling the duck "Don't worry about the noisy kids. They won't hurt you."

He named it "Hope" after a quote I had in the senior yearbook, and I hear that the duck went to live at the grade school petting zoo.

Joan Amy '80

There was an amazing opportunity to see some of the world's best entertainers of the time, plus the local plays, featuring many teachers, as well as our own school productions led my Mr. Flynn. Choir concerts, plays, musical extravaganzas, etc.   *Barb Schwerdtmann '79*

Before working at HKIS I didn't see many plays and visited concerts and art exhibits only marginally more. As a teacher, you get to know the kids and to see them reach beyond themselves as they do in the fine arts is special. I can't count the number of times I have mentioned to our Fine Arts teachers that so-and-so's life was deeply impacted or changed because of their participation in a certain play or concert or exhibition.

Dave Elliott, teacher '82 - '07
•The Swimming Pool

The Driskill's arrived in 1975 stayed until 1991. Jorie, Debbie Lynne with Helena born in HK. First years rough - no pool, no apartment at Repulse Bay lived out at Cape Mansions Road past the pig market every day through Aberdeen. Eating at Pok Fu Lam...Christmas caroling at the old folks home in PFL...The Pool opened a year later

after we arrived and had 6 major leaks. I watched the bus lady put kids on buses while holding her umbrella from the leaky pool. And watched the gardener kill all the flowers from using chlorinated water. Swimming lessons were in Repulse Bay at first. We grew a swim program that touched K - 12th grade. Jorie and Debbie graduated from HKIS...Helena left after her sophomore year.

Lynne taught PE in elementary grades. I almost broke my thumbs trying to catch Darrel Van Luchene going off the diving board during Adult swimming lessons. As Athletic Director, we had A B C grades based on age and height, a definite disadvantage for the middle school boys. I received a letter of reprimand from the HK sports association for having a coach that was too tall in Pastor Tuchardt, because he was "intimating" the referees. Carl Schiefer often had to shovel cement off of the Wan Chai playground before we could begin a basketball game.

We had visits by Mary Lou Retton after she had won the gymnastic gold medals. Faculty often played tennis on the 7th floor playground with Rowold, Thomas & Schiefer on Saturday afternoons. We'd put typhoon boards up after the typhoon began to hit. One board flew out of my hands and down the mountain! There were pancakes with Oettings on Fat Tuesday. Annual Thanksgivings on Lantau were special, even having our tent blow away, but oh what fun. The Seder meal at CAN put on by the Youth was meaningful. Early morning swims. Six bomb scares and evacuating Tai Tam in one week. Christmas basketball tournaments....and having a rule where we needed 6 buckets of sand on hand in case of fire. Friendly matches where if you tied an opponent the game was over – no overtimes.

I taught oriental Brush painting after being introduced to the art by a student - Thomas (now Dr.) Wong. Dave Kohl and I also took a class from Shirley Smith, a HKIS mom. Then I began teaching it in the Evening Program.

Bill Driskill, teacher, '75-'91

I had never painted with Chinese brush before, but I went to the YMCA for a class and fell in love with it. An old gentleman, who spoke no English was the teacher. His daughter translated for him. I was the only one in the group who spoke Chinese so he took special time with me. Although I later had other teachers, I felt he helped me most because he'd explain the meaning of the painting and the time period it represented.

When I taught the class at HKIS, it was at his urging. His philosphy was, "You don't know how much you know or don't know until you teach it." I began with fear and trembling, but eventually enjoyed sharing with others what I had learned. I hoped I wasn't hurting anyone by trying to teach it.

I don't do Chinese painting much anymore because it is difficult to find a place to mount them in the US.

Shirley Smith, HKIS mom & Evening Program teacher

•The French eclectic

Mrs. Cooper, the French teacher, is a scrounge who goes regularly to "Cat" Street, which is the place where junk dealers and peddlers sell all sorts of antiques, hand-me-downs,and used items. We were at her flat to see a huge 14-foot long board she got a month ago there, which she is now cleaning up and under centuries of grime is finding a beautifully carved entrance linterl to an old Taoist exmple, complete with elaborate Taoist symbols, lacquered and gold inlay.

Dave Kohl, art teacher, '73-'80, 1973 letter

Paul Kan was the crewcut man. Mr. Nandkmar Hussien Bhatti was the school driver and was always around the ground floor.

Steve Chiu '69

•Autoshop

Paul Kan had his wood shop, where the old workers met on the ground floor. Earl moved them out and he and I turned that space into the real auto shop for the students. Then, I did the community thing with many wives coming in to try to take care of themselves, automotively.

Dave Meyer, science teacher, '75-'81

•Life Skills

The high school faculty had a major meeting one spring day at Maggie Gordon's house up in the Mid-levels someplace - Tavistock I think it was. We felt the school curriculum was too academic and didn't meet the needs of "normal" American kids, in that there was no Industrial Arts/Home arts track at HKIS. No "hands-on" experiences. The re-

sult of the day of meetings and a fantastic lunch was a program we ended up calling "Life Skills" for lack of a more suitable title – under which we incorporated courses in Auto Mechanics (thank you, Dave Meyer), Wood Shop (yeah Fritz Voeltz) and an attempt at Home Economics, thanks to the willingness of my wife Katy to teach two singleton courses. Katy's teaching meant lots of prep time for not much salary....but she did it because it was good for kids. She had already taught a year as a "para-professional" in the elementary, and a year with high school English and social studies. She also taught piano lessons and accompanied a Ballet School at the Repulse Bay Hotel. The first semester of 75-76 she taught a cooking class in the late afternooon in the school cafeteria kitchen after the Ping Shan and Mac Donald's people left. She had many interesting adventures trying to use western-style pots and pans under the wary eye of Mrs. Chan.

Katy spent hours shopping and lugging plastic bags of groceries up the hill from Park n' Shop or Wellcome. They compiled their own cookbooks, and made some pretty amazing meals. The students ate well, but weren't very fond of cleaning up.

The second semester, the plan was to teach sewing. I can't remember if she did this in the cafeteria or they found a vacant classroom. But Earl Westrick tried to be helpful by financing the purchase of a couple of sewing machines. The kids made everything from aprons to prom dresses on machines that they had to put away after each session. Very innovative and adaptive...flexability was the name of the game. I think there was quite a bit of Saturday work, also. From my point of view, Katy thrived on combining her heritage from a mother under whom she had learned to sew in a family of five kids, plus Katy's curiosity in sorting through the ladder streets and Lee Yuen Street East for fabrics from around the world, threads and notions, and all sorts of domestic paraphanalia.

Despite everyone's best efforts, I don't think either program was ever offered again....and I wonder what ever happened to the sewing machines.

Dave Kohl, art teacher '73-'80

I guess my stretch would have to be cooking class on the 4th floor stairs! Cooking by Burner 101. I also have my cooking recipe book when we had cooking class on the stairwell between floors. We had an extension cord and an electric burner. The biscuit cake and chicken a la king were brilliant!

Barbara Schwerdtmann '77

• Student hindsight

I didn't have much use for many of my teachers at HKIS, or my school in the states for that matter. Until the very last day of school, Dean Fritts was one teacher that was low on my list. (Actually, he was the vice principal) But he showed me his true colors that day in June, 1980. I guess he thought it better to let me graduate than to cause me and my family pain during a time when everything should have been a celebration. I never said this to him, but please tell Dean THANK YOU. But looking back for me, and not the other poeple involved, getting busted may have been the wake up call I needed.   *Mike Skolnick '80*

• Ovid Wong
We were quite a large group at a dinner Ovid Wong organized to bid farewell to Sharon Prechtl in '74. He was the faculty social chairman.
                    Bev Larson, teacher '73-'74

• Faculty socials from letters in 1973

"We've just had another faculty "eat-in." That means that Ovid Wong, the Cantonese teacher in charge of inter-cultural events, arranged a dinner for a group of teachers at the Nathan Hotel (which a friend of his happens to manage). So we got a custom menu – bird's nest soup, fancy shredded meat and vegetable dishes, pinecone-shaped fish, sweet and sour seafood, good luck chicken(?), and a bunch of other stuff. There were about 30 of us, and it cost HK$ 25 per person. This was in Kowloon, so we rode the ferry over, and after dinner, walked through a"poor man's night club." Each hawker lights up his stand with one or more kerosene lanterns, and the place is noisy as all get-out from the merchants playing radios and demonstration records and tapes. They sell everything you can imagine, from tooth paste to silk, scrubbers to jewelry, and the closed-off streets fill up with crowds more dense than any traffic jam."Last night,we were at a buffet cocktail party at Dottie Mache's, on Headland Road. She's my department chairman and her husband is the chairman of the Board of Managers of the school. What a flat!!! Three times the size of ours, and ours is large by HK standards. The view they have from their 40-foot balcony takes in Stanley, Repulse Bay, Aberdeen, and the Peak. Furnishings include their

souvenirs from Bali, Indonesia, Japan, Borneo, and of course, China."   *Dave Kohl, Art teacher '73-'80*

• Chinese New Year Staff Dinners --

The annual dinners for the non-teaching staff have always been highlights for Mary Jane and myself over the years. When I first started attending them the faculty and administration were asked to provide entertainment which was of dubious quality but certainly gave the staff reason to laugh. The spirit of these events remains deeply honoring and simple and caring and just outrageous fun.
The administration takes pains to honor staff in a very Chinese way. Recently Mary Ewing, Anthony Hui and Tom Woo have made the event so special. Where else would a mixed group of secretaries and accountants from various countries, Chinese cleaners and maintenance workers and Nepali guards all be entertained by a Kenyan woman singing love songs in Cantonese while poking light-hearted fun at the Head of School? Perhaps this sense of compassion and spirit is HKIS at its best.   *Dave Elliott teacher, '82-'07*

5. In Memorium.....

• Ed Brackmann
Our father Edward Brackmann, gym teacher, math teacher and basketball and tennis coach from '68-'70 passed away in 1989 from a sudden brain tumor. He was the guy who made all the PE classes run laps, and he was still a physical fitness nut at age 60 when the tumor got him. He was Athletic Director at Concordia Lutheeran High School in Ft. Wayne at the time.   *Mark Brackmann '74*

• Jay Knisley
When Jay died, I was overwhelmed. I have 10 letters from grown up students of his telling how he changed their lives around. One cheated and the way Jay talked to the student changed their future, another wrote that Jay just made life so exciting that they wanted to get going and be a part of it. Jay was an actor and in many British plays and American plays. Made actors out of many of his students. He always expected the best and and almost always got the best. He loved to act and direct. But he would do anything that needed done to make the play a success in the classroom or on

the stage, even to cleaning the toilets or straightened up the mess. The play must go on and go on well.

Dusty Knisely, wife and librarian, '75-'79

•Betty Lazenby

Mrs. Lazenby was the mother of Scott, John, Ann, and Mary and she was also a teacher at HKIS. I don't know how many years she actually taught but she was my 4th grade teacher and she was wonderful. Of all my teachers at HKIS I think that she was the one who taught me the most because she gave me a love of books – good books (beyond the comic books that my brother and I devoured.) She was there when the light dawned and I discovered books- much to my family's everlasting dismay- I have not yet ever met a book that I didn't want to keep forever!!! Plus she was just a cool Mom and I envied the Lazenby kids!!

Tami Whitrock '77

Mrs. Lazenby just made everyone feel so safe and welcome. *Barb Schwerdtmann '77*

Betty Lazenby was a teacher to some of the early HKIS students but to me she was a neighbor. Her sons Scott, John, and daughters Anne and Mary were some of the nicest people around. I used to be invited out with them on weekends to go sailing out to Lamma Island or around to the harbor to sail around the ships at anchor including the wreck of the QEI. *Eric Lee ' 75*

• Bill Mahlke

Bill really loved being in Hong Kong and working at HKIS. He enjoyed the good relationships that he had with the staff and students and being able to give encouragement and enlightenment to his students. He also appreciated the respect that the people of Hong Kong had for teachers. He did enjoy Chinese food.

When Rhoda, my wife, and I visited Bill in HK he was a fantastic guide and tour director. We dined at the Victoria Peak restaurant, taking the tram, dined at a high-rise hotel that had the buffet lunch at the very top, had lunch at a floating restaurant, enjoyed the beggar's chicken with several other HKIS faculty, had lunch at the Repulse Bay Hotel-----walking there during the first typhoon to arrive after the high-rise apartments were built plus dinner at the Foreign Correspondent's

Club and other local restaurants.

Bill arranged for us to be among some of the first non-Chinese to go into mainland China and crossed over at LoWu on the train from HK. He had a friend at the Chinese Travel Bureau that arranged this for us.

Bill also enjoyed having a Chinese lady keep his flat clean and she even shampooed his hair.

Dick Mahlke, brother

As a student at HKIS, one of my favorite teachers had been Bill Mahlke … because of his teaching skills, his always interesting travel stories, and his cool Morris Minor Convertible. Because of the great respect I had for him, I found it nearly impossible to stop calling him "Mr. Mahlke" even though we later became colleagues.

Dave Christian '69

My wife and I recently vacationed in South Africa and I thought of Bill Mahlke because *Cry, the Beloved Country* was the first book we read in tenth grade. He was a very special teacher.

Peter Wang '71

Bill Mahlke was one of my absolute favorite teachers and I have many fond memories of him. I can remember working on Junto, the high school newspaper, with him. He was always so patient. Mr. Mahlke was my ESL teacher when I first came to HKIS. I remember when I came in for registration in the summer before the start of the school year, he was the one who sat down with me in the 4th floor cafeteria to help me plan out the class schedule. Besides teaching us English, Mr. Mahlke also from time to time illustrated to us slices of American culture and different aspects of life. Later, I also had the pleasure of working with him in Junto and learning about journalism. He was always the soft spoken, low key, methodological, gentleman teacher who at all times showed a keen interest in his students. He always had this slight smile on his face; however, that smile wasn't there on one particular day when he sent me to Mr. Von Behren's office for being "slightly" out of uniform. Mr. Mahlke, you are greatly missed.

Patrick Pang '80

Bill was a dear and dedicated friend and colleague. I always appreciated his gentle manner and the twinkle in his eye. He always extended a help-

ing hand and was certainly an inspiration to many. Bill Mahlke was one of the teachers we all knew. I am particularly sorry that I didn't have a chance to visit him when we were in Arizona for my father's funeral. Both my brother, Dwight, and one of my sisters, I believe, Sheryl, had been to visit him on previous occasions. They had thoroughly enjoyed being with Bill, hearing about his present adventures and sharing many memories of the "early days" at HKIS. He was certainly a special colleague to me when I was teaching at HKIS in the 70's. He will be sorely missed by the many he inspired.
Sandra (Scarbrough) Walters, French teacher '70-'74

Mr Mahlke was THE BEST English teacher I had in High School, or College for that matter.
Gail Storey

Mr. Mahlke was one of the best teachers/advisors I ever had. He always showed great kindness, encouraged me to stand up for what I believed in and had confidence in me. I am deeply sorry to hear of his passing and wish him well in his journey.
Bobbie Tse '72

Mr. Mahlke was one of my most admired persons and a teacher. I have described him as a "GENTLEMAN" who had a BIG heart. Anybody had him as a teacher would have agreed. Even though he's not with us anymore. I still would like to vote him as the "Most favorable teacher" of all time at H.K.I.S. I am very sad that he's gone because he was one of those persons who impacted many lives, one of those is mine. He will be in my heart forever.
Gabe Lau '77

I remember Mr. Mahlke as gentle man. Though I was never in any of his classes I always heard that he was very good as a teacher. Pun battles at the Drift Inn with him would have been a lot of fun.
Ed Ketterer 75

Bill Mahlke's been a fixture for a huge number of us HKISers of the 60's and 70's. I was fortunate to have attended alot of his classes when I was in High School. He got me into journalism and I'll never forget the times we spent together working on "Junto." I've always hoped to be involved in a reunion where we can meet up with Mr. Mahlke again. He's always been a quiet man, a gentleman and a person that I'll always remember as "Mr. HKIS."
Ken Koo '79

I did not personally have him as an instructor at HKIS. I do remember passing him in the hallways of HKIS and the impressions he left me was that of a large gentle man. Perhaps, if he was an instructor of mine I may have turned out a better writer. Cheers to Bill!

His invitation to a party, that we will all eventually attend, came first. God Speed Bill.
Eric Lee ' 75

I had class with Mr. Mahlke for one year. Although my memory fades about some specifics, I do remember him as a kind, soft-spoken man, well liked by his students. I remember his creative writing class being a bit challenging at first, but with his encouragment, it became interesting and fun, and I grew to love writing. I hope that our new alumni will carry similar memories of the teachers who've changed their lives. And don't the good ones change us all for life?

Thank you, Bill.
Mark Shostrom '74

I will remember him as a gentle, caring man who was a dedicated educator and continued to be interested in the well-being of his students long after they had left his classroom. It was Mr. Mahlke who taught me to write something I will always be grateful for. I hope he's up there reading some of this. He was definitely one of the good guys.
Robert Dorfman `72

Although my dad had worked for the same company for thirty years, home, life, and work life were as separate as they could be in a line of work that took the entire family around the world. I don't think that we appreciated how many people's lives Bill had touched in a positive way until an overwhelming number of people attended his memorial service. Some traveled a long way to attend, and many of them took the time to "say a few kind words."

I'm still touched by those words, and I still take some comfort in knowing that he was every bit as good a person in their eyes as he was in ours. I'll bet that a teacher's family (and many teachers themselves) don't know how many students have really been touched and changed for life by that teacher.
Mark Woodruff

teacher. *Mark Woodruff*

Someone asked a general question to the 'train' about who our favorite teacher was at HKIS. My thoughts turned to Mr. Mahlke immediately - before hearing about his passing. I really appreciated his teaching style. I pray that his family will have comfort in knowing he is in a better place.
June Steagall '77

Bill Mahlke was my teacher before there was an HKIS. Back in Los Angeles in 1962, he first taught me journalism. I later became very interested in writing and was editor-in-chief of our high school newspaper. When I arrived in Hong Kong, imagine my surprize to see my old teacher now as a collegue.

He was a true friend to my wife and me, and we had many expoits throughout the Colony over the years. We even met up in London for a week of attending plays and shared a bed-and-breakfast there. For years, I admired his '67 Morris Minor, and was only too delighted to be able to purchase it when he decided to be a pedestrian.
Dave Kohl, art teacher '73 - '80

•Dave Rittmann

One day I had an appointment to see Dave Rittmann. I came out from one of the offices and saw Dave standing in front of the window at the business office. He saw me, extended his arm, and together we skipped all the way down the hall to his office. Another time Dave showed the clown inside, that always makes me smile when I remember it, was the afternoon I was walking down toward the office at the end of the hall – Dave saw me walking by the first office and by the time I reached his office, he had plastered his face against the glass, completely distorting his features.
Judy Butler, teacher '76 - '83

While most people remember him as headmaster, I was lucky enough to have Mr. Rittmann as an English teacher. In addition to AP English, he was willing to arrange an independent study for credit for Kathy Peaslee and me, in which we read, discussed, and wrote about works of literature that we chose together. Our AP English class bonded over Dickens, Joseph Conrad (we would quote lines to each other outside of class), and *One Flew Over the Cuckoo's Nest* (remember the field trip?).

I always thought that Mr. Rittman should have been a college professor, but I am grateful that he chose to teach high school students. Although I ended up as a history professor, I owe my love of literature to him. I think I wrote and told him some of this after I left HKIS for college, but I'm not sure whether I actually did or just meant to. I hope I did, and that he knew what an important influence he had on my life. *Linda Lierheimer '77*

I've always admired the way Dave could convey in one short paragraph what would take me a full page to communicate. Actually, Arleen and I have known the Rittmanns since they came to serve on our staff at Our Saviour Lutheran School in the Bronx. He was fresh out of college in the early 1960s. It was that relationship and our knowledge of them as superb teachers that led HKIS to bring them out.
Bob Christian, first headmaster '66 - '77

I've always been a voracious reader, and the summer between Jr and Sr year we had just moved to The Peak. I was bored bored BORED - so when we started AP English, we were asked to list what we had read that summer. My list included *War and Peace*, *Les Miserables*, all the Michner and Clavell I could get my hands on, and a lot of Dickens as well. I remember Mr. Rittmann asking if I enjoyed "light" reading. I laughed and said I just wanted to be prepared for the class. We read, discussed, and debated - and the entire AP class smoked the exam!!

• Marie Von Behren

We have all lost a kindred spirit, a diligent worker for the Kingdom, a loving mother/grandmother, and an enthusiastic friend. She was usually the first to arrive and one of the last to leave my annual holiday open house, and we shared a lot of wonderful laughter. There's probably a library in some corner of paradise that she's already evaluating for re-arrangement. Rest in peace, sweet lady. *Dave Kohl, art teacher '73-'80*

I loved the teachers at HKIS, those wonderful German-named Lutherans. Thoughtful, patient, funny--great guys and gals. Special mention to the late, great Marie Von Behren. I was a library assistant and she was a joy to talk to, to work for, and to just hang with. So funny and she liked kids a lot.

get-well card when I was in Adventist hospital.

Ann Sullivan '75

•Werner Von Behren

I remember our WONDERFUL choir teacher and elementary principal Mr. Werner VonBehren- I "sing with an egg in my mouth" always- just as he taught. He is probably the teacher who made the most lasting impression on me

Tami Whitrock '77

I had some great teachers at HKIS though the one who still holds a special place in my heart and mind was Mr. Von Behren. What a trooper....and what a name for choir director! I can still picture him instructing us to "make your mouth oval, like an egg", while he demonstrated, and all our faces were reflecting the stained glass colours in the chapel balcony.....:O....but he got us to sing our little hearts out, even when singing, "Rain Drops Are Falling On My Head"....ha, ha--we were so hip.

Jill Liddiard '77

Mr. Von Behren would really get into "If I Had a Hammer"...we sang every morning in his class in 8th grade.

Barb Schwerdtman '77

•Marge Westrick

We used to pretend to feel sick so we could go see Mrs. Westrick, the school nurse. It didn't take her long to figure out we were faking it, and the open invitation was given to drop by any time. So we did. Just a quick hello and a hug and we were on our way.

Barb Schwerdtmann '77

Marge and Earl Westrick had the kind of influence on my life that changed me forever. Their love and confidence in me carried me through the teenage years and inspired me to try to live with compassion, as they always did. I spent many long evenings at their Cabin #24 at Laan Tau Camp. We had fun, laughed a lot and talked "deeply." I always felt like I was part of the family. I will always remember the dark and misty walk home to our Cabin #5. My flashlight would be dim as I passed cabins down one mountain, passed the mess hall, crossed the saddle and then hiked up the other side. Laan Tau Camp is the most special place in my life and the Westricks are amazing people. My gratitude to both of them is unending!!!

Debbie Noren '73

Chapter 5
Students

HKIS Students represented over 30 countries during most school years. Some were from long-term local Chinese families, or some the children of traders and diplomats; others from missionary parentage. Many American and multi-national firms made Hong Kong their East Asia headquarters in the '60s and '70s, which meant recruiting personel from abroad and from the home office. Many students were moved to HK with a few weeks' notice, some up-rooted from secure roles in their American schools back home. Some were delighted. Some were NOT happy.

David Pollack wrote the definitive book identifying the phenomenon of these students and their survival and success in such a setting. "Third Culture Kids" are the young who were raised in a culture neither their own, nor their parents', nor that of the geographic locality where they lived. They had some things in common with the local children, some things in common with their cousins and friends back home, but more in common with each other - thrown into a millieu of sophistication, international associations, new local language and custom, with generally enough money to take advantage of a unique opportunity. They may have had more in common with their friends than their parents, who often were fully involved in business, government, religious, or domestic issues.

-Ed.

1. Third Culture stories:

One time on a job interview they were questioning about my education. "HKIS? You mean you went to school in Hong Kong?" They thought that I was making it up. They were wrong about that, but not about my grade point average.

Mark Feldman '75

I got my Third Culture Kid book by David Pollock in the mail today. Already I can see what it is that I have felt all these years and never realized. I think that is part of the feeling that I get from all of you on the Dragontrain – that we are all in this together. I feel like I have found a big family out there!!!

Tami Whitrock '77

When I read the TCK book, I cried through parts of it, because I suddenly realized "Hey, I'm not so crazy after all!" For the first time, I was being told not only that a lot of what I had felt for the last 30 very odd years was normal, but that I wasn't alone in feeling that way. I think it should be required reading for any family moving to a foreign country.

Deborah Smith '80

It is funny to belong but not quite all the way. I can remember one morning when Bobby Yamashita, Chris Reaves, Rob Reiner and John Cammarata were sitting on the bench in front of the elevator on seventh floor when I came up the stairs. One of those guys called me a 'banana' and I thought, "no way was I a banana".

I said, "I'm not a banana."

Chris replied, "Then what are you?"

Of course my last name being 'Lee', I said, "A pear".

Chris retorted, "So, you're still a fruit." Laughter resounded, and Rob explained that I was a 'banana' because I was 'Yellow' on the outside and 'White' on the inside. The Asian analogy to an 'Oreo.'

It really is a strange feeling to be with a group of people into which you don't totally fit. I mean if it looks like a duck, flies like a duck, quacks like a duck; it probably is a duck. Well not exactly, I am of Chinese ancestry, I look Chinese and that is about it. At 5'10", I am too tall to fit in, I do not speak the language, I dress by western standards, and in the city of HK I stick out of the crowd pretty badly. Now take all this to Hawaii, I fit in by appearance, but my inability to speak pidgin (a mix of colloquial broken English, Japanese, Korean, Filipino, Hawaiian, and Chinese) is a sure give away that I am not truly a "\'local.'

Having been moved around a lot during my younger years leaves me a lot of room on how to answer the question of " Where are you from?"

Eric Lee ' 75

• Attending a British School

The American community in Hong Kong had been eager enough for an American type school and so a "Provisional School" was established to fill the gap until the first HKIS building was completed. Grades 1-6 met in a rented apartment building on Chung Hom Kok Road, while some older students pursued Dow-Midland correspondence classes in the same building.

My sister, Ann (then age 13) and I (then age 15) did not follow the correspondence route, but instead enrolled at KGV (King George V School) in Kowloon. Fortunately, a neighbor in our apartment building worked very close to KGV, so we were able to ride with him in the morning. This was long before any cross-harbor tunnel, so we took a vehicular ferry every morning, and got quite good at mimicking the "Smoking is not allowed on the vehicular deck…" announcement that was made at the beginning of every trip. Each afternoon we made our own way home by public bus (usually a #7 down Waterloo Road), the Star Ferry, and another public bus (the #6 to Repulse Bay.)

KGV was a new experience in any number of ways. After taking an entrance exam, I was placed in Form 4 … or more accurately, in Form 4B. That meant I was (theoretically, at least) smarter than the students in 4C, 4D. And 4E … but not as smart as the kids in 4A. During final exams just before Christmas break, several 4B students, including me, scored high enough that we were promoted to 4A … while some of the lower scoring students in 4A moved "down" to 4B. It was an interesting sort of hierarchy. (Ann, by the way, was placed in Form 2A right from the start.)

KGV offered many glimpses into British culture. Our schoolwork not only took place in ranked classes, but also relied heavily on examinations. I recall very little homework, little call for "outside research." Those who were good at taking notes and cramming for exams did well … while those who didn't … wound up in the "C," "D," and "E." sections. The oldest students, those "Upper 6" students who were preparing for their final exams, were "prefects," and responsible for much school discipline.

We also saw British culture on a more popular level. Worldwide, youth culture was highly influenced by the British invasion in music (think Beatles, Rolling Stones, the Who, the Kinks, etc.) and fashion (think Carnaby Street, Twiggy, etc.) I remember that wide belts and low riding "hip hugger" pants were popular among many of the boys, along with polka dot or paisley shirts with white collars and cuffs. Some favored a "military" dress look, while others preferred their "Nehru" jackets.

One of my KGV friends lived in the New Territories, as his dad taught at the Chinese University near Tolo Harbor. David's family had a small motorboat that we rode past Plover Cover out to Mirs Bay, (the site of occasionally desperate and dramatic "swims for freedom.") Our outing was recreational, however, as we pulled up on a sandy island and spent the afternoon snorkeling amidst very colorful tropical fish and other vibrant sea life.

At this time, fireworks were readily available throughout Hong Kong, particularly around Chinese New Year. I brought home a sizable collection of bottle rockets and launched them from my bedroom window over the Deep Water Bay hillsides. For better or worse, that was the last year that fireworks were easily available to the public, as the civil unrest later that spring led to significant government restrictions.

Before we had left the US for Hong Kong, we had all gotten a battery of shots. (In addition to passports, we had to show "shot cards" when going through immigration at the airport.) There was a small outbreak of cholera during our first year in Hong Kong, and in response the health departments set up public inoculation sites around the city. I recall stopping and casually getting a cholera booster one day on my way home from school.   *Dave Christian '69*

You know you're a 3rd Culture Kid when:

• You can't answer the question, "Where are you from?"
• You speak two languages but can't spell in either.
• You flew before you could walk.
• You have a passport but no driver's license
• You have a time zone map next to your telephone.
• Your life story uses the phrase "Then we went to..." five times.
• Reading National Geographic makes you homesick.
• You read the international section before

the comics.
- You don't know where home is.
- Someone brings up a team name, and you get the sport wrong.
- You watch a movie set in a foreign country, and you know what the nationals are really saying into the camera.
- You haggle with the check out clerk for a lower price.
- Your high school memories include those days that school was cancelled due to bomb scares.
- You think VISA is a stamp in your passport & not a plastic card carried in your wallet.
- You know it really is a small world after all.

2. The Provisional School - 1966-67

The Provisional School, operating in an apartment was, in a way, a home school. Recess was divided by class groups, but we still played in the courtyard with kids from a wide range of backgrounds, and a wide spread in ages. It did feel like a family setting. We lost some of it when we moved into the new building in Repulse Bay, but I still saw my own brother and sisters when we wound down the staircase to PE, and later my mother taught fourth grade, and I would see her during the day too. It seemed the older kids looked out for the younger ones, and the junior high kids never got too big for their britches, like they always seem to do in the US medium security compounds (i.e., middle schools).

We convinced some of our teachers to hold class on the beach. Not surprisingly, I can't recall a thing that we might have been taught there, but I do remember the humid tropical air and warm water and chasing girls around on the beach in the goofball games that junior high kids come up with.

Scott Lazenby '72

I attended the original HKIS School. I was in sixth grade, in the living room of the apartment on the 2nd floor. Other classes were in the bedrooms. Our old home at 56 Chung Hom Kok Road has been knocked down and something big went up. There is a new road across the street, called Cape Road, which now connects Chung Hom Kok directly with Stanley.

Carolyn Cole '73

The Provisional School on Chung Hom Kok brings back so many 4th grade memories. As I think about them all they are very disjointed. I remember the 5-inch red centipedes that lurked at the edge of the road that wound down to school. The big kids told me they were poisonous. I still have a fascination for creepy crawlies and science today. Leaving the house at 6 AM to walk down the mountain in the dark via 500 plus stairs (North Point didn't have a bus route yet to where we lived) to get bus #10 to Central, transfer to bus #6 at Star Ferry and ride out to Chung Hom Kok Road for the long walk to school.

Walking that mile plus in the pouring rain and getting picked up by the Ketterer's driver. Some times it was the small black car, other times it was the Limo. Once (in the small car) they picked up so many of us drenched kiddos that I had to lay all across their laps, soaking them all. That's what I got for being the smallest. At least we got to school faster! A field trip to the beach that was on the side of the peninsula away from Stanley. I think there were banana trees growing at the edge of it. Having a British actress named Mrs. Cutler as my 4th grade teacher. I remember how she read King Arthur and other British tales aloud to us daily, in her wonderful accent. Then we taught her how to sing "I've Been Working on the Railroad." Big kids walked through our room to get to theirs. We were in the living room, the 7/8th grades were in one bedroom and 9-12 were in another one. Both my sisters (Becky and Debbie) were in those other rooms. Playing "swords" at recess time. It was a bit like marbles but we used cocktail swords. I don't even know where I got them from, but you captured your opponent's sword, arrow, spear, javelin, etc. and got to keep it. It kept us very busy! Playing Chinese jump rope and jumping higher than I ever thought I could. I could jump the ones on my friend's shoulders. I think it was because we walked so much that I was in such good shape. Buying Joysticks, Wonderbars, and Popsies on hot days from the bicycle vendor outside of the school at the end of the day.

Mary Jo Luedtke '75

My first year at HKIS was in the second grade in 1966 at Chung Hung Kok Road. I remained at HKIS until the end of my 10th grade year in 1975.

Some memories that have come back to mind: the shack, eating grilled cheese sandwiches made by Chris Myers at the American Club, cottillion, the Go Down, Thingamees , and many more. My family was then transferred to Tehran where I finished high school before going to college in North Carolina.   *Chris Caluori '77*

3. The First HKIS building 1967

During our first year in Hong Kong, I enjoyed regular trips through the HKIS construction site with Dad. Progress continued, and somehow, in the midst of a historical water shortage, the building was completed. Dad had assembled a teaching staff, books and furniture arrived, and school was ready to start in September.

Certain events and activities stand out as I look back at those first two years. Among other things, the opening of HKIS returned me to a familiar situation, that of being a student in a school where my dad was an administrator. For the most part, I had gotten used to that role … I certainly had plenty of practice. But occasionally ….

These were the years when "hippie" values influenced youth culture, even in Hong Kong. While some teachers and administrators made sure that the girls' uniform skirts were long enough, others made sure than the boys were keeping their hair short enough. One day my dad stood at the door as we exited from the chapel, and pulled a number of us out of line. Although it may have been a bit shaggy, my hair was hardly very long, but I suppose my dad wanted me to set a good example … and so, like the other transgressors, I had to make a trip to the barber that afternoon.

HKIS began to emerge as a force in local sports, particularly in track and field. With Bob Burns as coach, we "made do" with unusual training venues. Distance runners regularly ran down to the end of South Bay Road. We occasionally met to sprint and/or stretch on the beach at Repulse Bay. We regularly met on the road above the school (South Bay Close) and did repeated intervals back and forth around traffic cones. Occasionally we would use a van to travel to the St. Stephens field in Stanley, and once or twice we even went over to the grass track at KGV.

Because interschool track happened entirely during one three day meet in the spring, we regularly entered both senior and junior athletic meets at South China Stadium, Government Stadium, or the only all weather track in HK, the Boundary Street track in Kowloon, and we fared quite well against other students and club athletes.

My sister Ann stood out in both running events and hurdles, and Jody Saunders complemented her in the shorter sprints. Etsuro Hayakawa became a colony-wide force in the sprints, while Alex Koperburg and I were frequently near the front in middle distance events. Debbie Mushett, Julie Newport, and Valerie Smith helped round out the girls' team, while Barry Laubach, Rick Hum, Wilfred Koo, and Rick Brackman added depth to the boys' team.

Dave Christian '69

My three children, Debbie, Kathy and Patricia Smiley were practically spoonfed their education at the Hong Kong International School from the day it opened in 1966 until our family moved back to Atlanta in 1971.

Jacqueline Smiley, mother '66-'71

• Elementary adventures:

As hangouts go, mine was decidedly at the less glamorous end of the spectrum: the elementary school library. I spent second, third, fourth and half of fifth grades at HKIS, and frequent trips to the library were a mainstay. As I recall, the library was on the east side of one of the hallways running north from the main staircase in what is now the Upper Primary building in Repulse Bay. The library was a rectangular room that stretched off to the right as you entered it, and I think the librarian's desk was in the far corner, not at the entrance the way it is now. The adventure books that I most enjoyed were in the middle of the wall facing the door, and I devoured them shelf by shelf. I remember heroic figures who descended into the mouths of volcanos, fought bad guys who tried to trap their feet in giant clams at low tide, and much, much more.

Recess was fun, too. Sometimes my friends and I played soccer and other times we shot baskets for the game of "horse"; the fifth floor playground, which was on the fourth floor then, had a net that was only seven feet high, in addition to a couple regulation-height nets, and the lower net was a natural favorite for younger students. The lower net is no longer there, unfortunately.

Elementary school was not just about the library and recess, of course – there were classes, too. Starting in fourth grade, we struggled to learn Cantonese in a program that was much more basic than the Mandarin instruction offered today. Math was taught with more of an emphasis then on memorizing multiplication tables and so forth, without the more elaborate and complex syllabus that HKIS follows today, which includes exposing children to negative numbers at a much earlier age. Term papers were a lot of work –I remember doing one on Jupiter –and did not include the fancy Powerpoint presentations and oral presentations that are common today. The mainstay of HKIS then and now was the presence of great teachers. They kept us in line, corrected us when we strayed and prepared us for the frenzied world that lay ahead of us. *Keith Bradsher '82*

•Construction

In 1972 there was the "Moving A Mountain" theme that saw gongs going off several times a day as the construction workers blew up a good chunk of hillside to put up the Elementary School across South Bay Close. I still have the pictures of each Elementary School class taking a class photo at the site with a sign in bold print reading "Moving a Mountain" Grade...! *Ken Koo '79*

When we built the new building, I don't remember if we consulted a feng shui master. Maybe one of the architects did, at their own cost and never told us. We were just concerned about fitting square footage requirements on the side of a mountain and holding the mountain in place with the best construction methods. I haven't run across any mention of feng shui in either of the Old or New Testaments, but then, I haven't read Revelations or all of the Old Testament prophets that carefully. *Bob Christian, first headmaster '66 - '77*

Building the new school across the road, anticipating the blasting days, standing at the window waiting for it to go, think it was around noonish. I think the power or heating would also go off that year, we wore hats and scarves, like it was really cold!! The new school was so colorful, especially against the deep green of the hill side. *Barb Schwerdtmann '77*

•Kids say the darndest things (actually heard in the HKIS elementary school):

John: "Mrs. Chan is going to be 6 years old on her birthday."
Ben: "No she isn't. When you're 6, your teeth are falling down and hers aren't."

——·——

Mrs. Elliot: "When they rolled the stone away, Jesus wasn't there. He was gone."
Mary: "They probably moved him to a cemetery."

——·——

Christian opened a snow pea and found only one pea inside. "It's a tsunami pea. He lost his Mom and Dad. They got washed away in the water." (He made this comment one month after the Sumatra event.)

——·——

Who made God? "Whose tummy did he come out of?"

——·——

Christian: "My sock is every time jumping down in my shoe."

——·——

Stephanie: "Will my heart turn black if I say bad things to other people?"

——·——

Max: "Did you teach here for 20 years?"
Mrs. Elliott: "Yes"
Max: "I wasn't even born when you started to teach!"

——·——

Kane was excited to hear about an upcoming fire drill. "We'll get to slide down the fireman pole!"

——·——

Anne: "When the sun goes up and down and up and down and up and down it gets so dizzy that it makes it rain."

——·——

Hannah: "To make the air clean we need to paint soap all over the road. Let the bubbles get bigger and bigger and bigger...so big that they hit the sky,. When they pop they will come down with the rain and wash the air."

———

Frederick: "I wish everyday was Christmas and we had a birthday every Saturday and Sunday."

———

Celia: "You shouldn't eat with your mouth open or someone might snatch your food."
Mary Jane Elliott, teacher '80-'07

I remember the wonderful quotes from some of my students – one I have quoted scores of times. This came from a small sage in grade 3. "Life is never straightforward. Everyone has to face difficulties." One day a 2nd grader and I were taking things off the bulletin board and my student looked at me and asked, "Miss Butler, do you work?" *Judy Butler, teacher '76 - '83*

I had a great time on a class trip to the Mountain Cream ice-cream factory with Mrs. Geenwald.
Patrick Pang '79

The school buses always parked on the 4th floor playground and K-6 graders waited in the covered area shivering in the cold during the winters waiting for the 8:15 bell to ring and the doors to open............mad stampede time !
Ken Koo '79

I remember a time when the girls started wearing the boy's uniform ties to school. Then we had an assembly just for the girls and were made to vote on adding the ties as a mandatory part of the uniform. We voted "no" and that squelched the fad. I remember being impressed by the way the administration handled that. *Wendy Liddiard '73*

I had one Joseph Kilpatrick who reminded me of "Dragnet" and Joe Friday….he wanted "just the facts!" Never give him too many instructions or don't expect more than the basics from him. He had a great sense of humor. Another student was Tony Welsh, whose goal in life is to become the Prime Minister of Canada! Smart and savvy…we might one day hear about him in politics. William

Stevenson became the most recognized HKIS student in all of HK. He appeared on every major billboard and on multiple tram signs dressed as a hotel delivery boy advertising the new "Mall Shopping Centre" in Central across from Admiralty. No matter where I went in HK, I could not escape William.

I have wonderful memories of my HK students and I just want to say that I was blessed by their motivation to learn, to enjoy everything we threw at them, they were respectful of each other and of diversity that made HKIS a great place to be. *Zita Thompson, teacher '81 - '93*

My mom, Marlene Seeley, directed a production of Sesame Street. They actually put it on TV! We had to do another production for that, and we actually still have it on video tape. I was Harry Monster, it was a great deal of fun to do.
Dean Seeley, '85

Marlene Seeley and Dottie Mache were inseperable friends, and since I taught art with Dottie, I knew all about most goings on in the Elementary. My favorite memory was when Marlene produced the musical "Sesame Street" in the chapel. The costumes were amazing and the kids were really good. There were large set pieces and backdrops, which had to be moved out into the outside hallway so church could happen Sunday morning. The Chinese maintenance people thought they were trash and hauled them downstairs. When Marlene showed up to put the stage back together and the sets were gone, there was a hue and cry heard across Repulse Bay. You never saw Chinese workers quiver like they did that day. Somehow, the sets were restored in time for the show. *Dave Kohl, art teacher '73-'80*

I had Mrs. Rupprecht for second grade and was in Mrs. Burns' class in third grade. I was back in Hong Kong in 1998 for the first time since 1970, and I turned on the hotel TV. As I flipped channels, you will never guess the identity of the economic correspondent for MSNBC--our very own Martin Soong! Other famous HKIS names on the TV include Andrea Koppel at CNN (daughter of Ted Koppel) and Trey Wingo (featured on ESPN's Sports Center). I suppose having all those Vietnam correspondents in HK in the late 60's bears fruit in the next generation.

I have fond memories of Mr. Brackmann. I

only wish I could tell him that I am a much better basketball player now than when I was in fourth grade.   *Jeffrey M. Trinklein '74*

I remember the first day of school (my junior year) and going through the motions, but then lo and behold, I see Tony Betts! We had lived down the street from each other in Korea, a few years prior to Hong Kong. He was great friends with my brother, but then we lost touch. Tony introduced us to his friends at HKIS and from then on, life was good at school.   *Linda Reizman '80*

There was a field trip to the USS Coral Sea, with Merrilee Block's 5th grade class. Her husband was the Commander of the aircraft carrier, and we all got to have our pictures taken sitting in the fighter jets on the deck. In the galley, there was a huge cake welcoming our class aboard the ship. We each had a sailor assigned to us, and mine gave me his monogrammed cap to keep when the day was over. Mrs. Block was a fun teacher, who re-minded me of Marlo Thomas. Once, she came back from a school break with every finger bandaged and swollen. She'd dived straight into a bed of sea urchins, fingers first. It looked so painful.
Jill Liddiard '77

Our family came in mid-1967 and I started school in the Bristish run Hong Kong Kennedy Road School while waiting for admission to HKIS. I attended HKIS between1967 and 1969. I was in Mrs. Bentley's class (1967-68) and Mrs Burns'class (1968-69) and I believe a Mr. Brackmann in the gym and Mrs. Duval.

I left in 1969. I can tell you for a fact, that de-spite the very short 18 months there, I have never been to a better school and coming home to Swe-den in July 1968 felt terrible, and it took several years before I adapted to the Swedish way of think-ing or the school system for that matter. Revisiting my dear beloved Hong Kong in 1981 the first time - a lot had changed. The Repulse Bay Hotel was doomed, our house in Repulse Bay Rd was to be demolished, the old Casino near the beaches derelict, and HKIS students without uniforms.
Henrik Mjoman '78

I remember walking up and down the end-lessly circular stairwell at the the 'old' 7- story HKIS building. I always got dizzy.
Scott Schroth '77

I would lop down the stairs 2 or 3 at a time, until Mr. Christian would tell me again... to slow down!

The "covered area" under the chapel was where we played ping pong all the time, hockey for PE, golf with real clubs where my pal Cindy Palmer got a golf club in her neck and I went to the hospital with her. I vividly remember the time the kid went running outside and got wrapped up with the cord around his neck. They filled in the wall to stop that from happening again.

The 4th Floor courtyard was where we lined up every morning, being jealous of the kids who got to ride the bus, while I had a driver. Playing kickball, choosing teams, I was a good kicker and catcher, so I got picked early, feeling sad for my pals who were always last, but I picked them first when I got to be captain. The courtyard was also the site of group pictures taken for the yearbook, our graduating class photo!

We often had PE on South Bay Close, in front of Church of All Nations – Years of playing 4-square! Go Robbie! My brother went swinging on the big steel gates and got smashed in the head when he didn't stop in time. My first experience with a goose egg. Those of us that went to church knew about the bathroom inside at the bottom of the stairs - an insider's secret! Going in to visit with Pastor Tuchardt and then listen to the Doobie Brothers!   *Barb Schwerdtman '68-'77*

• Elevators

We all wanted to take the elevator in the original H.S. It was the slowest thing in the world, but the most fun! I remember being able to stop in between floors and physically open the doors and haul yourself out, thereby "stalling" the elevator for everyone else's use! (Did I just give too much away?)

My freshman year I broke my foot at the pool at the Lantau Cabins. Dr.'s orders were to use the elevator, but the darn thing was so slow I was al-ways 10-15 mins. late to class! So, I ended up hop-ping up and down the stairs! I remember the irony at the time--allowed to use it but didn't want to! Go figure!   *Trina McCormick '81*

Getting into the lift one day, I became aware that there was some rumbling in the ceiling. Not knowing what to expect, and thinking it was some-

73

thing mechanical, I moved the light grill. I guess I wasn't totally surprized, but there, crouched above the lift was Missy Preston!! What a strange place to sneak a cigarette.

Earl Westrick, principal et al '71-'96

I know ALL about elevators... The administration and Headmaster in 73/74 would verify that.... my bad? *Melissa Preston '77*

• Living and Growing with HKIS

I was a 7 year old when I took my first steps into the school. Now, 39 years later, I'm a parent and I can look back to the days when my kids took their first steps into HKIS ! From performing in the "Chicken Fat" exercise routines (ask any mid to late 70's HKIS alum and they'll remember Chicken Fat !!!) in the late 60's under then Athletic Director Ed Brachman's strict but benevolent scrutiny to watching my son's Grade 5 Civil War re-enactments in 2000 under Terry Quinn's exquisite choreography. From my singing "Onwards Christian Soldiers" back in 1968 as a 2nd Grader in the Church of All Nations led by Werner Von Behren's orchestration on the organ to watching my youngest daughter sing "We are the Kids of HKIS" with her 2nd Grade choir under Beth Hoepner's direction. I've watched with pride how, despite a gap of three decades, what I experienced as an HKIS student and what my children are now experiencing as HKIS students are, in many ways, the same.

From the mists of HKIS genesis when the first Christmas basketball tourney tipped off and the first Day of Giving kicked off both at what is now the Upper Primary gym, there were many traditions that have lasted and many traditions that have faded…Sadie Hawkins Day, Slave Day, the Dance Marathon, the Mok Cup and Rice Bowl intramurals. *Ken Koo '79*

The day Pam Wong joined our 4th grade class, Lois Christian got to take her around, and then we all ended up being best friends!

Barb Schwerdtmann, '77

I dreaded my first day at school but quickly learned that the solid cliques in American schools did not exist at HKIS. Because kids moved around a lot, it didn't make sense to be exclusionary. During my first hour at school--8A, homeroom with Mr. Holliday (whom I think the teachers called Doc Holliday), a pretty girl named Libby Adcock introduced herself and we became instant friends. On a Christmas shopping trip to Daimaru (I loved the aisles of merchandise at Daimaru!) we bought each other ceramic animals--Libby got the cat, I got the dog. This is a strange comment, but Libby taught me about kindness. She was so thoughtful, so friendly, and so genuine. Everyone loved her. I remember the view of the Happy Valley Race Track from her balcony. We used to jog around that race track to lose weight.

There were three eighth-grade classes--8A, 8B, and 8C. We all took Mr. Rupprecht's Earth Sciences class. He gave the same test to all three classes. Somehow, we started a cheating ring. All three classes shared the tests so we knew the answers ahead of time. Eventually, Mr. Rupprecht found out and he was SO nice and understanding. Back, in Beltsville, the teachers would have screamed and clobbered us.

While in 8th grade, Larry Burroughs, the famous Vietnam War photographer, died, and his daughter who was in my grade withdrew from school.

In ninth grade my best friend was Ginger McElroy, who was tall like me. She was so funny. Made me laugh every day. A shout-out to another girl who definitely had the humor gene--Mary McIntosh. In tenth grade my buddy was Violette Li. I was on the Varsity Basketball Team and she was the statistician and team assistant. Although one year younger than me, she was a junior and I was a sophomore. Super smart. We co-taught Vacation Bible School at CAN.

In ninth grade I made the junior varsity basketball team. On the first play of my first game, I grabbed the ball after the opening toss-up and dribbled it down the court for an easy lay-up. I missed the lay-up. Good thing. I was shooting at the wrong basket. BUT, I improved and set a record in tenth grade for most rebounds. I loved being on a sports team and Mr. Pfaff was such an understanding coach. *Ann Sullivan '75*

• Memories of a K-12 alumni

HKIS didn't have the pre-primary education when I started. It was just Kindergarten and there were a number of us that went K-12 together that

DRAGON TALES

graduated in '97. The class shirts were 'End of an Empire'... and it had meaning in more than one way for a goodly number of us. Kindergarten was good – Mrs. Chapman. Remember dressing up cabbage patch dolls with a friend, Lisa Shaw, in HKIS uniforms for show and tell one time... On up through the grades. Probably going to forget some but Alan Link, Mike Lambert, Mrs. Oberg (for fourth and fifth). Then on to middle school... Hoeppner for sixth. McGregor-Brown for eighth.

Virginia Thompson was significant in High School. People of influence that immediately come to mind (aside from the folks mentioned above) in no particular order... Bickel, Handrich, Westrick, Oetting, Black, Elliott, Woodford, Rohrs, Woodall, Temme, Chaveriat (probably butchered the spelling on that one), Koehneke, Klammer, Eichert, Frerking, Schmidt, and of course many more.

While there certainly were cliques that formed in our class, I really felt as though we still stood together and while we did have a few of our odd ones, I don't think any of us felt as though we didn't belong and I would even say most of us actually crossed several clique borders. While I knew I didn't necessarily "fit-in" with the some of the groups, it was never as though they wouldn't talk to me if a conversation was struck. Back then just about everybody at least knew everybody else's name if not where they were from and what they were about. Perhaps we might have seemed fractured but towards the end of our time there, I at least felt we had a close-knit community.

Jason Weber '97

My HKIS years were interrupted by a home leave to Atlanta my sophomore year. Many adjustments...Like knowing that Burger King was a restaurant and not royalty. Or learning that you're really not supposed to pick up the cereal bowl and shove it into your face, congee style. Or that Laht Hot was not English (Laht meaning spicy). And American kids were so obsessed with cars and getting a license. Give me a double-decker!

The wierdest thing in Atlanta was being the only new kid in my high school, not just Atlanta but, in just about the whole of Fulton County. There was a kid in my social studies class from Chad 10 years back and we became fast friends...mostly because we seemed to be the only people who understood that there was a real world out there.

My HKIS education must have been good, they thought I was a genius. I made the "super" honor roll and was on the Academic Bowl team with a bunch of seniors. I was a nerd at 14. All I can say is "Thank you," Mrs Chern, Mrs. Banwell, Mr. Carlton, Mr. Matthews and all the other great teachers I had.   *Deborah Smith '80*

I certainly can remember more about those two short years than I can about my junior and senior years back in Minnesota, returning after my father's contract expired. Some of those memories include:

The first time eating pigeon, or squab, with its head still intact staring up at me from my plate.

Finding Asian "squatter" toilets with masses of flies waiting for their next supper! How appetizing!

My brother's first reaction to watching British comedy on TV, in particular, Man About the House – (known as Three's Company in the USA), when one of the roommates took her top off to reveal her "boobies!" My parents all of a sudden had to sensor TV during daylight hours!

My first "small world experience" when we discovered that Mr. Voeltz knew my aunt in a small town in Wisconsin;

Meagan O'Keefe asking me if Minnesota was any where near Chicago (and I thought I was bad in geography!)

-Playing Hearts and Whist in the cafeteria and Tara Whitehill's announcement to Mike McCoy that it was a "red letter" day!

My first "C" – Mrs Banwell Ancient History class – Libby Wallis and I only figured out how to study for the tests in order to get "As" at the end of the term!

Playing basketball against the Chinese Schools at public playgrounds with the "old" men squatting right on the edge of the court and the LOUD spitting when attempting to throw a free throw (subsequently Mr. Voeltz doing the same thing during practice so we wouldn't get distracted!)

Pete Reiner asking our tenth grade substitute (the band teacher?) biology teacher "how to do it" when he was passing around a pop quiz on human reproduction and the teacher misinterpreting the question and turning nine shades of red when Pete responded, "Not that, I know how to do that! I want to know how to do the quiz"

75

Sailing a laser with Tony Cahill in Repulse Bay only to lose my bikini top as we tacked.

My first kiss – Rob Janssen on Repulse Bay Beach after walking amidst the Chinese lanterns for the Autumn festival – only to be embarrassed when Rob later told Cathy McCoy, one of my best friends, I didn't know how to French!

My first drunk with Cathy drinking a bottle of Mateus Rose in the stairwell at Repulse Bay Towers, using a ballpoint pen to jam the cork into the bottle. The beginning of our motto, "Mateus is our juice."

Gregg Saunders and Todd Kehoe coming over to the flat to wish me a"Happy 15th Birthday" and Greg letting me drive his MG convertible in the car park. I don't know who I had the bigger crush on – Gregg or Todd.

Kathy Dewinter and I sharing a plate of food at a banquet in Manila during a Sports Exchange Tournament. I convinced the boy's basketball coach that I needed to go along as the student manager since the girl's team wasn't invited! After 26 years, I met up with Kathy in Seattle and it felt like we started just where we left off in HK!

Renee Doyle '78

I skipped the last few classes of the day with Bey Chen to go to Stanley for won ton noodles. On our way home on the #6 bus, the teacher whose class I skipped got on (karma!) and we had to avoid him until he got off at his stop - a very bumpy ride!

Anita Lau '84

4. High School School life

After a boring summer, the school season could not have come soon enough. I could walk to the South Bay campus and I began to take the trip at least once per day to shoot baskets in the front courtyard. It wasn't long before I met the HKIS basketball star, Brad Sandler. Brad was friendly and gracious. He seemed to know that I was desperate for contact with anyone other than my family. He immediately invited me on the first of many trips to the American Club in Wanchai and then to Kowloon to Ned Kelly's Last Stand. Finally, I felt like I might survive this whole ordeal. I met Steve Koch, Sean O'Keefe, Todd Kehoe, John Trepanier and Mike McCoy through Brad. I naturally went out for the basketball team since these were all of the guys who played for HKIS.

The most significant event that fall was a Halloween party in the Mid-Levels. I am not sure who I went to the party with but I will never forget who I left with. I met Kari Shimasaki that night. I can remember it like it was yesterday. Life for the next 18 months was defined and framed by my affairs with Kari. So many taxi rides to No. 6 Po Shan Do. I was happy, maybe as happy as I had ever been and possibly ever would be. Everything came easy in that framework. School, family life, sports, and friendship just naturally flowed from the energy of being connected to someone like Kari. I am sure that the whole first love experience was intensified by being in a foreign environment but never-the-less it was wonderful.

I spent more time in church in those days with Kari during lunch hour (with the 8th Grade choir practicing in the balcony) than I ever did for Sunday Service. Sorry Mr. Himmler and Pastor Tuchardt. You could hardly classify our purpose for your chapel visit as spiritual! Our friendship was the type I never thought could end even though we were always very aware that when high school was over we would most likely be apart. As a result I took her for granted and she found someone else that would give her the attention she deserved. I lost a great love. I finished my senior year and went to Ann Arbor and the University of Michigan a changed person. *Brad Doyle '76*

I remember lining up for F-1 student visas at 7:00 a.m. at the US Consulate on Garden Road that used to really be a Garden Road. Now...."cough ! gag !" *Patrick Pang '80*

•Cafeteria Life

There was an intrepid group that put a VW bug up on chairs in the cafeteria!

Tami Whitrock '77

The cafeteria was the hub of school. But whose idea was it to call it the Village Green?? Never did figure that one out.

For a while, the Chinese food was better than the Western food, and I hated the Spaghetti sauce, used to get noodles only. McDonald's was a real treat, and none of the kids in the US could believe we got to have McDonald's.

The Jukebox was always a hit, especially when the new songs were put on. Spaghetti dinners were a madhouse back in the kitchen. My Mom was in charge a couple of times, so of course I ended up in the kitchen helping. We still make the same recipe! Pancake breakfasts, sewing class, dance marathons, etc. Then there was the infamous making of the garlic escargot we stunk up the cafeteria with for French class. What a smell! They were disgusting as well, and we HAD to try them.

In later years, it was where we always played bridge and just hung out with friends.

Best time in the Cafeteria: When the announcement came that the Vietnam was over.

Barb Schwerdtmann '77

I recall Kelvin Limm skateboarding in the cafeteria, and telling us he could jump over a table and land on his board on the other side. It didn't quite work out that way, and Kelvin broke his ankle in the process. Immediately upon returning to school with a cast, Tom Burkhardt took Kelvin to the art room and fashioned a pair of plaster tits that he affixed to the front of the cast...which Kelvin proudly wore for the next six weeks. Life is art!

Mike McCormick '80

I NEVER knew what was going on in the Photo lab! Was I that clueless? Wish I had known! I loved photography class. In fact, I still dable in it. I have a new digital SLR I am playing with on my grandchild. In one of my boxes is my scraps and castings from jewelry class. I wasn't very good, but loved the creativity. I find it amazing today what a different kind of education I had from what kids get today stateside. I feel fortunate that we were able to experience what we did. What kid has a death & dying class? I remember the class trip to the mortuary and crematorium. I wish I hadn't opened the window on the oven. EEEWWWWWWW!! I loved journalism and have dabbled in it on occasion since. *Cindi Webb '78*

The Sullivan boys and I were in Doc Malmin's chemistry class and he had this fixture for light tubes (like a fluorescent light fixture), he would put tubes in there with different gases and they would emit different colors depending on the gas.

We were told DO NOT TOUCH THIS fixture.

Well Tom decided to grab the 2 ends of this deal – thus passing a MASSIVE amount of electric-

ity through his body. His hair stood straight up and his eyes bugged out of his head. As long as I live I will never forget that day. *Kelvin Limm '79*

Two HKIS students made the Hong Kong Standard in '78 when they found a rare specimen of a scorpion. Steve Karsten and David Ho were amateur herpetologists, and discovered the scorpion while searching for reptiles and amphibians under rocks in Tai Po Kau Forest. Their specimen of Hormurus australasiae was only the fifth actual living example of this rare breed, and there was a story and photo in the March 12 Weekender section of the Standard.

Richard Schrock, science teacher '75-'78

i just got out
of the shower
i hadn't taken one
in a week
it was great to
watch my sins
wash down
the little hole
in the floor -
again.

he keeps staring
and pointing his finger
at
me
it follows me all
around the room.
i'm only 17 and
i want to stay at
home
and eat hot
biscuits

James Langford, '80, from Impact 3

There was a reason why we took drama at the end of the day - so we could get out of the uniforms! I still laugh at Mark Feldman as Estragon in *Waiting for Godot*, as he disclaimed: "An erection?! and later "Let's hang ourselves immediately!" He loved that part. *Marcy Brooks '75*

• Modeling & Fashion

I did some modeling for a one-time shoot. The pictures were taken in the original HKIS Sanctuary. I was supposed to be praying with this serene look on my face. I don't know if the pictures were ever used for anything. I was also an extra for a B-Rated James Bond type movie where the shoot was on Kowloon side somewhere. I don't remember the name of the movie or the lead actor. The scene was a cock fight and my role was to be one of the crowd and to be totally horrified at the kill. Of course there was no cock fight, no blood and it was just a room full of people acting. It was rather fun.

Diane Reynolds

In a Sunkist commercial I did, they had me stand in front of a sky blue backdrop and drink Sunkist Orange soda from a can with my other arm straight out to my side at shoulder height. At the time I thought it was strange, but since I was getting paid to be strange, I did what they asked. When the commerical aired, there I was with my arm around a gorgeous blonde girl at Fisherman's Wharf! Now, where was that girl when I needed her? And, I sure don't remember being in San Francisco. I also did a Pepsi commerical where I skateboarded toward a vendor cart full of Pepsi's, and jumped over the cart landing on the board as it scooted under the cart.

Another commerical I remember was for Dors jeans and clothing. There was a whole group of us at the Lee Theater which served as the nightclub we were supposed to be in. I played the drums in the "band." Stuart Pearce was on guitar, and I think John Lutz was part of the band, too. I remember Traci Birnie was there, too, along with a couple dozen other Crusaders (pardon the PI term).

Kelvin Limm '79

Did I mention modeling was boring? Went all the way to some studio in Kowloon and sat under HOT lights all day wearing makeup. What a boring way to spend those Saturdays. Hated it! I had to sit very still for many hours (probably not really as long as it would have seemed to me at that age!)....and the staff was all Chinese. There were two makeup artists, a man and a woman who could not agree on how to do my makeup. One would spend an eternity putting it on me, then leave the room. The other would return and wipe it all off with tissues! After several sessions, they had a big argument and the woman departed.

My younger sister Anne was also at the first modeling session, but she cleverly made a big fuss so that they would let her out of it, which worked

right away. I spent many Saturdays doing this, and I teased my Dad years later about the fact that I got no payment from that gig! *Jill Liddiard '73*

There was a big bash at the Train Station following the Impuse and Ready to Wear fashion week. I got to be a part of with Keith, Nick, Barb B., Michelle, and Gilbert. That was awesome!

Barb Schwerdtmann '77

Towards the end of the '75 school year Apple Jeans did photo shoots with HKIS students. They were supposedly doing 6 shots. I was involved in the first two before I left. Some of the people that I remember being in them were: Karen Heck, Sally Lord, Libby Wallace, Julie Peterson, Cliff Raborn, Mark Feldman, Ken Westrick, John Trepanier... and quite a few more. As I remember there were 12 - 15 people in each shot. *David Knisely '75*

The Phoenix Hellraisers: The story of how the Phoenix Hellraisers came to be, is a classic in foreign cultural clashes. We see many great examples of mistakes made in spelling for signs, menus, instructions etc. A group of guys were going for "Phoenixes' Hellraisers." As in the Phoenix the bird that rises from the ashes, (and the original movie *Flight of the Phoenix* where they recycle & build a plane from a wrecked plane). Howard Hsu, Scott Bearden, Randy Bright, Kevin Kinne, Bob Roth, Brian Anderson, Cindy Webb, & myself (seems like there was 1-2 more) originally "formed" the group in 77. I think we initiated a couple new members in 78

We ordered jackets from a typical Hong Kong tailor in Wanchai. Well, in a classic misprint he made us the "Phoenix Hellraisers." As a joke, it was almost better than the reason we had the jackets made in the first place.

The idea was along the lines of a sophomoric prank... What would happen if we all got matching jackets and showed up all at the same time wearing them in the cafeteria. We expected a big laugh as everyone got the 'joke.' I'm not sure why we thought it would be funny, but we didn't get the reaction we thought. I'm sure there was some laughing, but not enough to make a joke out of it. So, the prank turned a bunch of friends, into a group, with an identity no-one really understood. Best of all, no-one was from Phoenix, although we were asked that question many times!

Ike Eichelberger '78

I still have Phoenix Hellraiser jacket, somewhere in my closet. Seems to me Renee Mordini also had one of those jackets.   *Scott Bearden '78*

•Sports

I was a budding and enthusiastic track and cross country runner in those days, but quickly discovered that sports at KGV were run on a completely different basis than what I had been used to. For the most part, teams did not have a season during which they regularly practiced together. For example, the cross-country team was assembled by holding an intramural competition, and then simply entering those athletes in interschool competition.

However, I had become used to training on a more regular basis … that is especially important for distance runners. Because we had an hour and fifteen-minute lunch break every day, I was able to use that mid-day time to change clothes, run intervals on the school field, and then change back into my uniform for afternoon classes. (Those who sat close to me were probably glad that the classroom walls consisted of many open windows.)
Dave Christian '69

Playing sports in general at HKIS and Rugby in particular was memorable. Not only for the joy of the sports but for the incredible comaraderie especially the Rugby team. Needless to say it was spectacular to start a team in a sport that at the time was not native to the Americans and go undefeated in the first season

We were marked young men after that. How dare we upstart Americans beat the Brits at their own game. Oh, I was a bit torn on that, being English at an American school. I think owed a lot of our success that first year to Mr Chambers the coach and Tal Albertson who would take the ball and run like a bat out of hell. I don't think anyone could catch him in those days.   *Gavin Birnie '75*

I took the independent physical education course where they gave us credit for participating in and writing about community sports. I played softball and Ruby on the weekends, joined a bowling league, and took parachuting lessons from British paratroopers with Phil Jordan. HKIS is the only high school where I could have done that. I still remember the early morning treks out to the

drop zone. First we would take the double decker #6 bus downtown, have breakfast on the ferry, and then another bus through the hills into the New Territories. We would be gone all day just to jump a few times. Yes, we really had a lot of freedom in Hong Kong.   *J. R. McMullen '76*

•A Sports Center discussion between Mark Wallis '76 and son, Mark Wallis II '07

HKIS has always had a strong interest in Baseball. In the seventies, the school supported an intramural program with games held in Aberdeen. Today, the school sponsors a High School team and competes in regional tournaments against other International schools.
-Ed.

Mark '76: You know son, you played on a pretty good baseball team this year winning both tournaments in Shanghai and Beijing. But head-to-head, I think a fantasy All-star team from 1976 would have given your team a real run for the money in 2007.

Mark '07: No way dad. We went 9-0 in tournament ball and nobody even came close to challenging us. We had excellent hitting, pitching, and of course speed on the base paths. Our team had 6 seniors and the benefit of a couple of future superstars who "played up" from the Middle School.

Mark '76: Well, your team could hit, but you didn't have a long ball hitter like Brian Leonard '76. Brian once hit a ball Mark McGwire-style over 400 feet into left field. The ball landed in the swamp area just next to the famous center-field duck pen.

Mark '07: You know dad, our pitching this year was outstanding with Corbin Russell'07, TJ Gavlik'09, "big Ian" Hosford'07, myself and, of course "little Wallis", my brother Andrew'11.

Mark '76: Yeah, agree. I'll admit you had some pitching, but you didn't have Brad Doyle'76 who could throw real heat. When Brad left HK, he made the U of Michigan team as a freshman walk-on. Brad could really throw hard – I know because I faced him as a hitter! I just know we played some great games and great memories.

• On the Bench

Our 1972-73 Boys Varsity Basketball team was one of the best. With starter seniors Jim Richards, Tal Albertson, Jon von Behren, Bob McCoy, Mike Sullivan'74, Ken Westrick '75, and Brad Challberg '75, the team was virtually unbeatable. The team easily won the Holiday Tournament and even such strong local rivals like Lingnan College proved to be no competition. (The team was also well-known for its fondness for macramé headbands.)

Having such strength on the court allowed Coach Bob Rogalski to bring along a few younger players like Mike McCoy'75 and myself (Mark Wallis'76) to gain some valuable experience. As we quickly learned, our primary role on the team was to provide practice defense and challenge the other players when running horse races. Particularly exciting was the "Yucca" full court press drill.

In fact, being part of the team was a great experience and we quickly found ourselves writing a fictitious book titled "On the Bench." The book was never published, but in the end, the bench proved to be one of the best seats in the house.

Mark Wallis '76

• Bobby Knight's visit to HKIS

In May of 1975, Coach Bobby Knight of Indiana and Texas Tech Fame came to Hong Kong with his team on their way to play a series of exhibition games in China. The Coach was always looking for talent to recruit and his stop at HKIS was memorable.

For nearly 3 hours in the High School gym, the Coach and his player-assistants put the HKIS boys Varsity and Junior Varsity teams through a WORK OUT. One of the Coach's favorite drills was the "Eagle" defensive drill that covered all parts and corners of the gym. Finally, after running horse races for "conditioning" purposes, the Coach introduced a short movie about basketball at Indiana.

Years later, I met the Coach at a St. Louis Cardinals Spring Training game and thanked him for his visit to HKIS – and the workout. Without missing a beat, the Coach replied "You survived that workout?"

MarkWallis '76

• Track/Cross Country

I was friends with Mike Kinne through Jr High. He should have been class of '80 unless he took the fast track..I remember he was great at track short legs and all, we were a great team at Rice Bowl, still have my ribbons. I remember in 8th grade we were doing balance beam work in gym and he thought it would be funny to push me off the beam. Being as short as he was he pushed me at my ankles and my legs flew out and I landed on the beam flat on my back. I though I was dying, couldnt breath, made quite a scene and Mike looked so horrified.

Chris O'Keefe '80

I remember 7B with Mr. Matthews! Chris O'-Keefe was the one who taught me shot putt for Rice Bowl in 8th grade. It saved me from having to do a lot of jogging in track practice in high school. So, thanks!

Deborah Smith '80

I remember those grueling practices with Mr. Matthews. I still stretch the way he taught us, even though the trainers at the club tell me I'm going to hurt myself doing it that way. I remember Mr. Matthews would give me his track shoes when I would run my races. My feet were so big, 13, I couldnt find any shoes my size.   *Chris O'Keefe '80*

I also miss the sleepy fishing village with squatter areas that Stanley used to be. I miss the more primitive and quaint shopping alleys that used to be there. I also miss the little paths and roads that we used to run through on the cross country course, complete with those little wheeled carts and chickens to trip over.

I still remember the one chicken that stepped into my path on the home stretch of a cross country run, which I managed to kick into the bay at full stride, leaving lots of squawking and a cloud of feathers in my path (not too humane, but funny at the time). I was there the day after they burned down the squatter area after having evacuated everyone to resettlement areas. I'm sure the people are better off with better housing, but somehow, I miss the quaintness and atmosphere (both meanings of the word) that it added to the area.

Stanley is just an example of many areas that I miss from the old days. But I realized after a while as I visited the few landmarks that were still there, what I really missed was the people and the circumstances that made us young, carefree, adventurous, and full of a love for life. *Bill Steagall '75*

5. Pranks

The best one I heard was in my sister Julia's 7th grade art class. While the teacher was out, Tommy Anderer took a shoe, painted the bottom of it, and somehow got it on a broomstick and put footprints on the ceiling.

When Julia was at Junior High Camp, Howard Hsu was one of the camp counselors. Somehow the guys in his cabin managed to get a cow and herd it into another group's cabin. I'm sure he had nothing to do with it, though.

Sheila Baker '82

What about when John MacMillan and Tom Burkard blew a hole in the gym floor with a home-made firecracker in a remote control car? I think that was in '70 or '71, or something.

Kelvin Limm '79

I, Tom Burkard, solemly swear that I never did, nor ever new anything about blowing any hole in the gym floor. Maybe John was part of that, but you've got me mixed up with someone else. If my memory serves me correctly, I believe Robert Bradlaw was the explosives expert. Could it have been him? *Tom Burkard '76*

We, as teachers often bloc out (or never knew) the morbid details of daily adventure in school (Blew a hole in the gym floor? That explains why they were just refinishing the gym floor the year I moved to HKIS (73) and Bob Christian asked me to design "something" to put in the center of the court – which ended up becoming the current HKIS Logo.) *Dave Kohl '73-'80*

• Bruce Lee

Shocking and saddening news of his death July 20 1973 opened up a portal of discussion amongst us. Some of us knew who he was and some did not. Some knew of his role as Kato in *The Green Hornet*, some of his early movies some of us had seen. The most astounding aspect of the whole event was the response of the H.K. community. It was like an American president had died. We had no idea of the popularity of this young man within the British Colony. We gathered together in the cafeteria in various groups over several days discussing his past and the growing martial arts culture to find out who he was and what he meant to the H.K. Chinese. We watched the papers and the media as outsiders seeing how another part of the world responds to a significant event.

Eric Lee '75

6. A Life Turning Point

When anyone looks back to his life, he will sure find some important turning points. For me, studying at HKIS was definitely one of those important points in my life.

Prior to studying at HKIS, I was a student in regular local grammar school. I devoted most of my time to extra curricular activities such as organizing activities in school, scouting etc. My then perception of studying was that no matter how hard you study, usually the results would not have fairly reflected it. Hence, my attitude towards schoolwork was to get a pass, and continued to enjoy myself in extracurricular activities. Fortunately, every year I was marginally promoted to next grade.

My parents noted my wrong attitude towards my study, and they were fully aware that with this attitude, I sure would not pass the regular public examinations. They planned to send me aboard to study in Montreal, Canada.

After all things were set on this course, I attended farewell parties from my school and classmates. However, my parents had to attend to some important matters and could not accompany me to Canada. At that time, I was only fourteen and they were not ready to let me go on my own. Accordingly, I did not go to Montreal, nor did I return to my previous grammar school since it would be hard for me to explain to my teachers and schoolmates about my situations. Finally, I had not attended school for about half a year.

Somehow, my Kung-Fu master reminded my parents to consider sending me to International School for further education. Since my mother had given a talk in HKIS before and she had had a good impression about HKIS. Since the application deadline for the entrance to class in 1975 was almost due, Mrs. Tuchardt, the Admission Director, asked my mother to bring me along for an examination as soon as possible.

Mr. Earl Westrick, the High School Principal, accepted me as a Grade 10 student. As I had to prepare for the entrance examination, I had given up my trip to attend the Scout World Jamboree in Norway that year and attended the HKIS summer school.

I understood that it was my last chance to deal with the whole new environment. For the first couple weeks of school, I focused entirely on my study with no extracurricular activities. Of course, there were quiz and tests but soon I found I could get good grades in all subjects. All of a sudden, I realized that my grades did reflect my efforts expended and it was proportional. With good grades attained, study was no longer a problem for me. I enjoyed the most in ESL classes taught by Mr. Bill Mahkle and the fine arts classes with Mr. Dave Kohl. I did the best in mathematics and even challenge tests to advance courses. Later on, I must thank to Dr. Malmin whom aroused my interest in chemistry and sciences.

Soon I found myself totally suited into the American education system. I enjoyed studying as well as in all extracurricular activities. Furthermore, I also expressed my art talents and my paintings were displayed all around the school. I had also designed the covers of two yearbooks (Orientals - 1977 and 1978). I was elected into the National Honors Society only after studying in HKIS for a year. Finally, I also received the Service and Citizenship Award of 1978 in the graduation ceremony.

I was encouraged by Dr. Mary K. Heisler to apply to The College of William and Mary, Virginia for my undergraduate study in Chemistry and Fine Arts. Thereafter I obtained my doctorate degree in Chiropractic in Los Angeles Chiropractic College and elected as one of the Outstanding Young Men of America in 1988.

This explains why once I returned to Hong Kong in 1988, I volunteered myself to serve HKIS in different committees and as President of the Alumni Association without any reservation. Now looking back, HKIS really provided me with wonderful memories of "Life is positive and promising".
                                        Dr. Thomas Wong '78

Chapter 6
Repulse Bay

Repulse Bay, named after the famous British frigate HMS Repulse, must be one of the most beautiful locations for a school anywhere in the world. Rugged granite mountains back clean sand beaches, tropical lush vegetation, and secluded homes dating back to the 1920s.

At the time HKIS was constructed in the gulch off South Bay Road, only a few large structures broke thru the forest of bauhinia and bamboo. Barren rock cliffs were scarred with a catchment high above, but the hillside would turn white with cascading torrents during the frequent monsoons and typhoons of summer. Europeans had taken to living on the south side of Hong Kong Island, far away from the hustle of Central and the densely packed residential towers of the Midlevels and The Peak.

Students often had P.E. classes at the beach, about a ten-minute walk downhill from school. After classes, there were several stands, vendors, and after 1975, a McDonald's. A small business complex housed a Citibank (later Bank of America), a post office, and the Park 'n Shop. Upstairs was a hair salon and the offices of Doctors Oram and Howard, where most school families sought medical services.

The historic Repulse Bay Hotel stood majestically above Repulse Bay Road, its fountains dribbling water while the uniformed wait staff attended dinners on the wide verandah. Hong Kong & Shanghai Hotels operated the grand dame of aristocratic elegance, where the British and Japanese troops fought the final skirmish of the Battle of Hong Kong in 1941. The view over the Bay included Eucliff, a neo-gothic castle, one of several homes owned by the Eu family, whose children attended HKIS.

But most significant to many HKIS students was a small non-descript tin-roofed noodle shed at the foot of South Bay Close where local Chinese workers and drivers slurped hot noodles and enjoyed San Miguel Beer from several water-chilled coolers. It was a favorite stopping place before, after, and - most significantly - during school hours. Many a truant student could be found, cigarette and/or beer in hand, within the dark entrails of The Shack. It was an institution.

-*Ed.*

1. The Shack

It wasn't very long ago,
But it seems like many years,
Since I was at the shack,
With a nice refreshing beer.

The smell of noodles cooking,
A crack of a peanut shell,
And somewhere in the distance,
You hear the school's last bell.

The tables soon fill up,
Friends sit all around,
Talking of the day's events,
And drinking a couple rounds.

The dust on the dog disperses,
As he walks on by,
The bird jumps around in his cage,
Wishing he could fly.

The rooster tries to crow,
The bird tries to bite,
And everyone's talking,
Of plans for Friday night.

As the sun starts to set,
It's time to head on home,
But we all know we'll be back
For the Shack is our second home.

It is where we can laugh,
It is where we can play,
We'll be back there soon,
Nothing keeps us away.

-- I wrote this soon after moving from Hong Kong to California in the middle of my junior year. I was quite depressed to learn that the big after school hangout in Redondo Beach was the local Burger King. Of course, I refused to ever go there.
Gretchen Likins '87

I was in the shack after its "renovation" (move this tin wall here, put that one over there) and the cockroaches had all been stirred up. They were particularly active that day. Some people were having noodles on the "upper deck" and I saw Kim Semken jump up from her chair. She started waving her hair about – a cockroach had flown into her hair. And such hair she had! That was really something watching her try to get it out. People were laughing, myself included, and then it flew out of her hair and straight into mine. More laughter ensued, but not from me that time. It didn't take quite as long to get it out of my hair but I remember VIVIDLY the feeling. (On a side note, my sister Julia vividly remembers my sister Leslie and myself always making her dispatch the cockroaches we found at home. "Julia! Come here! There's a cockroach! Come here!" Leslie and I have no such recollection.) *Sheila Baker '82*

I remember shooting rats at night in the shack with a slingshot. *Eric Lee '75*

Do you guys remember how the owner at the shack prepared the Noo-do? They purposely over-cooked the instant noodle for it looks bigger and more in the plastic soup bowl. Then they pan fried an egg, put that on the noodle, then sprinkled chopped up green onion on top. "One Dala priest." *Gabe Lau '77*

The Shack! Lord what a place! Low ceilings, low light, hazy smoke, beer, sodas, card games, noodles... *Cindi Webb '78*

Grab a glass-bottled chocolate Vitasoy out of the 4 inches of dark water from the floor model cooler while grandma sweeps the bok choi outer leaves into the mossy gutter with a splash from the ubiquitous red bucket and a bare-assed baby chases the chicken. We had 2 choices on the Vitasoy. White or brown. The cold ones were from the water cooler. On the cooler it says " Hall How Hall Loc" in Chinese translates into "Coca Cola." Imagine we used drink it out of the bottle straight from the cooler. The only reason we are robustly healthful today is because of drinking straight out of those dripping bottles. Never mind the eccenaesia. For stout intestinal flora and other immunities I credit thrice frozen coconut ice-cream, sun-softened salt cream Swiss rolls and other delicacies. _ I think we could franchise The Shack. Imagine

them, coast to coast, nestled between the Burger King and a muffler shop! *Eric Allen '75*

Those noodles at the shack were kinda scary, but the 60-cent liter of San Mig beer was great. How convenient on the way home from a hard day's work at school....and at the right price!! *Ian Goepfert '80*

Beer and noodles was a lunch staple at the shack. I was there the day it was torn down - came around the corner and a dozer was turning it to rubble, it was 1985 or 1988. Nor will I forget Dave Meyer asking a number of us to delay our usual afternoon trip to the Drift Inn for a pint because the faculty was going to be there for a casual after school staff meeting. *Mike McCormick '80*

My brother remembers a brawl in McDonalds at Repulse Bay and going to jail during that incident and having to be bailed out by Mike Heeney's mother. He was also a member of GMBH Club (Good Morning Bong Hit Club), something like "420" these days. *Linda Reizman '80*

Everyone remembers the 3rd Floor Lounge (an escape zone) at the High School. Almost as good as "The Shack." *Jerry Cashman '78*

2. Eucliff

I share the sentiment about the changing landscape of Hong Kong! When I returned to Hong Kong in 1996 and took a nostalgic walk down Repulse Bay beach, I was disheartened to see Eucliff replaced by condos and my own house at #8 South Bay Road in the final stages of being knocked down. In 1997, when my sister Cindy ('74) and I returned for the HKIS Reunion, she jogged Bowen Road one morning and discovered that Fairlane Towers, our first HK residence, was completely gone and replaced by a new building. It was as if all traces of our having been in HK were being obliterated. But, I guess HK is a place where no one has time to bemoan the past. *Carolyn Cole '73*

I am really sorry to see our old homes knocked down and replaced. Fortunately, Prince Charles et al have succeeded in slowing down the destruction of some of the older buildings around HK, but many of our homes and other special places like Repulse Bay Hotel and Eucliff didn't es-

DRAGON TALES

cape that. I take consolation in the fact that they can't take away our memories.

Diane Anderson '69

I went to Euston once with Doug Eu once. The place has five stories and an elevator, also saw a grand piano by Steinway very old and very nice. Eucliff was a great place too... got to go there often to play tennis with Doug and Robert, Mark, Lisa, Sharon, and Tracey... life was good.

Derek Dooley '79

Karen Eu was in my advisee group in '75. As we talked about events we could do to get to know the students in the group better, it was suggested that we have a pot luck supper. After a few thoughts about where to hold this dinner, Karen volunteered that we could use her place. The family castle overlooking Repulse Bay built by her ancestor Eu-Tong Sen, in the shipping trade. At the time of WW 2, it was known as Eu Castle.

Of course, we all jumped at the chance to get inside this famous place. So it was all arranged for a school evening in the fall. We arrived and were greeted in the courtyard by uniformed staff. No one lived at the place, but they maintained it for social functions. The staff had set up a long elegant table in an inner courtyard, with white linen tablecloths and elegantly folded napkins. The silverware bore the Eu crest (I can't believe I didn't take one!).

While we were digesting our meal of American hot dogs, macaroni & cheese, and other gweilo favorites that the kids had provided, we roamed freely through the grounds and building. This was supposedly the last place the British held out against the Japanese in December of 1941. The story goes that the Hong Kong defenders ended up either jumping or being bayoneted over the edge into Repulse Bay below, and that only one survivor made it out to Stanley to tell the tale. So Eric Allen and I are climbing up into a turret, and come to an empty room coated with peeling cream paint. There in the paint are scratchings and names and short messages gouged into the finish, and one had a 1941 date!! Amazing!

Dave Kohl, art teacher '73 - '80

3. The Repulse Bay Hotel

The Repulse Bay Hotel was where we had

Sunday school and I remember the hotdogs they made at the beach, with mayo and butter on the toasted buns!

Liz Jackson '72

We lived at the Repulse Bay Hotel. I remember the toast being put in a rack for breakfast and the food was yummy. It was also a great place to explore there were so many places to investigate. We got there in the summer so having the beach was perfect. What were the names of the parts of the beach? Lido was down by Eucliff, then there was the middle part that had the outside restaurant and the far end by the rocks with that big cement Chinese building, later McDonald's, etc. We used to go and drink Mateus wine and eat bread and cheese bought from Park 'n Shop.

Rosemary Garvey '77

We stayed at the Repulse Bay Hotel when we arrived in December 1972 or January 1973 (it was summer break for us, coming from Australia) and when we left in June 1981. In the years in between, we would go to the hotel coffee shop after school performances. I seem to remember French onion soup and milkshakes were excellent there. And, when I was older, the Singapore Slings were quite tasty also. When we left, my sister Julia and I shared one of their huge rooms. Their guest rooms were larger than my friends' apartments in NYC. We had a lot of fun with the ceiling fans – load all our underwear on them and then turn it on high, try to cut fruit by throwing it up into the fan, and things of that nature.

Sheila Baker '82

I spent a lot of time at the Hilton, but lived at the Repulse Bay for 3 months while waiting for our stuff to be shipped from South Africa. It was so great there, and the food was yummy!! And then the beach was right there... exploring the old Eucliff was the greatest...

June Steagall '77

We arrived in HK the summer of '67, and lived at the Repulse Bay Hotel for a while; I loved the ice cream presented in silver service on the verandah. I can remember the Sweets Shop with all that candy behind glass doors. I loved the garden areas around the hotel, where I found a litter of newborn kittens - and wandering around the beach all day. The climate was a shock, and I swam every day and drank Sunkist orange and lemon sodas in the heat.

Sheila Baker '82

"We celebrated our first wedding anniversary with a buffet lunch at the Repulse Bay Hotel.

Tables are on a verandah, which faces the bay, beautiful view of the water, islands, palms, etc. Overhead are crops of ceiling fans, circa1920. There's a waiter for each table, dressed in crisp white jacket and black trousers. Food is laid out inside the lobby, scrumptious hot and cold dishes, salads, and arranged intricately on huge sterling platters. Sculptures of Chinese creatures are molded out of both butter and ice. We went back twice for more.

All the silver utensils and flatware are emblazoned with the crest of the Hong Kong & Shanghai Hotels. Then there's the dessert table, with fruit, tortes, all sorts of brandied pastries, and cheeses. A nice leisurely meal - almost two hours - for HK $20 (+10%) each. Am I a big spender???

Dave Kohl, art teacher '73-'80, 1973 letter

The Repulse Bay Hotel was our first home in Hong Kong. It was our family's favorite haunt - Pepper Steak done by Mario, Coupe Geisha, and high tea. Right when the big #10 typhoon hit Hong Kong in 1968. Was it Rose? There was no beach and the hills were all covered with waterfalls. It remained our family's favorite place, taking all of the visitors there, watching the filming of the sequel to Love Story (Oliver's something...?), then sitting at the table next to Candace Bergan when they had lunch..... Having a graduation party there with family and friends.... My Mom and her friends Mrs. Wong and Surrency went there all the time for lunch and to talk about us kids.

Barbara Schwerdtmann '77

The Repulse Bay Hotel also had a marvelous restaurant where I had my first tantalizing taste of spaghetti carbonera - still one of my favorite pastas that they also prepared right at the table. The Hotel was also where my dentist had his office – can't remember his name but because I was terrified of needles he used to fill my teeth without anesthesia. He thought I was nuts but he did it and I guess that helped me have the high pain tolerance that I have today. How I wish fluoride had come about a bit earlier - my kids haven't had any cavities!

Lynn Barratt '73

Ed: The dentist was Rick Walters, husband of HKIS French teacher Sandra '68-'72

I never lived in any of the hotels, but I do remember going into the Repulse Bay Hotel to see the doctor on a regular basis, for cuts I got from rocks while surfing Eu Cliff during typhoons. I remember killer waves in Repulse Bay, but during typhoons? Is that what I learned from HKIS about sanity?

Kelvin Limm '79

We stayed at the Repulse Bay hotel for three months while apartment hunting. I will never forget the colonial feel and smell, the high ceilings, slow turning fans, tea on the veranda the wide hallways.... While there my sister Christina, then 7, met Lois Christian who was also staying at the hotel with her family. She asked Lois's dad, Mr. Christian, if she could go to his new school HKIS at Chong Hom Kok. So Christina went to Chong Hom Kok. Being in Kindergarten I went to the Kennedy Road Junior School. I don't believe there was a Kindergarten at the Chong Hom Kok flats. The next year, 1967, I moved to the just opened brand new HKIS in Repulse Bay for the first grade. I remember construction workers still working on the building's finishing touches.   *Liz Calouri '79*

I lived at the Repulse Bay Hotel when we left the colony. I have huge respect for my mother and father went on ahead by three months and we stayed until school finished- with my brother in the hospital (pneumonia) and me sick at the Repulse Bay. (I grieve to this day that I missed my last days at school). I was so upset when I heard that they had torn the hotel down that when we went back to HK I refused to even walk up and see the "terrace" that they re-created. What a beautiful place. I couldn't believe that the soldiers had ever rolled bombs along the corridors!!! (And they had a killer pastry shop!!) And the water balloons, ah yes!!! My children will never know the thrill of lowering them down on a string and swinging them into an apartment below!!!   *Tami Whitrock '77*

Our family lived for a month (when coming from Sweden) in The Mandarin in May to June, 1967, and from there went on to The Repulse Bay for another 3 months before moving in at our flat in South Bay Road. It was fantastically interesting as a kid to wander about in the shopping arcades, always discovering something new, having those exotic smells all around - yes, living in Repulse Bay had its charm and mystique. There was an old store where you could buy sweets and soft drinks. And then there were the gold fish fountains.

Henrik Mjoman, '78

We spent months in the Repulse Bay Hotel.

We got to know the staff really well, and they remained friends for the 30 years we were based out of Turtle Cove. Busboys and doormen became the generation of management in the 80s and 90s. Somehow, there was always a table at the best hotels, club, and restaurants in HK for us. It was because these guys had gone on, and yet remembered the three brothers who were polite and respectful as little kids. Thank you, Mr. Kadoorie for training the best guys in the business.

Jim Hoffman 84

4. Repulse Bay Beach

I have always loved Love is a Many Splendored Thing - we could see the house where it was filmed from our apartment in Repulse Bay...that film reminds me of HK when we first got there in the 60s – just as the building boom was starting.

Tami Whitrock '77

As for the jellyfish and plastic bags, here's a memory. I was entering the surf at Big Wave Bay and a wave hit me and left behind what I thought was a plastic bag on my shoulder. Just as I reached up to remove it I felt the stinging on my skin and realized it was a jellyfish. I ran back into the receding wave and washed it off, but having stayed on me for so long it left some pretty good scars. If I'd been at Repulse Bay I could have gone to the first aid station and they would have put that yellow iodine on it, their universal remedy!

Wendy Liddiard '73

I remember Allison Guilbertson's birthday party on their launch when the jellies came up under us. Then the boat boy made us jump back in the water! I still love the ocean!

Barbara Schwerdtmann '77

I think HK raises the biggest jellyfish in the world. I remember having to leave a spotter on the boat when we swam to warn us if one got to close. I remember the pain of the stings that spread all around my body when one got me. They were huge!

Debbie Smiley '72

Especially the plastic bags – I forgot about those – how could anyone living in Hong Kong not remember the plastic bags? I also remember some of the kids got stung, not directly, but by loose tentacles of a Portuguese-of-War. I heard stories of some students who went water skiing across the bay one summer when a whole pack was coming in. Fortunately, no one fell. *Diane Kasala '73*

Once while swimming in the Bay, I thought a plastic bag washed over my arm and it turned out to be a blue jellyfish. Goes to show two things:
• Waves washed the jellyfish colonies into Big Wave Bay.
• There were obviously a lot of plastic bags in the waters, otherwise many swimmers wouldn't have thought the jellyfish were plastic bags! Where is that darned Lap Sap Chong?
It must've been quite a sight for people who were watching me try to pee all over my arm!

Kelvin Limm '79

Wasn't it the "Osprey" that burned in Repulse Bay? It was a grand old 2-masted schooner.

Melissa Miller '79

When I was young, there was a playground for some of us in Repulse Bay. Our parents would frequently eat at the Life Savers (it was called something like that anyway) again on Repulse Bay. While they ate Chinese, we typically ate McDonald's from down the way a little bit and then ran a muck out in this courtyard. *Jason Weber '95*

Who could forget the smell of the sewer draining right in the middle of repulse bay!!!?? I remember that it smelled and we used to dare each other to follow it up and under the road and it came out up near the shack.

Tami Whitrock '77

In the 1980's you truly took your health into your hands by swimming in Repulse Bay. I was told recently that even with the new sewer (storm drains plus the other) that Repulse Bay still gets closed due to pollution. I remember Eric Lee telling me he once followed a sewer pipe into the Bay and that it was pitted all the way down - this when they were still made of metal. I'm sure Eric could tell us a lot about what he saw in Repulse Bay and Deep Water Bay. As I recollect he has dived all along that part of the island's coast.

Edward Ketterer '75

I certainly do remember diving along the edge of the bay by Eucliff and as I got further out toward the channel between the island and the bays Repulse and Deep the smell definitely got worse. The water didn't taste any different though, salty, if you must know. There at the point, the pipe ended and dumped directly into the bay. It was gross and revolting to find out what I was swimming in. I am surprised that I didn't get sick. Anyway I am saddened to find out the sewer outfall is in the bay. That pretty much takes care of what little marine life was there. Anybody for a swim in the toilet?   *Eric Lee '75*

4. Surf's Up

The year was 1977. Typhoon season was upon us, and I started taking my board to school, waiting for that perfect moment when the swell would hit, and I would cut out of school. So, I would cart my board from class to class. Mr. Von Behren finally called me into his office one day. He wanted to know why I was carrying that thing around to all my classes everyday. I explained that life in Hawaii was surfing all the time, and that because HK did not have a lot of it, I didn't want to miss out, and typhoon season was really the only time for potentially nice-sized waves. Much to my surprise, he seemed to understand. He then really surprised the crap out of me when he suggested I store my board in his office because it would be safer that way, and that I wouldn't risk injury to others in the halls and classes.

The fateful day finally came when a swell hit Repulse Bay. I scrambled into his office to grab my board and there he was. He knew I was going to cut out, and he also knew other students would cut out just to watch. He made no effort to stop me because he knew I would go no matter what. He was right.

My whole perspective about him changed that day. He wasn't a stonewall headmaster at all. He was a human! I wonder what parents thought when they saw my board in his office. Did they think he was from Malibu?   *Kelvin Limm '79*

I did a lot of shell collecting while in HK. Lots of cowries and murexes in Repulse Bay. Some of the most beautiful cone shells I collected were from Repulse Bay also. Bill Steagall (sp?) and I once swam out to South Bay Islands after a typhoon passed thru HK. I poked amongst the debris cast up on the sandbar (rock bar) for shells and whatever. I found the beat up remains of a pearl oyster torn up from the bottom and tumbled in the stones and gravel. There was not much left of the shell but the living part of the oyster was intact. I told Bill that this was the remains of a pearl oyster.

He said," Really?" sounding surprised.

I assured him it was and he said, "Can we crack it open?"

"Well, yes we can." I told him.

"Oh goody. If there is a pearl in there can I have it?" Bill replied with eager anticipation.

"Sure." I told Bill with the knowledge that pearls were rare in nature. I went to work and pried the shell open with some sharp piece of debris.   There, in the mantle of the dying animal was a small baroque pearl! I regretfully handed it to Bill and I think he still has it to this day.   *Eric Lee '75*

I actually remember our swim out to South Bay Islands where we dove around for a while. My memory of the event is similar to Eric's. I actually had the pearl made into a ring, which I gave to my mother, who still has it. Eric and I actually snorkeled Repulse Bay several times. Good times.   *Bill Steagall '75*

I remember many swim team practices with Mrs. Rose at Repulse Bay in the fall or winter (I remember it was cold!). When we went to Taiwan with the school to compete against TAS, it was winter and we were unprepared, we sat in our wet swimsuits with wet towels and shivered through the entire meet.   *Wendy Liddiard, '73*

I remember the early swim team and walking from South Bay Close down to the beach for swim practice. How about the winter practices in Repulse Bay in the cold water and waves? This was NOT my favorite part of the swim team, since we didn't have a pool we swam out to the rafts and went back and forth between them.

Diane Reynolds

Swim practices still continued in Repulse Bay during the fall. I remember a lot of swimmers complaining about being stung by jellyfish. I wish they knew about Portuguese-men-of- war, which would have limited the complaints. I just remember it being cold no matter what. Those first plunge into the water and flailing arms and legs till we warmed up our core body temp. Then it wasn't so bad.   *Eric Lee '75*

5. Hangin' Out

• Mothers Club

I have great memories of the Muther's Club at The Lido (not as wholesome a hang-out as the school seems to remember!) which was actually party central in '73-'74. Great music by local musicians and HKISers like Mark Shostrom, long weekends dancing and occasionally good surf in the Bay. We also danced the nights away at Thingames above Central and in the clubs of Wanchai---especially the 747! *Missy Preston '77*

I remember being at the Lido Beach in 1967 when a local man was pulled from the water, and surrounded by a crowd on the beach. Eventually someone nearly said that he had been bitten by a sea snake! Just the idea was so spooky that I ran away and wouldn't go back in the water for several days.

When we moved to a nearby apartment a few months later, I was told not to touch bags or boxes found near the playground or anywhere on the street - bombs were being set around Hong Kong by communist sympathizers. One day there was a gory front-page picture in the Post of a policeman who'd had his hands blown off almost to the forearms, while trying to dismantle one of those bombs. The photo must have been taken just seconds afterwards, and I've never forgotten that terrible image. *Debbie Smiley '72*

•Lido

My first kiss was with Marilee Mattson, playing spin the bottle in 7th grade. We had snuck into the Lido with a few others. I can honestly say she was the first girl I really pined over.
Gavin Birnie '75

June of '97- right before the handover, my husband actually consented to a China tour that ended in HK. We were on a cruise and docked at Ocean terminal. I was so proud of myself that I was actually able to find the ferry terminal (OK- ANYBODY could) but I remembered how to run for it when the bell began to ring. (My husband thought that I was nuts- but it was Pavlov's dog hear the bell- run down the ramps!) And then HK side I was totally lost until I rounded the corner and there was Battery Path!! (And how many of you remember that there was a GREAT magazine stand right near there that had 100's of comic books. We lived on comics in the 60's and now I wouldn't buy one for my kids they are all so depressing.)

After that I insisted on riding the bus to Repulse Bay (yep - found that number 6A, hey, when did they all get to be air-conditioned? I did miss the conductor clicking his punch) – on the ride through town I was totally lost again. But the absolute thrill of it all was rounding the corner on Repulse Bay and seeing the cross of the school against the sky...thank goodness THAT hasn't come down!!

Of course - it didn't hurt that I lived in South Bay Villas- and THOSE haven't come down yet either- but they were all gated off and I didn't have the guts to beard the gate man and try to explain what I was doing there.

I did walk up the Miles of steps that went up the hill by the A building (not the one closest to the school) and try to peer in our old apartment. I was sorely tempted to see if I could scale the fence by the bottom (they used to lock it in the 60's and we learned how to get over it then) - but I was out-voted.

My husband also quickly backed off his LOUD comments about the beach and how close we were - (he couldn't believe that as close as we lived that we did NOT go down there every day) once he had trekked the hill in the heat (it was pretty darn hot and humid that June day- and I made him walk from the beach to the school and back) he was a believer. Got a hankering for some "Green Spot" and peanuts....... *Tami Whitrock '77*

One of the things that stands out about Prom night is taking the bus back to Repulse Bay (after the post-prom party) in the morning with all the vendors headed out to set up shop for the coming day. We stood out just a bit! *Kris Brannigan '69*

We lived on South Bay Rd., and I spent a good bit of time hiking the hills above Repulse Bay. Old pillboxes served as rest stops and reference points, sometimes as supply caches too. There was a surprising amount of wildlife. Also camping on Lan Tau and in the hills above Kowloon. Those concrete "water slides" were a trip! Some of them ran nearly vertical with long drops!
Mark Woodruff '77

•Park 'n Shop

We did go down to Park n Shop all the time when we got older. Before that in elementary school was the Popsie man for goodies before going home; he had the best Japanese bubble gum.
Barb Schwerdtman '77

When we lived in South Bay Villas, by the Lazenbys and Whitrocks, there was a store that delivered groceries. We used to call them up and order all kinds of junk food when our parents were out. *Debbie Salter '74*

We moved to Repulse Bay, weird name. I learned it was named after the HMS Repulse, and had nothing to do with repulsiveness, Anything but! The flame trees in bloom were breathtaking. A quick walk to the "Park"n Shop", the "Dairy Lane" and the new "Mc Donald's" made life easy for an American. Needless to say I got my first bout of food poisoning from the golden arches! We had Sunday brunch on the veranda of the beautiful Repulse Bay Hotel. I have not since been to a grander, or more beautiful hotel. I remember the Eu Cliff Castle dares! Me...too chicken, too scared! All the brave souls that did... you are my teenage idols!

Sydney Henrietta '84

Our family settled into our two-floor flat at 80 B-2 Repulse Bay Villas. My dad was trying to win me over on the move and said "Hey, there's a beach real nearby. Just follow the path." I did and saw a huge, gross snail and then met my first local resident, a Chinese man who took a major spit on the stone path leading to the beach. Welcome to Hong Kong! It was then that I discovered that at 5'8" I often was as tall or even taller than the adult male population in Hong Kong. Strange feeling for a teenage girl. On our first day in our new apartment, we met teenage twins, Miep and Huib Pendratt, who lived at 78 Repulse Bay Villas. They were very cool, from Holland, and convinced us to take a taxi with them to school each morning. Yes, we lazy Americans, who lived three (very steep) blocks from school, took a taxi each morning. Sheesh! *Ann Sullivan '75*

At the Repulse Bay McDonalds, I remember squishing 15 people to a table, Consulate kids and their Oreo cookies and Doritos, and all the bomb threats called in before Biology and chemistry exams. *Bonnie Tucker '89*

•Drift Inn

There were two clubs in Repulse Bay, down by the beach. One was the Drift Inn, where Kerry Fogarty, the Demetros brothers and I used to play darts against the Brits, Sue Myers, Margaret Kim, and the like used to go there too.

The other was the Wellcome Inn, a bar/restaurant upstairs over the grocery store. There was a bunch of us there one afternoon in about '79. Gary Sousy had his feet on one of the ta-bles in the bar and one of the waiters (we thought they were all Triads) took exception. Of course, Gary being a cocky little bodybuilder did not budge. The waiter threw a glass ashtray at Gary. Gary got up and the waiter ran back into the kitchen. When the waiter re-appeared, he had a meat cleaver in his hand. I was sitting next to Gary, you never saw two gweilos run so fast!

One other night, a bunch of us were there, and several of the chefs came out with meat cleavers, and we all stood up to fight with them. Then the manager called the RHK Police, so we high-tailed it. *Ian Goepfert '80*

I can't forget the day Dave Meyer asked a number of us to delay our usual afternoon trip to the Drift Inn for a pint, because the faculty was going to be there for a casual after-school staff meeting. *Mike McCormick '80*

We took photos of the '79 senior class officers at the Nautilus Club, which would be upstairs from McD's. It was a pretty Posh place.

Ken Koo '79

nb. The origins of P.O.S.H. are quite interesting and very Colonial. When sailing to Asia aboard a P & O liner, if you had money, you had a cabin on the Port side of the ship outward bound, so as to be on the shady side of the liner. You would have a similar cabin on the Starboard side returning home to Britain - hence: Port Out Starboard Home -ed.

Food and Drink

The common elements of food and drink take on special significance for expatriates. When out of your familiar home environment, one of the most comforting aspects of life becomes the dependable tastes and smells of back-home foods and drinks. Great efforts went into obtaining food items from one's country of origin. Ex-pats seem to be willing to pay nearly any amount for a taste that's comforting.

Markets catering to the European and ex-pat Asian community were generally small, but stocked selected items that kept a loyal customer base. Frozen prepared foods were rare in the 1970s, but commodities like NZ lamb and cheese, Danish Chicken, American Turkeys, and rare lasagna noodles were but a few of the items that became familiar to food shoppers at Park 'n Shop, Wellcome, and Dairy Lane supermarkets. Smaller stores delivered goods, generally at the back door "tradesman's" entrance to flats - Alice Provisions, Stanley Store, and Asia Provisions being the most common.

Local open-air markets provided a plethora of fresh vegetables, locally grown, transported in from china, or flown produce from Israel, South Africa, SE Asia, and the States. Freshly slaughtered red meat animals, poultry fluttering in straw baskets, and freshly caught seafood were on sale daily. European shoppers mingled (contended?) with cook amahs at the stalls, where weight was determined with a string scale, and amounts calculated on an abacus, paid for only with coin and paper, or put on account.

Restaurants representing nearly every imaginable country and cuisine were present in Hong Kong. While Chinese eateries of many regions dominated the selection, the prevalence of south and SE Asian restaurants meant an abundance of curries. Hotels served up fantastic noontime buffets. Elegant dining at Jimmy's Kitchen, several steakhouses, and atop the best hotels added to the sophisticated nightlife of many families.

On the other end of the spectrum were the dai pai dongs or food stalls with their boiling pots of noodles and smoldering woks of hot oil ready for action on all sorts of pastry-covered rolls and nuggets.

Hong Kong remains, without doubt, a gourmand's paradise.

Ed.

I'm glad I risked the snack drools...teenagers are gluttons! And our taste buds so unjaded, so ripe, sensitive... and those flavour memories!

Fast food style western offerings in HK were nasty. White Castle...Maxims' burgers ...Kentucky fried...so unfresh, greazi.

However, world's best-grilled cheese was at Kai-Taks' cafeteria. Two types of cheese and fried in a mould. World's best Baked Alaska was at the Correspondents' Club. Best pepper steak at the Stanley Prison Club. Worst damn hotdog from Lai Chi Kok amusement park... never became that ill until I moved to Dehli!

Never became ill from anything bought off the street in Hong Kong, in stalls or other rickety, damp establishments. Au contraire had many a gut grabber from the '5' stars.   *Eric Allen '76*

1. Dai Pai dongs (food stalls)

Street Hawkers with deep fried squid legs... can't go wrong for 2 cents but you don't want to get up close and personal after a leg or two...phew...but yum yum. All that cholesterol...

We knew the secret vendors for specialty items as kids...Caine Road for Rock Sugar and Bazooka Joes, the Ritz in North Point for toast with Condensed milk all hot and buttery after a swim in the hotel pool. 70 cents for the swim 30 cents for the toast (5-6th grade Quarry Bay before there was a HKIS) then back on the bus to the bottom of Tai Hang Road...the shop with the HUGE, GIANT, NOT FROM THIS EARTH sour...make you GAG and shudder drink a whole Green Spot in one gulp SOUR PLUMS dba Wa Mui.3 for a HK dime ...and that lovely red ginger...stain your fingers and leave you with the RUNS...Mao's revenge if you ate too many.   *Rich Vaughn '72*

I am still making those Dai Pai Dong's Style French Toast. Flash back to Hong Kong instantly in 8 minutes. Take two thick slices of super soft Hong Kong style white bread (no crust please, otherwise there will be no flash back.) Spread generously with peanut butter on one slice, stick them together; dip them into the beaten egg, slightly deep-fry them into golden color. Then lay them on the paper towel to soak the excess oil out, spread margarine on top, and use either honey or syrup.

Whoa, slides so smoothly, "Mo Duck Ding"... give it a big thumb and a wink! Deadly though. Ha! We all only die once, might as well die happy!   *Gabe Lau '77*

My last year in Hong Kong I lived on my own at the YMCA in Kowloon. I was playing rugby for the YMCA club and after games on Saturdays I loved getting some Char Su (sp?). There was this vendor on the corner that had them on strings and oh so good with an iced down San Miguel.

Once during a visit to Wanchai with who knows who (at this stage of the game I am happy its the memory not working as well as it should) one of the vendors had cups of noodle soup. It was cold and it seemed like a good idea. Those were the hottest darn noodles I had ever tasted more like rolled Habanera peppers.

I liked the Leiches (sp?) nice cold sweet tasting fruit and Mango ice cream. Mixed with rum was not too bad.   *Mark Feldman '75*

If you didn't get 'Cup 'O Octopus' off a street vendor, you missed something I wish I had missed... but I try everything once ... twice if I like it... which is why I had this luscious bit of Asian food ONCE... it was like chewing an old wet suit... only the wet suit would have tasted better... I enjoy Chinese food over all else... but I have had to draw the line on things like "Chicken Feet and Calamari (a deceptively exotic name for another tenacled

beast...) w/ Oyster Sauce and Snow Peas..." Call me picky.... I did eat more than my share of the deep fat fried Fish and Chips in the soggy newspaper, covered and dripping with malt vinegar from the vendor in Wanchai... beyond yummmm.... and sooo good for you...   *Missy Preston '77*

Greasy fish and chips down in Wanchai, wrapped in newspaper should have killed us...but it was SO good.   *Marcy Brooks '75*

2. Restaurants

Eating at Chinese restaurants meant always-spectacular food. In addition, when we found out that being loud and messy were actually polite ways to show our appreciation for the quality of the food and service, we cut loose!! What better way for high school aged boys to act out!   *Scott Schroth '77*

I think it was when Sandra Walters was leaving, it was decided we should all go out to eat...so Ovid Wong arranged for all of us to have this magnificent meal. I remember one course was snake-- and it came in a silver dish with a snake coiled as its handle. I remember it tasted just fine.   *Bev Larson, teacher '74*

Ping Shan restaurant in Repulse Bay...I remember the salty jasmine tea they used to serve straight from the Repulse Bay, hopefully blessed by the sea goddess Kuan Yin. We emerged with stomachs of steel.   *Patrick Pang '80*

• The American

We'd often meet up with students before going to a movie, play, or social event, at the American Restaurant. For a while this meant confusion, since there was the Old American Restaurant on the northside of Lockhardt Road; then the New American Restaurant on Johnson Road; and then the Authentic American on the south side of Lockhardt, which is the embodiment of this heritage in 2007. The Chinese in their wisdom, use round tables, hence the number of sitters can be expanded far beyond what westerners are used to - a table for six can easily handle 10. With the same comfort of a Chinese elevator, it can handle up to 15.

"Warm-ups" meant the required chopstick contest... passing the vinegar & red pepper-marinated raw peanuts around from chopsticks to chopsticks until someone dropped the nut. Good-natured laughter covered the loss of "face" for the clumsy gweilo, who inevitably had to start the exercise again. I've never found a Chinese eatery anywhere that does those marinated cucumber and peanut starters.

Of course, a small army of emptied San Mig bottles filled the side table. And there were bottles of cold water (dung soi) available by request... the waiters thought I was somewhat strange for ordering water, since they assumed all gweilos only drank bei jau.

The tradition is that each person orders their own favorite dish, and then when it is served family-style, everyone digs in - chopsticks flying!!! More Chinese wisdom was present in the ever-handy lazy susan turntable in the center.... this meant you could turn the disc to get at your favorite dish, but also play tricks on your innocent table-mates who were trying to dish up on the other side of the susan.

Can you imagine a better set-up for hungry uninhibited high school kids?? Add to this the tradition that a messy table is an indicator of a successful meal - the kids loved this one - one night resulting in large smears of hoisin and oyster sauce on the white linen. Hardest tradition to honor was leaving at least a little bit of one dish, to indicate that we had, in fact, been satiated and filled beyond our capacity.

Never, in all my life of traveling, have I had better food and more fun that at the Old American.... I think it was the night we had a reunion of the kids who had gone on my first China trip in 1977 - David Trees, Patrick Pang, Anthony Anderson, Joan Amy, Rich and Sylvia Pearson, etc etc. It doesn't get much better.

What any of the three American Restaurants had in great food, they equally lacked in decor. A grungy facade, peeling paint on the walls, and a few non-descript pictures glued onto the cream walls. There was a tattoo place next door, and the California bar was on the corner. When my long-time friend Dennis Bartz got married to Connie Marrill (who was Bob Christian's secretary), they planned the rehearsal party dinner at the Old American. I drove his parents, who had just arrived in the Colony that day, to the spot where they would be hosting this ceremonial meal. His dad thought I was joking when I pulled up in front of the American..."Come on David, take us to the real place" "No, Al...this is it, really. It's good, you'll see." My wife had to re-assure them that I was not playing a prank on them. Dad liked it…and the price was right!   *Dave Kohl, art teacher '73-'80*

Eating at The American Restaurant was always a highlight…of course we all had our favorite dishes; that corn and crab soup and those onion cakes were delicious. And to this day, no one makes them like the American Restaurant. The more people we could gather to go to dinner, the more fun it was and what a noisy group we were. My kids were reluctant to try much the first few times we ate at the American, but they soon realized that the McDonald's burger or peanut butter and jelly sandwiches we brought for them "didn't hold a chopstick" to sizzling beef and pancakes, chicken and cashews, and broccoli dishes. Then there was the dessert, bananas and apples.
      Zita Thompson, teacher '81-'93

•Maxim's

Maxim's along with Maria have the best bake goods. I love their black forest cake and the chestnut cake. The lunch box from Maxim is a Hong Kong institution (I think they might have invented that).   *Patrick Pang '80*

Well, there was no McDonalds when I lived there, 1966-1971, but we did have a great hamburger hangout called Whimpey's. It was that or the American Club for hamburgers.
      Debbie Smiley '72

Maxim's was probably still the best caterer at HKIS compared to the expensive and tasteless stuff my kids eat at school now. Sloppy Joe's, hot lunches. I still remember helping out. That's one of my earliest memories of HKIS.   *Steve Chiu '69*

Maxim's, best tuna fish sandwiches and beef stroganoff. Pastries to die for, éclairs especially. The restaurants far exceeded the lunchroom food.
      Barb Schwerdtman '77

Were those "Maxim" hamburgers the served at school really that bad or was it just me?
      Mark Shostrom '74

• McDonald's

In the fall of 1974, McDonalds opened in Hong Kong for the first time. Until then, the only decent burgers were available at Wimpey's (D'Agular St.) or the Chuckwagon (members only at the American Club).

The first McDonalds opened on Patterson Street in Causeway Bay in early 1975 and the grand opening featured employees walking with full trays food – for free! Later that week, at the official opening of the store, Rev. Paul Tuchardt and I were the first customers. This McDonalds was very popular on the weekends and before intramural bowling at the South China Recreation Club.

The second McDonalds opened in Repulse Bay later that same year and the High School Jazz Band (directed by Mr. Chet Passarella) was featured at the grand opening. This restaurant was soon the lunch provider for the entire school three days a week. It was very popular after school and basketball practice where a few players were known to have eaten as many as 4 Quarter-Pounders w/cheese at one seating.

Today McDonalds has more than 200 restaurants in Hong Kong and employs over 10,000 people!

Mark Wallis '76

I worked at the first McDonalds in Causeway Bay. I craved American fast food and it was a sure way to get some. The problem was that when I worked at the register none of the Chinese patrons would come to me. The line was out the door at the Chinese register and mine was empty.

Also the pay STUNK!!! We got .25/hour US (I don't remember what that is in HK dollar). I barely made enough to take a cab ride home. So net/net it was not the right career path for me. Besides I didn't need the calories. I think Denise Trepanier worked there as well. It did not end up being a long-term thing. I think they liked having a handful of Americans employees at the opening but it did not last long.

The American Club cheeseburgers were by far better. I still dream about them. I used to get two (can you believe what a pig I was (am)??) then I would forge one of my brother's names to the 2nd chit. My father eventually caught on to me and the 2 cheeseburger practice came to an abrupt halt. I have a newspaper clipping of opening day at McDonalds with employee of the month prominently displayed (me); it looks like I'm thinking about my next cheeseburger.

Megan O'Keefe '76

The only food we got was McDonalds, who actually delivered to HKIS in the mornings. You could order your lunch ahead of time for each day with colored tickets. In fact, it was the only 'hot lunch' available for a while. By the time the stuff got to us at lunchtime, the fries were all soggy and the burgers were quite disgusting.

Anita Lau '84

Mark Wallis and Pastor Paul Tuchardt bought and consumed the first 3 McDonalds hamburgers served in Hong Kong, after getting up at 4:30 am to be the first customers in line when McD's opened in Causeway Bay.

Wally Tuchardt '81

nb: Before McDonalds opened in Hong Kong, students going back to the States over Christmas would take orders from their HK friends, and bring back sacks of tepid mushy burgers and fries that they had purchased on the way to the San Francisco airport - Mmmmm 10-hour old McFood. Yuck... but desperate times call for desperate actions -ed.

McDonald's, Pizza Hut, and KFC were the only fast foods there in my time. I remember how awestruck we were went we ran in to a Burger King at City Plaza. Of course there was a Dunkin' Donuts early on, that my parents used to drive quite a ways to get to occasionally. But it eventually closed.

Jason Weber '95

Ah the naughty things we did, I seem to recall I was one, yes the butter ice sculptures were beautiful and the ginger bread houses too!!! Christmas time hanging out waiting to meet friends in the upper lobby of the now gone Hilton, cheeseburgers at the Original American Club at the old Hong Kong and Shanghai Bank, Christmas cotillion at the Club with our little white Mickey Mouse gloves (5 fingers though). T'was a good life, but more fun to be drinking Mateus wine on the old Cricket Club green after a Friday/Saturday night movie listening to AJ, Tad, Robbie and the rest strum guitars and singing songs while we lay back and looked up at the Hilton. I think it was one of those evenings that led us up to sit on the edge of the roof.... memories.

Rich Vaughn '72

Marco Polo Pizza was, hands down, the best pizza I have ever, ever had. It was typically served at The Lunar New Year festivities... The World's Fairs... The big international basketball tournaments... The Halloween Fairs, free even at the annual welcome' party for the US rugby team there for the Sevens.   *Jason Weber '97*

Some of my favorite memories...Cheeseburgers at the Chuckwagon (American Club), Happy Valley (loved to watch the races with binoculars from our WongNeiChong Gap Rd. Apartment), Darts and beer at the Bull and the Bear, The revolving restaurant on top the Furama Hotel, junk daytrips out to surrounding islands and waterskiing in Deep Water Bay, The New Territories in the 70s.when you got off a bus there you felt like you were somewhere else, Landing at KaiTak Airport, Moon Cakes (yes, the sweet ones), the night market, shopping anywhere...and many more...
                    Renee Mordini '78

I have fond memories Dan Ryan's Chicago Grill (The Mall), Shooters 52 (Times Square), Kublais, Pine and Bamboo, Casa Mexicana (the early years), San Francisco Steak House, The American Restaurant...   *Jason Weber '97*

• Dim Sum

There is also a shark fin dumpling, which is pork or shrimp paste with shark fin mixed in as the filling. It comes with a few slices of tiny ginger stalks in a red vinegar sauce. It is essentially a few spoonful of shark fin soup steamed in a giant dumpling.   *Patrick Pang '80*

3. Eating on the Sampans

Marge and Earl Westrick took us out for a dinner in Causebay Bay… on the Bay, actually the typhoon shelter, which is adjacent to the Royal Yacht Club. We rented a sampan with a table set for four and little squatty stools not made for big gweilo bodies, and were paddled around the shelter by a very wiry short Chinese lady wearing her silk pajama outfit and a straw hat. Small boats serving different kinds of food pull alongside, and you barter and buy food, which they then cook and you continue to eat and order and eat and order and eat and order till you are full. It was amazing.

One boat for noodles, one for vegetables, etc. The best was the guy selling seafood. We bought two catties of live shrimp (a catty is about 1 1/3 lb). He then stirfried them for about 2 minutes in a sizzling wok, with a chili sauce. Then came clams, fried in the shell with a great spicy soy sauce. We had live cooked crab also. Meanwhile, the lights of the city are coming on as the sunsets, and the harbour is full of reflections and activity. Another sampan with four musicians pulled along side, and we were given a choice from about 25 different songs on a hand-lettered cardboard - they played 3, and all sounded alike. They won't be getting any recording contracts in the near future. When we were all done, the sampan lady very carefully rolled up the paper table cloths full of shrimp and clam shells; made a tight wad of the papers, plates, and chopsticks; and ceremoniously dumped the entire lot overboard!!!! So much for the clean harbor movement.
                    letter 1973, Dave Kohl, art teacher '73-'80

I remember going out for dinner. Went to the waterfront, where it had a wall that kept small boats docked. We ate on a boat at a card table, with brown paper on it. We bought drinks and fish, all sorts of goodies and they cooked it for us on the boat. It was wonderful! As we finished, the lady came to take the stuff away. She picked up all four corners on the brown paper (and I knew what she was going to do!) She gathered it all up garbage, paper and cans and threw them overboard *&^&^^%$#$%%! I knew then that someday soon that would reclaimed land. I don't think she thought that.
                    Dusty Knisley, high school librarian, '74-'79

4. Snacks:

Dim Sum is great but I remember the snack van that would park by the school at 3:30. Blue and white, sold the nourishing goods we all needed.
    -Chocolate flavored Vita-Soy.
    -The unforgettable tubes of Hua Flakes that looked smelled and tasted like gold fish food.
    -Always treats were the packs of dried squid whose indestructible contents could be chewed non-stop from Repulse Bay to the Midlevels with still a tentacle left over.
    -My favorite were the many varieties of succulent, chewy, salty, tart, licorice, spicy and un-

matched by any other purple preserved plums (I called them wama-wei).

Best of all (also available from the Peoples Merchandise Emporium) were the "White Rabbit' individually wrapped white, milky caramels.

Durian-flavored hard-boiled sweets one could taste hours later.

Coconut flavored ice cream from 'Dairy Farm'.

And those deep-fried sticky sweet squares of yellow crispy bloated-up spaghetti things.

And while on the topic why not pay homage to the wonderful bakery goods.... those salty, creamy, sweet Swiss roll slices in green, yellow, pink and white. And that gum from China, Wrigglies a la Chine? Real spearmint extract but it'd never be chewable but dissolve to nothing!

And Sugus!! Little wrapped squares of fruit flavored ecstasy.

Delisio extrodinario are my memories no?
Eric Allen '76

When I just think of wah-mui, my both sides of saliva glands are tingling with sensations.

There was frozen pickled papaya. They were usually orange in color.

The popcorns they used to sell at the cinemas were buttered and caramelized. Yumm!

Mentos - the minty candies,
Cadbury fruit/nut chocolate bars,
Malteses balls?

Those fresh peanut chewy candies were made fresh and cut in pieces sold at most of the ferries entrances. Well, except Tsim Sha Tsui (Star Ferry), I wonder why?
Gabe Lau '77

-Wam wois, the bane of my dental existence - caused major deterioration of the gum lines on the left, where I used to keep mine for hours.

-I used to get kids to buy me Bazooka bubble gum from Stanley - on the HKIS black market.
Barb Schwerdtmann '77

-Black currant jelly candies that we ALWAYS used to eat in class - they are a British candy but don't know the brand or anything - we used to get them from Park n' hoc (I mean Park 'n Shop) and pass them around in the back of class - Toblerone gigantic chocolate bars...those bring back chocolate memories.
Karen Limm '77

Menthos and Aero bars

Steamed peanuts I would buy from the carts at the Hong Kong Island Bus Terminal after coming in on the #6 bus from Repulse Bay and waiting for a #11 bus to MacDonald Road. This was my daily commute home after track and field practice when we lived on Bowen Road.

I also indulged heavily in Cadbury chocolate bars, sometimes up to 7 a day - frozen pineapple from the Bowen Road ice cream man.

Unsweetened Dairy Farm yogurt, right from the carton. I'd walk by Park 'n shop every afternoon after track and field and down a full quart as I walked home. Mmmmmmmmmm
Carolyn Cole '73

Those frozen orange pickley things, papaya, were from the Popsi vendor, but they were my favorite snack! Absolute YUM!

I'll never forget my astonishment when I bought popcorn at a theatre in Atlanta in 10th grade and it was salty... Yuck! WHAT a disappointment! ;-)

Smarties! I got so excited when a friend of mine said he had gotten Smarties for us to give out at Halloween... then I saw that he meant some sort of sweet-tart thing instead of the something nearer to M&Ms that I was expecting. Man, I love these memories... (I just never realized so many of them involved food!)
Deborah Smith '80

Joysticks... Let's not forget Nutty Nibbles!! Served by Mrs. Chan, the sweet Chinese lady in the cafeteria who fed us such niceties. Long live Dairy Farm.
Mark Shostrom '74

Wa muis, which I still eat almost every day, also dried salted lemon peel (yum) especially good for sore throats

-Rollos were my favorite chocolate at the Star Ferry

-Sweetened condensed milk was my favorite, right from the tube, and also the thick malted sugar that we wound onto sticks
Liz Jackson '72

-You can't beat the tried, true and proven remedy for sore throat...dried lemon peel. Although today though I brush off the extra salt!!!!!!
Rich Vaughn '72

Lyle's Golden Syrup was a favorite. I used to come in a green and gold tin. Believe it or not, I've found other TCK friends who also know Golden Syrup (and Wheetabix) from living in Africa - try asking about it next time you meet another non-HK TCK.   *Diane Anderson '69*

Cinnamon paper was this edible paper covered in sugar and cinnamon. I believe it was sold "black market" by some enterprising kids in elementary school. I think that dads would bring it home from business trips to Taiwan or wherever. And certain enterprising kids (Tim Tyler may have been one of them?) would sell it to their classmates. It was a good candy for eating in class because you could just pop it in your mouth and it would dissolve.   *Julia Baker, '84*

Pumpkin seeds were my favorite snack, and the caramel corn in little brown sacks we got in the theaters.   *Debbie Smiley'72*

Patrick Pang left a lasting impression on me when we went into China the first time in 1979 for an interim trip. He had two suitcases, one with clothing and traditional traveler's items. The other larger case was chock full of snack food. Tubes of Pringles, which were very hard to get in Hong Kong then, plus all manner of western candy bars and snacks. Not a piece of quality nourishment in the lot. When I asked him if he was afraid we wouldn't get enough to eat, he simply said he didn't like Chinese food! Such is the conundrum of life with Third Culture Kids!!
                              Dave Kohl, art teacher '73-'80

•Chestnuts roasting....

Hot Roasted Chestnuts after a steaming bowl of soup at the midnight side stalls on cold icy nights in Wanchai and the... great preventor of hangovers.   *Rich Vaughn '72*

In wintertime, every once in a while, a finger of smoke, a tendril of scent, would draw my attention to a tucked-away part of an alley or blind corner where a Chinese vendor would be roasting chestnuts over a fire fueled by propane -35-40,000 BTUs heating a cylinder topped with a wok-full of blackened pea gravel. There, nestled amongst the hot stones would be richly browned chestnuts,

ready for consumption by hungry passers-by. The scent was much like fresh roasted coffee only sweeter. A couple of coins exchanged, a few courteous ritual words, and I would have in my hand a brown bag full of hot chestnuts ...to help warm my hands and insides as I made my way to the #6 bus for home.   *Eric Lee '75*

The Chinese name for these chestnuts is also interesting to ponder, in the sense that they are called "sugar stir-fried chestnuts." The way they stir them around in that gigantic wok full of gravel with the ol' kerosene stove roaring away - talk about major league fire hazard! I know the method is used to prevent the chestnuts from bursting because of the high temperatures they're prepared under. I think they pierce them first.
                              Gabe lau '77

"BEANO" a huge deception! I remember arriving on the beach "suffering" from heat exhaustion in '69 and being thrilled to find a man selling ice lollies and ice-cream. I bought what I thought was a "fudgecicle"! Yuk! The texture of the beano was AWFUL! Such a disappointment. It's amazing how one's tastes change.... I ended up liking 'beano' ice lollies.
                              Sandra Walters, Prof. de François '70-'74

Vita soy...blech!...right up there with Beanos.
                              Barb Schwerdtman '77

That's it. That was the Red Bean popsicles you were eating!! Beanos were the all time favorite in Hong Kong.   *Gabe Lau '77*

There was a "popsie man," as we fondly called him, waiting for the Provisional School students to walk up the long hill to the top of Chung Hum Kuk Rd. We were usually dripping with sweat by the time we reached the top, and a "popsie" (aka popsicle) was the perfect treat to cool us off. The popsie man was on his motorized scooter with a small metal cooler attached. The first time I pointed to a chocolate ice cream bar with chocolate chips in it. I took a huge bite and promptly spit it out. That was my first experience with a Beano Pop. Ugh! A frozen soybean popsicle with small soybeans spread throughout was NOT my idea of refreshing. I never made that mistake again!
                              Becky Luedtke '72

After a swim meet one day I needed a bit of sustenance and went to get a popsicle. They were out of coconut (my all time fav), so I picked up what looked like a fudgesicle. WHAT is up with the bean popsicles!? And it was my last 30 cents, too. So much for that memory! Wow.

June Steagall '77

• Ice Cream treats

Dairy Farm - It used to have those white three-wheel Vespa scooters with an icebox all over the city selling ice cream. When I was very young, my mother used to take me to this playground off Magazine Gap road almost everyday. I got friendly with the ice cream man. He let me climb all over his little Vespa and even help him sell ice cream. I had never even heard of dry ice until he showed it to me. I knew how to operate that Vespa even before I knew how to ride a bicycle. Those memories from so many years ago have been etched permanently in me and sparked my interest in Vespa scooters so much that I bought a basket case vintage Vespa a few years ago and restored it myself. Loved the Dairy Farm Nutty Nibble. It still slips out of my tongue as "Nutty Nipple" sometimes. It is still one of my all time most favorite ice cream treat.

Patrick Pang '80

5 Bei Jau and other libations

Nothing better than ice-cold San Miquel in the brown bottles after a long, hot hike (or at any other time for that matter!) Or those famous San Miguel brewery "tours."   *Wally Tuchardt '81*

My favorite beer ritual was to go out to Stanley after school, where there was a Chinese shop across from Ma Tai Kee's. In front, there was a display of tourist trinkets for sale and school supplies for the Chinese school kids. Often two or three children would be sitting on tiny stools, practicing writing their characters in blue-ruled practice booklets. But the Squaddies hung out there.... Squaddies... is that what the British soldiers were called? And this narrow shop had ice cold San Mig in the cooler. You could have a good chat with the Brits and hear their fantastic accents, and watch the Chinese kids still in their school uniforms doing their practice drills making careful characters that I could never do.

Following this, we'd retire to have a plate of fried noodles at the Stanley Restaurant, up those slimy narrow stairs. Oh yes, with the little squatting ladies in their pajama suits washing the dishes and chopsticks out back in their red plastic buckets on the pavement. Where's the health department?

Dave Kohl, art teacher '73-'80

nb: San Miguel or San Mig was San mig ahhhh or Ho Pang Yau (A real friend). Ed.

A very popular concoction was a Shandy. It was a mixture of half beer and half 7-up or something similar. That was the only way I would drink beer. Everybody looked at me like I was nuts. Sure killed the taste of the beer.

Eric Lee '75

I remember a Shandy product that was called "seen-day" in Cantonese. That was they way I drank beer back in the days of Alcoholics 101.

Ken Koo '79

Green Spot

I remember Green Spot- I LOVED that stuff- they have never had anything near it here in the US- I can't stand carbonated orange pop- only the stuff like Green Spot. I even remember the commercial for it-always in Cantonese with that awful rich Chinese kid who asked for Green Spot (sounded like 'lok bau" to me) and then after he gets his drink of Green Spot he says something (evidently) really rude to the butler (probably something like "this drink isn't very cold, so my father is going to cut off your head!!) and the butler sweats and gulps. And all the time a Strauss Waltz is playing. (If I went down and checked my piano book I could even tell you the name – it may be Vienna woods to you– but it's the Green Spot theme to me!!!)   *Tami Whitrock '77*

I remember the Green Spot orange pop commercial. I think it was filmed in the Peninsula Hotel. The kid actually said Green Spot is so delicious and the butler kinda gulped 'coz he was probably ready to tear the little spoilt brat's head off and take a swig of the stuff himself! Yeah, they don't make it like that anymore or anywhere.

Ken Koo '79

Remember those Watson's Cola, they were only half of the price of the regular Coke? Schweppes Ginger Beer, Cream Soda. They were so delicious!! The icicles were double, with 2 sticks. Either stick the two sticks in your own face or stick one in your friend's cheeks. Those were the "Melody Fair Days." *Gabe Lau '77*

Since we could not get neither Dr. Pepper or Vernor's Ginger Ale in Hong Kong, there was an active attempt to bring back as much of those drinks whenever we went to Tai Pei... there is was very easily obtained at the PX or in the shops. I got six six-packs in my soft-side suitcase coming back from Interchange. *Dave Kohl, art teacher '73-'80*

Back in HK I was hooked on Kalamansi juice. No one here even knows what a Kalamansi is. In those days, it was sold in a single-portion box made by VitaSoy, and you punched a sharpened straw into the foil circle for a airtight seal. I also liked those yummy little coconut tarts we had in the cafeteria. I also liked Haw flakes - the little round slices of dried plums. *Melissa Miller '79*

•Water and water rationing

Cold Water had to requested specifically when we sat down in most Chinese restaurants...so they would not automatically open up a couple beers (I guess that was the assumed ritual for gwei-los). So I learned to say dung soi very early on. Supposedly it was bottled water, but I don't remember often seeing them pop off the cap. Hmmmmm. *Dave Kohl '73-'80*

China instigated the leftist groups in HK to march in the Colony chanting Mao slogans and waving his Little Red Book. Giant revolution banners were hung outside the Bank of China. This was '67.

With the riot and a natural draught, China also decided to turn off the water supply. At the worst point, water was turned on for 4 hours every 4th day. May parents went out and bought several big metal drums, and put them in the middle of the living room. With the riot, curfew, and everything else that was going on, we were afraid to be outside, therefore spent a lot of time playing inside our small apartment, while co-habitating with these big water drums. I had a train set, so one day I built the train tracks around the circular drums. I got a good beating from my mom for that...how would a 6-year old boy know that water and elec-

tricity do not mix? *Patrick Pang '80*

My mom loved it when someone came to visit us during the water rations and stayed in a hotel. Mom would go down top their hotel and shower in their room before gong out to dinner. We had to fill up all the containers we had with fresh water to get through the 4 days. Just another reason to hang out at the beach! The parents definitely suffered more than we kids with that episode. *Anonymous*

6. Markets, etc

What would old HK be without all the dark and hidden treasures? The alleys with a glimpse into HK 100 years ago. And of course the open air markets. That was like a biology lesson hanging on hooks! I also recall at the fish market they would fillet the fish just enough so you could see its heart still beating. It was an odd sight with maybe 100 of them lined up at a stall. Not sure if that standard of freshness would go over well at your local (USA) grocery store. *Ian Goepfert '80*

So many of my special HK memories revolve around food, food preparations, and dinners out, buying food. One of my best memories is the first time that Donna Oetting took me by the arm down to Wanchai to buy Chinese pork and chicken. I had never seen meat displayed hanging from meat hooks outside or in the windows. Since my uncles were butchers and owned their own meat market, I was sure that anything I bought in Wanchai had to be subject to some disease, and that my family wouldn't survive the experience. Donna just laughed and said, "Don't worry!" She was right and for many months, I made the trek by bus to Wanchai to buy pork and chicken.
Zita Thompson, teacher '81-'93

Ah Yick store in Stanley was where we'd meet the Squaddies, also get huge live prawns and fireworks. *Jim Hoffmann '79*

I liked to watch them process fish at the outdoor markets. The hawker at the fish stall would put his hand into a barrel of water and haul out a live fish and slam it down on a cutting board with a splat. Then a sharp knife was passed behind the gills and down the entire length of the fish body. There laid out on the counter was a fish freshly filleted out still semi-alive with all of its organs intact and the heart still beating.   AMAZING!

Eric Lee '75

My very first morning in H-K was spent 'alone' in an adventure stroll through Western Market. Sensory overload! I can see in vivid detail to this day the shining green legs of living frogs cleavered off by the deft whacks of a market merchant. Being 15 there was only one appropriate response...COOL! Anyhow, to the treat.

On the way out my nostrils were slamhammered by the fumes of a cooking stall, and figured "why not?" I got my cone of newspaper containing grey/brown mystery tubes, placed a chunk in my tentative mouth and promptly retched the offensive morsel onto the ground. Tripe! I've avoided ever since.

Eric Allen '76

One day after baseball practice in Aberdeen, a few of us went across the street to get a drink or drumsticks from one of the hawkers. We saw a dog trotting across the road toward us. It suddenly stopped in the middle of the road to do its "business." We were laughing when all of a sudden an orange BMW 2002 came roaring down the road at high speed.

Wham! It hit the dog dead on. Incredibly, the dog managed to get up, and whining the whole time, limp its way across the street, where it laid in a patch of mud right at our feet. We were just standing there looking at this dog dying in the mud, when a Chinese hawker, who also saw the whole thing from across the street, approached us. He motioned to the dog and then to us in a questioning manner. We assumed he was asking if it was our dog. When we all shook our heads, "No", he thanked us in Chinese, then picked the dog up and went along his merry way. We knew right then that he had really asked us if we were going to want it (for dinner?!). That's one time I happily gave up "first dibs"!

Kelvin Limm '79

• The Fishy Man

The Fishy Man came to our condo in Jardine's Lookout with a basket on his shoulder and gum in his pocket. He sold fresh fish, cut on a plank in front of our door. We always bought groupa, fresh from the sea... well ...fresh from the fishy man's basket. As a kid, I followed him, house to house and gathered fish offal and heads to feed my cat. He would walk into our neighborhood and sing "fishy man, fishy man!" Everytime he would see me, he would smile his goldtooth grin, and give me a fishy smelling stick of gum. Wrigley's spearmint fish gum! Yum! Many years later he made it to Repulse Bay...and the divine fish-gum was still offered.

Sydney Henrietta '84

BAY COURT

127
REPULSE BAY ROAD

Chapter 8
Family Life

Students at HKIS came from a full range of family backgrounds. Husbands and fathers were working in Hong Kong for a wide variety of employers, missions, consulates, and other schools. Some were self-employed. Some were 'China Watchers." In some cases, students knew intimately what their dads were about; others were totally oblivious. Some dads didn't or couldn't talk about their "other" life(s).

Most mothers were not employed, thus able to participate in activities both at school and in Hong Kong. A few women were able to teach at HKIS and other local schools. A few started their own businesses. Membership in various exclusive clubs was common - from the Royal Hong Kong Yacht Club to the American Club, HK Country Club, Ladies Recreation Club, etc. Others chose to participate in local church, educational, or informal groups. Life was made easy because inexpensive household help (amahs) could be employed on a daily or live-in basis.

Families ranged from having one to as many as seven kids at HKIS. Some expatriates stayed less than a year, others settled in for decades. Several long-established Hong Kong families sent their students to the school.

For many, the Church of All Nations was a second home. Most of the overseas staff and their families worshipped there, as did many school families, despite their various Christian backgrounds.

Living in Hong Kong, or any overseas situation, could be very hard on family life, and the separation/divorce rate during and after time in HK was higher than the average for the times. The community could be small and incestuous. One or both parents could be out of HK while kids continued to attend school, cared for by the amah. HKIS insisted that a non-servant adult live with kids when parents were gone. Kids and moms weren't always happy being so far away from the familiarity of their homes "back home."

But, domestic life was definitely a unique experience, with lots of memories.

Ed.

1. The Impact of Hong Kong live on a family

Arleen and I and our families look back on eleven very special years spent in Hong Kong - August, 1966 through June, 1977, years which are filled with experiences and memories that have proven to have a lasting impact on us. The hand of God has been so very evident as we recognize God's presence, blessings on HKIS, personally in our family, and and professionally in our ministry.

Arleen experienced this in her personal responsibilities and opportunities. She was first of all mother, providing a home for the family, maintaining that "home." Then, as the Headmaster's wife, she was especially involved in welcoming new families, particularly those of the overseas teaching staff, helping them to find their home in Hong Kong and to be part of the HKIS community. In the latter years, she also served on the staff of the school's kindergarten program.

Teachers, students, families, and staff members (from gardeners to watchmen, business office employees, and drivers of our vehicles), from around the world, added to my life experiences. So did the dozen or so personal secretaries, American, British, and Chinese, who worked with me and put up with me for the 11 years at HKIS. (This list included one newly employed young lady who began her first day of work with me at 8:00 AM, went out for lunch at noon, and never returned! Was I really that bad a taskmaster and a poor headmaster?)

Our children experienced God's blessings in their living within a multi-cultural community, where there also was a diversity of religious and non-religious backgrounds. They attended a school where facilities, program, and standards of education were outstanding. As part of home leave travel, they were able to move around the world, stopping in various countries in the Far East and in Europe. And they were able to examine and understand the direction of their own lives in the light of all they were able to see and do and experience.

Arleen and I thank God for our rich experiences in life and in ministry in New York City, Hong Kong, and the Pacific Northwest. We are very thankful for our five children and their families, for our nine wonderful grandchildren, and for the openness and world outlook we can share with the members of our families as we see the need to be God's people and communicate His love with others throughout the world.

Praise the Lord! Bob and Arleen Christian, founding Headmaster '66-'77

One of the more charming surprises in our new apartment was a fish vendor who appeared at our back door. He brought what looked to be different kinds of fish each week in his wicker basket, but he referred to almost all of them as pomfret. We were always eager to watch him use his simple but accurate hand scale and then deftly clean the fish with his extremely sharp Chinese knife.

Dave Christian '69

HKIS furnished stoves and refrigerators to the overseas faculty at the time. When I knew that someone was coming in my first few months I would go buy the items and say that I wanted them delivered on August 1 because the person was coming on the 5th of the month. However, I hadn't compensated for the fact that their time and mine were not the same. So it might come on the 15th of the month. I very quickly learned that I had to tell them to deliver things like this two weeks ahead of when I actually had to have it for the new folks coming and then it would be there on time.

Finding apartments or flats and being the sponsor with the Hong Kong Government was also my responsibility. I would hear from Bob Christian that a new family had been hired. I would get their file from him and find out how many children they had, if it was a single person etc. I would then start a search for an apartment. My family and I made many trips to various apartments and would finally settle on one. I would sign a contract to lease the apartment. Many times I would have to look for weeks as there was an apartment shortage. I was asked many times how did you decide to rent a particular place. I finally came to the conclusion that if I felt I would put my family in a particular place then I would hope it would be adequate for those coming.

I also had to complete forms for the Hong Kong Immigration department that we in fact would be hiring the particular family member. This was an interesting process. The main thing was to make sure that the incoming faculty person had to understand that they could not arrive in Hong Kong before they had their visa. If they came to soon it caused many problems with the Immigration Dept.

One couple sent their items by airfreight to Hong Kong. They had their name and HKIS on the boxes. Customs would not hold the items but they would not let them in either without examining the contents. So I went with Paul Kan to Kai Tak airport customs and we had to open all the boxes and then take them. You would be surprised at some of the interesting clothing items we discovered and much to the surprise of the wife whose items we had to go through.

Ed Dollase business manager '67 - '74

I always thought the impression that my dad succumbing to the "Geisha Syndrome" was unique. He even married one of those 26-year old "geishas" and had another daughter. Talking about it always seemed taboo, but after talking with other alum, I found that the same went on in other families...dads with Chinese mistresses, that is. I think several families left the Colony over this issue, and then split up. HK had a unique lifestyle in so many ways   *Anonymous*

My dad left us the year I graduated, and my parents divorced a few year later. He remarried and neither my mom nor brother has contact with him. I'm the only one   *Anonymous*

My parents tried to make their marriage work in Hong Kong. We saw way more of him there than when we lived in the States. Seems once he got things running smoothly at the factory, he didn't have much to do. He would often come home early and go to the beach with us or do other things with us. It was actually nice to get to know my dad. My parents went on trips together, socialized together much more than back home.

Renee Doyle '78

2. Missionary Kids

What was it like being a MK in HK? I knew my friends had many amah's, a driver, club memberships, etc. but I was the recipient of their invitations, so I also enjoyed their wealth. It really didn't matter. I did wish we didn't have so many kids in the family, at times, because money was tight and who wanted to invite 8 people over? It was a ready-made party on the other hand, and I have fond memories of popping popcorn, making special drinks of OJ, and 7UP, and having game nights. Mom and dad would put the youngest 3 to bed and we got to stay up late. Birthdays were coveted because only the birthday girl was taken out to eat with mom and dad. *Rebecca Luedtke, '66-'72*

My dad and mom were both Southern Baptist medical missionaries, employed by the "Foreign Mission Board of the Southern Baptist Convention." Dad was a surgeon and Mom was a nurse. When they first moved to HK in 1960, Dad was supposed to work at the Baptist Hospital in Kowloon (up on Waterloo Road), which would have been fine... had it existed yet. He ended being the administrator of building the hospital and then I *think* he was Chief of Surgery for a while - maybe alternated with Don Langford.

We spent three years in the states 1969-1972 and shortly after we came back, my Dad and Uncle Don decided to open a "private" charity practice, which became the Langford and Smith Medical Group. My understanding was that they were at odds with the mission board to do this, getting donations from people varying sources like the Levines (a Jewish family that was very good friends with us), Sham Shui Po Baptist Church and Run Run Shaw. Basically, it ended up being a really successful idea - giving people the opportunity to see a doctor without going to a hospital, and giving them the treatment they needed, even if they couldn't pay for it, but NOT making them feel like they were charity cases. If a patient came in who couldn't pay the entire cost of whatever surgery they might need, they worked with a social worker who helped them figure out how much they *could* pay and then the practice would work with doctors/hospitals to bring down the costs as much as possible and then pay the rest. (I'm a little proud of those guys for what they did. Can you tell?)

Cantonese was really my first language. But when my family came back to the States on furlough (I was five), something scared me about speaking Chinese, so I refused to speak it anymore (I don't remember this at all). We were in the States for three years after that and when we went back to HK, I was just old enough to start shopping at

Kowloon City regularly, so I picked up the same stuff most expats did -- numbers, "gei doh chien-ah?" etc. And I as I entered Jr. High and High School (and followed my brother Dave around like a puppy), I picked up the swear words, and the all-important "bei jau" and "ying jai". When HKIS decided not to have a Cantonese class my Sr. year (lack of interest -- only three people signed up!), I thought that would be the extent of my Chinese language.

When I lived in Atlanta and people kept asking me to speak Chinese. When I got tired of saying 1-2-3-4-5-6-7-8-9-10 (in Chinese, yat-ye-sam...) and let out a string of curse words, an Asian girl walking by stopped and gaped at me and then said, in the strongest Southern accent ever, "I cayn't beleeeeve you say-id thayat!" I responded, "I can't believe YOU said THAT!" Totally illustrated the weirdness of Chinese coming out of blonde-haired, blue-eyed girl vs. Southern drawl coming out of Asian girl. ;-)

A few years later, I decided to try Chinese again in college, even though the only Chinese class they had was Mandarin. It was five-credit class, and I admit I struggled. But, by the time of the final exam, an oral exam, I was feeling pretty confident. I completed the exam with a feeling of pride and relief because I had understood everything Mr. Ma had asked me and I knew that I had answered him correctly!

But he looked at me sadly and informed me that he would have to give me a "C" on the exam... Why? Because I had answered everything in Cantonese! "But Mr. Ma," I said, "I don't SPEAK Cantonese!" "Yes, Ms. Smith, you do... and very well!" SIGH!

So, although I couldn't put a sentence together in Cantonese if you paid me, I know the language is lurking SOMEWHERE in the (deep, deep) recesses of my mind! ;-) *Deborah Smith '80*

Both sets of my grandparents were YMCA missionaries in China from around 1910 to 1936 leaving Shanghai when the Japanese bombed. Both of my parents were born in China, both grew up in Shanghai and went to the Shanghai American School. My father did all 12 years there.

They met after WWII, married, had five kids in various places in NY and NJ then picked up and moved to Tokyo. We lived in Tokyo from 1965 to 1971. My twin brother and I went to Nishimachi

School, then St. Mary's. The older brothers went to ASIJ. After a six-month stint back in the US, we moved to HK in 1972 where I joined in sixth grade.

Actually, ALL of my aunts and uncles (10) were born in China. Of their group, most were involved in careers that involved China or Asia or life outside the US. But interestingly enough, of the approx 35 third generation only two (me and a cousin) have ended up back in Asia. Most have pursued lives back in the US. (What does that mean?)

If I get the time, I'll have to share some of my Grandfather's memoirs, which he pulled together from his weekly letters he wrote back to his parents faithfully for 26 years.   *James Barnett '78*

My great grandfather (from my mom's side) was saved by missionaries from the west. I was told it was wartime and he was in Shantung and was basically homeless and was a pauper. All his relatives were dying off because there was not enough food. Some missionaries took him in, fed him and kept him in the missionary compound. He ended up staying in the compound for many years thereafter.

One of his sons, my grandfather's brother, was sent to Japan for education by the missionaries. My grandfather was able to become an engineer after completing college due to help by the missionaries. I am forever grateful to the many missionaries who sacrificed their families, and even their lives for the good of the Chinese people. The greatest gift of all is that, after five generations, we all become Christians. Watching our kids saying their prayers each night is most gratifying.
Linda Lau, wife of Gabe '77

My mother, "Dusty" Knisely, HKIS High School Librarian '74-'79, was born in China. Her folks, Charles and Mazie Reinbrecht, were missionaries in China for 20 years before being kicked out by the communists. From there they went to HK for 19 years until my Grandfather retired. While I lived in HK in '74/'75 he died, and they had a memorial service for him in the New Territories, at the church in Yuen Long he had started many years before.

My mom was born during the time they were in Tsing Tao and spent the majority of her first 16 years there (except for sabbaticals in the US and up until they were kicked into HK). Her "first" language was English/Mandarin. She was there during WW II and was in concentration camp for 3 years (age 8 - 11) under the Japanese. The only hardships she remembers was always being hungry, but the guards had it no better - there just wasn't any food available. (Which might explain why she hasn't stopped eating since she got out! -sorry mom) The person who the movie, "Chariots of Fire" was about was also in the same concentration camp and, if memory serves me, he died while there. There was a book written about the camp she was in, called, "Shantung Compound" (I wouldn't bet on the spelling) I picked the book up to read when I was in HK but it was a physiological book and not the historical novel I was looking for. So I abandoned it in favor of "Tai-Pan".

My father and us kids were born and/or raised on or near the farms of PA. I assume that my mom's background was the impetus for us to leave there and head off to Japan in 1969. All I can say is that it was the best thing that happened to me, the best education a person could hope for. Especially since I live by the creed, "Don't let school get in the way of your education!"

I spent a year working in Japan ('86/'87) where I met my wife, Keiko. It is my plan to have my children go to elementary school in Japan so that they learn the written language. They have dual citizenships at this time and when they turn 22 they must make a decision as to which country they want to be civilized (!?) with. So I guess you could say my kids are 4th generation TCK, if you start with my grandparents. I would not want it any other way!   *David Knisely '75*

Church of All Nations was where I had Confirmation with Lois, Eric, Pam, and Martin and Rev. Boemke.   *Barb Schwerdtmann '77*

3. Adjustments

Our family had always moved around and we were usually the only new students in school. "So, you're the new family that moved from California?" was what we used to hear. It made me feel so different. It was hard to break into those long-established groups of friends.

Then we moved to Hong Kong in 1980. I was in the middle of 8th grade. While I was waiting to see Mr. Reimer, the Jr. Hi principal, for my first-day-of-school tour, I looked through the tall windows in the office door. I saw many faces crammed in the small window frame, all staring at me and my '80s permed hair. They finally came in and surrounded me, peering down on me as I sat in the chair. They fired questions at me:

"Are you new?"
"Where are you from ?"
"What's your name?"
"Who's your teacher?"
"Do you want to have lunch with us?"
"When's your free period?"

They all wanted to be friends! It was great. I learned later that the new bunch of friends in the window were what turned out to be HKIS longtimers. Not exactly sure of the names anymore, but many became good and long-time friends.

As an adult and military spouse, I still continue to move every few years and know it can be difficult at times. But if you have a good attitude and search out new friends, you will be happy and have great experiences. My fellow HKIS classmates found me. They made me feel comfortable and welcome and helped me begin a great era of experiences at HKIS.

The part of the story I do not usually tell is that when my new friends had lunch with me, it was not in the cafeteria, and it was not lunch. It was cheese doodles and a diet Pepsi and Marlboros in the girls' locker room by the gym, so they could smoke! Ahhh Hong Kong memories.

Tiffany Likins, '84

I was raised in a military family, dad in the Air Force and a French mother. My sister, mother and I lived in Switzerland in 1970 while my dad was doing one of several tours in Vietnam. Upon his return we found out he had an opportunity of working at the Consulate in Hong Kong for a 3 year tour. My dad took 18 months of Mandarin Chinese in Presidio in Monterey California before we left for Hong Kong.

One time I caused some trouble while playing around on the beach at Repulse Bay and got chewed out by a Navy Commander. Then seeing him show up for dinner at our apartment that night! Small world even with 7 million people!

John Morris '76

Thanks to the Smileys, our transition to HK was made easier and more fun   *Nancy Israel '72*

The most important event in my life to date was the day my parents gathered my brother Brad and me, ages 16 and 14 respectively, around our dining room table to announce, "We are moving to Hong Kong".

"Where?" was my immediate response. As a family we had moved several times but always within the State of Minnesota. That was traumatic enough. Up to that point my whole world was Minnesota. I remember being upset with a junior high friend who was considering going to college in Colorado.

I didn't even know what continent Hong Kong was, much less able to point it out on a map! Then to add insult to injury our father told us we would be going to a school that required its students to wear uniforms! Brad and I were upset to say the least. However, Brad eventually convinced me it would be a good move.

When the time came to move we flew (my first plane ride) to Washington State to visit our grandparents who needed reassurance Chairman Mao would not harm their daughter or her family. We went from one heat record to the next with each stop becoming hotter and in the case of HK more humid! Who can forget the moment when the plane doors opened only to be bowled over by the humidity and that peculiar smell HK can claim as its own!   *Renee Doyle '78*

I left my beloved Beltsville, MD (suburb of Wash. DC) kicking and screaming. I did NOT want to go to Hong Kong. We arrived in the summer of 1970--thirteen-year-old me and my fifteen-year-old brother Mike, a major jock. I had a great thing going in Beltsville--major friends, major activities. I wanted to break a leg or do something in order to not go and was so happy when my required physical showed a heart murmur, or something like that, that required a second exam. Alas, I ultimately passed with flying colors, although I did develop a major crush on the doctor.

Ann Sullivan '75

Everyone needed an international yellow shot record card (PHS # 731)! I remember going as a little kid, 4 months before we moved to start getting the shots, sort of put a damper on moving. I hated getting the Cholera shots every 6 months, my arm would get a huge red lump and be really hot, hurt for days. Here's the list: Yellow Fever -

once Cholera - first 2 shots a week apart then every 6 mos. Typhoid - 3 shots a week apart only once. Typhus - 2 a week apart only once. Diphtheria– Orimune Rubella TB every year

Barbara Schwerdtman '77

We used to get a day off from school when we got those charming cholera/typhoid booster shots every six months. They produced terrible pain and we'd be up all night with mini-cases of these awful diseases. The affected arm would be stiff. School would let us stay home, so no one would bump the arm! Good grief, It really hit me how privileged we actually were...when scores of poorer Chinese would die from cholera following a typhoon.

Jill Liddiard '77

My Father's company finally found us a home, much to my dismay. I had enjoyed life in a hotel, it had become home. The oatmeal was never quite right for some reason though, and the men always came into the restroom. I later learned it was I who walked into the "boys room" all the time. Oh well..."So what?" said a red faced kid...."we are going to our home in Jardines Look-out!" I found out the name of our "home" was Falcon Lodge. Wow! Cool!

Off to school.... a uniform and new friends. It was called Hong Kong International School, I was in the first grade! And life was never the same!

I experienced a lot of heartache, yet what I remember most are the color and smells of our quasi-colonial island. A mixture or two cultures... Chinese and British. We celebrated Chinese New Year and the Queen's birthday, Moon festival and Boxing Day. We drank Ribeana (I did) and drank Vitasoy.... (not!) noodles at the shack...and great meals at "The New American Restaurant "in Wan Chai. I sailed with my father on the sea that was ours... the South China Sea, and said my farewells to him there, as well. His soul remains in Hong Kong, as does mine. At times I have wondered if I have been blessed or damned to have lived my youth in Hong Kong. The answer can be answered by my fellow students from HKIS... I think, well I know, the answer to that is.... we are blessed beyond belief.

Sydney Henrietta '84

Whew!! My Mom helped make Braille books but she must have been bored out of her skull- she never learned to drive in HK. I don't know that I could have done all that she did at 34 years of age-move to an unstable part of the world (who could forget the riots of '67!?), interview non-English speaking amah's (in our hotel room at the Hilton) send her children to the far reaches of the New Territories for riding lessons (I always wanted to ride the train that one more last stop to the border) and packed up the kids and the household BY HER-SELF when dad got transferred back stateside and she stayed that extra month or two so we could finish the school year. (My brother ended up in the Adventist hospital with pneumonia and I was sick the whole last two weeks of school while we were living at the Repulse Bay hotel.) So a tribute to our Moms!!! I don't know how they coped. I think my life is bad because I have to do my own dishes.

Tami Whitrock '77

Our moms may have had servants, but think of all they had to give up. My mother had to follow my father wherever he went and never really had much of a chance to make a life of her own. And being a diplomat's wife was a JOB--there were lots of unofficial duties that she had to perform (entertaining, etc.) that she received no paycheck for.

When I was 9, my mom had to move back to the states with two children (while my Dad stayed behind for a few months) because she was 8 months pregnant and there weren't any decent medical facilities in Jakarta. *Linda Lierheimer '77*

There was a Catholic orphanage located in the NTs where my mother and younger sister and I would set up a Christmas party for the kids each year. My mother got to know the French nuns there and we would decorate and give out gifts of toys my dad's company donated. The kids had been abandoned by their families out in the rice paddies because they were "defective" and all were severely handicapped. It was a good education for us, but hard to take, sometimes. *Jill Liddiard '77*

I have a strong conviction that my mother spent many an hour on the streets and alleys of HK and Kowloon scouring the little shops for unique treasures and irresistible bargains. There was a lot of high quality merchandise in our family home. I'm pretty sure my Mom wore out a lot of shoe leather doing her comparisons from shop to shop. Cat Street, Wing On, and Yue Hwa seem to come back to me as frequent parts of family dinner conversations. My favorite line to pass on to people I work with is that "We had a 'Lawn Boy'" who came every weekend and cut the grass around the house with a set of hand shears, polished all the brass cabinet hardware with brasso, polished the parquet teak floor to a brilliant shine with paste wax and a buffer, and washed and waxed the car all for a few dollars. People around here have lawn-boys that have to be filled with gas and pushed around the yard, and it doesn't do any of the extra stuff.

Eric Lee '75

My brother Johnny and I moved to Hong Kong in 1979 from San Francisco. Our father was offered a position to manage Crocker Bank for Southeast Asia or South Africa. He asked us where we would rather live, Hong Kong or Africa. Definitely Hong Kong!

We stayed at the Hilton Hotel for a couple of summer months while our flat on Magazine Gap Road was being renovated and decorated. School was starting soon and we were so nervous and excited at the same time. You would think after moving around our whole lives, we would get used to it.

My Korean mother wasn't happy living in Hong Kong. It must have been so hard for her because English was her second language and she didn't speak Chinese, but it was always assumed she was a native because of her appearance. My father was so busy with work and away on business trips so my brother and I never really felt grounded. I'm sure that is why we latched onto our HKIS friends and they meant the world to us.

Linda Reizman '80

We moved from Tokyo where I had lived since I was five... I was part way through my 6th grade year and was 10 years old and was miserable leaving ISSH (International School of the Sacred Heart). My dad was in the FBI and was transferred to HK. My mom was extremely pregnant and we lived in the Repulse Bay Hotel for four months because my dad was looking for a residence that could accommodate all of us. My sister Kim and I had such fun in that hotel. My dad still recalls leaving for work every day and seeing his 6th and 8th grade daughters being served their breakfast on the verandah prior to going to school and being amazed at his (and our) circumstances.

Unfortunately, my mom lost that baby in the last month of her pregnancy and so it is a bit sur-

real that I have a "relative" buried there.

Kelly Prechtl '78

In our life of Embassy deployment we usually moved in diplomatic, cultural and commercial circles not normally associated with government civil servants in the U.S. To give my children a sense of responsibility in the successful performance of family events, we taught them how to serve at the table whenever we had non-formal dinners. I remember how surprised the Kohl's and Voeltz's were, when Isabelle (HS) and Stephen (MS), dressed in white tops and black skirt and pants, served our entire dinner (and didn't spill anything on our guests).

I had thought of a farewell party to thank all for making HKIS an unforgettable memory. Then I remembered many teachers' meetings on organization, school policy, items requiring further discussion, more informal discussions between, teachers, departments, etc. - just the usual stuff of large, formal meetings. I suggested we have a "brainstorm day" at my very large, conveniently located apartment on Tavistock Road, near the tram.

We began at nine, with coffee and pastries; moved to lunch at noon with paella and trimmings and dessert; had afternoon tea and/or drinks at 3:00 and closed down at about 4 to 4:30pm. During that time, conversation flowed and ebbed, groups formed, broke up and reformed with others. Individuals with little contact within and without their departments met with others to exchange, discuss and refine ideas, projects, etc.

It was a wonderful day for me, especially, since HKIS had given me so much, I was glad to be able to provide the space and the atmosphere for helping the school move ahead. If I had stayed longer I would have had one every year -- it was so much fun and so rewarding.

Lastly, I remember our weekends when Stephen was on the baseball team. Those were the days we drove down to Stanley, deposited on the field (if no game) and then went to the beach at Stanley to read, watch the junks and have a wonderful lunch of the fresh catch of the day, served over a heaping mound of hot, fluffy rice in the local fishermen's simple snack bar. DEE-LI-CI-OUS!!! How my life would have been less fulfilling had there been no HKIS and no Hong Kong.

Maggie Gordon foreign language teacher, '73- 75

113

4. Life with (or without) Dad

Joe Lelyveld, who went on to become the executive editor of *The New York Times*, had his two daughters at HKIS for a year, and my mother taught one of them. He and his family fondly recall their instruction. He was the NYT reporter here in 1971-72, as I recall, but did not like Hong Kong so they moved on. The NYT had other correspondents in Vietnam so he was only covering China and could not get inside in those days, which he found very frustrating. I entered HKIS when school started in 1971, and I left in February 1975. I would have been in the class of 1982 if I had stayed.

My father did not talk much about the Vietnam War or the other stories he did, although he did bring back a small curio from each trip -- a face painted on the side of a coconut, a tiny sandstone lion and so forth. My father had more room for travel, as he was the only Washington Star correspondent in Asia. It was some strain on my mother to have him travel so much, but my brother and I accepted it. *Keith Bradsher '82*

nb: In addition to Henry Bradsher, other correspondents with students at HKIS included Larry Burroughs, Steve Bell, Jim Bennett, Ted Koppel, and Roy Rowan - Ed.

When we lived in HK, (1966-1971) I met Steve and Joyce Bell. Their kids went to HKIS also. Steve was ABC Bureau Chief for the Far East. Joyce and I sang with the British group named the Robin Boyle Singers. One day she invited me to have lunch with her at the Peninsula Hotel so we could talk about Atlanta, Georgia. After a wonderful lunch and a VERY long question and answer period, I asked her just why she was so interested in Atlanta. She then told me it had not been announced yet, but they were moving to Atlanta in a few months or less. That was when the fun began. I told her it had not been announced yet, but our family was moving back to Atlanta around the same time. Back in Atlanta we were still friends and Joyce joined the Robert Shaw Choral, then Steve joined Good Morning America and later became a professor at Perdue University in Indiana. *Jackie Smiley, mom*

One Saturday I had to come to school to do some make up work, and was surprised to find someone in my artroom/woodshop. Turned out to be Mr. Hoenig, hammering and sawing away on something. I introduced myself and inquired what he was working on.... In his thick Germanic accent he said that his daughter was in a play, and they needed some sets. So he was building them.

My comment was to the effect that it seemed like a lot of work. His reply? "Well yes...but it's for my daughter!!" *Dave Kohl art teacher ' 73 - '80*

The story about my Dad is priceless. Yes, he was working for Lufthansa at the time. It was the only time he came into school and I was so happy that he helped with the scenes. It was the French Revolution and I was the song voice of the King. It was 7th or 8th grade. My Dad is well and will be 85 in 2007! *Helen Hoenig '77*

5. Television

Debbie Buroughs ('74) and her Mum lived on Headland Road with the Mache's. We were there for about 6 months with them in 1968 and Debbie and I were pals. At their flat in Headland Road, there was a little switch down on the baseboard next to the TV that you used to change the channel. The Dusty Springfield show is what I remember watching then. My favorite Chinese show was Bonanza with voice-overs, and when I stayed home sick from school, the Cisco Kid was on the Chinese channel in English around 1pm once TV started being on at odd times during the day. I remember watching Daniel Boone and the Wonderful World of Disney on Pearl in the late 60's and early 70's. Then we really got modern and had the satellite news in the morning with Hal Archer. *Barbara Schwerdtman '77*

Some of the HK TV programs I remember in 1968 was 'Skippy The Bush Kangaroo'; BATMAN (great!!!) TV series; Superman (in colour) TV series; Flipper, series-series; "Fireball XL5" (with the famous puppets) 'Lamb-chop' (British puppet with known British actress running it was probably called something else (Shari's Playhouse in the US); "Marine Boy" animated about a boy who lived under the sea and fought enemies (as usual) (in English); 'Gold dar' - Japanese series about fighting Jurassic Park type monsters (animated); 12 o'clock high - series (not film) - among others with Spencer Tracy - loved it (despite I was only 8 y.o); 'Lawman' (cowboy series); Iron Horse' (ditto) 'Cimmarron Strip' (the same); 'Dundee & Chalhain' (cowboy-like series); 'Mission Impossible' (original series); The Man from U.N.C.L.E.; 'The Village' (John Drake - Birtish series - terribly frightening); The department store "Wing-On's "Soundbeat" 67 followed by 68 and then in 1969 I left so ..I didn't see that one.

Henrik Mjoman, '78

The safety commercials aired on TV were unique! The tossed beer bottle from a high-rise, dismemberment by industrial machines, jaywalking, etc.

Wally Tuchardt '81

There were two English TV channels: TV-B Pearl and RTV-2(?) (Rediffusion), and about six Chinese channels I think: TV-B Jade and the rest were RTV-###

During Jr High and High school, TV-B started (M-F) at 4pm with Sesame Street, followed by RTV at 5pm with Electric Company. I think we watched the 1/2 hour soap opera Young & the Restless during dinner (6:30ish).

When I was in 11th/12th grade, they started having Saturday morning shows and I particularly enjoyed one called Raffles about the gentleman burglar. I also fell in love with Bruce Boxleitner as Luke Macahan in How the West Was Won. I remember watching old movies during typhoons because they had to have something on TV so they could keep us informed of the storm progress, but they didn't have any regular programming. So, I enjoyed The Party (still one of my favorite Peter Sellers movies), along with classics like The Philadelphia Story, Bringing Up Baby, Arsenic and Old Lace. etc. etc. etc. And people wonder how I do so well with the Entertainment category in Trivial Pursuit! Marine Boy was my FAVORITE cartoon! Marine Boy and his Oxy-Gum!

And I was a big fan of the Chinese Bonanza as well! It was hilarious to watch it dubbed into Chinese because the voices really didn't apply! Then there were the subtitles. I appreciated the Chinese subtitles on the English programs because we lived under the flight path to Kai Tak, so my dad could tell me what I missed when a plane flew overhead.

Deborah Smith '80

My family is fragmented and spread all over. For most of my life, we've been on several continents. Yet, I also got a good bit of time with them. Yes, I've missed weddings, funerals, births, and a lot of birthdays, but I don't know that I'd trade them for the experiences I've had living overseas. And there were some family times. I spent the better part of several summers with my grandparents, and there was quite a reunion on my mother's side when we returned from HK. Just the same, I was quite glad when Dad moved home. It meant that I got to share more time with him for a couple of years before he died, although we didn't know that was coming when he returned.

While I wouldn't trade the experiences, or friends, from those overseas years, I wonder if the fragmentation has influenced my choice of spouse? Her family is tight, almost all live in the same state, and nearly every family holiday is spent together. I like this too, and wouldn't trade that feeling of family away easily either, especially now with kids of my own to raise. They're more globally aware than their friends, but not nearly as much as we were. They can't believe that I went to 6 schools in 12 years, and sometimes I can't either. With all of the curriculum changes, it's amazing that I learned anything! Anyway, I think I've had the best of both worlds!

Mark Woodruff '77

The summer of '72 we had thirty-nine inches of rain in three days in June. I had kidded Earl Westrick, the high school principal, when he came that he would see it rain, but not much in the fall of the year. The following summer it rained and many of our apartments had to be vacated because of structural damage to them. Including the Westricks. The government actually condemned them. So finding new apartments in such a time was very stressful. However, the Good Lord provided as He always did.

Ed Dollase, business manager '67-'74

6. Unintended housemates

In our old apartment on the ground floor apartment on Shouson Hill Road East by the street, our bedroom floor had a huge crack by the wall where millions of cockroaches came up. The last year we were there, we had 50" of rain in 48 hours with the back yard flooded, and Westrick's flat was undermined. I used two cans of roach killer that day and sprayed the thousands of roaches that taken cover outside under the windowsills. Following that we had a great reduction of roaches for the rest of our stay.

Bob Ruprecht, teacher '67-'73

There is nothing in the world like the huge cockroaches we all grew up with in Hong Kong. I used to have bad dreams about them when I was little.
Sheila Baker '82

The joys of Hong Kong life! Larry Neuman called up the other night and said, "I was just coming down the stairs and a rat ran into the 10th floor lift lobby. I closed the door, so that I'm, pretty sure it is still in there. How's your big dog with rats?"

I remembered Mahal's previous encounters in the presence of the experts - Shiefer's Cindy and Fudge, and how she just sort of wandered around wondering what all the fuss was about. I related to l Larry that I'd be willing to bring her down, but I wasn't sure that Mahal would be any good. I remembered that when dachshunds are classified as ratters, some can be categorized as "Cindy-Fudgers," but others are Pepperers (Driskill's wonder dog). I feared that Mahal was in category two.

I brought Mahal down to the 10th floor and Larry and Dennis Oetting were suitably armed with broomsticks. We opened the door and Mahal began to sniff around and then focus in on something under the white cabinet. A little shaking of things and out popped Mr./Ms rat! With Mahal in hot pursuit, the rat scurried across the lift lobby floor weaving amongst the various bikes, pots, and dancing human legs. Then retreated back under the white cabinet. Now with Mahal barking and chewing at the bottom of the cabinet, another few shakes brought out the rat again. It took Mahal only one snap and a shake to have said rat reduced to a lifeless lump.

Mahal has therefore borne through her dachshund bar mitzvah and arrived as a mature dog following in the great traditions of International Towers canines. Fortunately, our telephone has not been ringing off the hook for additional service requests.
Ken Rohrs, middle school teacher, '73 - current, from a 1985 letter

• Puppy Love

Our family had just moved into our apartment on the 6th floor on the midlevels at 15 Magazine Gap Road on Hong Kong Island. The building was raised up on pillars so that the parking lot fit nicely under the building.

As most apartment buildings, the caretaker at ours had a watchdog. This watchdog was a fierce looking and sometimes bad tempered Chao or Chao mix, male dog. You never knew if he was going to let you pet him or not, so we didn't even try, although he did like the food scraps we'd give him. He was a work dog and was treated as such by the caretaker.

On one of those days when my mother had picked me up from school something was different at our building. We saw a small puppy by the door that lead to the caretaker's room. He was so young - it seemed to us too young to be away from his mother. Well, we fell in love with him from the first moment we saw him. The caretaker had named him Lucky.

Within a very short time, Lucky recognized the sound of our car engine and would come running out from wherever he was sleeping when he heard the VW Bug coming into the car park. We fed him lots of "good" table scraps, which included cooked meat we put aside especially for him and of course since he was still so young he got his ration of milk every day. For a while it looked as though the caretaker had gotten him to replace the older dog.

One day Mom asked the caretaker why he had gotten the little dog. He wasn't feeding him properly or hadn't taken him to the vet for his shots, etc. Lucky had to sleep in a rolled up piece of water hose and was very dirty. The caretaker just grinned at my mother. Lucky was doing well and developing into a healthy small sized dog with our help. We took him to the vet for his shots.

One day, after parking our VW, and expecting Lucky to come running, we saw it. The dog had been in some kind of accident. Lucky's eye was hanging out of its socket. He didn't seem to be in any pain and wagged his tale as he always did when he came to meet us. My mother screamed for the caretaker and asked him what had happened? He stammered something about the older dog having attacked Lucky. Of course he hadn't done anything and so the poor little dog had been in that condition all night.

My mother grabbed the dog and off we went to the vet. The caretaker screamed something back at us in Cantonese, but we were gone. Lucky lost his eye that day because it had been too many hours since the attack. A few days later after we picked him up from the vet, we brought him home.

My mother called the caretaker to let him know we were going to keep the dog. He was furious and said it was his dog and then shouted something else we didn't understand. And then we found out why he was so mad. He told us that they were going to eat him for Chinese New Year! That was it! We walked away and left the man shouting. Now Lucky was officially our dog.

When my mother left Hong Kong after my brother had graduated many years later, Lucky traveled with her. He flew to Germany one summer and then accompanied her when she went to California.

And so it turned out that we took a little something more with us than just memories when our family left Hong Kong.   *Helen Hoenig '79*

We had charming rooftop flat on the beach at Ting Kau. It had a HUGE terrace overlooking the beach, and shortly after moving in I noticed that a beautiful young German Shepherd was apparently living wild on the beach below. One day I found her roughly tethered to a tree by an old Chinese woman who I learned, through my limited language skills, was taking her home for dinner. Wow, did we have a fight! But after a lot of yelling (and a couple hundred HK dollars) I convinced her to let me have the dog.

When I left HK just after the handover in '97 Lassy, of course, came with me. A school for the disabled built her a huge wooden crate for the trip and decorated it with flower stickers and smiley faces, and she even had her own doggie passport! It was quite a sight wheeling this monstrous crate through Kai Tak!   *Melissa Miller '79*

We stayed at the Hong Kong Hotel 4 months. Because of the import restrictions, our black Labrador had to stay in quarantine for six months. The impound location was right up a hill next to Happy Valley Race Course. Every day after school, I took the school bus that would let me off at the racetrack. I walked up the hill and visited with Milady for about an hour and then took a regular bus back to the Star Ferry.

At some point I decided that Milady would enjoy some good food. So, before leaving for school each morning, I would order my room service breakfast and include pork chops or steak or chicken. I would wrap it up and take it to school. After school I would take it to Milady at the quar-

antine location. She grew very fond of her afternoon meals!

This went on for a few weeks until one evening I arrived back at the hotel and my stepfather and mother came into my room. He was not too happy and wanted to know where all this food was going and how was he going to explain the room service bill to his boss. I remember, after explaining what I had been doing, my mother was smiling but my stepfather didn't see the humor in it. So, the extra food had to stop. Instead, I saved some of my breakfast and took it to Milady each day.   *Patrick Gould 1970-1974*

7. Moms and Domestic life

My memory of moving to Turtle Cove well before it was finished centers on the coolies carrying the furniture down those two turns over planks and dirt roads. OSHA would have a fit.
        Jim Hoffman '79

• A K-12 life

I grew up in Hong Kong. I first remember days of living on Shouson Hill. Playing in the courtyard. Riding my bicycle with my Grandfather over for a visit. There was a fountain that never had water in it in the middle of courtyard. We would find frogs under planters and put them in the fountain. Also a playground. A big huge bush in the middle as well. "Chun Kee", the man who basically drove a mobile food store. For us kids he was a mobile candy store! "Chi Wow." the car repair guy at the bottom of the hill. *(Ed: in the '70s, HKIS families fondly knew this place as "Shady Tree")*

After a few years on the Hill we moved to 11A International Towers. My best friend was Adam Oetting (Oettings were in 10B). Good times. The big fish barrels that were used as coolers... Using Gary Woodford's gas grill up on 13. Jumping down the half story flights of stairs in a single hop. Jumping the railing a half story up to get directly on to the 7th floor monkey bars. 7th floor playground. Only two English channels on TV for most of my time there... The pool. Later on, Project Adventure. The basketball court and playground across the street at 6 South Bay... Church of All Nations. Spending time in the garden area outside the administrative offices. Sometimes climbing up and down the trees to get back in there. The monster stairs just to the left of the church...at least seven flights and seven landings!!!

        Jason Weber '97

As a parent, I was grateful for HKIS. My children's teachers found something to love and appreciate in every child and yet allowed them to be themselves. It was a place where my daughter Katy could watch the movie "Bronchiogenic Carcinoma" in the library viewing room over and over, daughter Jenny could get away with wearing roller skates for a day, and son Robert could wear no shoes at all, since he lost them so often. Robert could be himself – sitting in the wastebasket if he wanted, or representing his third grade in student council and convincing his teachers (including Judy Stringer) that third graders, too, could have an overnight camping trip.

It pushed both Katy and Jenny to stretch their minds and bodies (swim team!) and offered a loving and safe harbor from which to begin to explore their worlds, independently and with cherished friends. We were lucky enough to be there for five years, between 1973 and 1978, and we remember it fondly.   *Kathy Isaacs, teacher, '73-'78*

We arrived with several other faculty families in 1967, and were the first to use the new building. We lived with a bunch of other faculty out at Cape Mansions on Mount Davis Rd, and had many adventures there. The commute, including coming through Aberdeen, was quite memorable, with fresh and drying fish aromas coming from the fish market, and usually a farmer out walking an enormous pig along Wong Chuk Hang many mornings.
Liz Von Behren '71

• Raising a family in Stanley

Our first three years, we lived on Shouson Hill Rd. The apartment area had a little grassy patch, which was good for the kids to play. They had a number of British friends and learned some phrases from them that they used frequently! We were on the third floor and had wonderful British neighbors right across from us.

Kristine started Kindergarten in Sept. of 1970 so I (Lois) was forced to drive right away to get her back and forth, taking her to school. At that time, there was a waiting list for most grades, and I was able to tutor these children in our home and keep them up with their classes...a perfect job for me.

We had not sent much furniture to HK so had some things made right away. The things we ordered turned out all wrong so we purchased used furniture from a school family and used it for

many years, even shipping it back to the States. Do you remember "two weeks"? Everything we seemed to order would be ready in two weeks. That didn't happen!

Later, also living in our building were the Wallis' and Silzer's. The Wallis's lived below us and Mark was learning the drums. But we got even because our Dave was learning the trumpet and Tim, the sax! It was great living so close to friends.

We enjoyed the fish man coming door to door, selling us fish.

HKIS decided to house faculty in the new building behind us. That included two apartments to house all the Westrick's (7 kids). It was difficult to get a phone at the time, so all of the calls that came to Westrick's, Tieman's, Paul Carlton and Fred Pfaff came to us (we were there one year ahead of them) and we were running to get them. Finally, Walt came up with a solution. He told each flat to hang keys or something to make noise in the window. He attached that to a long string to our flat. When there was a call for one of them, we pulled on their string making a noise on their window, they came to the window and we could tell them to come and answer a call for them. Ingenious!

Then the rains came and the building had to be evacuated. All the Westrick's came to our building, including Czar, the dog. An empty flat took care of the guys, and everyone else came to stay with us. We had people sleeping everywhere. I remember Earl walking into our bedroom by mistake the first night looking for Marge! We all had a good laugh!

Three years passed...the landlord was raising the rent so we were told to move, either to the new apartments at the new school or to Stanley. We chose Stanley. I remember my first exposure to Stanley three years before. The smells overwhelmed me and I thought, "Who would ever want to live here." Now, 3 years later, we loved being there. With windows open, we could hear the South China Sea waves lapping up, and the carts coming from the shacks early in the morning heading to the winery. We made friends with the Chinese merchants and our British neighbors as well.

Adjustments to living in Hong Kong included getting used to the small loaves of bread...at first, I was always running out. Ordering groceries over the phone and having them delivered in a big basket to your back door. In Stanley, shopping at Stanley Store, where the owner (I've forgotten his name) tried so hard to please us Americans. He even tried making chocolate chips one time to accommodate us. When he finally got lasagna noodles, he tried cooking them at home and then asked me why we liked them...they are so bland. I explained all of the other things needed to make them tasty.

We worked on making quilts at church for Lutheran World Relief and later, Walt saw them hanging as privacy screens in the Vietnamese Refugee Camp where he worked.

Once a week, we hosted Bill Mahlke and Jay Frazell for dinner and often ended the meal playing the "dictionary game." Since we lived right among the Chinese community, we hosted a breakfast open house for everyone from HKIS and friends from CAN, at Chinese New Year. The dragon dancers came right into our building on Stanley Main St. We started making waffles the night before.

I taught English to children in the school in Stanley once a week. The teacher worked that into their curriculum.

As a family, we explored Hong Kong. We had what we called the "Mystery Trip." Each one of the five of us had to plan a Saturday, going to someplace we had not been before. Parents were consulted when necessary, but otherwise, it was a surprise. We still talk about the one Walt planned, waking all of us up at 4 AM to watch the fisherman bring in their catch into Aberdeen! We saw all kinds of unusual fish, then went back home and into bed.

Those 11 years were the best years of our lives. We feel so blessed by the Lord to have been able to serve Him in Hong Kong and meet so many wonderful people.

Lois Schmidt, faculty wife & mom, '71-'83

• Growing up at Sea and Sky Court

Our first place of residence was at Sea and Sky Court in Stanley on Main St. It was right across the street from the Stanley beach. It was not a swimming beach as Stanley sported a winery and pig farms amongst the shacks in those days. My room was on the first floor off to the side of this ten-story building, and my window stuck out just enough that I could see the ocean. Chinese fishing boats or junks, the ones with the giant rounded sails would set anchor in the bay and they would sampan their way to the beach. The fishermen would sell their catch in mornings in the Stanley market and others would layout seaweed on the seawall to dry.

Greg Pearson and I would often play on that sea wall. It was a steep enough angle that with cardboard you could slide down the wall into the sand. There were a couple of drainage channels too. We would make these popsi (popsicle) boats and float them down the channels into these elaborate hand dug sand channels to have races. I shudder to think what was in that liquid propelling our boats. Further down the beach when the tide was low you could walk the sand all the way to the rocks at the other end of Stanley. I am told this is all cemented in today. Back then you had to time it just right with the tide and you would literally walk under the stilts of a few buildings right up against the beach. Down about where the winery was on the beach, we would often find small ceramic wine bottles in the sand. Some had wine others were spent. But to this day I always thought that was cool finding these vase like shaped bottles in the sand that had washed ashore, perhaps they were rejects from the factory.

Another vivid image...Laying in my bed I would hear the rattle of pushcarts laden with pig swill go by my window. The pig farmers would gather the food scraps from the local restaurants and the waste from the winery to create this foul smelling swill destined for the pigs in the shacks. But then the inevitable would happen and a Lori would periodically go by filled with pigs on the way to market. I especially remember the metal cages that they would use. They would bind up the feet and stuff them in a cage that was roughly the girth of their torso. Then they would stack them one on top of the other. Boy they squealed as they went past. Just a side note–There were a few times when a pig would wash ashore on the beach all bloated and covered with flies. It was all interesting stuff for a kid running around Stanley back in the 70's.

The sounds and smells are always the best triggers for memory. I can almost hear the Opera too. Sea and Sky Court was at the end of Main St., so looking out my window was basically dense brush and trees. The next thing beyond the trees was a giant courtyard of sorts that once or twice a year they would build this giant Opera house out of bamboo scaffolding. If I remember right they would cover the entire structure with plastic sheeting, not unlike the red/white and blue bags we all came to love living overseas. So lying in bed I would hear Chinese Opera coming through the night air. It was really traditional stuff with full costume, make-up, and music. If I had to guess it was around the Chinese New Year or Moon Festival, I just don't recall.

For anyone that ever lived at Sea and Sky Court, they would surely remember Ah Tim the caretaker. He was this wiry and sometimes crotchety old man that had a funny bend in his back. I'm sure he loathed seeing us kids around. We were always up to something, somewhere in that building.

One final memory of Stanley…. the wild dogs. There was this one curved stretch on the way to Main St. I had to walk on the way home. At the curve was the Chinese Fishermen Club and an ancient Banyan tree towering over the road. It was this corner that these dogs would always be hanging out. Some were rabid and others mangy, lots of Chow mix in most of them. During the years I lived in Stanley I always hated walking past this spot. Then one day, they were all gone, animal control had made a visit.   *Mark Rittmann '87*

Colonial Housing: "House sitting for the Taylors has been grand. Sitting on the verandah, I can see two tankers steaming across Deepwater bay on their way to the Harbour. The house is a colonial building, built supposedly by a shipping magnate, occupied during WW2 by Japanese officers for a mess but now owned by the US consulate. The verandah is complete with Doric columns, overlooking the whole bay. Three tables and wrought iron chairs give us plenty of seating to watch the sunsets. Our Amah, Linda, is very nice, a quiet Philippine girl who cooks, cleans, and washes for the household. She cooks a big breakfast each morning, makes the girl's lunches, and has dinner ready exactly at 6:30, as per Mrs. Taylors schedule.

The rest of the house is equally impressive. Off of our bedroom suite is Jay Taylor's China Library. The dining room is a high ceiling with gothic arches, and a doorway into the verandah. There are 3 other bedrooms, two baths, and a nice living room. Linda has her own quarters, and so does the

gardener, who takes care of the lawn (a rarity in HK) the grass tennis court, and the flower and vegetable garden.
          Dave Kohl, art teacher, '73-'80, '73 letter

•Room with a view

I still remember visitors to our home droping their jaws at the view from our midlevels flat. My Dad had a big couch placed on our veranda, with a telescope and binoculars to watch the planes coming and going from Kai Tak, among other interesting things...   *Jill Liddiard '77*

•Appliances   from a letter in 1973

Appliance repair here is something else. We've located the trouble with our washer. This is the one that was left in our flat because the new owners (Voeltz's) could not fit it into their apartment. The repair guy comes out on a little motor scooter, with very few tools and no spare parts. He surmises the situation, then goes back to the company. They must have some round-table conference about what to do. When I call Mr Ling at Goodyear, he says "our engineers have decided...." Sounds strange to me. The guy came out three times, all the way from Kowloon, replaced a belt that had worn thin, and the total service charge was HK $ 40.   *Dave Kohl, art teacher '73-'80*

Wonderful amahs in Hong Kong? It was everything you can think about, exciting, crowded, luxurious, ever changing, hectic, incredible, and amazing. I cannot say often enough how lucky I was to have lived there. Our family, which included mother, father, younger sister, and younger brother, soon came to include our amah, Ko Mui Ling, which we referred to as Ah Moi. She lived with us, cooking, cleaning, and generally providing a wonderful Cantonese flair to our home. One of her specialties was fried prawns and fried slices of eggplant, which were so light and delicious you could not stop eating them. As children ages 12, 10, and 6, Ah Moi would take us to central market…what a place. I will never forget the smell. It was horrid. It was a large building with a tiled interior, which I assumed was easier to wash away the various animal and vegetable debris at the end of the day. However, the odor would cling for quite a long time. Upon entering, it was common to see a sweating, white tank-top clad Chinese man hoisting a dead pig over his shoulder, its body flapping as he carried it upstairs to the pork vendor's stall.

When we shopped for the prawns, Ah Moi would always take us to a specific stall and he would carefully weigh out one or two catties for us to purchase. One time we went and they had just beheaded some chickens in a nearby stall and I saw them running around, literally like the expression "a chicken with its head cut off"...yikes. You never see that at Safeway.

Another place both Ah Moi and my mother took us was a lovely world called "the alleys". They were close to central market and truly a shopping wonderland. One would walk down the alleys, which were literally stall-filled fire hazards full of purses, fabric, tailors, pots & pans, toys, electronics, etc. etc. All the while, the vendors would be shouting," hey lady, come over here, buy my..." fill-in-the blank.

We soon realized that the way of business in the alleys was to bargain. Soon, my sister and I became good at the "walk-away" from the initial offer when we were buying purses, clothing, etc., then returning when the shouts of "price come down" lowered the cost to our level, or close to it. They always had the top designer knock-offs and it was so much fun to go shopping there. I will never forget the first pair of bikini underwear I bought in the alleys,–red nylon with black lace trim… talk about whorish, hahaha! But at age 12, I thought they were great! We lived in 3 different apartments while in Hong Kong. The first apartment was on Garden Road and I remember shopping for small paper lanterns with wheels in which we placed candles and participated in some type of lantern festival. I also remember hearing festival firecrackers although at the time, 1966-1968, the Cultural Revolution was going on in China and we were not allowed to purchase fireworks. Guess what my dad and brother immediately bought when we moved to Tokyo soon after.... yup, you guessed it, lots of fireworks! *Kendra Lannom '66-'70*

Just before the start of the school season we moved into a new flat at Repulse Bay Towers and life took a major step in the right direction. The flat came with a ten-story view of Repulse Bay and the beach. The best feature was the new amah, Gloria. She called me "master." Well that lasted about two days. "Mum" put a halt to that immediately.

Never-the-less, Gloria still meant that laundry would be done, meals would be made, beds would be made, and I would not be included in any such activity. Certainly there has to be a God!

Gloria was the envy of all of her Pilipino friends since she had her own room with a private telephone line and television. She spent most evenings with us watching TV as part of the family. My mom insisted that Gloria walk beside her and that she be treated as an equal. Evidently this was unusual, especially among the service help that worked in British households. I will never forget Gloria asking me each night before she retired, "What for breakfast tomorrow, Master Brad?" And if we didn't have it, she would get up early and go to the market so that it would be on the table when I got up. How awesome was that!
Brad Doyle '76

Continuing my "ugly American-ess," I never appreciated our amah, Ah Fung. My friends all had younger, prettier, more chic amahs. Ah Fung was fifty-seven years old, grumpy (at least she seemed that way to me), and couldn't pronounce my name when calling me to come to the phone. "EE-on!" My brother still calls me that. *Ann Sullivan '75*

So many Kids lived in The Monster block A-H, Repulse Bay Towers, between the old Repulse Bay Hotel and the turn into South Bay Rd. Behind the Mansions. 15 stories w/ blue and yellow small terraces on the front, wonderful 4-floor split level apartments, huge square footage.
Rich Vaughn '72

We lived in Fairlane Towers on Bowen Road in the mid-levels. During a typhoon, Christina and I could see the typhoon signals down by the harbor from our balcony. I remember hoping for signal number 3, which meant no school!! The McCoy's, Steele's, Masons, Ellis', Cole's all lived in our building. Of course the Cole's moved to a bigger place in Repulse Bay following their ninth or tenth child!

I remember our amah keeping live ducks in a tub full of water in the servants quarters for her dinners during the week, nothing like fresh duck! I also remember her tales from her childhood in China, apparently her mother would stay up at night to catch cockroaches to make into a curative brew for colds and fevers. She would have to drink the brew and yes it was perfectly awful. She and

her brother also had a harrowing escape from China.
Liz Calouri '79

I lived on a boat for two years with my parents before going stateside. We were moored at the Yacht Club in Causeway Bay, aboard a 51 ft ketch. We had moorings both in Causeway Bay by the RHKYC and the gweilo side of Aberdeen in the typhoon shelter. Rode out a few typhoons there too. Spent most of our weekends racing smaller boats and trekking up to Snake Bay where we rafted up 15 plus boats across with the RHKYC sailing crowd. On longer weekends we headed up to the New Territory Beaches just this side of the border. One time a Chinese gunboat came out and said we were on their side of the territory line and threatened to take us in. I didn't see a dotted line, but we weren't going to argue. Occasionally we'd anchor in Repulse Bay and row to the beach and walk up to the school.

Once during a typhoon signal #3 there was supposed to be school the next day. When we rowed ashore, the following morning, some smaller boats and a catamaran were capsized. We drove as far as the bend coming around into Repulse Bay where there was a landslide blocking the road. My mom (Mrs. Kasala, 1st grade teacher at HKIS) & I peeled off our stockings and shoes and squished through the mud barefoot up to our knees. There was a taxi on the other side, which drove us to the school. We arrived only to find out that school was closed for the day! We didn't have a means of communication on the boat other than a ham radio, and the local radio news said nothing of the school being closed, so no one could call us. Cell phones would have been great back then.

I played the harp consistently up through college and now that my youngest daughter has left the nest I am toying with the thought of doing some more than sporadic playing.
Diane Kasala '72

I remember going on the Kasala's junk with my Parents. On the bunks they had Chinese wedding quilts, beautifully stitched with the dragon and Pheonix on plum colored satin. We put down anchor near "Mirs Bay?" and were awoken early morning by? Were we too close to China? I will never forget the harsh Mandarin voices and the rude intrusion of the flashlites on our sleeping faces. I was in the first grade, and Mrs. kasala was my teacher.
Sydney Henrietta '84

• Shopping *from a letter in 1973*

"I feel so materialistic I can hardly stand myself. Friday was payday, so between us, we got about HK $4600 in pay. Well, it didn't last long, as we had decided months ago what we would do with our first check after the flat was set up. So Friday I bought my camera at Mark's, a Minolta like my last one. Then yesterday, we went shopping. Kate bought wads of material and a new sewing machine, a Swiss-made Elna. At the China Fleet Club, she paid HK $900. Seems to be a great machine, does everything but make love, and weighs only 14 lbs, plus runs on 220v here and 110v in the US. I also love the curry at the cheapo little restaurant inside the Club. We also took our friends with us, as they wanted to make major purchases at the Fleet Club, and use my car to haul their loot back over the hill---so the Voeltz's bought a sewing machine also, a set of pots and pans, typewriter and other little junk. Dennis' roommate, Gary Barnes, bought a stereo amp, turntable, and two huge speakers...so we were quite a laden Ford Cortina coming back over Wong Nei Chong Gap Road. Happy capitalists!
Dave Kohl, art teacher '73-'80

I remember the vegetable and fish mongers that came to the flats, one guy had a piece of iron he's ring as a chime, and one came in a little Morris panel truck. They came on a regular schedule, so you could actually plan on their arrival and plan your meals accordingly. Then there was a fellow who played the flute outside your window for a few coins tossed. And most importantly, there was "Rassule Dazzule - the Pakistani rug "agent" who carried a huge quantity of rolled up hand-made rugs in a huge white sack he'd sling over his shoulder. Amazing.
Anonymous

8. Holidays

Long Summers! We arrived in Hong Kong in the summer of 1974 between my sophomore and junior years in high school. My parents had been separated for several years and my father took an overseas assignment. My mom agreed to reunite as a family to take on this new adventure and maybe they could salvage the marriage in the deal. They divorced later, but they had several great years together while in Hong Kong. That summer was one of the most difficult of my life. I remember the first flat we lived in was in Kowloon Tong. It was hot and planes were flying into Kai Tak airport just a few hundred feet over head all day and what seemed to be all night. I just wanted to be on one those planes to take me back to the life I had just left. I was born near Philadelphia but I was definitely a Midwestern kid from Minneapolis, Minnesota.

I was such a "jock." Football, hockey, and baseball were the activities that filled all my days all year long. One sports season lead into the next sport, year after year. Suddenly I found myself in Hong Kong with nothing to do and no friends. No sports to play and just long hot boring days. I could not believe that I would have to wait until 4 PM each day before the TV would broadcast and then it was slim picking as to the program choices. It would be later that watching Bonanzain Cantonese would actually be entertaining.

The worst culture shock of all was the lack of sports news. I was lucky to get day old scores in the Stars and Stripes. To read about the Super Bowl three days after it was over was just cruel and unusual punishment. My younger sister Renee and my mother spent most of our time trying to fill the empty hours and we shared one thing in common: boredom. My older brother stayed in the US since he had just been married and had a newborn and another on the way. I remember thinking how everything was so different; smell – oh the smell - the air was different – so humid – grass and concrete were a different texture and of course there was the racial differences. I had never experienced being a minority. *Brad Doyle '76*

There was a large group of faculty living out at Cape Mansions on Mount Davis Rd past Pokfulam, including Brackmans, Bill Mahlke, Thelma Prellwitz and Sue ???, Bev Arnett, Dennis Bartz, Schroeders, Dollases, and Zimmermans. There were others, but I don't remember all of them off the top of my head. We played a lot of cards together (especially the kids) and it brought me quite a few babysitting jobs too. We had good times out there. There was often a U.S. aircraft carrier anchored out between HK island and Lantau. Those were the days of having sailors over for Thanksgiving and seeing scads of them on R&R in Wanchai. My experience of the Vietnam War was rather removed, since we had no TV, and the sailors we saw were partying. I missed that dinnertime "war-

on-TV" thing that I have heard about so often, with graphic images. *Liz Von Behren '71*

We use to have sailors over for Thanksgiving. Usually a couple of Officers and an enlisted man. They were always pleasant. But they were on their best behavior when invited to your house. In Wan Chai they were out of control…but I suppose it kept many Wan Chai residents in business and brought food to their table, too. *Ian Goepfert '80*

I always had a super early curfew but was not allowed out at all when the Seventh Fleet was in town. Not that I hung out with sailors or anything, but my dad knew the fleet was in town and he was adamant. I remember my mom tried to have some sailors over for Thanksgiving one year and my dad said there was absolutely no way he was bringing sailors into the house to meet his teenage daughters. *Sheila Baker '82*

I have a great memory of inviting military personnel who were on leave in HK during Thanksgiving and Christmas holidays. The Boyds and the Days as well as the Oettings, Webers, and Driskills were among those families who invited sailors to enjoy a home cooked meal with "real families." We got to meet many interesting men and then had fun taking them for an evening of bargain shopping at the Night Market in Kowloon. Of course, the street side food vendors left them wondering about the sanity of eating at a place like that…I considered it "fast food" HK style. But I'll admit, I wasn't too adventuresome myself when it came to eating the chicken feet…spring rolls were one thing but chicken feet?! Ugh!
Zita Thompson, teacher '81-'93

"As Christmas nears, we find ourselves becoming aware and contemplative of the distance to our families. Last Friday when I went to the Park n' Shop in Repulse Bay, they were unloading a truckload of freshly arrived Washington State Christmas trees, and the fantastic pine smell really brought back both fond memories of Christmas' past and a few near tears of happiness for those good times. The school has a ten-foot tree in the lobby, waiting to be decorated by the elementary moppets. By the way, the fresh trees looked better here than most I'd seen during my years in Chicago, and the cost was HK$ 10 per foot."
letter in 1973, Dave Kohl, art teacher '73-'80

FAMILY LIFE

On Christmas Eve, 1968, our family attended services at Church of All Nations, after which, I assumed, we would go home and open presents. I was eagerly anticipating a new Simon and Garfunkel album, the lyrics of which were especially relevant to my 17-year-old state of mind. Before we could attack the gifts, however, dad got us all together and drove to a resettlement estate, a government built complex that provided one room "apartments" for qualifying families. Conditions there were crowded, but they offered more stability than hillside squatter shacks. As a 17 year old, I would have preferred being at home listening to "I am a rock, I am an island," but the memory of that night has stayed with me as a particularly strong symbol for the great disparity of living conditions in Hong Kong then, and still throughout much of the world today.   *Dave Christian '69*

• Holiday travels

Our family Trips to Thailand were wonderful. Bangkok, Pattaya & Chiang Mai. My Favorite of all time was the last trip we took I believe it was '74 when there were a lot of HKIS families staying at the Royal Cliff Hotel. The Trepaniers, McCoys, O'Keefes, Pendergasts, Reaves. We probably could have sold a video of the times we had "Kids gone wild." Horsing around in the pool after sampling the local herb. Someone not being able to find the end of the diving board. Almost jumping off the balcony of the hotel in my haste to escape the hotel room because I thought we were being busted. Not one of my prouder moments but one a lot of people remember and remind me of.
Gavin Birnie '75

One day before we were to depart for home (USA) in the summer of 1975, we were granted travel visas to enter China (PRC). We dropped everything, reconfigured our suitcases and went. I still remember hearing the Noon Day cannon from across the harbor as we left on the train.

My father had applied for visas but held out little hope that the opportunity would arise. Pretty slim chance, since he was an employee of the American Embassy. The embassy staff laughed at the thought, knowing that the PRC would never go for that.

We had a wonderful three-week tour of the costal cities of Canton, Tiensin, Nanking, Shanghai,

Beijing and a couple of others I don't remember. Stood in the middle of Tiananmen Square and walked from one end to the other, walked on the Great Wall, walked in the empty courtyards of the Forbidden City, and the Summer Palace. This was our family together as our own little tour group, no one else was with us. It was awesome. I could not believe the amount of food that was presented to us at every meal, breakfast, lunch, and dinner.
Eric Lee ' 75

9. Completing the cycle

Last year I had Mark Wallis II join my homeroom and learned that he was the grandchild of the man who hired me years ago, Darryl Wallis. The family was always special and helpful to my wife and I as we were getting started in Hong Kong in the '80s. I hope that the Wallis' continue to bring generations of people to Hong Kong.
Dave Elliott, teacher, '82-'07

In 1999 I accepted a Call to Lutheran South Academy in Houston and one of my first experiences was the yearly District Administrators' Conference at Camp Lone Star. To my surprise, there as an assistant director of the camp was my former HKIS student Adam Oetting. My 4th grader, now grown and professional! After completing HKIS he had earned a sports scholarship to Concordia University in Seward, Nebraska. During his third year at CU I accepted a Call to St. John's, the elementary school across the street. We had reconnected then and I was able to celebrate his milestones of graduation, marriage, and his entering the Lord's Service as an outdoor educational/recreational specialist.

Our shared memories of MAG camp at Wu Kwai Sha and my desire to have our 4th graders at LSA have a yearly outdoor education experience resulted in our now yearly 4th grade excursions. For the next five years I was able to watch this former HKIS student grow in leadership and maturity – until he, his wife, and adorable twins moved to Walcamp in Northern Illinois.

Full Circle – but not so much in parallel geographical locations as in watching what a loving, Christian family, and a phenomenal Christian school and church can produce – a young man who loves his Lord, who was in a caring environment with excellent teachers and curriculum that allowed him to gain the confidence and strategies he needed to overcome a learning disability and rise to his full potential, and who will now pass that faith and legacy on to his two children and all the young lives he will touch.

Jan Yung, teacher and administrator, '84-96

We left HK on February 1st of my 10th grade year ironically to return to ISSH in Tokyo… as miserable as I was when I got to HK in 1971, I was doubly miserable to leave. I remember crying my eyes out at the thought of leaving HK and Carol Ann Patterson was at the airport witnessing it all…it was pitiful. Fortunately for me I was able to return my senior year as a cheerleader at the tournament, but so far that is the last time I was there. I have four children now and plan to return to the land of WWII pillboxes, incredible sights, wonderful culture and fabulous food!   *Kelly Prechtl '76*

I remember how easy it was to get used to seeing the temperature reported in Celsius rather than Fahrenheit. You just knew that 33 degree Celsius was hot and humid. Same with the currency conversion. When I got back to the States, I had to convert every amount into Hong Kong dollars for the first few months.   *Ann Sullivan '75*

It was the bi-centennial summer of 1976 when our family left New Jersey for Hong Kong. I was only 14 years old when we moved so far from home. Little did I know I was in for quite an adventure! My sister and I left 3 brothers back in the States, the youngest to finish out his senior year in High School and the other two were in college.

My sister, a lot younger than me was completely culture shocked. I on the other hand had quite a different experience. I can remember the excitement of such a different culture. The smells of Hong Kong, the humidity, double decker buses, crowded streets, taping our windows on the 17th floor of our flat for a typhoon. All of it was so new and exhilarating. I quickly adjusted and soaked everything in. I can remember longing for American food and candy when I first arrived in HK, but other than that I was never homesick at all.

School proved to be a "home away from home." HKIS was full of warm and compassionate teachers who were some of the most dedicated teachers I've ever had. Being so far from home it seemed we were so eager to make friends and connect with each other that it all happened so effort-

lessly. It was a huge melting pot of teenagers thrown onto this island in the 70's, free to explore and discover more about themselves than they ever imagined.

My parents traveled often with us all over South East Asia, discovering Macau, Indonesia, Thailand and so on. Plus Lantau and the New Territories. But a lot of the time we were largely unsupervised while my parents traveled alone. Not always a good idea! I can remember nights at the GoDown, partying out in Tai Tam, hanging out on the 3rd floor lounge, eating a bowl of noodles at the Shack (if my teenagers could see me then!) eating McDonalds at Repulse Bay Beach, junk excursions and so much more, all of it very free and VERY fun!

And then suddenly one day it all ends over a dinner at The American Club, when your Father says, "I have some news to share with you, we're being transferred again."

Even though my time in Hong Kong was short (3yrs) …it didn't really matter. What mattered was the quality of the time spent in exchanging beliefs, attitudes and connecting with each other. Hong Kong was a life changing experience for me in those formidable years. It opened my eyes to the reality of a new culture and some very wonderful people, teachers and friendships that I'll never forget.   *Mary Pat Brennan '81, attended '76-'79*

In the early '70s, everything had to come basically by ship from either the U S, Australia, New Zealand or some other overseas source. The ships came only about every six weeks. One Saturday I told my wife that I was going to Stanley to get a haircut. She asked if I would you go to Stanley Store and pick up some breakfast cereal. However, when I got home I told her the guy said "next boat six weeks."

She was upset. Later that evening as we were eating our evening meal our son asked why mom seemed upset because she couldn't get something at the store. I said "your mother was upset because we would have to wait six more weeks to get the cereal that we could get anytime in the US." He said "Well if things are so great in the US, what are we doing here?"

Later my wife and I talked about his comment and realized that our children didn't know what it's like to live in the US, as they were only 5 and 1 when we came to Hong Kong and this was

125

almost six years later. So we decided that maybe we should return so they could find out what living in the US was like.

I know that they and we two will never forget our experiences at HKIS and feel it was one of the best decisions we ever made of going to Hong Kong and the quality education our children received. *Ed Dollase, Business Manager '67-'75*

Barry Kolb, who came the same year we did in 1973. When he decided to return to the US after just three years, I was kind of surprised, and asked him the reason. He said, "When my kids start saying 'biscuits' instead of 'cookies,' it's time to get back to America." *Dave Kohl art teacher '73-'80*

10. HKIS Romance

I wonder if the number of couples that have paired up at HKIS over the years is anywhere near the average for a school.... or an International School. I'm sure I've left someone out, but in asking friends and alumni, we came up with the following couples that met at HKIS, and eventually wed.

- Ed.

Randy Chadwick '78 and Cindy Newnam '79
John Lazenby ' 74 and Christa Ebert '75
Chris Reaves '75 and Pam Peterson '76
John Trepanier '75 and Karen Heck '75
Cindy Kinne '78 and John MacMillian '77
Brent Smith '78 and Sandra Koo '78
Larry West '79 and Odile Seciniaz '79
York Wong and Elizabeth Wong '77
Lillian Tantosubroto '73 and Raul Pangilinan '74
Scott Lazenby '72 and Sandy Grimsley '72
Jonathan Slayton '72 and Barbara Fehler '74
Chris Tuchardt '83 and Bill Kuhn (faculty)
Greg Westrick '73 and Jan Schalk (Faculty)
Paul Carlton and Becky Raborn '68 (both faculty)
Mary Kaye Heissler and Frank Soderlind (both faculty)
Scott Sorenson and Joyce Ho (faculty and staff)
Rachael Ranta '72and Fred Pfaff (teacher)

One of HKIS' greatest love stories. Rachael left for the U.S. thinking the Rachael–Fred romance was over. He left HK within 24 hours, caught up

her in CA and proposed.
Earl Westrick, principal and more '71-'96

Unbeknownst to the basketball team, Coach Pfaff had been dating Pastor Ranta's daughter, Rachel. As Rachel was taking off for the States, Mr. Pfaff ran to the airport and proposed. What romance! *Ann Sullivan '75*

127

Chapter 9
Transportation

Seems like people never stopped moving in Hong Kong.

We were people on a mission to get someplace then go someplace else, on our way to someplace else. And there were so many ways to accomplish this - private automobiles being the least common choice. It was said that if all the cars in Hong Kong could be on the road system at the same time, they wouldn't all fit. Considering the scarcity of major roadways in the '60s and '70s, that may well have been a true statement. A drive into the New Territories usually meant winding up, over, and through Lion Rock tunnel, past Amah Rock, then a meandering system of two lane roads connecting rural towns and villages before the advent of new towns and multiple-lane highways.

Far more common were systems of public transportation - Kowloon and China Motor busses - double-decker leftovers from the London Transport system. There were also a multitude of public light busses - vans that were limited to 14 passengers that stopped anywhere. Fleets of taxis roamed the streets or lined up at hotels and ferry terminals - except at cab-changing time - 4pm - when every cab zooming past seemed to have a cloth over the meter. Unique to Hong Kong were private hire-cars - pak pais -, which meant any arrangement from having a regular car and driver, ones you could arrange for by phone, or ones you hailed on an as-needed basis. Several drivers and car companies served HKIS families; the most infamous was "Six-fingers", based under a tree near the foot of South Bay Road.

For those ambitious in getting into the New Territories, there was the Kowloon-Canton railway, with hourly green trains heading north to Sheung Shui or the occasional train to Lo Wu and the un-crossable Chinese border. Villagers and market ladies, loaded with baskets and bales of produce balanced on shoulder poles squatted on the floors of the open baggage cars, jostled with bands of uniformed school children on outings or returning to village homes for the weekend.

Rails also carried a legion of trams along the waterfront from Western Market to Shau Kei Wan at cheap prices, but without guarantee of a speedy ride. The electric double-deck trams were not built for passengers over 6 feet tall, nor were they noted for their comfortable Victorian wooden seating. But they could be rented in the evenings as a venue for parties and celebrations, a tradition that soon caught on with HKIS senior classes. The Peak Tram, an engineering marvel, was always popular not only for residents of the mid-levels, but for folks seeking the cool and relative solace of the Peak, its restaurant, cafe, and trail around Victoria Peak. The views, especially on the south face and over Pok Fu Lam, could be breath taking.

In Victoria Harbor and amongst the outlying islands, Hong Kong's fleet of regular ferries, both passenger and vehicular, formed the major link between points on both sides of the fragrant waters. Despite the opening of cross-harbour tunnels and the later addition of the MTR, both HYF and Star Ferries carry their capacities in passengers and vehicles.

Once on the route of the great steamships, Whampoa Docks and Ocean Terminal saw a marked decline in passenger services in the 1960s, as 707 and 747 jetliners became the standard means of transport in and out of Hong Kong. Cruise ships made the occasional call in Hong Kong, but the fleets of American President and P & O liners became a thing of the past.

Most significant of all was the umbilical connection with the rest of the world - that strip of tarmac surrounded on 3 sides by Kowloon Bay - Kai Tak, truly one of the most unique world airports. The approach over Kowloon brought white-knuckled passengers to eye-level with residents under the approach path. The greeting area witnessed so may tearful greetings, parties for new friends and colleagues, and many a thwarted romance.
                                                                    -Ed.

1. Kai Tak Airport

The Rittmann family arrived in the summer of 1973 and I was just turning four. As a little kid what I remember was the black ridged rubberized flooring through out the airport. Once you had your bags at customs and loaded them onto a cart, you'd hear this constant bizzzzzzzzzz of the cart rolling across the ridges on the floor. You'd clear customs and pass through these double glass doors into a no-man's zone. It was from there that you would prepare for the onslaught of humanity. Pushing the cart up to the sliding glass doors, they would open and there in front of you was this sea of black hair, hundreds of Chinese awaiting the arrivals. In contrast I was this platinum blond kid half the height of the crowd ahead. The final step was descending this long ramp down into the crowd, and there you had arrived in Hong Kong.

Mark Rittmann '87

Katy hated flying, figured some day our "number" would be up, but it was the only reasonable way to get into and out of Hong Kong. The landing at Kai Tak didn't help, but I sure found it fascinating. We did come back to Hong Kong by sea the summer of 1977. We had been in the USSR, taking the Tans-Siberian Railway from Irkutsk to Nahotka, where we boarded a Russian steamer requiring 10 days to sail into Kowloon Wharf via Yokohama.

Dave Kohl, art teacher '73-'80

Some of you veteran folks may have had the "privilege" of landing at the Old Hong Kong Airport. Below are the memories of an unidentified retired airline pilot:

"Fond memories?

I showed the Jepp approach plates for Hong Kong to an air traffic Controller at the Denver Center. His comment was close to, "You gotta be kidding!" There were a few other words in there that I have deleted. The ILS approach was to a hill, not the runway. If you followed it all the way, you wound up flying into in that checkerboard pattern on the rise. The drill was to fly to minimums, and then crank it over into a hard right turn and dive for the runway.

There was usually a cross wind, which explains some of the other problems. It was pretty easy to get a wing tip, or an outboard engine. Some of the lucky ones got outboard engines, the first at impact and the second trying to recover from the first engine strike. And you couldn't cheat by going below glide slope or turning in early. Large buildings downtown! And if the approach wasn't enough fun note that the runway is short. More than one went off the end, or the side, into the bay. Missed approach? Remember the hills. Yep, another hard right turn and climb, baby, climb! The weather was usually not clear. Clouds were the norm, with a bit of fog or mist, and sometimes heavy rain. It's a tropical place.

There was an approach to the other end of that single runway over Lye Yue Mun. It wasn't much better. More hills and the missed approach was a hard left turn to avoid the hills and the big buildings. Yeah just another day at the office. The new airport is almost easy. There are still the hills all around the bay, but at least the ILS takes you to pavement. And you don't have to look up at the people in the higher floors. You don't really appreciate flying in America until you have flown out of Kai Tak. There were some airports in South America that were almost the equal of Hong Kong. Did I mention what braking was like on a rainy day on that short runway? Or the huge puddles that formed because the airport was sinking, and no one wanted to spend any money because they were building the new airport? Fond memories! Yeah, right!.

Fritz Voeltz, social studies teacher, '73 - '80; '95 - '03

I have flying fears, following a plane accident in the Yucatan in '84, in which only one passenger was injured, but the rest of us were badly shaken. Up until that point I always loved to fly. Now my husband says he feels perfectly safe flying with me, in that the statistics are in my favour....but tell that to my stomach.

Jill Liddiard '77

The best was taking the helicopter back and forth to Kai Tak. That was really fun. I also remember when the Concord came into Hong Kong it flew right past our window on Magazine Gap, right at eye level as it made the pass over the harbour.

Barb Schwerdtmann, '77

2. Ocean Liners

Our dad was transferred to Hong Kong from Switzerland in 1966. We took the MS Victoria ship from Venice, Italy to Hong Kong. It took us over a month to make the journey with all our furniture and household effects on board. Contrast that to today where one's expected on the new job yesterday! During our years in HK we took several ships to destinations in Asia for vacations – did anyone take the President Lines, the Roosevelt, Cleveland or Wilson? I remember once taking a President liner and being the only ship leaving HK harbor while dozens of sampans were making their way back in the wake of an impending typhoon – our captain skirted the typhoon while we lay green in our cabin beds. Returning to HK harbor was always interesting with the hordes of sampans and boat boys pleading for us to throw anything into the water, oranges, apples, and money. When thrown they would dive into the water and miraculously get the item regardless of the shot.

Christina Calouri '79

I spent almost three weeks aboard an ocean liner--in fact I did it three different times. Now days, one has to pay a fortune for those cruises. I still remember what fun we kids had roaming the decks and sneaking into first class. Anyone else experience the cruise liners going to and from HK?

Nancy Shirey '79

It was an August morning in 1975 when Norma Schroeder and I found ourselves standing on the Wampoa Docks, literally wondering where in the world we were. Thank Heavens Arlene Christian stayed home from Church of all Nations that day or we might still be standing there.

Mary-Kaye Soderlind '75 - '80

3. Star Ferry

All I can remember is standing at the Star Ferry Terminal wearing a Christmas hat, ringing a bell, and collecting money for "Operation Santa Claus." I think we even made the front page of the South China Morning Post.   *Debbie Smiley '72*

The best known ferries are Meridian Star, Twinkling Star, Silver Star, Celestial Star, Guiding Star, Evening, Rising, Day Star, Morning Star, Night Star, Electric Star, Golden Star, and World Star.   *Barb Schwerdtmann '77*

When it comes to crossing the harbor by Star Ferry, I would ride the 2nd class. Reasons: That there kept me toasty and warm by the engine room

in the winter, having fun watching those sailors operating the engine below. And the money saved was for a pack of Wrigley gum. Further, the 2nd class passengers always got to jump before the 1st class!! So you would beat the traffic at the taxi stand or the bus stop. Ha!   *Gabe Lau '77*

4. Trams

I remember the 50s party the faculty held on a tram. We all dressed in 50s clothes and Bob Scripko was decked out in a full nun's habit as the "head" of our school – St. Prissy High School.

Judy Butler, elementary teacher '76 - '83

Tram parties -- and losing people along the way as they had to get off to find toilet facilities.

Sheila Baker '82

We had a tram party - after graduation 1977. What a great way to say good by.
Loved the Peak Tram, especially getting a chance to see that Hong Kong was truly in the Mid Tropics when you got to see all the foliage on the hill. The walk around the Peak really shows the changes everywhere.   *Barb Schwerdtmann '77*

5. Busses ("bahzi")

Ever wondered how the famed HK movie stuntsmen landed so much fame in Hollywood? Probably by sitting on the top deck first row, listening to the alarming creaks, groans on the #6 bus to Stanley...like the thing's gonna fall apart any minute as you go careening around the bend off Eu Cliff.
Our family also stayed 3 months in a hotel when we first arrived, but it was on the Kowloon side so we had to get to the Star Ferry, take the boat across, and take a bus from Central to Repulse Bay. As I recall, it took over 2 hours and we became adept at pushing to get all three of us on the bus at the same time. No politeness there!

Rebecca Luedtke, '66-'72

The Egg Story: Kids from the mid-levels going to HKIS had a same daily ordeal - a 45 minute bus trip across the winding maze of spaghetti thin roads to make our way to school. Might seem tame by Kowloon kid standards but let's face it - for young humans bursting with energy - going 7 miles by the compass in nearly an hour is simply - torture. I was over six feet tall and had to lean my head down (because the public transport bus ceiling is only 5'9") into some local yokels oily recipe of hair with dandruff flakes so large the lice are skiing, with no place to turn, move, only to occasionally dive further into this follicular compost pile during various turns in the road. But, I digress. So, here's our busload of "international" kids riding along. Every morning they pass a local school doing the attendance thing in front of their school. Manning the crosswalks are guys dressed up in military-like garb - light khakis suits with epaulets, matching hats with stiff shiny black visors, shiny black shoes - and topped off with a large white "X" banding across their chests. Very serious stuff. The few, the proud, yadda, yadda, yadda. They put up their hand and traffic comes to a halt, kids cross, hand comes down, traffic resumes.

The thing is, these are kid cops. And it's the late 1960's where rebels vs. authority is very chic. It helped spawn the bad haircuts and revolting clothes that we all wore to show off how cool we thought we were. A whole era of "fashion emergencies". To help ignite the revolution, this bored busload of America's best and brightest decided to help foreign relations by having one kid in the middle of the bus reach out of an open bus window and knock the cap off of one of the crossing guards, followed by a guy at the back end of the bus reach out and smack an egg on top of the newly hatless victim's scalp! Daring. Exhilarating. Something to look forward to. And so it began.

The first success produced such rapture and no repercussions that it was quickly followed by a second and so on. Nice story, huh? These kids, your fellow students wreaking havoc on the system, showing a little Yankee Imperialist "running dog" one-upmanship. Not so fast. After over a month of such hijinks and shenanigans the contented laxity that follows such unchallenged taunts set in. So when a Chinese holiday meant school as usual for HKIS and a day off for the crossing guards, the stage was set. Those idle minds that inhabited the devils' playground wrapped in a school bus rolled by for another day of academic instruction on a typically humid Hong Kong day. Yawn, empty schoolyard. No hat check today, Oh well...

But as we rounded the corner past the school...Yup, you guessed it. Our bus was pummeled with eggs. Bathed in eggs. Drenched in yolks. Submerged in shells. Omeletted! It was probably the only time you could see a yellow school bus in HK. By-the-way, the windows were open.

Every, I mean EVERY, HKIS kid was battered (and fried). No white shirt/navy panted or sky blue gunny sacked-student was left untainted. These Crusaders arrived at school that morning with more than egg on their (collective) face. It may have been the great Confucius (he who fart in church sit in own pew) who first said, "Revenge is a dish best served cold, or souffléd."

Brad Sandler '75

I was at school the day they came in covered with eggs. The story is true! There were a lot of interesting things that happened on that bus.

Rosemary Garvey '77

Back of the bus song on elementary field trip. From the halls of HKIS to the shores of Repulse Bay We will fight our classroom battles With spit balls, gum, and clay. We will fight for lunch and recess We will keep our desks a mess, What a mess! We are proud to claim the title of the teacher's greatest pest.

Barb Schwerdtmann '77

6. Motorcycles

I'm sure early HKIS faculty have memories of pre-school meetings that went on for weeks. Apparently the admin folks were getting the message that these gatherings needed to be spiced up. So.... in 1974 Mark Silzer, junior high principal, told us (junior high faculty) that AC had decided that each division would have an "opening" for the pre-school meetings. Their hope was that this would create some enthusiasm and also allow each division the chance to showcase their uniqueness.

(If I remember correctly, that was also the year of the famous line-up of all the HKIS men who had facial hair. Remember Chet Passarella's famous line?)

It didn't take long for the junior high folks to determine what was unique about us. We were motorcycle people! In our group that year the motorcycle owners were Mark Silzer (an old single-cylinder Triumph dubbed "the pig"), Bob Matthews (Honda), David Christian (Honda), Ken Rohrs (I think he had a Honda too), Fritz Voeltz

(Honda 125), and Sue Hampe, the Algebra teacher. Turned out we had enough bikes to get everyone on one.

The day came, the doors were opened, and the junior high faculty motorcycled into CAN. It was quite the endeavor as it took considerable gyrations to get the bikes turned around once we had them in there. Remember Elise Forester, junior high secretary? She was on the back of Silzer's bike! Dave Landdeck was on the back of mine. The other passengers I can't recall.

Understandably some folks weren't too keen on our demonstration of uniqueness. The really bad part was the church smelled of motorcycles for quite some time afterward.

Fritz Voeltz. Junior High teacher '73-'80

The event was a teacher introductory meeting before the school year started. You also need to remember that Elise Forester, Chet Passarela (sp) and Sue Hampe were with us. We had turned off the motors before entering because some of the bikes (THE PIG) had emission issues. As was often the case with the team, we thought it was a good idea at the time but the rest of the world was not real happy with us. I spent lots of time later living down this decision, and the "Too macho" title we had just won. Note that in these days of Green, all bikes fit in my reserved car park at school!

Mark Silzer, junior high principal '72'-78

However the chapel incident wasn't half as memorable as when we rode over planks in the NTs over trenches, or rode down Tai mo Shan with no hands on the handlebars. Helmets? Of course we had them. Mine was bright orange with "Jesus saves" on the back in fluorescent green. He still saves by the way.

Love in Jesus, Mr. Matthews

I have a lasting memory of the HKIS "rebels without a cause" biker 'gang' comprised of Mark Silzer, Fritz Voeltz, David Christian, Ken Rohrs, Mark Reinking, and Bob Matthews.

Wally Tuchardt '81

I was one of the "on the back riders"...the occassion was either our opening assembly for the year or a Chapel service.

Dave Landdeck, teacher '72-'78

My first year at HKIS, 1975, we had a very large number of new hires, so we were meeting for a chapel service in Church of All Nations, when in roared these motorcycles. I remember looking at Bob Christian and expected some strong condemnation of this action, but he just shrugged his shoulders, smiled his impish smile, and said nothing. I also remember being asked that day why I was bearded at that point, and gave some lame excuse. Chuck Passarella, the new instrumental music teacher heard this and said, "It's just his nose hairs that have grown long."

"Doc" Jon Malmin, science teacher, '75- 79

7. Taxis ("dixie")

One of my best Hong Kong memories was a result of one of the most immature things I've ever done. All I can say is, thank goodness for immaturity.

My friends and fellow basketball teammates Karen Goepfert '87 and Rachel Dall'Alba '86 and I had just finished playing a game at the annual holiday basketball tournament. Maybe it was all the tournament excitement. I don't know. But, we three started to think a silly thought. We wondered what would happen to a taxicab meter after it went over $100. Back then, in 1984, the money meters only had two digits before the decimal point. Cab fares never went over about $40.00 anyway.

So, we couldn't get it out of our minds. What would happen if someone went past $99? How would the driver know how much you should pay? Oh, our curiosity would not rest until we uncovered this mystery of the taximeter.

We pooled our money and had over $100. (Well, of course we did!) We hopped in a cab and enthusiastically said "Around the island!"

Of course, we were met with confusion. Although our driver did not understand our desire to make the meter hit $100, he did understand that we wanted to drive around - the long way. And we were off.

We had a new-fangled Disc camera to record our journey. (If you are thinking compact disc, you are in the wrong era, my friend.)

From our school in Repulse Bay, we went around the island toward the east - past Chung Hom Kok with its dense trees, past Tai Tam and what would one day be the new school campus. Somewhere around Causeway Bay I leaned out the window and took a picture of the Esprit store - it was a favorite of mine.

We continued through Wan Chai - it didn't look as familiar during the day. And we drove through Central and got out at the docks to take a picture with some attractive U.S. Marines who didn't know what to think of us. No time to talk, we were on a mission. We got back into the cab and drove past all the tall, downtown office buildings.

We continued to drive around and saw places that were unfamiliar. Places that we didn't normally visit. I think it was Pok Fu Lam with its dense apartment buildings and clothes hanging off the balconies to dry. We continued around the boat villages at Aberdeen and the beach at Deep Water Bay.

Finally, we came back around to Repulse Bay up the hill to the high school. Our excitement grew. But, the meter was only at $99.20. Ugh! We were so close to the $100 mark. The driver did not understand why we were so disappointed to reach our destination.

We motioned for him to continue. To continue up the hill toward the elementary school. Still, we had not broken the $100 mark. So, around the bus turnaround we went. You know the one, the curving driveway under the school pool where we caught the buses home. Once was not enough. We went around again. And finally, the meter clicked and we all cheered. We achieved our goal and solved the mystery. It turned out to be not very exciting. The meter read "-0.20."

It wasn't until I got the film developed that I realized what a great experience that cab ride had been. Besides being a crazy adventure, it was a quick snapshot of the many different sides of Hong Kong. Rarely does anyone get to see all the different sides of Hong Kong, let alone in one day. I am so grateful that my friends and I were crazy enough to do it. *Gretchen Likins '87*

8. Pak Pais

Pak-pai drivers, who drove the private hire-cars, were unique. We had a specific driver that my friends and I hired on several occasions. He drove an older black Mercedes, as so many of them did, and we called him "six fingers" because he had two extra appendages growing from the sides of his thumbs. When he drove with his hands at 10 and 2, you could see the 4 thumbs clutching the steering wheel. *Kendra Lannom '79 attended '66-'70*

We had a driver for a while, and then he became a Pak Pai, still a family friend. Used to pick up other kids on the way to and from school. I even sold my old bed frame to 6 fingers. Took taxis everywhere, loved when the Public Light Bus started, went right up my street.

The new underground opened in '72, which was really cool. Used to like taking the car ferry across also. Great fun to take the # 6 bus to & from Repulse Bay and sitting in the front on the top was the best also. Long walk down Magazine Gap though to #17. *Barb Schwerdtmann '77*

Hong Kong offered everything...color, culture, an ever-alluring magic and of course easy access to all! Who didn't love being on a double decker bus, topside on the seats in the front! Didn't it seen like we were running over everything? Weird feeling of vertigo! Wan Chai? Equally assessable to us, even cooler! Waking up pak pai drivers in the middle of the night? Was he not called "6 finger pak pai?" MTR and around the clock cheap taxis from aforementioned Wan Chai bars! You know what? Those liberties, granted us at an ungodly early age, probably have forged some very hard resilient souls.

Sydney Henrietta '84

9. Cars

For a while we had one of those big gray Daimler limousines like the black ones the Governor and the Queen rode around in. One Sunday morning my father decided that we should all get in the Daimler and go look at a farm our family owned way out in the New Territories... someplace very close to the border at Lok Ma Chau. To get to there we ended up having to travel down this extremely narrow one lane road, which we did and which was fine, except however when it came time to leave.

It was only then that our driver pointed out that there was no place to turn the Daimler around. So we continued down the road getting closer and closer to the Chinese border - the "Red Chinese" border as all Americans called it back then. Being 12 years old in 1972 I found it all rather exciting, especially after the farm and the boring two-and-a-half hour car ride to get there. Within just a few minutes we came to the HK government-run check point, complete with armed border guards and one of those red and white barriers across the road with the weighted block at one end like you see in all the old war movies. Meanwhile the terrain had rather quickly changed from farmland to thickly forested and there was still no place to turn around.

A quite animated and concerned series of discussions in Cantonese ensued between our driver, the border guards and my father about our predicament. The border guards assured us that there was a place a couple hundred yards up, out of sight in the no-man's land between the borders, that we would see when we got closer and where we would be able to turn the Daimler around. They assured us that lorries often used it and that it was perfectly legal and perfectly safe for us to do so too.

I could see that my father had become quite concerned. First of all, a Daimler limo was bound to attract a lot more attention than a lorry. Secondly, what if there was no turn around up ahead? What if the guards thought it might be great fun to send a Daimler limo full of white people up to their counter-parts at the Chinese checkpoint? My father and his family had spent WW II essentially under house arrest in Shanghai in order to stay out of the Japanese camps. After that, he experienced first hand the war between the Nationalists and the Communists, the Communist takeover, and the ultimately the Communist nationalization of all property and businesses interests in China. In addition, there had been a number of well-publicized incidents over the years, in Hong Kong and elsewhere, of the Chinese government grabbing people near their borders and throwing them in jail for years under trumped-up espionage charges.

I remember suggesting to my father that because he was not an American he shouldn't have as much to worry about as the rest of us and because we were children they probably wouldn't want to make an example out of us. My father quickly pointed out that not being an American meant he could not rely on the US consul like the rest of us if trouble arose. Moreover, since he was born in Shanghai in his case they would not have needed to trump up espionage charges, they might have just said "welcome home Joe, we've missed you." At that time, Chinese nationals were NEVER allowed to leave. Whereas my siblings and I might have been held there for years, he might have been stuck there for life.

Accordingly, he had a decision to make. He could either trust in Peter, our driver, to drive our big car 4 miles in reverse down a narrow winding country road without scratching it or putting it into a ditch, or he could trust in the guards' assurances that the turn around indeed existed up ahead and that we would not be grabbed and held as spies by the Chinese whilst trying to make use of it. Ultimately, we went forward. Obviously, we made it in and out. I remember immediate and absolute silence being ordered, and obeyed by all. Although, thinking back I guess the order was probably directed mostly at me, having seen a few too many John Wayne movies. Also, I remember how visibly nervous my father was the entire time we were in the no man's land. I guess I was still at the age where it was hard to believe that there might be something my father couldn't handle.

Pat Hotung, '77

I remember sneaking out at night to hook up with Jim Pendergast & Bob Yamashita to ride around in Mr. Pendergast's car that Jim had rolled down the driveway in neutral so as not to wake up his parents. To this day I am not sure how Jim's Dad ever explained to himself the case of missing gas in the car. *Gavin Birnie '75*

Hong Kong was a tough place to grow up as an American kid if you had taste of driving before you arrived. I had driven with my Dad a couple times in the US, rode motorcycles & mini-bikes, & we had a mini car, the kind they drive in parades (2 cycle engine would go 30-40 mph). But Hong Kong was a tough place to drive, legally or otherwise. Some of us solved that problem by borrowing the folk's car. To get out of the apartments at night, we also used the bamboo scaffoldings. It's pretty easy to climb them – as many people probably can attest. This worked well, until in quick succession we all began to have accidents. Just bad luck and being cocky, unpracticed, young drivers.

I crashed my Dad's Vauxhall on the way back to Repulse Bay from Wong Nei Chong gap. Somewhere along one of the turns, I started to lose control. I was probably going too fast for conditions & hit some water draining off the hillside. All of a sudden, I was headed for the wall off the cliffside. Luckily I corrected towards the slide, and didn't go straight through the wall. I bounced the car sideways off that wall, and then headed across the road towards the rock wall of the hill. Once, more I slewed the car around and bounced off the other wall.

I finally came to a halt in the roadway facing the correct way, but with a flat tire & both sides slightly crumpled. The police came by about 10 minutes later, and asked if I needed help with the tire, but I was almost done changing it and declined the help. I limped the car home, checked the damages, and knew there was no way to get out of it.

That was a tough conversation with my Dad, and it cost me most of my college savings (of my own personal expense money) about 1100.00 US dollars in 1978. That was my 1st accident, but wasn't the last... *"Ike" Eichelberger '78*

I remember sneaking out my dad's 1976 Chevy Malibu and driving around the island. Never crossed over to Kowloon side with it though. *Scott Bearden, '78*

There weren't many cars in Hong Kong in the early '70s. To own one meant you had basically paid double the cost of the car, since the Hong Kong tax on cars was 100%...and that didn't include the sea freight to get it shipped. Hong Kong had 3 taxes, and one was on cars,which were considered a luxury. For many people, if you could afford a car, you could afford to have a driver,who also kept the car immaculately clean (remember the uniformed drivers using feather dusters on shinny cars while waiting outside government officers or by the banks?) *Pat Hotung '77*

There was a Rolls Royce that was often parked in a driveway across from the McDonald's on Repulse Bay beach. The car and the mansion the driveway led to seemed completely abandoned. My guess was that it was left (either just abandoned or someone was killed) during WWII, etc. As I understand, the whole area has since gone through a redevelopment and is probably gone. But it was something that I had looked upon and wondered many, many times. *Jason Elliott '94*

I loved driving Hong Kong Roads, both the crazy curving ones like Repulse Bay Road, but the little out-of-the-way roads like Chung Hom Kok out by the Chelsea Home, and out into the New Territories...always used having out of town com-

pany as an excuse to motor thru a different part of the NTs, and found some awesome villages. In 1976, my godparents came to visit, and we drove the circuit of visitor sights, stopping in Tai Po for gas. Somehow I wasn't paying attention with the attendant asked about gas or petrol, so I said gas. When I went to pay, I realized he had put diesel into the tank! Fortunately, I hadn't started it yet. But...how does one drain a full tank of fuel?

The embarrassed and frustrated attendants first tried to syphon out the tank, but in priming the siphon, got several mouthfuls of diesel. Then they tried to tip the car onto its side is the stuff would drain out. That didn't work. Finally I motioned to their hydraulic lift and conveyed the idea that we could remove the tank and drain it.... success...after about 3 hours of very animated discussions! Then there was the question if I should pay for one tank of fuel or two.

The last year we discovered the road out to Cape d'Aguliar - beautiful, curvy but level, and NO traffic at all... guess we could only go as far as the fenced off area around the telecom installation. MY little green Morris Minor Convertible was the perfect little put-put car for excursions. One time we loaded it up with another couple and our two babies and drove to the top of Kowloon Peak, had a picnic and looked down on the Kai Tak runways. *Dave Kohl, art teacher '73-'80*

Our first few cars... A brown Renault was first, then a white Honda and then the little yellow Mazda 121. I learned to parallel park in that car in the round high school parking lot... (Find the irony... round... parallel park... first time behind the wheel...Didn't do any damage though). *Jason Weber '97*

My mother always refueled her light blue Volkswagen Beetle at a Shell service station on Macdonnell Road close to the top of Cotton Tree Drive, close to our apartment then on Macdonnell Road. My questions about high gasoline prices one day in 1973 led to her giving me a copy of Newsweek to read about Arab-Israeli War. I was fascinated, and began reading the magazine almost every week. Many years later, I happened to see the same issue of Newsweek in a display on the media at the Pompidou Center in Paris. And I now live close to the same service station in Hong Kong, now a Sinopec station. *Keith Bradsher, '82*

• AG 6622 - The White '66 MGB

Over the years, HKIS students have generally preferred (or resorted to) public transportation to personal driving. Taxis were cheap and there was never a worry about parking, petrol, or flat tires. Gregg Saunders'75 was the exception, driving a white '66 MGB (whenever his mom wasn't) to Repulse Bay, South Bay, Stanley, The Peak – wherever! He was an expert at the use of the dual air-horns and he always had a personal pit crew with him.

One evening after a Holiday Tournament Basketball game, Gregg returned to find the right rear tire completely flat. No Problem, however! With his personal pit crew of Mike McCoy'75, Steve Koch'75, and me, we managed to lift the back end of the car off the ground while Gregg spun the chrome lug nut off and put the new tire in place. Seventy five seconds later (slightly slower than NASCAR), the job was done!

In later years, Gregg started an unofficial MGB owners club with Mike McCoy and me - at one point owning 4 MGBs between the three of us. With MGBs, it was always good to have a full set of spare parts! *Mark Wallis '76*

Dennis Bartz also owned a "B," and I owned a second one upon return to the US -Ed.

• Chinese Fire Drill

We owned an old beater '67 Ford Cortina wagon - which I bought sight unseen from Mel Schroeder in 1973. I had always given my cars a name, and my wife Katy dubbed this vehicle "Magnolia" the first time she saw it...that name stuck.... but Chris Myers called it "The Washing Machine" I think because it sounded like a washer stuck in the "agitate" cycle. We were "family" since Katy and I often house-sat with Chris and Sue when their dad was out of the colony. Their amah, Ah Kan, had Scotch ready for us, everyday when we got home ... so we could take in the vista of the South China Sea from the balcony. And she could cook...but I digress....

Huib and Miep Pendraadt used to come along with me and Chris to play squash at the Yacht Club, where they all had memberships, and I was a gracious guest. The route back to Repulse Bay took us up Blue Pool Road, past Art Himmler's flat. It was a steep road, and every time you had to stop in traffic going up, you needed to do the two-handed thing with the parking brake and advancing the clutch as you released the brake so you wouldn't coast backwards into the guy behind you. One time as we got to the top of Blue Pool, at Tai Hang Road, we had to wait a very long time for the traffic so we could make the right turn. All of a sudden, the other three doors of my little Cortina wagon open up and the three bored kids all do a parade around the car and switch seats!!!! I think of that episode every time someone yells "Chinese Fire Drill!" *Dave Kohl, art teacher '73-'80*

Driving in Hong Kong is an adventure. Besides driving on the left side of the road (it's proper to say the "opposite" side, not the "wrong" side) the gearshift is also reversed. It's only confusing when you remember how you used to do it in the States. I also went through a time, when I'd get into the driver's side, only to realize I was on the passenger side!!!

Drivers here are quite aggressive, and there are as many busses as there are cars. They have myriads of van-sized busses, which are called Public Light Busses (PLBs). They go everywhere, and the drivers are not far short of maniacal. Learner drivers can drive everywhere except on streets where it is posted that they can't. They are SLOW and have to have a metal sign on the back of the car with a huge red "L", indicating they are learners. One learns to avoid Blue Pool and other roads that are popular with learns and instructors.

The only direct road to Central from our side is torn up now while they put in some under-street wiring. So you either go early, or drive around through Aberdeen and Pok Fu lam. Gas costs HK $4 an Imperial gallon, but oil is only HK $3 per Imperia quart. Magnolia (our '63 Ford Cortina we bought from Mel Schroeder) is good on oil, and reasonable on gas, if the car isn't loaded with 6 or 8 people (which it often seems to be). To park downtown (Central, opps) you almost have to use a parking garage (multi-storey car park), which costs a whopping HK 1.50 per hour.

letter in 1973...Dave Kohl, art teacher '73-'80

137

Chapter 10
Adventures in Hong Kong

Past the Island School, French School, and Old Hospital on Bowen Road led a path to the park. It's name I've now forgotten. The path wound along the hillside. On the right the thick bushes, rock faces, small trees and stands of bamboo. Through the same foliage, on the left, the din and odor of Central, Wanchai and North-Point.

One would pass the occasional walker, amah with toddlers and heavy load of plastic shopping bags. On weekends came the orderly and fun-seeking groups of picnic bound, singsong chanting high school chums. Early in the morning the elderly walked their slow, erect loose armed shuffle or swung legs and arms, some did Tai-chi, some took their birds for the view.

Some ways along one arrived at a clearing in which stood a small concrete Pagoda. A few park benches faced a small but occasionally virile waterfall and brook. The water spilled down between beige granite. Some of the granite faces were painted with white Chinese characters.

There were sometimes young men playing bamboo flutes. The slow and low-pitched pentatonic melodies were free of a steady tempo. The men told me they were students of Buddhism and played thus in the park as part of their study.

Some visits to the park were completely private and solitary. And yet, only a short distance away bustled millions of people. I'd visit the park at all hours of day and night, all times of year and never saw violence, vandalism, or litter. I was never accosted nor troubled. I always left the park feeling peaceful and content.

Most importantly, it was there I'd experienced a number of firsts, first feelings about where I was on the planet and how profoundly `Oriental' (for lack of better) my South-East Asian surroundings truly were. The sounds and smells of it all, the incredible energy of it were almost more tangible from the quiet of the Pagoda than from in the middle of town. The music of it (often in concert with the flute players) was made by the combined din of as small a thing as voices to the great horns of the ships in harbor. This sound I can conjure up to this day.

Anonymous

1. The Hotels

•Hong Kong Hilton

"Meet at the Hilton"

Dave Kinsely, '75

When I was in 9th grade, a new crop of friends arrived and they were all staying at the Hilton. I spent the first two or three months down there – with Linda and Johnny Reizman, Mitch Disney, Ian Goepfert, Richard Van Dusen, Chris Thorne, among others. We would have full-blown meals for after-school snack at the coffee shop – charged to some corporation or other, no doubt. That was also the time we saw "Grease" in the theaters NINE times. Yes, nine. And that movie had such an uplifting message for a new high-schooler.

Sheila Baker '82

My family spent a few months in the Hilton before our apartment in Repulse Bay was finished. I had already had a few years of freedom using the Swiss public transit system, but Hong Kong's was even better, with double deck buses that careened around corners. We had the run of the city, an experience that few American kids now enjoy as they are imprisoned in their suburbs, dependent on mom to drive them to soccer practice. But I digress…

Scott Lazenby '72

We lived in the Hilton for several months in '76 waiting for our furniture to arrive from the States. I have two Hilton coat hangers that I still use in my closet!

Kathy Grimes Velchoff 78

I remember the butter sculptures. We used to explore all the hidden rooms at the Hilton. There was some really neat stuff. I also remember going up to the roof and dangling our legs over the edge.

Debbie Smiley '72

How many Christmas masses/religious services can a nice Jewish girl go to in one night? I remember many on Xmas eve...and the giant snowman cake at the Hilton that was, supposedly, donated to charity.

Audrey Sandler '76

I "lived" in the Hilton in 1967 for over a month while we (the Coles) waited for our furniture to arrive from the US. If I remember correctly, this may have been where we first met many families. It was so bizarre going to and from the newly opened HKIS School in a pak-pai from a hotel and doing homework in a hotel room. I had a perpetual cold from the air conditioning. Two of my brothers broke their front teeth on the side of the pool and another brother gashed his head on the nightstand while jumping on the beds. Having dinner alone with my parents at the Eagle's Nest was my introduction to society.

I can still feel the chill of the AC (air conditioning) as I rode the escalator up to the Lobby and the smell of the fabric shops as I passed the first floor, the slam of the taxi doors at the entrance, the ding of the elevators arriving at your floor, and the taste of the pastries from the Coffee Shop. When I go to Heaven, I hope the Hilton is there too.

Carolyn Cole '73

My family spent our first few months living at the Hilton in January 1970. I used to look forward to the chocolate mints under the pillows after homework. I still have a love for chocolate mints and room service. And still hate to make my own bed. Seeing the Hilton from a vehicular ferry is my first memory of Hong Kong. I still remember the feelings of excitement crossing the harbour. It's almost 30 years ago to the day, yet the moment is still crystal clear. As a 13-year-old kid who had hardly left the mid-west, it felt like a whole new world opening up. Indeed, it was.

Mark Shostrom '74

The Hilton was our downtown favorite place...I remember the paper lampshades stall at the end of the Hilton footpath.

Barb Schwerdtman '79

My dad used to take us to the Cat Street coffee shop for breakfast on Sunday. And those shops

in the mall there! My Mom loved to window-shop there with me when I was a very small kid. I stayed there in May 1989 and watched the people demonstrate in Charter Garden in support of the students in Tiananmen Square from my room. It was a big hole in the ground in 1996 when I returned. I miss that place.

Patrick Pang '80

Cat Street was the HKIS hangout for the sophisticated shopping crowd, the prom morning crowd, and the pre and post Den crowd from the Peninsula. –Ed.

I think we lived in the Hilton for 3 or 4 months I remember how the elevator didn't go to the 3rd floor, as that was the kitchen, but we figured out how to sneak in and get some extras of those chocolates they used to put on your pillow each night.

Debbie Salter Jackson '74

Half of our 'good times' as young adults 'happened' at the Hilton, Cat's Street, the Eagle Nest for anniversary dinners, and the Den for dancing. Yes, even the teachers had fun there.

Sandra Walters, Prof. de Français 70-74

I remember hanging out at the Hilton - even getting caught there one night after telling parents that we were at a sleep over!

Liz Jackson '72

I think my funniest memory of the Hilton was while we were waiting for our parents one afternoon in the lobby, a group of Japanese tourists came in with their guide, who was carrying a small flag and they were obviously supposed to go where ever the flag guy went. They followed him to the front desk, over to the baggage carriers and then... after getting them all seated in the lobby, the flag carrier headed for the Men's Loo... and each and every man, woman and child in the tour group got up and followed him in there, single file. It was hilarious watching him try to get them all back out of the men's room.

My sister and I also made up our own "language" while we were staying in the Hilton while waiting for our flat next to the Island School. We got tired of riding in elevators with people who were speaking languages we could not understand, so I got my sister (then 7) to play along with the French/German/Spanish mish-mash I pretended to speak and when we would get in the elevators together, we would start rattling off in this gibberish that sounded surprisingly enough like a language... the people then stared at us for speaking some foreign 'tongue' they could not understand and we felt like we were pulling one off on the grown-ups. Too much fun!

Melissa (Missy) Preston '73-'74

We lucked out on both ends of our life in HK - stayed at the Hilton on our way in and at the Repulse Bay Hotel on our way out - Great experiences! I can understand why the HK Hilton didn't last any longer than it did - all of those out of control American kids all over the place.

And then there was the drive to the school in Chung Hom Kok.

Another Hilton memory was the protestors throwing rocks at the big glass entrance as we were on our way to Sue Israel's birthday party at Louigi's. We really got in the thick of it in those years - not realizing the major part of history we were observing. Anyone else remember the phrase "Yankee go home!"

Barbara Fehler '72

We were at the Hilton in the fall of '66-the Stones and the Lazenbys were there at the same time that I can remember. I never got to eat in the Eagle's nest- it was the grill and the coffee shop for us!! (And room service- to this day I have a real thing for room service- but I never get to order it!!!) I can remember watching soccer games out the window- and walking down the street to Queensway- there was a newspaper stand there that had TONS of comic books! (And the Hilton is no longer there- but that little street is still there leading up to the Botanical Gardens. Talk about nostalgia hitting you in the face!!!)

Tami Whitrock '77

We arrived in the Colony on New Year's Day 1967, and I remember that first harbor crossing on the car ferry - waves splashing over the bow, and that unique "fragrant" harbor smell. A surreal feeling - you're kind of wiped out from the long flight (we moved from Zurich to HK), so everything's kind of hazy, a group of Dow families that I didn't know had just met us, and boom you're surrounded by lots of people speaking a very sing-song language. It was all pretty confusing and amazing to a 9 1/2 year old at the time.

We took up residence at the Hilton for a month or so, and I remember commuting to the first school in an old VW van that any Deadhead would be proud to own. We had to walk down to Queen's Pier to pick it up. For some reason, I seem to remember the Coles either rode the van with us, or maybe were just living at the HH at the same time. A couple of other visual memories from the Hilton era: looking down on the Cricket Club on Saturday mornings and seeing all the kids in their uniforms; and seeing the wafts of smoke along Queens Rd. Central from the communist protests.

Kerry Prielipp '75

My memories of the Hilton include going there for some sort of dinner which had a Middle Eastern theme and seeing a belly dancer perform for the first time, and also getting some wonderful jewelry at the shop in the Hilton. I still have the ring and earring set with beautiful amethysts, which my parents had made there for me for senior prom/grad.

Lynn Barrett '72

We moved to HK in late February 1967, height of tension in HK due to the Cultural Revolution. Norman Hill, curfews. Etc. I remember my first glimpse of "real" communists across the street from the Hilton (where we stayed for about a month) marching in front of the Bank of China (a modest structure in those days) chanting the name of Mao as they raised their little red books above their heads. What a thrill!

I also remember the chocolates, but they weren't mints, they were little Cadbury Dairy Milks. We used to go into the kitchens and all sorts of out-of-bounds places. I remember watching the cooks prepare the ice and butter sculptures. And then there were the water balloons my brother and friends would drop from the 18th floor window onto Garden Road....

Nancy Israel '72

Our favorite family dinner was at the Eagles Nest - onion rye bread. Shopping at Dynasty with my Mom. I bought my daughter a crimson vest on E-bay from Dynasty from the 60's! Used to meet my Dad there after an afternoon in town as he parked his car there when his office was in town. There was the little old lady in white looking for her lost son. The guy selling the paper lamp shades, the peddlers making palm frond crickets and hats. That awful smell coming from the toilets, and that great camphor tree.

Barbara Schwerdtmann '77

I never dreamed anyone could live in a hotel

for three months! We arrived in the worst heat - Aug '67-—after 17 lovely days on an ocean liner with the Addingtons. We were in a ground floor apartment with a walled garden - think, no breeze - and a very slow moving fan. The water came on every 4 days for four hours. Everywhere you went places were cordoned off due to some bomb threat or other. I still don't like to run over anything in the road because it might be a bomb! *Linda Schock '77*

I grew up in HK but the Hilton holds vivid memories for me as we lived (literally) right up the street (or road... Garden Road). I remember swimming in that "L" shaped pool they had, and the American Giant Hot Dogs at the ol' coffee shop that became Cat Street. I remember the huge buffet spreads they used to have at the Lotus Room and picking up the Stars & Stripes at the lobby shop. They turned the Eagle's Nest into a disco after dinner hours for a while also in the mid-70's. Too bad, the entire hotel/building is now gone. In its place is a 60? 70? story office building called Cheung Kong Center. The hotel came down (I think) around 1997 about a year after it went thru a multi-million dollar facelift. The old staff was transferred to another hotel in Hunghom over at Kowloon.

It was real sad to see the hotel taken down. A piece of history and a piece of ourselves went with this grand old lady. *Ken Koo '79*

Seanna (Laughlin) Desmond and I were official babysitters for the Hilton hotel. We came up with the idea, applied and we were contacted when Americans requested a babysitter. It was great. They always sent us home via taxi (not a pak pai). Although we babysat individually, since I lived in North Pointand Seanna lived in Repulse Bay, the taxi ride alone was hefty. I did it from 1970-1972 and I believe we told people we were paid HK $5.00 per hour. It was about $1 per hour US. They were so thrilled to be getting an American babysitter, that the tips were very generous. I wonder if any other HKIS girls did that or if it just stopped when we left for college.

Rebecca Luedtke, '66-'72

We lived at the Hilton coming to and leaving HK. And we made great use of the Eagles' Nest at night. They had a band in '74-'75 that could speak nothing but Cantonese, until they started to sing and play, then they were the Beatles, the Doors, the Stones, any band who had a recording they could mimic like nothing you ever heard. Had to be careful to watch out for flying deadly kung fu MARS BARS. We would pay our 10 dollars HK to get in (which included 2 mixed drinks for each and every underage kid in the group) and would stay till they closed. Way fun. *Melissa (Missy) Preston '73-'74*

• Mandarin Hotel

We lived at the Mandarin Hotel when we first arrived - that's where I encountered Mrs. Burvett, the HKIS guidance counselor, meeting her for the first time in the Captain's Bar of the Mandarin! My other first residence in HK was the Canosa Hospital since I missed the first week or two of school with a stomach infection.

The Mandarin Hotel was very posh with excellent service. It also had a fabulous restaurant, which I believe was on the roof, where they prepared some dishes at your tableside with the biggest set of chopsticks ever seen. My father impressed all the staff there because he was able to use them. *Lynn Barrett '72*

• Peninsula Hotel

"The Scene" was in the basement of the Peninsula Hotel. If you were out too late, you'd have to take a Wahla Wahla back to the HK side because the Star Ferry closed for the night and then a pak-pai back to Repulse Bay. I remember my brother Dave getting in trouble w/ his friend Steve Gaston from KG5 a couple years earlier because they took a Wahla Wahla over, due to the closing of the Star Ferry because of a typhoon and the signals going up and closing the ferry.

Rich Vaughn '72

• Hong Kong Hotel

My first impression of Hong Kong was living for 6 months with my parents in the Hong Kong Hotel on Kowloon side. It was Christmas for a 5 year old kid. The room was small, but the hotel was big. The Christmas tree seemed a ridiculous prop, but there it was... Merry Christmas!!! I was more interested in the top of the parking lot of the hotel. I could see the harbour, and smell diesel and something else, something very different than I had ever smelled. There where large ships and Chinese junks in full sail. It was 1972, America was at war with Vietnam and American cars were lined up at the gas pumps. Little did I know the political engine of the world. I was in heaven.

The Cricket man set up his umbrella close to the Ocean Terminal, at times he would shift, and find the corner next to China Arts and Crafts...his sometime home. He set up his little black umbrella and pulled his palm fronds out of a bag. He made crickets and mantis, with red matchstick eyes. They found themselves stuck in the black umbrella, as if they were perched and ready to fly, or jump away. Many came home with me. Alas, they shriveled.

Then off to school! It required driving under the harbour tunnel from Kowloon to Hong Kong Island. Pretty scary, stinky and dark. Cars, lorries, taxis and pigs? We are under water!!!

Sydney Henrietta '84

We lived in the Hong Kong Hotel at the Star Ferry dock on the Kowloon side of the harbor. There was a cool "museum" of sorts in the lower levels, with a wax museum of Chinese history. It included the Opium Wars, complete with silk cloth and light "fire" to represent the burning of the opium. I also remember the recreation of the ever-popular habit of "feet binding" that was done to women (still is I'm sure somewhere remote...) to make them ever so more beautiful (like anorexia today...). The hotel looked across the harbor to Victoria Island and was a truly remarkable view, even for a 16 year old to be sure. Happy memories.

Melissa (Missy) Preston '73-'74

I remember the wax museum- wasn't it at the Ocean Terminal. My friend Patty Butner and I used to go there and scare the bejesus out of ourselves because we would be the only people in there and it was so dark and quiet. I remember the guy getting the bamboo shoved under his fingernails in particular.... *Tami Whitrock '77*

We spent the first three months at the Hong Kong Hotel on Kowloon side attached to Ocean Terminal. Spoiled rotten we were. Tracy and I riding up and down the elevators to the coffee shop for a lot of our meals signing them away to our room. *Gavin Birnie '75*

2. Clubs

• Foreign Correspondent's Club

My father, Henry Bradsher, was a member back when it was in the building that has since been torn down to make way for what is now the Ritz Carlton. The FCC moved to its current location, on Ice House Street, in 1982. I am very active at the club as first vice president and also as the convener of the speakers committee. The main value of the club these days lies in all the great speakers who come through town; most of them want to talk at the FCC, and sometimes they say something interesting. Hong Kong is so safe that we don't worry much about security.

Keith Bradsher '82

Thanks to Andy Chworowsky, I was able to hang out at the FCC during the Handover in '97. He took me there the first night I was in town, and there was little security, just sign-in at a table. They said about 500 correspondents were present in Hong Kong for the big event, but since there was no trauma or confrontation, the reporters had little to do but find human interest stories and schmooze. The smoke-filled FCC was a cacophonous space, glasses clinking, animated discussions, and a good time was being had by all.

Dave Kohl, art teacher '73-'80

• American Club

The old American Club down in central was in the HK Shanghai bank building, I think. It was very Spartan, and we all really liked the Cream of Chicken soup. Then the kitchen door was left open and I saw the tall stack of Campbell's Cream of Chicken soup and one of the cooks opening the can. That burst our bubble. I spent a lot of time at the American Club in St. George's building, and it was really cool when my Dad was president of the club. Go Dad. Dad and I also went to the weekly football games at the Chuck Wagon. Rocky would see us coming, having already poured my Dad's ice tea and my coke, and our cheese burgers and fries would be served about 5 minutes after we arrived.

We loved the Sunday brunch after church, steaks at the Grill, green goddess dressing, Thanksgiving, Maine Lobster night, dinner and play nights, the Filipino guitar player, Cotillion, and hanging out with friends. Then they started flying over Dryer's ice cream. Locky load was the favorite. Eventually a store on Kowloon side imported it, and then it made it to Park 'n Shop. American salad was a riot: a wedge of iceberg lettuce, flown over from the states of course.

Some guy in the American Club arranged for a friend in the States to tape the game and gave the tape to a pilot friend who had the HK route. The best part were the commercials, a link to what was going on in the States. One time, they arrived without the commercials and everyone threw a fit. We found out that the guy taping thought he would be nice and paused during all the commercials! Got him to quit that pretty quick! The super bowl was the best, everyone had divided up on their favorite side and the game began!

Barb Schwerdtman '68-'77

I remember once when my father confronted me with the bills from the American Club and the Country Club. They were something like $5000 apiece for one month. I nonchalantly replied, "Those must be YOUR bills, Dad." To which he replied, "I don't even GO to those clubs, I only go to the Jockey Club!". Yikes! *Kelvin Limm '79*

One major surprise was having a club sandwich at the American Club, and having it contain ox tongue! *Dave Porter '73*

•HK Country Club

My friends and I spent loads of time there, bowling, swimming, squash with Renee, tennis, parties, dances, great Chinese food, and almond pancake crepes. A kid's dream set up. Just sign the chit for anything you wanted. Getting my high bowling game at my birthday party, 205 - took 20 years to beat it! *Barb Schwerdtman '77*

A group of us would organize tram parties (ten dollars Hong Kong a person) and it would be a wild night. I remember one time Michele Disney and I jumping off because we had to use a bathroom and then running like maniacs to get back on the tram. Fights would break out (in Wanchai and once in front of the Bull and Bear). Kids would be running for their lives (looking for taxis mainly) but a few of the brave would stay and fight it out. *Linda Reizman '80*

Circa 1981. Henry Hamel was riding the last #6 bus back from Central (around midnight). On the bus were some locals who were looking for a fight and chose Henry as a target. Henry managed to keep things calm, but was very worried about what might happen to him when he got off the bus at the dark and remote Chung Hom Kok stop. Luck was with Henry that night as who should get on the bus in Repulse Bay? None other than his 6' 3" 190 pound friend, Wally Tuchardt. Henry describes the story as having heard the "Hymn of the Val Kyrie" as Wally walked toward him on the bus while the would be fighters scattered.

Circa 1975? Mark Wallis and Rev. Paul Tuchardt getting up at 4:00am to be the first and second consumers of the first McDonalds hamburgers ever served in SE Asia (Causeway Bay). *Wally Tuchardt '73-'81*

•CYF - Christian Youth Fellowship

C.Y.F. met in Kowloon Tong, usually at the house of one of the missionaries. I attended these clubs from around age 5 through high school. The different age groups had different names - Joy Club, Sentinels, Crusaders, CYF. I remember Mr. Bauman reading us "The Cross and the Switchblade". We often would ride the #7 bus downtown after the meeting to have some more fun. *Debbie Noren '73*

CYF met on Friday nights at Kowloon Tong. Julie Whitehill was the one who got us to go. *Ken Koo '79*

Adventures in the Colony - Annual Walk for a Million Trek. That was way fun. Eating out was a big part of Hong Kong. Favorite Chinese restaurant was the American and the New American restaurants. Peacock and Pheasant in the early years, Kingbo - Kingsburg for dim sum, Luigis for meatball pizza, and the clubs, see below.

Going to Alison Gilbertson's birthday party on their boat and while we were all swimming off the boat, a bunch of jellyfish came up under us and I was stung all over my legs and stomach. They made me jump back in the water to help neutralize the sting, I really didn't want to go back in but finally did. That or urine, water won out when they presented the alternative.

Wanchai, Seeing the soldiers throw up all

over the street all the time during the Vietnam war. All the lights I could see from my apartment on Magazine Gap. I took tons of time-lapse pictures from my bedroom and the lights were wonderful.

Kowloon, taking second-class on the Star Ferry, wiggling our way up to the front and running down the gangplank. Best times were during a typhoon and it was really choppy. Messing around in the Ocean Terminal, Mrs. Wong organizing a special lunch for us after bowling that had octopus tentacle bits in it, which grossed everyone out, so no one ate it. I think it was at the Oceania restaurant.

Field trips, 5th grade field trip to the Coral Sea, getting a hat, sitting in the plane that was really cool.

Trekking all over the islands with Mr. Von-Behren. Painting the Glory Boat, singing at the TB hospitals all of the other places with choir. Macau's Ready to Wear Festival.

Our camp, can't remember if it was 6th grade or Junior High, but rolling what seemed like a million meatballs with Mrs. Hotung.

Worst Field trip - Peng Chau (I think), a bus took us to a beach and left us there all day. Some kid (yes, I remember who) dumped out my sunscreen as a joke, so I stayed in the water all day so I wouldn't get burned. My face and shoulders were so badly burned, I had to stay off school for a week and now I can't be out in the sun much at all. Not a highlight. *Barb Schwerdtman. '68-'77*

3. Wanchai

I have lots of memories of basketball games against Navy teams. A vivid one was the damage done to the rims by those teams dunking during warm-ups, half-time, and during the games. By the time the game was done the rims were no longer level, or even close. Always amazed me too that there seemed to be a token white guy on those Navy teams.

As athletic director I ended up over at Kowloon Sports getting custom rims made with supports welded under the rims to keep them level during the dunk fests. Good move, except that Andrew Ellis ended up sliding his hand down one of those supports when he was dunking at the end of a PE class and ended up with three fingers sliced. *Fritz Voeltz '73-'80; '96 -'03*

When the USS Enterprise was in HK, the Varsity B Ball Team got go on a tour of the ship. At that time there were approximately 5,000 troops on board, including Marines.

The Varsity used to play the teams from whatever ship was in port. We usually played twice a week. This was our best competition, we only had one true Chinese School rival LingNan. The team from the USS Oklahoma City could have beaten some college teams. It was quite a sight seeing the "Cheerleaders" that they brought from Wan Chai. The sailors couldn't wait to get back to their true R & R. *Steve Koch '75*

When we played basketball in Wan Chai on the outdoor courts. The 'out-of-bounds' was defined by the crowds of local Chinese spectators who ringed the court, 3 or 4 deep, right up to the line. If the ball hit the crowd, it was out of bounds! *Scott Schroth '77*

Anyone remember the Red Lips Bar in TST ? It's still there as are the toothless wonders who's apparently been working there for the last 4 decades *Ken Koo '79*

In Wanchai, there was both a Nebraska Bar and a California Bar...isn't the Calif where Chris Myers used to keep a change of street clothes? I remember he would take the bus down to Wanchai after school, and change into his wanchai duds, then carouse Lockhardt Road. I learned "fai jai" ("fat boy") from him, named after one of the Calif Bar waiters.

Once a year, some of the male faculty would take a "wonton walk thru Wanchai" just to say we had done it. Once we did this in January when a ship was in...And we went into some Suzie Wong place where two little bare topped Chinese girls were huddling round a kerosene space heater. Their goose bumps were larger than their mammaries. Memories? Hmmmmm

But, Scotchman that I was, I could not bring myself to waste a HK$ 100 bill on a watery glass of orange juice to keep the mama-san happy. *Dave Kohl, teacher '73-'80*

The Suzie Wong was nothing special. I recall having a beer there with a group of HKIS folks and these old Mama sans without teeth would try to catch your attention. *Ian Goepfert '80*

ADVENTURES IN HK

Lan Kwai Fong was/is good fun, but sedate compared to Wan Chai on a weekend in the mid seventies when ten US Navy ships were in town from Vietnam for R&R. The Front Page had a good house band and there were usually a couple of well known musicians passing through at any given time. Things really started to pick up after midnight. *Mike McCormick '80*

We had such freedom and innocence in those days. In my senior year ('78) I went to classes in the morning, tutored English in the afternoons and frequented the clubs at night. I remember some of us would go to the bars near The American Club and dance disco. We would do the bump and tantalize the Japanese businessmen, get them to buy us drinks and food, then just leave then with their mouths hangin' open. Oh.... we felt such power! *Cindi Webb '78*

One time I remember being down in Wanchai with Colleen Fogarty and we were down there to go to the Levi's store or something and along came some American sailors. We were friendly and smiled back at them. They came over to talk to us and right then it became apparent that they were looking for some SERIOUS fun!! We seemed to be way in over our heads. I don't remember how we got out of that one! *Sally Lawton '77*

As high schoolers, Seanna Laughlin and her twin brother, Mike, and his friends, and I frequented the pool hall and billiard rooms and bars. (My parents had no clue what we were doing, and I never fessed up.) I remember someone breaking a beer bottle to fight with and Seanna and I quickly slipped out the back. Pool is still a favorite game of mine to this day! The bars and nightclubs always wanted more girls in them, (so many men on R&R) so we never had to pay a cover charge. I always felt safe with the "boys" around and we saw some pretty awesome shows for free. One was pretty raunchy (involving animals), but we just left. As I recall, we had to drag the guys out...

One night we were together as a group at a nightclub and an American soldier (or sailor?) asked me to dance. I accepted and he was a beautiful dancer. We were PERFECTLY in sync. (OK, it was a slow dance.) At the end of the song, he whispered in my ear, "How much do you charge?" I was so dumfounded that I didn't say a word, walked back to the table, and told everyone there what happened. Wow, was I naive.

Seanna and I once met a U.S. fighter pilot on the street, during the day. He asked directions and we hit it off. He was only 1 year older than we were (?) and he was on R&R from Vietnam. He never talked about the war, even though we asked. We had a great time taking him to Ladder Street, (or was it Cat St.?), touring HK and hanging out. He even requested to return to HK the following year for R&R and we met up again. He was from the USS Kitty Hawk, which was the largest aircraft carrier at the time in the US Navy. He gave us a private tour of the boat and they announced by loudspeaker "women on deck" to make sure the men were all clothed. After reading "The Things They Carried," I have a better appreciation for why he totally wanted to escape talking about Vietnam, and just wanted to be around normal American girls. We did have a blast, and it was all very innocent.

I never felt scared, because we knew HK like the back of our hand, knew enough Chinese language to get by, and felt it was home. I take that back. I did feel scared once. A filthy homeless guy came up behind me, in broad daylight, and put his arms tightly around me, pinning my arms down. I froze and we stood there like that for a long 10 seconds. The streets were full of people AND NO ONE DID ANYTHING.

He released me and I ran for the Hilltop Apt. mini bus got on and was shaking all over. I have since been aware of my surroundings at all times, esp. when I am in Chicago.

Rebecca Luedtke, '66-'72

My sister Sheila and I got tattoos on one of our last nights in HK before we moved. A final act of rebellion - I thought it was the perfect souvenir. *Julia Baker '84*

Star Bowl over at Star House; the American Pool next to the Central police station; Thingumees; I'll bet the rugby guys remember that one. Mickey-D's first foray into Asia and Kevin Keimig's memorable and impeccable timing in "answering" the question "What do you think of McDonald's hamburgers ?". "It tastes like s--t"! *Kelvin Limm '79*

Who could forget the filthy delicious hawker stalls in Wanchai. At 4 a.m. drunk as skunks trying to balance atop the planks with those tiny little stools (so the lo shiu wouldn't scurry over your feet). In the wintertime, collars were pulled up, electrical lines dangling from the flats above jaffed, twisting down to the 11pm to 5am hawker stall. The roof covering and the sides of the stall were propped up with sticks of bamboo. The delicious brisket w/ egg noodels, the wiff of allspices, garbage, booze, burnt wiring and sparks cascading from above... ah the times of youth....lucky we had strong stomachs and immune systems back then. God, I would love a bowl of it now.

Richard Vaughn '72

I have not forgotten those Dai Pai Dongs (food stalls) were mostly located right next to a public lavatory. They were, indeed! So, besides the allspices, garbage, booze, burnt wiring you also had those incense smells that the Dai Pai Dong owners were burning. The incenses was for their ground & stove gods. However, no more hawkers by the lavatories in Hong Kong. They are all now centralized at certain buildings.

In fact, at the Dai Pai Dong, they are still serving the egg noodles with the briskets, which is on the dry side, top with oyster sauce, add a little oil, garnish with Choy Sum. Boy, that stuff goes down slowly and killing you so softly, remember?

The Won Ton Mein, ooh. I used to dream of it when I was going to school in Chicago when the wind was howling with the wind chill factors at -45 degrees outside. Frost and crystals were formed on the windows. I wished someone would deliver a bowl of that stuff to my bedside. Maybe we can flag a cab down, you can tell the driver to make a brief stop at Jaffe Rd., then I can tell him head to Kowloon side to the Temple St., at Yau Ma Tei where the night starts around this time.

Dream on!! *Gabe Lau '77*

4. Outdoor Adventures

• Hiking

One of the cool things about growing up in a city like Hong Kong is that, while it is densely populated, it is not a concentrated city. You have the downtown central district, Kowloon, Aberdeen, but then you have the beaches, the islands, the mountains and those great mountain trails. I used to walk with my family and my dog along Bowen Path when we lived at Woodland Heights and then up around the Peak when we lived up there. I loved hiking the Walk for a Million each year. I used to like going hiking up in the mountains above Repulse Bay with my friends – no-one would ever know what we were up to. We used to hang out in the pillboxes left over from the Second World War. Mr. Sorenson took us on all manner of cool hikes all over HK and the New Territories when we were training for our Nepal trip. I remember once his girlfriend came (I can't remember her name, but she was really nice) and she hiked with us for a few hours – in high heels! Really high heels! I was very impressed.

Sheila Baker '82

Tim Schmidt and Henry Hamel were detained at a random immigration checkpoint on Wong Nei Chong Gap Rd for not carrying their HK ID cards. Neither set of parents could be reached so Henry instructed his brother to find his card and then hike down to Stanley from Chung Hom Kok, find the Schmidt's hidden key and dig up Tim's card. Walt and Lois were very surprised when they came home to find Jimmy Hamel rifling through Tim's room to find Tim's ID card.

Wally Tuchardt, '73-'81

Behind our flat on Bowen Road (Baht ho say Bowan Do) rose a steep wall of earth and vegetation. A surprising number of acres were free of habitation (this being the mid-levels). I enjoyed exploring this area and would encounter a number of frightening species of bugs, lizards and snakes. Of the plant life I can say little save for that it was lush enough, creepers, giant leafed bushes, tangly masses of branches. Total privacy was available, looking upwards one could just make out the outlines of the adjacent `Borret Mansions.' Best of all were the sweeping lines of concrete water culverts, which meandered across the hillside to collect up the monsoon rains. *Eric Allen '76*

More significant to a 12-year-old boy, the hillside across the street had real bunkers and tunnels that had been used twenty years earlier, first by the British and then the Japanese armies. The adults didn't really want us playing in them...but how could you stop a bunch of junior high boys? The marvels kept coming: you could buy all sorts of plastic toys (most seemed to be James Bond-type guns) that were cheap, and at Chinese New Years, we could buy bags full of powerful firecrackers for just a few dollars (before they were banned due to the mayhem caused by the Cultural Revolution). We spent summer sailing a Sunfish on Repulse Bay and snorkeling around the islands at the end of South Bay. It seemed like paradise to me.

Scott Lazenby '72

It was great, exploring the caves and old army batteries in the Hills over Poshan Rd and various other places around HK Island. What an adventure of the imagination that was for 11 & 12 year olds.

Gavin Birnie '75

My Dad was the Air Attaché at the Embassy. Col. Webb. We lived up near the peak in a two building complex. Nice large apartment. There was a path under the parking pad that led down the mountain to the city below. Along the way you would find small temples, possibly graves. The path was like a jungle. I loved that walk. A few people would jog it, but mostly it was a silent walk down... maybe a mile? At our apartment building we had a guard and his own shack. He got so tired of us wanting to use his phone to call cabs that he finally gave me a key to it. I still have that key today. It is an old brass skeleton key type.

Cindi Webb '78

Shortly after we arrived, Hong Kong hosted a "round the island walking race" that attracted international race walkers. We watched some of the walkers in the Repulse Bay area, and then, that evening, drove to one of the Happy Valley stadiums to watch the finish. As far as I know, that event never happened again.

Dave Christian '69

How about playing Tarzan (or Spiderman) on the bamboo scaffolding and enormous sand piles of a hundred different building construction sites, ... or exploring the caves on Mt. Butler and Mt. Davis, and writing our own history of their creation (I was convinced for years that the cave above Black's Link went to the center of the earth).

David Vaughn '69

•Bicycles and Cyclo-cross

Nowadays the common name for off road bicycling is mountain biking but back in the 70s it was called cyclo-cross. There wasn't the specialized equipment that is around today and the fun of the sport was just to see how far one could go on a bicycle without crashing or having to touch your feet on the ground. John Lazenby, John Korteum, and I used to ride our bicycles up on the hillside after school and follow the catchments around to the reservoir or up towards Stanley Village area. We even rode in the rain to make it even more challenging. It was really amazing to learn how far one could get in an afternoon of bicycling following some tricky beaten trails to who knew where. There were some very spectacular views of Repulse Bay, the hotel, Deepwater Bay, and the Chung Hom Kok Headland from the trails we rode on. I don't think anyone took any real nasty spills but I know we had some really fun afternoons up on the hillside above the school.

Eric Lee '75

I was active as a leader of Cub Scout Pack # 1 in Hong Kong. We had various outings. One time we took all the Cub Scouts and their fathers if they could go to Lantau Island for a weekend camping trip. We went on a Friday afternoon.

On Saturdays, to have some fun a number of us rented bicycles to take a trip around the island or at least part of it. As you got away from the beach the terrain got to be fairly steep but they had little concrete walkways, equal to say a small sidewalk in the US. As these paved passage ways wound through rice paddies on either side you had to steer your bicycle with some level of expertise.

On one of the last stretches one of our faculty members who had accompanied me with his son and mine missed a turn and went face first with the bicycle as well into one of the rice paddies. They had about two feet of water in them. The faculty member was not a happy camper to have gotten soaked. However, the Chinese farmer was less happy and started to chase us with his hoe. He had been in the paddy working his rice crop. Needless to say we did not do any additional bicycle riding.

Ed Dollase, first Business Manager

•Skateboards

We loved skateboarding Stubbs Road, all the way from Magazine Gap to the Sikh Temple at Queen's Road East (gravity played a part here, too). We'd also put on raincoats in pre-typhoon weather (signal 3), and used them to land-sail skateboards at breakneck speed down the wind tunnel behind Repulse Bay Towers (never walk when you can ride).   *David Vaughn '69*

Keith Challberg would skateboard down Repulse Bay Road from Wong Nei Chong Gap all the way to The Hotel, very late at night.
                                            Wally Tuchardt '81

My brother Johnny was a member of the Peak Riders club, which included Mike Heeney, Bog Tan, Gary Coonan, Chris Thorne and Mike Roth. They introduced skateboarding to Hong Kong in a scary way. They would luge down from the Peak and make it all the way down to Central while avoiding cars, buses and taxis without getting run over. Now that was a miracle! The police were called numerous times, but they were never caught because they were all fast runners. A couple of times Ian Goepfert would drive Gary Coonan's Mercedes and I would clock them to see how fast they were going. The car was going 40 mph so I can't believe they survived Peak riding without major injuries!   *Linda Reizman '80*

• Missioning - Adventures off the Beaten Path

Mary Chen ('98 and teacher '02-'03) and I used to go on adventures. We both majored in geology at some point in time – because we love being outside – so you can imagine what kind of things we got in our heads to do – missioning – a term that an in-country interim leader in Nepal used for going on adventures off the beaten path. Mary and I adopted the term for our adventures. Two particular ones come to mind.

Once we got senior privileges with the quasi-open campus at Tai Tam (we could leave and return once during a class period), Mary and I decided that when we had long lunch periods because we had a free adjacent to lunch, we were going to go have lunch in Tai Tam Country Park.

So, the first day that we had this amazing long lunch set up, we hiked down to the field, past the guard station, across the street, and into the park. We walked into the park to the first big picnic and playground area and looked for a place to eat. Quickly we both came to the same conclusion. The best and most obvious place to eat was in the beautiful big tree in the middle of the picnic area. So,

we climbed up in the tree, arranged ourselves comfortably and started eating lunch. We regularly went and had our picnic in the tree. Over time we developed a code for different things that might have to be handed or moved around in the tree. The tree was item 0, Amanda's lunch item 1, Mary's lunch item 2, a backpack item 3, Amanda item 4, Mary item 5, and so on. We had at least 10 or 12 items.

The other missioning experience we had happened less often and started in a less pre-meditated fashion. One day we decided to go on a run after school. The plan was that we would go do the jungle run in the country park and then catch the 4:20 bus. About halfway through the run we crossed a bridge and stopped to look at the beautiful pool at the bottom of a nearby waterfall. We looked over the rocks, looked at each other, and one of us said "I don't mind getting wet, do you mind getting wet?" and we were off. We down climbed the waterfall, swam across the pool with our shoes and t-shirts held over our heads (Mary had on a swim suit and shorts, I had on a sports bra and shorts), and climbed out the other side. As I remember it, we both ended up with socks and shirts tucked into the waistband of our shorts and shoes on with no socks. It was probably February, so the water level was high in the river we were now following and the banks quite muddy.

Mary started to get a bit hysterical about the adventure we were on and since we had just finished college apps, she was composing college essays out loud as we went. As I remember it, one was about rationality. Item 5 was rational, item 4 was never rational. At this particular time, item 5 was being particularly rational and item 4 was being particularly irrational. Eventually the two of us made it back to the banks of the reservoir (we never actually went in the reservoir itself) and climbed back onto the main paved road in the park.

About ten minutes later, we ran into Mr. and Mrs. Voeltz taking a walk. We looked at them and they looked at us. Mrs. Voeltz said something along the lines of "we won't ask" and we kept going in our respective directions. Mary and I made it back barely in time for the 5:15 bus. The next day I ran in to Mrs. Voeltz first thing in morning and she looked at me and commented, "I see you are clean and dry now." Nothing was said about this experience until today (20 April 2007) when Mrs. Voeltz and I started talking about this book.

We repeated the missioning adventure a few more times that year and again when Mary taught at HKIS. *Amanda Henck '98*

4. Exploring the Outlying Islands

"We took a special chartered ferry to Hay Ling Chau, an island nearby where the joint council of churches of HK run a leprosarium (leper colony). There is no regular ferry service to this island, so this was a special opportunity. They have open house once a year, and we were invited since we're members of Church of All Nations. Bill Mahlke was our guide, as he's worked with them before. The day was beautiful and the island as picturesque as possible. You could see back to Hong Kong, and out to Lantau and other islands. The leprosy business was spooky (I suppose because of all the biblical images), but not eerie. People there were in different stages of the disease, some quite old, some confined to hospital beds, but most living and working in little communes, taking care of themselves. Many of the inmates there do handicrafts, which were for sale, so we got some very nice and quite inexpensive items.

Last Saturday, we got up at 6 am and took the bus to the outlying ferry pier and caught the early boat for Cheung Chau, an island near Lantau. It was super. The island has one very Chinese village on it, which had a full Saturday market going (we later bought fruit, eggs, fish, and some greens). We walked through the village, amongst fishermen's shacks and grazing chickens. Then we walked around the hills of the southern part of the island, finding a resettlement village built by CARE, another built by Lutherans, and a picturesque isolated farmer's settlement and terraced fields, where the families were out watering, weeding, and picking greens to haul to market. The scene, needless to say, was idyllic. We later walked back into "town" and found a quiet semi-deserted beach. At the far end of the beach was the island dump, where I spotted an old brown Chinese crockery storage jug. I've been looking for one since we got here, and this one was perfect - no chips or anything, so I liberated it, cleaned it out in the ocean, and hauled it back on the ferry and bus. Katy thinks I'm a little nuts...but the jug makes a great table base. *Dave Kohl, art teacher, '73-'80*

•The Lantau Cabin

The primary group my family belonged to was the Methodist Church. The other missionary families became our 'relatives.' Unlike most of the mothers of my classmates, my mother actually had a job. Our group had a house on Cheung Chau and a couple of times a year we would go there en masse. We ran all over that island, exploring the smugglers cave and the Japanese caves. We would salvage driftwood and have fires at night. There was a small orphanage next door and we would play with those kids.

Through our brethren in the English Methodist church we had access to a cabin (#8) on Lantau. The journey was made by ferry, then cab to the base of the mountain, then a very long semi-vertical hike. In the mountains it was very cool up there in the summer. Our recreation consisted of an icy cold fresh water pool and running around. Virtually all of the cabins were owned by one church group or another, so all of the residents were missionaries. Church services were a very big deal and the slightest medical problem was treated by several doctors. We all ate together. Luggage and groceries were transported by coolie women. These women appeared to be quite elderly, mouths full of gold teeth and jade bracelets on their wrists. They jogged up the mountain, stopping only to smoke at the top before heading back down. *Mark McIntosh '73*

"Tim Harvey, one of my senior students, invited me to hike along with him up to the top of Lan Tau peak. It's the biggest island in the Colony, and totally under populated. We took a ferry to another island (Cheung Chau), which went on to Lan Tau. Tim was carrying a home-made wooden backpack, made up of 2 x 4 wood, holding what must have been a 30-gallon drum of kerosene, to be used for cooking and lighting fuel in the cabins atop the island.

The trail was steep, rocky, and just clung to the side of the mountain. There are only a few villages on Lan Tau, so there were no people anywhere, and the landscape, views of the water as we climbed higher, and finally the vista of China and Macau were really breath-taking - picture postcard stuff!

Tim must be some sort of half-breed pack animal/coolie - he easily had at least 200 lbs on his back. Guess he did this almost everyday during the summer, and has done so for a few years, since the cabins are owned by the Baptist Mission his dad is part of." *Dave Kohl, art teacher '73-'80, letter 1973*

Our mission group (United Church of Christ -- one of those liberal ones) comprised the Whiteheads, Whiteners and Whitehills! (And also the Bergmanns and Carl Smith). We owned Cabin 9 and Cabin 13 on Lantau. It was Cabin 13, which was sold to HKIS. *Tara Whitehill '75*

My favorite place of all was camping in the cabins up on Lantau.

That's where I was always homesick for when I was in college. And to think of the airplanes and develop out there now. *Linda Schock '77*

The guys took camping trips to Lantao and the girls would get kicked off the island as girls weren't allowed to spend the night – and the mysterious disappearance of my sweatshirt once.
Renee Doyle '78

God what great memories of camping there in the 60's, I too had a salamander from the pool. The American Women's Assoc. organized Treks and we would be taken up the mountain by 2 teenage US sons, one w/ a giant machete w/ the famous Knotch in the handle...a "rabid" dog had attacked the group and he had to put it down to save them, or so the story went, 20 kids and 2 teenagers cost per kid HK$20.00. What a deal. Kick the can, storm the fort, recover the flag, ghost stories, and "the runs" from drinking pond water (probably would kill us today), we didn't care we were young and it was fun, life was great.
Rich Vaughn '72

The school owned cabin 13 on top of Lantau for many years. Dad and I frequently camped there and were pretty much always working on a project with it. I remember a number of trips... Our first, and I believe last trip my Mom took... One where my Dad actually brought a new inner door and frame up... There was an outcropping of rocks in the back of the cabin that I used to love to climb on... Also one at a friends' cabin called Cathedral rock if I recall correctly. Good times.

Some times the fog was so thick you could barely even see your own feet.

I remember the cow paddies, the 'pool', and

the walks back down in pouring rain. Being up there in bad storms. Fond memories.
Jason Weber '97

The natural rock pools out near the beach we frequented in Lantau were unforgettable.
Sheila Baker '82

Mr. Kohl took a bunch of us camping overnight on a beach on Lantau. What an amazing thing it was to sleep on the sand in our bathing suits, then wake up with the sun and walk right into the ocean. *Joan Amy '80*

Life in Hong Kong continued to offer excitement apart from school events. I recall many trips out to "Long White Beach" on Lantau Island. We'd take a ferry to Silvermine Bay and then board a public bus to the almost always-deserted beach. Lantau was not at all developed at that time, and from those untouched white sands, civilization seemed pretty distant. *Dave Christian '69*

• Lantau Thanksgiving

Earl and Marge Westrick invited Katy and myself to join their family for Thanksgiving, our first year, 1973. They had an idea about going camping over the four-day holiday and cooking and feasting on an American turkey on a beach on Lantau. What a great idea!!! Unfortunately, we had already committed to going to Macau with several other of the new teachers and had to decline Westrick's offer. But, we said, "for sure next year"

Comes Thanksgiving 1974 and Westricks plan the event again, including us, plus new teachers Mary Kaye Heissler and Norma Schroeder. We spent an evening at Westricks having a chili supper, planning the meals - who would bring and fix what, and each "family unit" took responsibility for a particular meal. The centerpiece was, of course, the American turkey, to be cooked by Earl. I love turkey stew, so we volunteered to make the leftover stew the next day, plus we'd do breakfast on Saturday.

Bright and early Thanksgiving morning, we meet at the Outlying Ferries Pier, tents, sleeping bags, food, and beach paraphernalia in hand. At Silvermine Bay this stuff is transferred into the light bus bound for Po Lin. Our destination, scouted a week earlier by several of the Westrick boys, was Tong Fuk, a pristine stretch of sand facing the channel where you can see the Macau hydrofoils go by. It is truly idyllic. There's a store a mile back, a waterfall and creek flowing into the sand, and a fair bit of driftwood for the campfires.

Setting up included digging a latrine behind some bushes down wind from the camping area. Earl located several large stones and reinforced a fire pit. Tables for drinks and snacks were set up. The day was spent tending the fire to cook the turkey, wrapped in four layers of foil. Other food items were cooked on a separate fire. When time came to eat, it was superb tender turkey, lots of side dishes, olives of course, and pumpkin pies for dessert, accompanied by a fine Australian wine. Later that night, picking turkey scraps off the bone and s'mores.

The remainder of the 3 days was spent basking in wonderful sunshine, hiking up the falls, building sandcastles, swimming, consuming a fair amount of San Miguel, taking lots of photos, and being generally indolent. Camelot, paradise, and sunburn, rolled into one. We came back so relaxed. Having taken lots of photos, we decided to have a viewing night a few weeks later. Everyone brought their slides, Westricks invited a few other faculty over, and we porked out on banana splits.

Word spread of our unique outing, and more folks were invited to join us the next year. Twenty-five campers in 1975. In 1976, there were about 40, including our 6-week old son Adam, who was quite content to sleep in a cardboard box in our tent. With succeeding years, the number eventually reached about 100, with more elaborate planning, and hiring lorries to take all the luggage to the beach. But the chili planning supper and the banana split slide show evenings remained part of the tradition. *Dave Kohl, art faculty '73 - '80*

Tong Fuk Thanksgiving circa 1980 was a disaster. Gale force winds from the sudden on-set of a monsoon brought down all tents and caused practically every food item to be "seasoned" with sand. The gathering had to retreat to the 4th floor cafeteria where turkey stew (with a hint of grit) was served. *Wally Tuchardt '81*

I used to live for the weekends because there was always something to do in Hong Kong. One of my favorite outings was going to Lantau. A group of us would bring beer, food and of course, smoking material. The guys would have to carry the heavy stuff, like camping gear, because we would camp out on the beach.

I'll never forget the one weekend that we got caught in a typhoon. Our tents were lost at sea after being blown around and everyone had to scramble for cover. The storm started getting worse and worse so Julie Schornstein and I found refuge in a small telephone booth. My brother and his friend Chris Thorne were drenched and hopping up and down begging us to let them into the phone booth, but we wouldn't let them in because it was just too small for four people. They were mad at us for days after that. *Linda Reizman '80*

All the overnight camping trips to the islands! All we did was drink beer, wine and smoke cigars. Funny thing was, all the parents knew what was going on but still allowed us to go. I guess they thought it was an opportunity to explode and explore without anyone around. *John Morris '76*

6. In the Fragrant Waters

I was out on a boat with Diane Adcock and her family when the QE 1 was on fire. We saw the smoke and went closer to see where it was coming from. It's amazing to think we were right there for such an historic event. *Wendy Liddiard '73*

Big Wave Bay was a popular destination for those of us who wanted to body surf or surf during typhoon warnings. The lifeguards would yell at us to get out of the water but we would stay out and ride the waves because they were too afraid to come to and get us. Besides the fact that most of us couldn't hear or understand them. During the wintertime, the water was cold, a wetsuit helped to stay out longer and there were NO lifeguards to yell at us. *Eric Lee '75*

The waves at Big Wave were much better than Shek-O or any other beach that I remember there. I remember body surfing there many times. Just about got myself killed a couple of times too. The waves here on the East Coast of the US seem positively tame compared to the waves on that beach, and they tend to close the beaches when the surf picks up because of the rip currents that develop. *Mark Woodruff '77*

Eric and David Lee, Tony Espro, and I surfed Big Wave Bay. Tom O'Sullivan and Pete Sullivan sometimes bodysurfed Big Wave Bay and Shek-O while I surfed. I loved how no other people ventured into the water at those times.

I remember once when our family once took our boat out to Big Wave Bay and anchored farther out so I could drop into the water for the outside sets. That was awesome. And to think, Master Surfer, Gerry Lopez, took a team of pro surfers from Hawaii to Big Wave Bay at the wrong time of year and deemed the place "a loser". All the better for us. *Kelvin Limm '79*

My sisters and I body surfed Big Wave Bay many times. I don't know if anyone remembers the Hoelsher's, they weren't in HK very long. They were neighbors in the same flat complex at 6 South Bay Close and we would go out to Big Wave Bay regularly to get sunburned, tumbled and jostled around in the waves. *Diane Kasala '73*

There were two times that I found myself swimming in the polluted waters of HK. Once Gregg Saunders and I had to swim the channel to pull our boat up when a typhoon threatened. The normal sampan rides (walla wallas) were shutdown so we took my surfboards and paddled across. The current was swift and the stench was horrible. I guess the current varied according to the tide and at that time it was running from Repulse Bay to Deep Bay. The current carried the sewer discharge through the channel.

The other time I went swimming in the toilet was when Gregg and I were out in HK harbor in a sailing regatta about this same time of year. I think we launched from the HK Yacht Club and I walked into the water and jumped into the boat when the smell got really bad. Each time I was out on the trapeze I tried to get dunked to wash off the smell. It never went away and I think we came in last. Sorry Gregg, I couldn't stand the thought that went with the odor, I could relay many stories about diving and underwater discoveries but I think save them for later. *Eric Lee '75*

•Sailing

I'm laying in the sun on the beach a picture-perfect near-tropical island somewhere off the coast of the New Territories. There is no one around. I am watching a fleet of small sailboats and waiting for the delivery of a group of middle school students I will supervise as they mess around in boats. I'm getting paid for this! This is one of my all-time favorite memories.

HKIS was the source of a lot of favorite memories. There was the year I "taught sailing" during the interim week but it was so windy we could never leave the shore. Instead we practiced outdoor cooking at Middle Island for five days in a row. On the last day I rigged one boat to go out, just to see if sailing was possible, and instead performed a graphic demonstration of righting a capsized boat for all my students.
Kathy Isaacs, teacher '73-'78

We would go sailing at the VRC and taking our VJ's out when the typhoon signals were at 3, returning later and no boat boys to help bring in the boats. "Sun ging gwai lohs" they would call us. Big brother Dave and I once snapped a mast in a gust coming in and almost lost it all in the surf that came up. Big trouble for that one when we got caught. Dave rescued the VJ but got badly cut from the barnacles and guy wires that got tangled in the rocks and sails. *Rich Vaughn '72*

Diane Kasala was an instrumental influence in my life, teaching me basic sailing in the old Bosuns. I remember Diane had a harp and I think she had it on her parent's boat. The first song I learned while in HK, Don MacLean's Miss American Pie, was one we heard a lot when we went to the sailing locker. I was often out on the Lazenby's sailboat in the Lamma Channel.

Gregg Saunders and I spent many Saturdays at the Yacht Club on a yellow 505 that we repainted orange and renamed it "Ripoff". We worked on the hull and got it ready to launch. That was an International 505 Class built in 1963. I had purchased my half from Eric Redheffer before he left. It was a great boat to sail in. I'd like to buy another one.

I remember the first time I heard the Noon Day Gun by the Yacht Club. I was walking from the bus stop to the RHKYC to meet Gregg for an afternoon sail when they fired the damn thing. Scared the S*** out of me. No one had told me about that thing! The last time I heard that gun was the day we left HK to tour China in 1975.
Eric Lee '75

153

Eric and I had to come up with something catchy for a name and we did spend some good money to keep "Ripoff" running. We had our fair share of fun with that 505 that we were constantly working on. He built the rudder and I did a centerboard and wow, they actually did the job well (his was better!). What great days. But the truth be told, was there any place better to be than out on any type of water craft in Hong Kong?

Racing sailboats on Saturday with Eric (great times and memories!) and then cruising with the Ketterer's or someone else that had a good boat to go out to Llama and veg for the day, eat great food at the restaurants along the water front, and listen to American Top 40 and catch up the happenings all the way back in the States. Then it was back home, nicely sun burned and getting ready to go to school on Monday. *Gregg Saunders '75*

I often ran into Eric Lee and Gregg Saunders on Saturdays down at the yacht club. What were those funny boats you used to sail? Hobie Cats? Or Sunfish, or something like that. I remember Hillard Ranta taught basic sailing with Walt Schmidt to faculty in Stanley at some club there. At least I learned how to tack and got a Helmsman's Certificate, which I practiced once under the Golden Gate Bridge on a friend's 45' Inca class.
Dave Kohl, art teacher '73-'80

Interim circa 1981: A weeklong excursion aboard the Huan sailing junk proved to be quite an adventure. A mid-week storm came up and made it necessary for the Huan to seek safe harbor. The main sail was badly damaged and had to be brought down. In doing so, the ship was destabilized causing most of the people on board to become sea sick. At the same time, Brad Westrick and Wally Tuchardt were below decks (seasoned Huan crew members from years past) preparing, of all things, tuna fish sandwiches for lunch. Just as the ship began to enter calmer waters, Brad brought a whole platter of sandwiches above deck whereupon the tops of the sandwiches were blown completely off by the wind and the odor of tuna fish salad caused another wave of nausea.
Wally Tuchardt '81

The HK School Sailing Association owned bosuns that HKIS used. They were about 16-18'. The bosun is the class of small boat. The school later purchased 6 Otters; they were about 12-14'.

We sailed them over to Wu Kai Sha and taught sailing at the Y camp there in the NT. Over and back was quite a hair-raising journey
Walt Schmidt, PE teacher '72-'83

I used to go and help with the 6th grade and Jr. High camps and learned to sail with Kris Schmidt, that and kyaking!
Barb Schwerdtmann '77

•Drama on the high seas - A notable dinner party:

Paul Carlton, the high school math teacher, arrived in 1971. He married Becky Raborn, the elementary music teacher, at Christmas in 1973. Sometime after that, Paul bought into a small pleasure junk, which I think he kept moored in Aberdeen, maybe at the ABC near Ap Lei Chau. I don't remember who the co-owner was, but he spent a lot of time working on it, fixing it up, and sailing on weekends. He also had led auto shop type activities with students, so he was pretty mechanical.

So one evening, he and Becky invited G. Barnes and his wife Anne, to have a dinner party over on Lamma Island. Lamma was noted for the fantastic seafood restaurants near Picnic Bay. Great seafood, freshly caught and cooked in excellent tradition, served with plenteous amounts of San Mig or Snowflake Beer. I think this was before Carlsberg had much of a presence in Hong Kong. The women dressed nicely, with the ubiquitous sweater anticipating the late evening chill.

Following the meal, they boarded Paul's junk to head back towards Aberdeen. As the story goes, a leak in the bow started producing a pretty sizeable quantity of water, which the women dutifully bailed overboard with plastic cups. The boat was not well balanced, and you had to move carefully on it, as it was prone to lurch.

The East Lamma Channel happens to be the main shipping lane into Hong Kong, and all varieties of ocean-going ships pass both ways there, at all times of the day and night. The wakes from said vessels bounced Mr. Carlton's craft enough so that the weakness producing the leak enlarged, and so the water in was more than the water out. Add to this that the pleasure junk did not have a very strong engine. One version says they ran out of petrol. Combine these factors, add gravity, and soon there was one sinking junk in the midst of this maritime freeway.

A channel marker or buoy - I never saw it - midway across the water, was their only hope for avoiding a basically hopeless nocturnal swim, and the four managed to get to the swaying pontoon, although obviously drenched. I guess it was pretty well covered with barnacles and their clothing got torn and they had lots of cuts on their skin. As I was told it, they valiantly tried for a few hours to signal these huge tankers bearing down the channel, but it was pitch dark, and basically a useless endeavor. Talk about a bad date!!!

Sometime near first light, the shivering couples begin actively hailing ships again, but by mid-morning, realized this was not going to work, and no marine police were around. Barnes' babysitter apparently had called the police that they hadn't come home, but if police boats tried to find them, they didn't. So, I guess it was Paul who finally realized that one of them would have to swim to one shore or the other to get rescue help.... and Lamma was the closer (or it appeared that way from their low viewpoint).

Shedding most of his already soaked clothing, he swims back towards Picnic Bay and manages to come ashore. Lamma on that side was basically a rural rock with a few rice paddies and choi patches. The story I heard was that Paul walked quite a ways in his soaked BVDs to a trail, then to a road, where eventually he encountered a local farmer. Imagine the thoughts in this Cantonese mind, with a pale gweilo in his underwear gesturing about who-only-knows-what, and babbling in American English...but it's gotta look pretty silly. Assuming the farmer would take pity on his plight, Paul somehow indicated that he needed to get to the village where they had dinner, and help would be available. Being a clever fellow, and no one's fool, the farmer charged Paul HK $200 for a ride into town!

A phone call led to the eventual rescue of the three on the buoy sometime that Sunday afternoon. Paul somehow never talked about this episode very much... but his dilapidated craft was seen a few weeks later on the beach in Tai Tam Tuk below the current High School campus. Whether it washed ashore, or was dredged up and hauled there, I never knew. I heard it was beyond salvage.

I think that was the end of Captain Carlton's sailing career.   *Dave Kohl, art teacher '73-'80*

•Swim Team

During my 8th grade year, we had swim team practices at the HK Country Club at 5:30 in the mornings. My dad sometimes drove several team members and us to these early practices when the driver was unavailable. Actually, the Country Club was just down Shouson Hill from our place at 35 Deep Water Bay Road. Scott McGee thought my dad was a bad driver. One time he told me "Your dad doesn't driver very much, does he?" Since dad rarely drove himself, I guess that's the reason.

My dad offered Mark Silzer the possibility that a smaller group from the team could use our pool for alternative practice sessions. Mark liked the idea, and often a group of up to 20 would show up at our place, and I got to swim with them. How could Silzer not let me join in the group? It was our pool. I think my dad did this so I could gain some confidence in my swimming. It worked!
Pat Hotung '77

I have a great newspaper article about the disrespectful American children who threw their teacher in the pool after winning a swim meet. It was a major deal for a while.   *Debbie Smiley '72*

I remember many swim team practices with Mrs. Rose at Repulse Bay in the fall or winter (I remember it was cold!). When we went to Taiwan with the school to compete against TAS, it was winter and we were unprepared, we sat in our wet swimsuits with wet towels and shivered through the entire meet. I was another swimmer who spent half my life in the pool. Being on the swim team was a wonderful experience, I was able to travel to Taipei, the Philippines and Bangkok as a member of the various teams I swam for.
Wendy Liddiard '73

Swim practice at Kennedy Town, wheezing after another 50-lap warm-up and greeted by the down-home aromas of the slaughterhouse (they used to call it the Kennedy Town Abattoir).

•Cross-Harbour Swim

I also remember an annual swim-across-the-harbor race where hundreds of people swam from

Hong Kong to Kowloon side, or maybe from Kowloon to Hong Kong. After riding the Star Ferry and staring into the polluted water, I could not imagine wanting to enter that race. However, my father had a speed boat that he kept at TaTam Harbor and he used to take us into Hong Kong harbor, right up next to some of the huge tankers and freighters and military ships that were coming in and out of the port. When I learned to water ski, I remember skiing right up next to huge vessels that were as tall as apartment buildings. Probably not the safest thing in the world, but what an experience!   *Kendra Lannom '66-'79*

I did swim the cross harbour a few times, which although filthy, was pleasantly warm! The last time I did was the oil slick incident. A huge oil slick floated across the finish line and caught everyone who was near the first of the race. Unfortunately there was a young man who died that year, and it was surmised that it was due to the oil fumes overcoming him. I remember being close to the end of the race when I swam into the oil and the fumes were horrible, right beneath my face with no way to escape. I put my head down and sprinted to the end.

Once ashore, I met up with friends who I could hardly recognize, all you could see was white teeth and the whites of our eyes, the rest was solid brown muck. We all went to our flat on Bowen Road and had showers, as most of them lived on Kowloon side, (our bathtubs were a mess afterwards)!   *Wendy Liddiard '73*

I also remember swimming, swimming and more swimming. I think I smelled perpetually like chlorine, especially in that last year. We trained over at the Morrison pool and raced in the championships, but I never did the cross harbour swim. My then friends from Island School had tales of oil and muck all over themselves afterward. Yeeech!!!   *Sally Lawton '77*

•Catchment Surfing

When there were heavy rains, we practiced the madness of water catchment rafting. This was on an old inner tube. We strung a rope over the top, about 200 feet from the spillway so you could grab on and escape. The tube to be collected later down the cliffs. Bloody foolish. So many kids in Happy

Valley, resettlement estates and the like, were swept down into drains and perished. We never even thought of the danger, just the hair-raising challenge and fun.   *Rich Vaughn '72*

Long before water slides came to be known in North America, my daring comrades and I would lower ourselves into these semicircular concrete expresses. Sitting on sheets of cardboard and greatly assisted by gravity and wet moldy concrete, we would wizz recklessly as far and as fast as we could travel (or until the cardboard wore out and we rode on our skins). I'm sure we cheated grim deaths more than once. The adventures ceased with a sudden loss of innocence over these giddy slides. One of the culverts explores rides unexpectedly ended at a vertical grate and eventually the hospital.   *Eric Allen '76*

I thought that I was the only crazy one to ride down the catchments when it rained hard. People think that there isn't anything fun to do when it's raining hard, like play in the catchments and the waterfalls. There are streams and rivers to kayak or canoe in elsewhere, but it isn't warm or challenging like it was in HK.   *Eric Lee ' 75*

7. In the New Territories

•Castle Peak

Give a kudo to Theo Jansen; he organized more than a few superb San Mig tours. There's nothing like being drunk as a skunk with a busload of your good friends at 11:00 a.m. and cajoling the bus driver to pull over on the side of the road so thirty people can hop out and take a leak.
                    Mike McCormick '80

Taking the train from Lo Wu into China in 1978 was like taking a giant step back in time. Hong Kong skylines to rice paddies and water buffalo and everyone wearing blue Mao suits and riding black bikes. We took one of the early tours to Canton, Kweilin, and Nanning. A snapshot in history.   *Barb Schwerdtmann '68-'77*

•Shatin

Shatin is a small village on the Kowloon Canton railway, toward the border. We took the train with the Landdecks and their 2- and 1-year old kids. We hiked up the hillside by the train station to the Temple of 10,000 Buddhas, a rather long steep hike, which took us through some sidewalk restaurants, then shanties, then open fields of rice and taro, and finally up a heavily wooded hillside. The Temple was interesting, in that actually 10,000 8" high Buddhas were set upon the shelves all around the inside of the temple. Actually, we didn't count them. Right in the middle of the sanctuary was a Sweden soft-serve ice cream machine!!! (Shades of Christ throwing the moneylenders out of the temple flashed through my ecclesiastical mind). Hiking back down the hill, we took the next train further out to Tai Po Kau, where we took a ferry around Tolo harbor.

Dave Kohl, art teacher '73-'80

• Horses

I remember those retired racehorses in Fanling too. The BG stables? Racehorse nags put to pasture, some w/ spunk and an attitude. I too remember the long train ride on the Kowloon-Canton Railroad... coal-driven locomotive, no a/c, gagging if your window was open going thru the Lion Rock tunnel. *Richard Vaughn '72*

I remember going horseback riding somewhere in the New Territories on Serendipity Days. I had to take a bus, a ferry, a train and then another bus just to get there but it was great! My kids think they're doing hard time if I won't give them a ride the couple of miles up to the mall! *Lynn Barrett*

My animal work actually has roots in HK, where I started out volunteering at the Island School mini-zoo as a kid; after I hung around so much that they finally put me to work chopping up food for gerbils, rabbits, etc. Eventually I "graduated" to working with the cool animals in the Nocturnal Room there (mostly from Australia and Indonesia) and even had my hair pulled by the resident chimpanzee. I've learned so much from working with animals, and enjoyed every minute! *Jill Liddiard '77*

• Junior High Camp at Suen Doh

As the Junior High faculty held a bunch of meetings to plan the weeklong outdoor camp, it seemed a good idea to incorporate some real life situations into the week. One idea that gained steam was "where does our food actually come from?" (Seems kind of lame as I type it now but it sure sounded good back then!) Ken Rohrs mentioned that at his wedding in the Philippines a pig roast was part of the festivities, which, as the groom, he was required to assist in the preparation. I added that, as a farm kid growing up in Wisconsin, I also had experienced pig slaughter. Both of us assumed the other had actually done the deed, which we found out later wasn't the case. Regardless, the plan was hatched to slaughter a pig(s), and chickens, at camp and prepare it (them) for eating.

We then contacted our liaison with the camp, John Bechtel, a CME missionary and fluent Cantonese speaker, to see if we could pull this off. He thought it would be great, and knew some area farmers from which we could buy the pigs. Rohrs made sure to request that the farmers be told not to feed the pigs a few days in advance, so they wouldn't have food in their stomachs when we did the butchering.

Finally the day arrived. Bechtel took us to the nearby farmer to fetch the pigs. Imagine our surprise when the farmer took us to the pens and the pigs were merrily eating away! As we didn't know how to purge pigs, we were stuck with well-fed ones.

We then got the pigs back to camp and tied them to the pillars outside the kitchen. A crowd gathered 'round as we got ready to do the deed. Rohrs wasn't keen to be the slaughterer, so that task fell to me. We went in to the kitchen to get an appropriate knife from the cook and were met with a look of distain. Never did figure that one out. Back outside, and with some holding down the pig I did the throat cutting deed. However, a two-fold problem surfaced. First, the knife was woefully dull. Rather than a nice clean cut, I ended up sawing! Second, I thought I was done but the pig wasn't showing signs of signing out. One of the mini-bus drivers, who had also gathered to watch this, bent down, looked at the pig, and made a frantic back and forth motion across this throat. Turned out I hadn't gotten deep enough to get through the artery. I thus resumed the cutting and now the pig was ready for the long anticipated roast.

Problem 3 now hit us in the face. For some reason we couldn't get the fire hot enough to cook the pig in a proper manner. The idea had been to

157

have it ready as part of the evening meal. It became obvious that it may be ready for a later evening meal, but not that day. While what I've written so far may be coloured by time, this next part I remember like yesterday. I think Mark Silzer suggested we cut our losses, and alert the cooks that he menu had changed. Here was Rohr's response: "No way, this has now become a point of honour. We are going to have pork, even if it is midnight!" He wasn't far off, as I think we finally ended up eating some fairly raspy pork around 10:30 pm.

Later on, as we had a chance to discuss the day, Rohrs and I found out that each of us thought the other was the "expert" at pig slaughter and preparation. Come to find out he had more or less been an observer at the one in the Philippines, and my expertise was as a hide scrapper when the farmer I did odd jobs for in Wisconsin slaughtered some pigs.

I'd love for Ken Rohrs to chime in on this too. I'm sure he could add, and possibly correct, much more. In a way those days were certainly golden for us as teachers in that we didn't get sued for animal cruelly, there weren't any nasty articles in the newspapers about the awfulness of the event, etc.
Fritz Voeltz middle school teacher '73-'80

While this is a story of cruelty, I can honestly say that these teachers did not intend such cruelty (Mr. Voeltz was cruel enough in PE).
Richard Grayson '77

I also went to the Suen Doh Camp in the 7th grade. I couldn't watch nor eat the infamous "pig." Remember being pretty hungry most of the time at camp, the food was not very appetizing. We had these big mosquito nets around our beds yet every morning many of us had misshapen eyelids or lips from their bites along with at least 20 – 30 other bites! I remember it rained a lot and we had fun playing games in the rain and mud, followed by umpteen showers. Another seventh grade highlight was Danny O'Keefe, my first boyfriend.
Liz Calouri '79

I went to the Suen Doh camp both in Jr. High and then as a high school student counselor throughout my high school years. I was there when Ken Rohrs and Fritz Voeltz did the pig slaughter, and I recall some chickens as well. We,

the student counselors, got together and wrote a song about the whole camp experience that year, and performed it for everyone on the last night, while we all sat around the campfire, and Bob Matthews played the guitar. The kids loved it -- thought it was hysterical. We were worried that we had offended the teachers, because we made fun of them in the song. I doubt if that was true -- we were lucky enough to have had some of the best teachers any one could wish for! I'd love to find a copy of that song.
Cindy Kinne '78

Junior High on the 7th Floor, Fritz Voeltz, Ken Rohrs, Dave Landeck, Dave Christian, Bob Matthews..............the motorcycle gang! Chapel was guitar-strumming concerts featuring Dave Christian and Bob Matthews. I still remember the songs: "to be alive, and feeling free, and to have everyone in your family". Suen Doh Camp in April and hearing news of the end of the Vietnam War the day we packed up and left camp back in '74. *Ken Koo '79*

I helped out with 6th and Jr High camping adventures. Once, I woke up in the middle of the night on the beach with a cow next to me lapping up our pancake mix we were supposed to eat for breakfast. Plus I found out that those were not only the biggest mosquitoes in the world, but we were in an area that still had live cholera. This was also the place that had the dead cows in the stream. We used to get the cholera booster shots every six months.
Barb Schwerdtmann '79

•Outward Bound

All 3 years of Outward Bound were a highlight. Crazy times, fun times, pushing the boundaries of self limitation. Life long friendships formed under stressful times and a pride of knowing you survived.

Some fantastic after parties as well. There was one in particular at the home (on a small island) of Simon Ackers-Jones (I believe that is how it is spelled) who's Dad was the Secretary of the New Territories or something of that nature. 17 year olds on their own with loads of booze and hormones. I was caught on the tennis court in a compromising situation when some wise cracker turned on the floodlights. *Gavin Birnie '75*

For Interim in 1980, I wound up sponsoring

a weeklong stint at the Outward Bound School in the New Territories, accompanied by a parent, and Anne Ellis, the French teacher.

Easter is a moveable feast but it often appears around the beginning of typhoon season, and for that reason the week was miserable. There were a few breaks in the weather with long periods of rain and cold. We found out what each day's schedule was after breakfast; there was no choice. Outward Bound was a British invention, like the Boy Scouts, and the tradition was to muck in and do what needed to be done. Two incidents stand out from that time.

One was a hike, of course in the rain, often uphill on a surface that slid away at most steps. We'd been wending our way up a particularly nasty slope for the best part of an hour, led by Brian, our relentless guide. Anne was bringing up the rear and, though a good tennis player, was not up for this kind of slogging. I was concerned and kept an eye out for her. But at one point she reached a place where, whenever she tried to take a step uphill, she slid back. I saw she was having difficulty and walked back to help. I tried to pull her out by hand but that only put us both in danger of falling into the mud. Anne gave up. "The hell with it," she said, all traces of British reserve knocked out of her. "Brian got me up here; he can get me out."

I thought that unlikely. Brian was leading the column; he had long ago crested this hill and was a couple of hundred yards away, probably with little or no thought for us. And it was raining.

I had my all-purpose day pack with me, crammed with fifteen or so pounds of what the Sierra Club says everyone walking away from their car in the woods absolutely has to have, and a good bit more besides. Among the latter items was a fifty-foot coil of quarter-inch nylon rope. I told Anne, "Hang on," and hiked about five yards away where I found some reliable footing. I took out the rope, knotted up one end and tossed it to her. I told her to tie it around her torso, underneath her arms, and hang on. Anne was no weakling but she was a petite person, whereas I have a bit more heft. I slowly pulled her uphill, taking it slowly so she could stay upright. The ground leveled out a bit farther on and we made it back to the main building to find the kids sipping cocoa and giving me unkind looks for having talked them into this wretched experience. But I did not care; I had

saved Anne, in a small way, and that was what Outward Bound was all about.

In all, a memorable Interim.

Andrew Grzeskowiak, teacher, '78-80

•Sai Kung

•Interim, 1981 (Bodies on the Beach).

The idea was conceived by Bill Kuhn in the Spring of 1981. Bill had arrived in Hong Kong from Chicago in August of 1980. He was a music teacher. He proposed that we offer a 5-day, 4-night hike to students who would traverse a major portion of the newly opened McLehose Trail... beginning where it started - at Pak Tam Cheung, and going as far as we could in 5 days and 4 nights on the trail. He would lead and I would assist as a "tail-end-charley." Bill did all of the intricate planning. I merely assisted. Nineteen students agreed to go on this strenuous hike. They came from 7 different nations - Japan, Korea, Italy, the U.S., the Philippines, Malaysia, and Canada. We later learned that most of the students had never before engaged in something like this. One young, spirited girl from Japan asked in a serious voice (after our presentation was completed) - "Where are the showers we will use on this hike?" I explained to all of them that there would be no showers and no baths at all for the entire duration of the hike. We would carry packs that weighed near, or over, 40 lbs apiece, and worse, we would sleep in our own sweat each night. We would carry our food and water, plus our shelter gear. We began to understand that most of the students had never 'endured' such hardships – as most had been raised in cosmopolitan cities under the care of gifted and educated parents. "Hiking" for almost all of them would be moving from the couch to a different room in their home or flat. The surprises were waiting for them...and for Bill and myself.

Our 1st day began early and by way of public transport we made our way to Pak Tam Cheung. The initial piece was a steep paved road up to the High Island Reservoir road and within minutes, all of us were sweating profusely. By Noon we had made it to an obscure area known as Long Ke Wan. Two hours later we walked into a small village named Sai Wan, and took a break. Some students were already whining about pains caused by their backpacks and feet problems. One young man from the US who fancied himself a bit on the tough side could no longer carry his pack. I carried it for him, plus my own which weighed over 50 lbs. I was younger then. By this time conversation among a number of the students had centered on how much they disliked having to live in Hong Kong, which to them was crowded (it was) and dirty (it was), and terribly hot (it was).

About 30 minutes out from Sai Wan, I came around a small cropping of rocks where the trail followed a narrow beach, and found the entire group halted. Bill came back to me and in a hushed tone announced: "There is a body on the beach ahead." I walked toward the area and saw the body. It was face up, slightly bloated, with life-less eyes staring at the sky. Most of the bodies' fingers and toes were missing which meant it had been subjected to fish in the water for some time. I advised we move on, and we did. As I was last to leave, I stood near the body of the man we had discovered.

A myriad of thoughts filled my mind. Who was he? Why had he risked his life trying to cross Mirs Bay? Did he leave a family whom he hoped to help? How ironic that several people who had been complaining about living in Hong Kong had found this person who desperately wanted to get to Hong Kong.

The incident made me think as well. Hong Kong was crowded for me as well. It was hot for at least 8 months of the year. With over 6 million people living in it, it was often less than pristine...and traffic by auto was always a challenge. There were times when I wondered why I still stayed on there. This incident - this discovery brought me up short. The trip would educate me even more in a short amount of time.

We reached the beach called Tai Long Wan late that first afternoon, pitched our camp near a small village known as Ham Tin, and settled in for some sleep. In the morning on arising Bill and I noticed what looked like dark lumps on the extended beach. I used my binoculars and found they were the same shape as bodies. We learned a bit later that 2 more bodies had washed up on the beach of Tai Long Wan...and we wondered why, and what might be happening near us. When we eventually returned to our homes/flats, we learned through the South China Morning Post that some 18 bodies had been discovered on the beaches in the area we had hiked through on that first day out. That sec-

ond morning, when the students learned that we had seen another two bodies on the beach not far from us, the conversation contained no traces of complaining about living in Hong Kong.

This Interim in the spring of 1981 remains stamped forever in my heart, soul, and memory.
Rev. Paul Tuchardt, Board of Managers, '73-'86

• Tai Long Wan and Ham Tin

Tai Long Wan, in the Sai Kung Peninsula, is one of the few places on the planet where I feel totally at peace. We first discovered this pristine and then unknown stretch of tropical sand with Ken and Urduha Rohrs on a hike in 1973. Just getting there was an adventure - bus to Central, Star Ferry to the KCR train station, train to Tai Po Kau, Tolo Harbour Ferry for two hours to Chek Keng, then an hour of steep hiking past Sharp's Peak. It was worth it.

Ham Tin, the little village a mile back from the beach was a traditional row village, one of several converted by Roman Catholic fathers before the NTs belonged to the British. A decrepit chapel stood next to our favorite drink place. An old Chinese man and his black pajama-clad wife sold cold drinks from their kerosene cooler. A sign over the door said "Victory Store." Once with Marge and Earl Westrick, we asked him about the name, and he pulled out a crumbling folded paper from his pocket. Carefully opening it, he was excited to point out that this was a certificate from King George VI, recognizing him for his help with the Underground Railroad during the Japanese occupation.

Hiking in one crisp and clear Saturday morning, we had noticed a large white yacht moored at Chek Keng. Coming toward us later on the trail was a very tall gweilo, decked in white walking shorts, high white socks, and accompanied by a few others in tow. It was Sir Murray! One of my kids recognized him, and said, "Aren't you the Governor?" as he briskly passed us. "Yes...I am." said Mr. MacLehose as he kept stride.

I often took groups of students camping there, and hauled our son there in the backpack before he was six months old. The quiet serenity of this unspoiled paradise, even with a few roaming cows that would nose into our food supplies, is a place of calm I always remember.
Dave Kohl, art teacher, '73 - '80

Hong Kong in the '70s continued to experience some effects of the Cultural Revolution in China. As the Red Guards continued their work, bodies would occasionally float down the Pearl River into Hong Kong waters. I recall at least one occasion when an HKIS student bumped into one of these bodies while out on a boat ride.

Dave Christian '69

I remember the Gurkas in Sai Kung were ferocious beasts. One summer in '73, I was assisting my Korean Taekwon-do instructor, Mr. Lee, to teach the Gurkas classes at the barracks. The Gurkas usually, I mean always, ended up with a few broken bones or bloody noses from the free sparrings. They usually, I mean always, ignored the word "Stop!" (No wonder the British Army hired them to be on the front lines.)

Just a few months before the Hand-over of H.K., I saw two Gurkas sitting in a Bently, with a huge "Crown" on the car door; they were waiting in front of the Botanic Garden on Garden Road for some big shot. So I went up to ask for direction how to get back to the hotel. Instead of giving directions, they gave me a ride instead. Boy! Oh boy! Did I arrive back in the hotel in style!! What a trip!!

I still regret that I sold my Gurkas knives, which were given to me by the Gurkas. Each one has two small daggers attached on side of the shields. What an idiot!! *Gabe Lau '77*

•Golf

I used to go golfing as a peewee at Deep Water Bay and the giant python that lived in the bushes on the 4th fairway, he would sometimes sun himself in a bunker. I had to learn not to put my golf bag down or reach into a hole w/out looking for a snake first. *Rich Vaughn '72*

There was an anti-litter campaign (Lap Sap Chung) in 1972 or thereabouts, my brother, Mike, remembers that they had a big kick-off campaign in Central with a huge paper/papier mache' figure of the infamous Lap Sap Chung--the litter monster (literally, Garbage Worm). The Kick-off culminated by blowing up the monster, scattering tons of paper litter all over Central. Too funny! *Ann Sullivan '75*

•Touring the New Territories

Dennis Bartz took us out for a drive into the New Territories last evening in his newly acquired MG-B. The muffler promptly fell off! Ah, shades of Bertha (my MG in Chicago). His doesn't run as well as mine did, but all his needs is some carburetor work. We also fixed the muffler. It fell off when we were by a roadside park. Dennis went into the loo and while there, swiped the wire on the handle of the pull-chain toilet and used that to wire his muffler back on. Clever!!

Dave Kohl, art teacher '73-'80, letter '73

•Refugees

I think the ship you're referring to was the KYLU, as she left Vietnam. By the time she arrived in HK, the name had been modified to SKYLUCK. What imagination! *Dave Meyer, science teacher*

•CY's University

When the Sea wise University ship burned in the harbour, it was January 9, 1972. The smoke was thick and black all across the water way past Kai Tak runway. We lived in the Midlevels on Magazine Gap and our living room wall was huge sliding glass windows. We watched it burn and the fireboats finally came within our telescope. Friends had a boat and they took us around the hulk a couple of months later and you could still smell the oily smoke. *Barb Schwerdtmann '77*

I remember the hulk of the incinerated Sea Wise. It had been the QE 1, owned by Cunard, and then belonged to C. Y. Tung, who was having it refitted into a college. It was planned to tour the world, as students would learn about peoples and places. The hull sat half submerged in the harbour for years, and the maps of Hong Kong had it drawn into the harbor space, just like an island. It was one of the Hong Kong "legends" we're told when we first arrived... the other legend was the Cotewall Road disaster/landslip, when an entire building slid down the slope above Western Market after intense rains. The scar on the hillside was clear and visible our entire 7 years in HK.

Dave Kohl, art teacher '73-'80

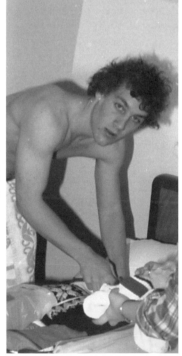

Chapter 11
Adventures Beyond

A school 'field trip' at HKIS usually involved airplanes, one or more other countries, and lots of spectacular experiences.

Scott Schroth '77

1. Macau

•The Grand Prix

Every year, our family went to Macau for the Grand Prix. At our previous home in Australia, our neighbor's son-in-law was the number one racing car driver in Australia (a Canadian named Allan Moffatt). We used to see him race over there and when we moved to Hong Kong, we continued our tradition of going to the races. We used to stay in that loopy space age looking Hotel Lisboa. One time, Allan showed up to race and we got pit passes. That was absolutely the coolest. He used to race in the sedan class, not formula one. At the time we knew him, he used to drive Fords (Trans Am Mustang, Falcon GTHO), and whenever we saw him, he would either win or his car would die. Allan only came to Macau once that I recall. Apparently it was super-expensive for the guys to get their cars and crews over to Macau.

Sheila Baker '82

•Macau Ferry from a letter "home" in 1973

The "family" group congregated Wednesday evening at the Macau Ferry pier about 10:30 pm. Since the ferry left at midnight, we walked around the "poor man's night club." which is an open market that gets set up every night and taken down about midnight. During the day it's a bus terminal. We ate some choi mein before boarding the ferry. The guys had one cabin, the women in the adjoining one. So we all got some sleep (?). The ferry arrives about 3 am, but you can't get off till 6 am, when Portuguese customs opens at Macau. We spent the day sight-seeing, walking over most of the city. It's a really Mediterranean place - in architecture, customs, and climate. The day was sunny and warm. For evening dinner, we met some other teachers who were also there for the holiday, and we had "African Chicken" at the Pousada, an old

hotel on the waterfront. Delicious.

We went down to the casino after dinner, but did precious little gambling. Our hotel was the Bella Vista, a classic ancient Portuguese hotel, complete with arched lobby, 12-foot ceilings, and a breakfast verandah overlooking the inner harbour. Next day we rented bicycles and rode over most of the colony, including a little known place, shown to us by Dave Christian, where you are separated from China only by a narrow 10-footside slough. The little man in the guardhouse across the water made sure we saw his gun, as he emerged from the cubicle and goose-stepped his way across his territory. Part of our cycling took us onto the Grand Prix course, which was run just last week here and is huge stuff. We returned the bikes, had a curry lunch, and shopped leisurely for Mateus wine. When we got back to HK, we met a group of HKIS teachers who had gotten group tickets for the new movie "GodSpell."

Dave Kohl, art teacher '73-'80

I can so picture the colorful chaos of Hong Kong nightlife. It was like watching a pageant unfold in front of me. I remember the lanterns and the night market before we boarded the ship to Macau. I picture the chickens squawking inside their woven baskets on the busses, the density of life happening all around.

Bev Larson, teacher '73-'74

•Macau Field Trip

My American History classes took a trip to Macau. We visited the historical sites, including the Protestant Missionary cemetery and still had about an hour left before we were to get our return ferry. Someone suggested that we stop at a casino nearby to see what it was like...it was still morning. When we entered, the place was packed with Japanese tourists that were placing bets - thousands and thousands of yen...and, fortunately, we watched

ADVENTURE BEYOND

them lose big time.

It was a great "economics" lesson and that is all they could talk about the rest of the day. I am afraid the rest of the sites were forgotten.

Sharon Prechtl, teacher '70-'74

On our class trip to Macau, I vividly remember making dark chocolate sandwiches on that amazing Portuguese bread, and our hikes in the mountain with Mateus we bought at the Park 'n Shop (charged to my parent's account)!

Linda Schock '75

2. Operation Interchange (1969)

In the summer of 1968 we began working on the first interchange with the American schools in Taiwan. The student body president at the Taipei American School (Bill McElroy?) visited Hong Kong and was hosted by Mike Swaine, our own student body president. (Earlier, Mike had penned the little red "Quotations from Chairman Mike" student handbook that began "Students of the world, unite.") The interchange project got off the ground, and in the spring of 1969 we filled a chartered 727 and flew to Taipei to compete in basketball, cross country, judo, swimming, tennis and volleyball, and to meet other American kids in Asia.

Dave Christian '69

There was an athletic competition between American schools in South East Asia held in Taiwan sometime that year. I was the most un-athletic person in the world, but I wanted to go on this trip badly! Fortunately for me, we needed to throw together a volleyball team, which is the only sport I was familiar with. Competition was such (maybe non-existent) that I made the team.

I remember staying in a hotel in Taiwan and the floors were alternately filled with male & female students. I do remember a lot of hanging out of windows & hollering to the floors above & below (besides throwing things up or down). I also remember the horror of our cheerleaders as we discovered how out of step we were with cheerleader outfits. Here we were in our longer skirts reminiscent of 50's poodle skirts in powder blue with an ordinary white sweatshirt with a makeshift HKIS logo on the front. The rest of the cheerleaders were of course in their short pleated skirts with matching slim-fitting sweaters, looking quite cute & put

together. One of our cheerleaders (who shall remain nameless) couldn't even do it. She refused to dress & go out there in front of everyone. It was pretty funny.

As far as our volleyball team went, not sure we won any games & I do remember how small we felt next to a rather tall Taiwanese team that seemed to us to be giants in comparison. They were indeed fierce & chewed us up and spit us out. Of course there was also time for sightseeing and shopping - especially all those pirated records. I remember coming home with various colored vinyl - albums in red and blue - wish I had saved them now. The trip was a blast & well worth the humiliation on the volleyball court and as a cheerleader.

Kris Brannigan '69

We did go to Taiwan once for sports, debate etc. exchange, and as I recall we got seriously beat, at least in sports. That must have been 1969. Other years we held a Holiday Tournament for basketball, and other schools came to HKIS from TAS (Taiwan American School), ASIJ, etc. The early years at HKIS didn't offer much opportunity for traveling as part of the curriculum. I know that later my mom took at least two groups to Bali, and both my parents took a group to Japan. When I was back in 80-81 working in the library I took a group of kids on the Huan-a junk trip to the New Territories during the travel time. *Liz Von Behren '71*

• Operation Interchange (1975)

We had an all HKIS inter-school meet with TAS and after that the senior class of '75 took buses to Toroko Gorge for our senior trip. I can't remember how long the bus trip was - at least 4 hours - and more than long enough for a number of students to get quite sloshed long before our arrival at the gorge. It was a beautiful place with hot springs and we had it all to ourselves except for the catering staff. Then flew back to Taipei and back to HK. There were some good black & white shots in the yearbook and I have a few of my own that I took to our last reunion in Long Beach.

David Knisely '75

Shirley and I were on the Taroko Gorge trip. I have a distinct recollection of my physics kids throwing large rocks into the gorge and timing the fall to verify the acceleration of gravity. We also participated in moving a large number of rocks around at the hot spring to create a hot tub with the water flow adjusted to comfortably hot.

Dave Meyer, science teacher, '75-'81

• Operation Interchange (1977)

Hey, how come we only went to Taipei? The adventure of staying at some stranger's house, at least they let us pick a friend to be with. Going out adventuring. Seeing an incredible Chinese show and eating the best whole shrimp with Pam Wong's grandma and grandpa! I just refused to suck out the heads, no way. I remember the beauty of Sun Moon Lake. Paul Anka tapes on the bus. Really strong cigarettes. Getting to know some kids better. Gilbert joining in with the band. Did all the Senior Class trips end up going to Taiwan and Sun Moon Lake? I think my brother also went in 75.

I remember the airline we took, FAT air, Far Eastern Air Transport, I think. One had gone down the month or so before our flight. I heard the kids after us started going to Nepal and other great places.

Barbara Schwerdtmann '77

I went on the final year in 1977. Interim replaced Interchange thereafter in '78. TAS was still in Shilin. I remember their gym was kinda dark and the walls were red brick. The varsity basketball team did really well, trashing both TAS and Morrison because Bill Keimig, who wasn't in town for the Holiday Tourney, came back for the Interchange tournament. We did a Don Quixote skit for the English part of Interchange. The fun, though, was off-campus. Cave records, the Mongolian BBQ in Tien Mu, Dairy Queen, bowling at the Grand Hotel lanes.

Ken Koo '79

3. Interim Program

This critical, long-term program has been foundational to so many students at HKIS. I would like to know how many college essays include a reference to a student's interim experiences. I suspect a huge number. Interim really does impact kids lives.

I was asked years ago to give a talk at South Island School as they were considering starting an interim type program. I started listing out the process we went through. a.) a year in advance interim proposals were due. b.) complete planning and budgets in September c.) a massive student

signup system was run in October and on and on.... Soon I noticed that they were giggling and rolling eyes at me. Afterwards someone told me that only at HKIS would a week-long trip turn into such a major production. We seem to have a reputation but the work is well worth it. The trips can be grand adventures of learning and personal growth.

Dave Elliott, teacher, '82-'07

I think Interim came as a result of a last minute scramble to replace Operation Interchange that used to be a once every 2 years' interaction between HKIS, TAS and Morrison Academy.

Ken Koo '79

• China

I had the pleasure of leading the first Interim China trip to Guilin in 1978, where I watched Patrick Pang talk his way out of responsibility for starting his hotel room curtains on fire. Turned out his buds had all bought fireworks, and tried to shoot them off from their balcony. When they missfired, they shot into the socialist lace curtains and became a fireball. Another trip was to Beijing and the Great Wall in 1980, where somebody took their skateboard, claiming to be the first to skate the wall.

Dave Kohl, art teacher '73 - '80

I was on the 1980 China trip. I also remember Hisae Sudoh, Antony Anderson and Dave Trees being there. I have a photo of all of us (including Patrick Pang) hanging out in the hotel room. I think we'd tried going for a walk but got bored 'cause they seemed to roll up the sidewalks by 8:00 pm back then. Wasn't that the trip where we had to stay and extra day or two because of the weather or some such thing? I remember calling Joyce Lu from the hotel, and she insisted that for weeks thereafter, her family got odd phone calls where no one said anything, and they were sure they were being spied on by the Chinese government. Hmmm.

Joan Amy '80

We had some pretty good times doing room parties with those snacks. It was the second trip to China in '80 when I brought the snacks. In retrospect, I should have sold those snacks to the Chinese people for money. I remember during the first trip, a few of us were walking down the main street of Hangzhou; before we knew it, it seemed the whole town had come out and followed us down the street. That was when China had just opened to the outside world, and the people in Hangzhou had never seen many foreigners. That was also at a time that 99.99 % of the people we encountered were wearing either green or blue Mao jackets, regardless of sex.

Remember when the Mao cap was a fashion statement in HKIS for a while?

My friend David Trees stole a ceramic roof tile off one of the ancient temple/palace buildings at one of the stops on the trip. On our way to our next stop, there was a truck full of PLA soldiers following our bus a few cars behind for a while at one point. We really thought that they were after him for the roof tile.

At the hotel that we stayed in Hangzhou, a few of us stumbled into the dining hall late one night after everybody had gone to sleep. It was full of local Chinese and they were all having big hot-pots of dog meat (at least that was what we were told). It had a very distinctive aroma.

One of the coolest things I saw in China was the 1940's style small suitcase size radio in my hotel room in Shanghai that used vacuum tubes. That wasn't a retro remake; it was the real thing from the '40's. I wanted to take that thing home.

One of the more interesting traveling moments in China was flying in that Chinese DC9 copy that had no seat belt. The floor tilted upward when the plane was on the ground. The seats were very wide and comfortable, but my seat back was broken and was in a semi-permanent reclined position, until the plane hit a bump.

I am glad that we had the opportunity to see China at that time when it was just opening to the outside world and everything seemed to be still frozen in a communist-era time wrap. It was a unique experience that nobody would be able to capture nowadays. China is so different today!

Light the curtain on fire? Never! A flaming mosquito net over the bed? May be….

Patrick Pang '80

It was May of 1978 and the PRC had just opened her gates to the Western world a few months before. After much planning and discussions with the Chinese Embassy in Hong Kong we were able to get permission to go to ol' Canton. With some sixty elementary students ready to travel and one parent for each student we boarded the train in Kowloon and made our run across the

boarder into China.

The 2 to 3 hour trip took us through the countryside with all the sights and expectations looming ahead. It was going to be a great adventure as we had planned to visit numerous elementary schools and meet Chinese students in their same grade level. Our sixth graders were ready and had some goals and projects to accomplish on this rather spectacular five-day field trip. When all of a sudden, no more than an hour into our train ride, a dozen or so 6th graders came running back to where I was sitting and screaming all the way; "...Mr. Lindner, Mr. Lindner, Mr. Lindner...Mary Tyler Moore is riding in the car behind us! Mary Tyler Moore! It's Mary Tyler Moore!"

Well so much for the field trip to Canton. Once we arrived at the station there were dozens of Chinese elementary school students lined up in two straight long rows ready to welcome the major film star traveling with us. As Mary Tyler Moore got off the train with her group, so did our HKIS 6th grade students. And lo and behold, what did the Chinese students start to scream when Mary Tyler Moore stepped into the crowd?

"American Kids! American Kids! American Kids!"

And Mary Tyler Moore was left to fend for herself as kids from the West met kids from the East!

Ah! God is good and just and has a sense of humor. *John T. Lindner 6th Grade Teacher '75-'78*

All of the class of '84 remembers our trip to Canton. Need I say more? The Dong Fang Hotel, full of loud, unruly American children, we all remember. After that, junior high, and on to high school. *Sydney Henrietta '84*

•Sapporo

Werner and Marie Von Behren took our little group of 10-12 kids to Hokkaido for its annual snow festival in '78 or '79. It was an awesome trip. We took over this little and very modest Japanese style inn with a communal bathroom. The first (or second) night we were there, we were all hanging out in the shared communal area making fun of each other's inn-supplied but ill-fitting Japanese kimono PJ's. We were all having a good time while, then, Werner and Marie, our high school principal and his wife, marched out of their room in their ill-fitting Japanese kimonos, towel tucked under their arms, paused, said hi, and then straight into the communal bathroom, announcing that they were going to take a bath. We all looked and each other in amazement and said, "Together..?" almost in unison after they shut the bathroom door behind them.

I guess they didn't get to see many foreigners there during those days. We were walking through some of the underground shopping area one day, when a shy but courteous Japanese man approached us. Using a combination of broken English and hand signals, he asked for a few strains of blonde hair from one of the girls who had a full head of shoulder length hair.

We had so much fun on this trip. Checking out the snow sculptures; cross country skiing; window shopping; laughing at the higher than human piles of snow on the side of the street with the occasional streaks of "yellow snow;" checking out the variety of vending machines on the street which even sold porno magazines…

One day, somebody found out that the Sapporo Beer factory had an all you can eat and drink Japanese BBQ dinner at its factory restaurant. It didn't take long for several taxis full of HKIS kids to decide that that wasn't a deal to miss. Nobody remembered how many plates of beef we had, but everybody remembered that the Sapporo beer only came in the larger 16oz bottles at the factory. And ….not all the kids came back to the inn under their own power. To this day, Sapporo is still one of my favorite beers!   *Patrick Pang '80*

•India

I couldn't wait for my first Interim trip. As soon as I moved to HK in 8th grade, and heard about this very cool program where we kids could travel to really exciting places in the spring, I was hooked. Luckily, I had parents who could see what a great and unique opportunity this was. In 9th grade, I remember standing at the bulletin board and checking out the trips. My best friend, Suzanne Norton, and I wanted to go together, and the India trip seemed about as fantastic as it could get. We both begged our parents, and I still can't believe that at age 14 I was going to go all the way to India, without my parents.

We spent a lot of time planning the trip. There were parent meetings. A list of things to bring. We had to get these tablets to put in the water, to make it safe to drink. Then we were off. We had a layover in Kuala Lumpur. If I remember correctly, we took Lufthansa airlines, and I think the plane had some issues with landing. I remember going down like we were going to land, but then went up really quickly. It was dark, but I looked out the window and it looked like the pilot had missed the airstrip, and we were in a field. Eventually we landed safely, all a little shaken.

I think it was in Thailand, we stayed a very old, Victorian-style hotel. The rooms were huge, with the tallest ceilings I have ever seen. The bathrooms were enormous, and I remember Suzanne or I were leaning on the sink, and it broke completely off of the wall. Water was gushing in the bathroom, like a fire hydrant unleashed. We screamed, and me in my robe ran down to get some help. The staff didn't understand anything I was saying. We were supposed to be out of the hotel in 15 minutes to meet the bus, and so we just packed up our stuff, and high tailed it down stairs to the bus. I think we told someone on the bus, but I always wondered how flooded that room ended up getting.

At the Taj Mahal, we stopped at a rest stop. There were these men who were snake charmers, and they had a whole bunch of snakes get loose from their baskets. I was in the bus, but that was really scary. Also, there were these dancing bears too. And kids who would run up to the bus begging. We were told not to give them anything, but that was really hard to do. I believe we all threw candy out the window anyway. All of this was unbelievable to me, and sad in a way. It was my first real experience seeing the 3rd world, outside of Hong Kong, and it made an impression on me to never take what we have for granted.

We then went up to Kashmir and stayed on houseboats on Dahl Lake. This was right out of a movie. Absolutely the most beautiful place I have ever been to this day. The houseboats were all hand carved, inside and out. The merchants would float their boats right up to our back porch, and display their wares for us to purchase. I got a great hookah for my father's pipe collection, and a beautiful brass teapot. We also took a boat (Shakira's) on Dahl Lake, and saw some beautiful gardens and ancient ruins. The history and the remoteness of the area were astounding. I still feel like it was a dream, and maybe I didn't really experience it.

Thank God for pictures.

We then went further up into the foothills of the Himalayas, by horseback. We rode these smaller Asian horses thru these vast fields full of wildflowers. I remember thinking there wasn't a telephone wire in sight. We stayed in these huge tents, and there were guides who took care of us. They fed us wonderful food. It was cold though. The snows had just melted, as it was early spring, and the ground was wet. I remember it being very far away from just about anywhere, and I still felt safe and secure.

I think of all of this now, and still can't believe my parents let me go. It was just an amazing experience and I learned so much about other cultures, who I was, and what I was capable of doing. I will always have a special place in my heart for India   *Suzanne Arneson '84*

•Darjeeling

Interim is one of my fondest memories. I went to Darjeeling, India (not once, but twice because I loved it so much there). I'll never forget getting off the plane in Calcutta and being mobbed by hungry children outside the airport. It was a good thing I had some Mentos and Fruit Gums with me.

We then took another plane north to Darjeeling. We got tours of the tea plantations, rode sucked up horses that definitely needed better grooming, visited temples and ate the best curry and naan ever. All the kids who asked for western food got sick, but those of us who ate the Indian cuisine were fine. Behind the inn we stayed in was the most beautiful view I've ever seen. Mt. Everest! We smoked a lot of Ganga while we were there too. A few of us smuggled some back into Hong Kong without thinking of the consequences if we got caught.

Unfortunately some students did get caught on their senior class trip bringing back P.I. bud and suffered major consequences. I'm sure none of us did that again after we heard about the ones who got caught.   *Linda Reizman '80*

•Nepal – Winterim

In the spring of 1980, when I was 16, Mr. Sorensen led a very lucky winterim group to Nepal to hike the Annapurna range in the Himalayan foothills. It was a small group and I met some great people. In the fall of 1979, Sheryl Wilcox dragged me to a slide show outlining the proposed trip. I told Sheryl there was no way my parents would go for it, but she talked me into hitting them up for it anyway. To my total surprise, they agreed. I had a (long) list of conditions that I had to meet, but I met them. In addition to Sheryl, there was her brother Greg, Joe Ziolkowski, Chris Christie, Mari Sekizawa, Mark Almond, and Carl Wollebek. Carl turned 16 when we were at our high point – with a view of Mt. Fishtail – and had a birthday cake made over the campfire. I remember our sherpa told us scary yeti stories that night, as we'd decided to sleep out of doors. Then, when we were almost asleep, I heard him making his high-pitched yeti noise from somewhere, trying to freak us out. Or at least I think it was him…

As a bonus, we stopped in Bangkok on the way to and from Kathmandu and got to hang out with some of our friends from ISB (International School in Bangkok – remember those winter tournament friends?). On the way back, we had connection problems and we had to spend the night in Bangkok. (Our parents hadn't been informed however, so it was a little tense at Kai Tak Airport.)

That trip was one of the greatest times I ever had. It was the most beautiful hiking ever, I got to meet a bunch of great people, and I became better friends with the ones I already knew. And it was my first vacation without my parents.
                                    Sheila Baker '82

4. Class Trips

Las Vegas has nothing on HKISers, twenty-five years after graduation they finally got around to adopting the motto of senior class trips: "What happens here, stays here." Probably an alum who came up with it for the city. The 1980 class went to Cebu. I recall walking into a restaurant/bar with a coat check closet that also bore a sign that said, "Check your guns here." No electricity at the hotel between 10:00 am and 4:00 pm, just hot sun, ice-cold beer and tropical fruits. The 1980 class wanted to go to Thailand, but after what happened to the 1979 class there, the school said no way. Cebu turned out to offer all the same thrills at half the price!!   *Mike McCormick '80*

Mr. Feia, the math and gym teacher went along on our senior class trip to Malaysia. He got his suitcase completely turned upside down at customs, losing everything. He also accidentally "left" two students behind. They had to catch the next flight home!!!   *Anita Lau '84*

While in Manila for the 1976 senior class trip, I got one of my best laughs ever. Earl, Mary Kaye and I were enjoying a late night cup of batangas coffee in the lobby of our semi-seedy hotel in Makati. I glanced towards the entrance in time to see Chris Collins, Tom Buckle, and my semi-adopted son Chris Myers trying to sneak past our guard post. Close by were three Filipino ladies-of-the-night, clinging to the guys' arms and giggling.

This was my spoiler moment!! Casually walking up to the six "young'ins" I politely informed the ladies that they were not permitted in the hotel, and that the boys were barely making curfew. These 3 ladies turned and quickly made their exit. The look of disappointment on the boy's faces was classic, but I thought I had merely intervened before these men made a commitment they couldn't honor. Simultaneously, all three yelled at me, "But...Mr. Kohl...we've already paid!"

I just smiled.

Dave Kohl, Art teacher '73-'80

There were two class trips for us '75 seniors - one to Taiwan and Taroko Gorge, including Taipei and the basketball tournament. What a night in Taroko Gorge pouring rice alcohol on things and watching it burn...things being hands, arms, and flagstones, to name a few.

The other was to Macau on the overnight ferry. There was a group that got off the boat really early after we arrived and managed to get into the Casino, even though most of us were underage. The group that slept in didn't get in the Casino, and spent the day touring   *Marci Brooks '75*

5. Faculty travel

Our second summer in HK was memorable! Along with SEVERAL HKIS faculty families, we traveled via a "slow boat to China" for about 15 or 16 days. The group was led by our favorite faculty guide, Donna Oetting, who along with her adventuresome hubby, Dennis, took on a massive job in planning an "educator's dream" trip to various Chinese cities and sites. We all met several times to work out where we would go and modes of transport between each city. We're told, "pack light!" and each of us took an oversized duffel bag along with a small cache of food for our adventure. I can't remember the name of the ship, but I remember looking at the rust on the exterior and thinking, this is not the "love boat." Our accommodations were scant but livable. The food was not worth remembering! But the entertainment one evening was interesting.... we were treated to a black and white movie in Mandarin about the Lone Ranger and Tonto...the only words we all understood were "Kee mo sabee." Those of us who were old enough to have watched that early television series, burst into laughter. On board ship, we celebrated birthdays, anniversaries, and any other event worth getting together.

Our tours to factories were unbelievable...what else do you do with Americans...take them shopping! Our flight experiences between cities were as amazing...one flight there weren't enough seat belts for everyone so we held on to the seat arms and prayed that the ascent and descents would be uneventful. Another flight had us all laughing while we watched the pilots wiping the condensation off the windows so they could see. Some pilots must have trained during the wars because we sometimes descended as though we were in "dive bomber" situations. Once we landed, we generally had to walk a ways to get to the terminal. My son, Mike, celebrated his 13th birthday on that trip – what a way to turn into a teenager.

One more thought about the trip, we had children that ranged from less than one year old (the Reinking baby) to Dave Anderson who was 14 or 15 at the time; many of our children were light skinned and had varying shades of blonde hair – we were a source of great interest for the Chinese who stood around our busses gawking at us and wanting to touch the blonde heads.

That trip included: The Oetting Family, the Bill and Terri Anderson Family, Arnie and Jan Holtberg Family, Carol and Bill Day, Jim Handrich and his brother and Milwaukee friends, Mrs. McGivern and daughter, Shaina McGivern, Mark and Libby Reinking Family, Al and Carole Feddersons, Larry and Darlene Neuman Family, and Bill and Zita Thompson Family.

Another trip that many faculty took was to the Philippines during Chinese New Year and it was also Valentine's Day. Of course, among us all, we had enough kids to start a summer camp...but the interesting thing was the vast number of school families that we ran into when we arrived at the resort. We could have easily taught school around the pool covering all grade levels and subjects. Sometimes, you just couldn't get away from everyone! The Bill and Lynne Driskill Family, the Mike and Reggie Smith Family, Bill and Carole Day, and the Bill and Zita Thompson Family were among those who were there. I can still remember Reggie following Mike around with a video camera capturing us all on film…those were the days of the super large cameras and the cords attached to the battery apparatus. Combining Chinese New Year with Valentine's Day was fun…the kids made out like bandits!

But the best part of returning to HK after a summer away was at SEATAC Airport – it was always a big reunion at the United Airlines waiting area for the long trip back to HK. We all great stories and bits of gossip to share! The flight attendants were often in awe at the camaraderie we enjoyed. *Zita Thompson teacher '82-'93*

6. Independent travels

After graduation, I left Hong Kong in early July of 1969 and traveled with Eric Mache' (whose mother taught Art at HKIS). We took a ship to Yokohama and Nakhodka, and then continued west on the Tran-Siberian Railroad. Our trip was in question until pretty close to our departure because of ongoing border tensions between China and the USSR. (The train runs fairly close to the border in places.) Tensions eased enough that we were able to follow through with our plans.

Apollo 11, America's first manned flight to the moon, launched while Eric and I were on the ship, en route to the USSR. We, of course, had little access to the news, and had to pick up little tidbits from other travelers. We knew that the landing was due to occur while we were on the train across Siberia, and we assumed we'd have to wait for news until we arrived in Moscow. However, one of the waitresses in the dining car had figured out that we were American. She spoke no English and we spoke no Russian, but she had heard of the successful moon landing and wanted to communicate that to us. She took out her order pad, turned it over, drew a little crescent moon and surrounded it with stars, and gave us a big "thumbs up." We didn't know the details, but she had clearly communicated to us that the landing had been successful.

(Interestingly, Eric and I landed in New York City and were there when the astronauts were greeted by a ticker tape parade.)
Dave Christian '69; '73-'75

Eric Caslow and I took a trip up to Canton our senior year. I ended up getting a smallpox vaccination at the border with everyone else because I had taken my father's shot record instead of my own. There were thousands upon thousands of bicycles everywhere. One night, after a huge meal and a show, Eric and I wandered around drinking a bottle of wine with a few other people. At night the streets were completely empty and dark. Sally Black was on the same trip, and people on the street would reach out and touch her hair.
J. R. McMullen '78

DRAGON taels

DRUGS

They are 10 time stronger
in Hong Kong
Help your buddy
dial 999
for emergency ambulance

Bust a Pusher Dial 5-271430
Anonymous calls accepted

172

Parties and Music

Hong Kong has always been a party town. Visiting military inspired the creation of numerous nightspots, and even entire districts. Music, recorded and live, added to the festive atmosphere. HKIS students had few difficulties merging into the evening scene - from Cotillion dances at the Hotels, to elegant clubs and lounges, to beer halls and bars in Wan Chai, Lan Kwei Fong, and Tsim Sha Tsui. Fortunately, the cabs never stop running.

Popular music suffered from a time lapse between America, Britain, and Hong Kong, and many students were starved for contemporary music and the latest new releases...which often arrived 6 to 12 months after they appeared in Europe and America. A few radio shows provided the only tie with up-to-date styles and hits.

These strong urges for music also manifested in active involvement in student instrumental and vocal programs. Several small musical groups played for school dances and other events since day one. Several noteworthy soloists performed with ensembles and teachers over the years, each with profoundly different styles.

Even the cinema was woefully behind in showing current hit movies. Hong Kong movie houses had their own culture, complete with vendors in the streets hawking an entirely different bill of fare from the sweet candies of American snack counters. But, one could purchase a specific seat for a specific showing days, sometimes weeks, in advance.... an enlightened practice far ahead of Stateside movie house practice.

Ed.

1. Popular Music

In the days before the Internet and music downloads, it was hard to keep up on what music was big in the States. As "Commercial Radio" was our only option, we didn't get to hear a whole lot – except Casey Kasem's weekly "American Top 40" show. I remember sitting there with my little yellow Panasonic tape deck taping David Bowie's "Golden Years" among others. I used to also put my tape deck up to the TV so I could tape TV theme songs like Barretta, SWAT, and the Rockford Files. My dad used to go to New York every November for a headquarters visit and he would go to Sam Goody and buy the top 20 singles. Then we would get them for Christmas. I still have my collection of caveman CDs.

A great way to hear good music (and not the top 40 stuff) was in Chet Passerella's music classes. Some days, after a late night gigging with his band (the Alley Cats?), Mr. Passerella would need to meditate and would leave us with his album collection. *Sheila Baker '82*

I believe it was Casey Kasem who did the American Top 40 From 1970 To 1978. I wish my fa-

ther-in-law was still alive because he was a radio air personality in the San Francisco Bay Area for many years working for KFRC and KYUU using the name "Rick Shaw" and knew the history of radio personalities. *Linda Cox*

Casey Kasem did the American Top 40 (hearing the jingle in my head now) and it was carried on the BBC once a week - Sunday afternoons. It was how we learned the Shaving Cream song - when Dr Demento recorded it in 1975.

Marcy Brooks '75

Listening to Casey Kasem do the American Top 40 countdown was big for me then. Sunday afternoons would find me with the cassette recorder ready to record those songs. I wanted to know what was going on with American music at the time but we also got the benefit of hearing a lot of British music too, didn't we? It's hard to believe I would walk around downtown Central to the album shops by myself and take a little minibus home whenever I was ready. *Sally Lawton '77*

Commercial Radio was the big station that carried Casey Kasem and the American Top 40, but

BFBS - British Armed Forces radio - was my favorite because it provided us with the new "New Wave" music coming from England. In the 70s, Commercial Radio basically played American Top 40, Elvis Presley, and songs from the '60s. I only listed to RHK radio to listen to classical music or the word shows, usually with my dad.

Deborah Smith '80

"Micky Mock, the Rock Jock" was a DJ in Hawaii, and came to HK to work for a couple of years. Or do you say Mick.E.Mock (?). His real name was Michael Pope and besides being on the air during the week, he "spun records" at a few bars, did special parties, etc. He had the Top 40 records sent over to him so that he could play them on the air at times other than during the Sunday program on BBC.

We found out then that the BBC recordings were fairly old when we got them in HK (six weeks? six months?) so Micky Mock's show became the #1 place for up to date "Ammurican" Music.

Marcy Brooks '75

I listened to Commercial Radio with Mike Souza on Saturday morning requests, with all those phone-ins for song dedications on weekday nights, which, admittedly, kinda got out of hand after a while.

And who can ever forget Johnny Quest!

Ken Koo '79

For me, no memory of HK can be complete without including the music of our times. How could we have made it through those times without Elton John's Crocodile Rock, or Carly Simon's You're So Vain, and, of course, James Brown's Sex Machine (a classic)?

I remember attending a Bee Gee's concert (before Saturday Night Fever), at a small outdoor stadium around Happy Valley. The venue was small and informal. That was the time when Bud Skennion and I replaced Mark Leonard's San Miquel with another liquid. For some reason, he didn't find the humor in it.

Patrick Gould '70-'74

The music I heard at the time was Gary Pucket's Young Girl - get out of my mind; Tijuana Brass; Tom Jones" Green, Green Grass of Home - these were regularly on the TV as the videos of that time. My friend Gardner Hatch, a year older, used to play the Chipmunks and 'DownTown' of Frank Sinatra fame. 'Frank Boy' was also very popular - Stranger's in The Night (learnt it by heart and I used to sing it to mom's office staff until she caught me at it - receiving chocolates - have accused her ever since of thwarting my career!

Henrik Mjoman '78

The best was the dedications on the radio, we still joke about those. "I like to make a dedication to Cinderella Chan, Bosco Wong, Napoleon Ng." Finally hearing the official Radio 1 announcement that they would no longer accept announcements about lost budgerigars. I remember one year someone's dad went back to the states for business and bought us new records for the juke box in the cafeteria! We were so with it!

Barbara Schwerdtmann '77

Best jazz in the Colony - I used to go to the Excelsior Hotel's Dicken's Bar every Sunday afternoon after the HK$ 18 buffet to listen to jazz and have a pint.

Wally Tuchardt '81

Jimmy Buffet captured my Hong Kong experience fairly well: "Some of it's been magic and some of it's been tragic, but I had a good life all the way."

Mike McCormick '80

Mark Feldman loved his rock and roll - and we used to complain about the horrible delay in music from the States. Then along came "Mickey Mock, the Rock Jock" all the way from Hawaii with the top 100 songs. Mark and I used to go down to the live shows Mickey Mock did, which was where we got to meet Christopher Lee when he was in town filming The Man with the Golden Gun. That was a big deal, with the production company there at the real Bottoms Up in Tsim Sha Tsui, with the entire street closed off. I still watch that movie with a laugh - it was never as quiet there as it's shown in the movie!

Marcy Brooks '75

We got the stateside songs 6 months after they were released because the means of communication was much slower then. How we relished the songs when they arrived. *Diane Kasala '73*

My daughter Rachel (20) was noting the other day that the groups she listened to just 5 - 10 years ago are mostly non-existent today, whereas almost all my favorites are not only still around, but still touring, doing benefits, etc. Even Ozzie! It was a cool time to be young and their staying power has made keeping "young" an easy venture. (Except for Ozzie...) Chris Myers was inquiring on where the ever-cute Emily Rose (da Rabbit, you know...) might be these days.... I was wondering if either of you remember Chris Green? English girl, great accent... where in my brain did I get that memory from... And shouldn't there be a kids game called "Where's Henry Wilson"?

Missy Preston '77

The Streak was by Ray Stevens...don't ask why I remember that one, and not many others... I'm glad to know it's not just me that suddenly starts to sing the words to what are now referred to as "golden oldies" from the '70s! Should see my kids' reaction when I sing the words to remade songs by new artists ("How do you know that song, mom?")...It's quite funny. Good to see old songs recycled. *Sharon Pearce '77*

2. HKIS music

After I graduated from HKIS I spent a year attending classes at HK University. During that time I joined my brother Robert (he played guitar and sang) and a guy playing electric violin on stage at one of the HKIS dances and played two Velvet Underground songs. The main band was the "Yellow Railroad" and we used their setup. We were pretty bad, but we were having a good time. It was the first time in my life I had ever been behind a drum set. Nobody knew what to make out of us except for Barry who was going crazy over the music.

We had another more conventional rock group in 1969 group with HKIS students Dennis Hoelscher on bass, Larry Otley on drums, my brother Robert on lead guitar, and me on vocals and organ. We had an article on us in the Star newspaper. We were called The Electric Chair.
Eric Mache '68

I was fortunate to be a member of "The Tribe" from 1970-72, playing keyboards. Our lead guitarist was Steve Mason. Robert Wang played rhythm guitar. We were all from the Class of '72. We had two additional members who were not HKIS students –Lionel Rocha who played bass guitar and Rick de Silva who played drums.

Occasionally, my brother (Class of '73) sat in on drums if Rick was unavailable. We specialized in the music of the Stones and Santana. I don't know how good we were but we were definitely loud. We had a regular gig at the Mother's Club and played numerous school dances, both at HKIS and at other schools and clubs.

Robert Dorfman '72

I enjoyed singing in the choir and performing in smaller groups, with Art Himler directing the choir. I also was involved behind the scenes in the musical play production of "Guys and Dolls". Art hired me to play bass along with a professional pianist and drummer to play the entire score for the play. I was the first student to be paid for performance in HKIS history. I also remember being involved (going to a music store) in the purchase of a PA system and mics for the play and future productions. Art was a great teacher and a good friend.

Music was a big part of my life. "Candle Light Dinners" at McDonalds/Repulse Bay on the weekends. Paul Westrick guitar/vocals, Cathy Clasper violin/vocals, and yours truly Jerry Cashman on guitar/vocals made some extra cash performing.

We did several musical performances in the cafeteria at the High School. We were playing under the direction the "master of rock and roll" Chet Passerella. The group included my brother John Cashman.

(I'm) Jerry Cashman (78) on keyboards, Dan Byrne (77) on guitar, John Hunter (77) guitar/vocals, Martin Ranta (77) on Bass, and various drummers. *Jerry Cashman '78*

I learned how to play the guitar with Mr. Matthews - *Amazing Grace* ...I once was lost, but now I'm found..." to the tune of The House of the Rising Sun! *James Barnett*

I remember our band," Signal 1," with fearless leader John MacMillan, "borrowing" the chapel for a "concert" and jamming with G. Barnes and Wally Tuchardt and Roger Anderson? I look back at photos in the yearbook...yikes! I can't believe I was wearing a HK Police canvas bag cut into a cape...in a chapel, no less!

What did the faculty think of us, then? What those teachers went through! Surprisingly they stayed on. I guess Voeltz got us back in 8th grade camp when he showed us how to slaughter a pig!

Kelvin Limm '79

3. The Movies, etc:

The movie theaters included the King and Queen in Central opposite each other on Queen's Road. Imperial in Wan Chai. President or Presidential in Causeway Bay. Lee Theater before you get to Happy Valley along the tram route. Jade and Pearl and New York in Causeway Bay by Daimaru. Hoover on Causeway Rd further down the road before the Victoria Park. And Ocean Cinemas by the Ocean Terminal.

Patrick Pang '80

The theater by Victoria Park was the Roxy Theater. Then there's the Park Theater at the foot of Tin Hau Temple Road. In North Point there were the Kwok Doe (can't remember the English name) and Nanyang theater in Wan Chai.

For those who were in HK during the mid-to-late 60's, there were the Central Theater near Sheung Wan and the infamous haunted theater East City (Tung Shing) Theater which is where the old Rigelletto's was.

Ken Koo '79

The theatre in North Point was the State Theatre. Don't forget the Hoover Theatre (Ho Wah in Cantonese), which was across the street from the Roxy in Causeway Bay.

Robert Dorfmann '72

Loved going to the Chinese movies and reading the subtitles, boy were they pathetic! That's what made them so funny. Remember going to see Jaws, with the Chinese subtitles, had people jumping and screaming before it happened in English. Totally weird. Still have Bruce, the plastic shark, they gave out somewhere.

Yes, I admit it. I also went to see David Cassidy with Cindy Palmer. Swoon. What can I say?

Barb Schwerdtmann '77

My memories of going to the movies in Hong Kong include the painted banners, and the feeling of going to a "grand" theatrical event (even though it was just a movie). The theatres were built up to be so "regal" -- bringing me to the memory of the "Loge." When we would buy tickets, we could reserve Loge seats for the movie, as if we were going to a Broadway show. The Loge was the best place to be when you were a kid, because you could throw the candy corn down to the lower level (if you were at the railing seats) and some people, who I won't name, might even spit their "chat hay" (7-up) over the rail just to see what people would do. I am embarrassed to realize the things we did at the time -- being just kids -- that were really "rude" toward the culture that has ultimately made us this 'third culture' that we are. I am proud to be that 'third culture' and realize that is why I embrace culture as an adult.

Cindy Kinne '78

We'd sneak into R-rated movies, only to find that the censors had stripped out anything that might be considered R-rated!! Very disappointing for post-pubescent teenagers.

Scott Schroth '77

We used to bring San Miguel beer to the movie theater and smoke too.

Linda Reizman '80

I was in 8th grade, when the movie Jaws came out. A bunch of kids came over to Kowloon side to see the movie at the Ocean theatre by the Ocean Terminal. I remember some of the kids being scared of taking a ferry and then having to go back to Repulse Bay where there were sharks!

Hong Kong had a casual "ratings" system: Suitable or Not Suitable for Children. My senior year I went with Keith Challberg to go see A Clockwork Orange. Well, for the first time, there was an age restriction on the movie, and since he hadn't turned 17 yet, we couldn't go. So we chose another film playing at the same theatre: The Fifth Musketeer. ey, it had Beau Bridges and I loved the Three Musketeers, couldn't be too bad, right? We didn't notice that the actual star of the movie was Sylvia Kristel, best known for the Emmanuelle movies... *blush*

And then there was the time I went to see Disney's Fantasia and the Chinese girl in front of us covered her boyfriend's eyes because the fairies were naked! And I remember laughing about Saturday Night Fever because I had seen it in the States (rated R) and then saw it again in HK -- it was a completely different movie because it had been chopped to bits by the censors. Even so, I heard that the film companies would send a copy to HK to be cut up and then it would go to the other countries in Asia for FURTHER censoring! And they didn't want them back!

Deborah Smith '80

At the movies I saw James Bond's You only Live Twice; some Steve McQueen film about Formula 1 where there were terrible car crashes and people got killed or were thrown into the trees on impact - terrible and saddening to me; and Doctor DooLittle which I loved as a 1st grader.

Henrik Mjoman '78

What I loved about the Hong Kong theaters (theatres) was that you could reserve your exact seat. I remember booking my tickets to Jaws six weeks in advance because it was sold out that far. I lamented the fact that they didn't have American style popcorn – the popcorn was always sugared.

I remember walking over to Ice House Street (heading to the American Club). I looked up and saw Spiderman climbing one of the buildings! They were filming a movie! It was a bit windy and he was having a hard time getting the shot. I watched for a little while, but the Chuckwagon was calling me.

Sheila Baker '82

We didn't go to many movies in HK, but did see the original Star Wars there in about '77. One of the unique aspects of Hong Kong movie houses was the huge painted signs that were displayed around the theater, so you could see these blocks away. Up close, I realized they were all hand painted on some type of cloth - beautiful reproduction work of scenes from the movie, with English and Chinese graphics. Some of them would have been worth framing - if you had a warehouse wall to hang them on.

Dave Kohl '73 - '80

4. Parties we remember...or don't

By the time I got to 7th grade and we had to choose our foreign language, Cantonese was no longer offered – only Mandarin. I decided since I was from New York, I should study Spanish since it would be quite useful there. In 9th or 10th grade, Lisa Pearce and I went to a movie in North Point and stopped off in a hotel lobby bar (for tea?) afterwards. We met these two guys who were with

the French Rugby team. I think I still have a signed picture of the team taken in Biarritz somewhere. These guys couldn't speak English and we couldn't speak French, so I spoke in Spanish with them. We spent quite a bit of time chatting, telling them all about Hong Kong, and we even shared a cab when we went home to Lisa's and they were heading to Stanley or somewhere.

When I got home that night, I told my mom about it. "Mom, we met these guys from the French rugby team and the only language we had in common was Spanish and we managed to keep a conversation going for over an hour! We never used English!" My mother mused on this and said, "Honey, that's great, but I don't think you should share that with your father…."

¡Gracias a Señor Wong-Russell!

Sheila Baker '82

Went out dancing a lot with friends, yes, this was the time of disco, and the hustle. Met some interesting people from all over the world at the bars. As I got older, was able to attend many functions with my parents, Chinese chows, wedding feasts, and entertaining many visitors from around the world.

Did you ever hear about the French Nuclear Aircraft carrier parties? It was the Joan d'Arc or something like that. The Dads at the embassy thought the daughters should act as escorts at the welcoming party. I got paired up with some fellow who pushed the champagne. To this day, I will not drink the stuff. I got so plastered! All the while I tried to act dignified and not let my parents know! Then the next night the ship threw a party for us. So, back we girls went in our ball gowns, all dolled up for the kill. The guys asked our Dads if they could show us the ship. Never, ever will I reveal what happened in the watchtower. But I bet most of the other girls know! I would kill if my kids did that today! I guess the shoe is on the other foot. When I am 90 in a nursing home, they are going to wonder what I am smiling about!

Cindi Webb '78

I would spoon-feed Cathy McCoy chocolate milk shakes in my bathroom after our many outings to the Back Door, Ned Kelly's or such other drinking establishments so we wouldn't have a hang-over the next day.

I remember throwing up over the terrace

railing at the Royal Yacht Club after Tony Cahill and Rob Janssen spiked (again and again and again) my rum and cokes with "151" while pretending to look for contact lenses. Cathy and I falling down the spiral staircase that led to the formal dinning room concluding the night when we had to stop in a park in Mid-Levels before reaching Cathy's flat so she could get sick before reaching her apartment and then playing a basketball game the next day – my highest scoring game!

Then there was getting locked out of the Back Door after I went to show a US Sailor where Ned Kelly's was located. He was kind enough to escort me home via Six Fingers (the Star Ferry had already closed) to Repulse Bay as I had left my purse in the bar so didn't have any money.

He offered to explain to my father what happened but I thought it best if he leave as fast as he could! I was only allowed to go out that night if Brad accompanied me. He was in a panic when he realized I was nowhere to be found. I was never so happy to see him when he returned home after escorting Kari home. (The following day we left on home leave for the States – only later did my Mom discover we weren't air sick but hung-ever – The true story didn't come out until YEARS later!)

Renee Doyle '78

The Godown was a firetrap that would never get a license in the States. The same doorman was still there ten years after we left. Lan Kwai Fong was/is good fun, but sedate compared to Wan Chai on a weekend in the mid-70's when ten US Navy ships were in town from Vietnam for R & R. The Front Page had a good house band and there were usually a couple of well-known musicians passing through at any given time. Things really started to pick up after midnight.

Anonymous

Ah.... the stories, which could be told! The only problem is – not sure the statute of limitations has run out. And as a forty-five year old, I'm not sure I'd want any of my kids reading about some of them. *Anonymous '80*

Oh my! Teenagers in Hong Kong. I think I got an "A" in mayhem and debauchery! Why didn't we have a class in that?

Sydney Henrietta '84

Since my father was always on a business trip and my mother was either visiting her relative in Korea or just there but naive, my brother and I would have parties and so many kids would show up. Beer pyramids and people pyramids in our living room. Wearing our Jordache and Gloria Vanderbilt jeans from Stanley market, our Nike tennis shoes, and listening to loud Led Zeppelin, The Cars, Foreigner, Boston, The Doobie Brothers, Van Halen and Aerosmith and even a little disco too. My Chinese neighbors probably hated us! Such crazy, wonderful times! *Linda Reizman '80*

My oldest sister did Cotillion in Hong Kong I remember all the "big girls" in white formal dresses with elbow-length gloves! I got the impression it was preparation for a social "coming out" announcing the girls as marriage material available for courting by eligible bachelors...?

Jill Liddiar '77

Ah the naughty things we did, I seem to recall I was one, yes the butter ice sculptures were beautiful and the ginger bread houses too!!! Christmas time hanging out waiting to meet friends in the upper lobby of the now gone Hilton, cheeseburgers at the Original American Club at the old Hong Kong and Shanghai Bank, Christmas cotillion at the Club with our little white Mickey Mouse gloves (5 fingers though). T'was a good life, but more fun to be drinking Mateus wine on the old Cricket Club green after a Friday/Saturday night movie listening to AJ, Tad, Robbie and the rest strum guitars and singing songs while we lay back and looked up at the Hilton, I think it was one of those evenings that led us up to sit on the edge of the roof.... memories. *Rich Vaughn '72*

We had the BEST of times with Mr. Kohl's Morris Minor in the summer of '77. Tom Burkhard was flat-sitting for him, and had the keys to his green convertible... We really put it through some trials. But don't get me wrong, with all due respect to Tom and John, they were always primarily concerned about the welfare of the car (yeh heh). However, it was the vehicle which transported us to the top of Mount Davis, where the army bunkers were far too steep to reach by car, but Mr. Dave Kohl, I am proud to tell you, we reached several times by your vehicle, and quite precariously if I may say so. I was the one who was screaming in the back seat, because I didn't want to die. But then we would reach the top, and John and Tom would launch their radio-controlled gliders, and we would enjoy some of the most memorable times over the mountains and valleys of Hong Kong Island. I remember those two guys thought it was so cool that they actually got your car to make it to the top of Mt. Davis -- what a harrowing experience from the back seat...those were some extremely steep bunkers!! That was some car...

Cindy Kinne '78

We had co-ed slumber parties (where we determined if people would look better in clothes or without), bomb scare parties and hurricane parties at our flat at Repulse Bay Towers.

Renee Doyle '78

A couple time I hosted "all-nighters" in the art room with students working on various projects or the potter wheels. I gave Werner Von Behren a bit of a go sometimes myself - he couldn't fathom why I had some volunteer kids working all night in the art room, and when Mr. Mok found a kid sleeping on the stairs at 4 am he called Werner, who showed up "incredulous" that ANYBODY would do something so crazy as to work all night with a bunch of high school art students. Hey it was fun, and of the moment.

Dave Kohl, art teacher '73-'80

•New Year's Eve

I remember the first time I was actually allowed out on New Year's Eve. It was my junior year and I was visiting HK from boarding school. My friend Elliot (from boarding school) and his family were visiting Hong Kong and we spent New Year's Eve together. We ate with the family at the Peninsula and then took off in one of Elliot's Hanukah presents – a hotel car for the evening.

We were traveling in high colonial style in one of the Peninsula's Rolls Royce's and we went over to the Hong Kong side and stopped by the Godown to meet some people. We left the car at the Furama and walked over. All of the sudden, I noticed an entire block packed with people running. The entire street was swarming with people and they were headed in a wave toward us and yelling. There were two people, a man and a woman with long blonde hair, at the front of the crowd and they

were running to get away from the throng. I had never seen anything like it. I though, "Whoa, things get pretty crazy on New Year's Eve. I thought it was just people out having cocktails and waiting for the cannon to go off." I told Elliot we had to get out of there.

We cleared out of the street and went into an alley to let the mob pass. After they went by, Elliot said, "Do you know who that was? At the front of the crowd?" I hadn't the foggiest idea. It was Mick Jagger and Jerry Hall trying to escape a horde of crazed fans. I said, "Oh, man! We could have whisked them away in the Rolls!"

Sheila Baker '82

I remember greeting the US Navy sailors and taking them on tours of Hong Kong. They in return took us on tours of the USS Enterprise.

Marcy Brooks '75

The faculty held a '50's party on a tram. We all dressed in 50's clothes and Bob Scripko was decked out in a full nun's habit as the "head" of our school - St. Prissy's. *Judy Butler, teacher '76-'83*

Strange and amazing things happen when alcohol, youth and little oversight converge. Of course, I was the kid who managed to get suspended for a year after my freshman year, so my experiences may be somewhat different than most. By the way - were we supposed to attend class? I was in school, from time to time, from 7th - 12th grade, starting with the 1974-1975 school year and ending in 1980. *Mike McCormick '80*

Another big plus in those days was the drinking parties and the weekend outings to Ned Kelly's on the Kowloon side for Pitchers of San Mig. *Gavin Birnie '75*

I'm not willing to put into print the point that what REALLY influenced us all in HK was that you could walk into a pharmacy and buy birth control pills over the counter.

But ya know what? We never had a HKIS high school pregnancy either! And there was plenty of opportunity for it! *Anonymous '74*

Chapter 13
Tough Times

I have to write some of this before it gets out of my mind. I find it hard to write about some of the people I went to school with not because they have gone on before us, but because they were a part of us. It wasn't all good and/or all bad, but a big part of growing up and trying to fit in with each other.

We were all together in the British Crown Colony because our parents were working in a part of the world that lent itself to opportunity and we were part of that. Maybe we didn't see it then but now maybe we can look back and reflect upon our interactions with each other, and can see how each of us influenced who we are today.

Eric Lee '75

1. We had a number of tragedies occur at HKIS.

In 1968, the child of one of the faculty died because of inadequate ventilation in the bathroom. He was Timothy Paul Von Behren, a 4th grader. We had all been told to leave the windows cracked to provide adequate ventilation as the geyser being used to heat hot water was gas. When a person ran hot water while taking a shower or bath, the geyser produced carbon monoxide. This was a very difficult time for all of us. We then put vents in all bathroom doors to help prevent this from happening again.

Our own son also fell through the windows in the base of the tower on the fourth level with the cross on top. He was leaning against it and it just gave way. He fell down three flights of stairs on to the concrete. They took him to Queen Mary hospital and he was there for three days. I know it was a tragedy. However, some humor came when I went to get him out of the hospital. The sister-in-charge told me that I owed HK$2.40. I was expecting a much higher bill and was very surprised at the amount. She said, "Well you have to take medicine home for your son and we will cover the cost of the medicine but you have to pay for the bottles."

We had yet another death occur but this time in the United States of the brother of one of the faculty. I remember Bob Christian calling me on a Sunday morning and asking me to make arrangements to get the faculty member on the way to the U. S. that morning if at all possible. So I was able to get the person on a flight that morning. I had to charge it on a credit card at the airport. Back then you had to take the ferry to get across the harbor as there wasn't a tunnel. We really leave almost within an hour to make the trip to the airport but we made it.

We also had the experience of the death of the daughter of Mrs. Chan on the Chinese staff who was hit by a lorry and killed. I had never been to a funeral at that point in Hong Kong of a Chinese person. I remember very well the fact that during the time at the funeral home, while the service was still going on, that the director came to Mrs. Chan and asked to be paid right then! That was an experience I will never forget.

Several summers later we had a new couple who were to start in mid-August. They came from Taiwan and stopped in Hong Kong to see their new home. They were going on to Europe for a vacation and then would in mid-August. I took them to their hotel and they said they would get to the airport on their own. The next morning, in the South China Morning Post was a small article on the front page that a Japan Airlines flight had crashed on its final approach in Bombay. Thirty minutes from reading the story, the HK Immigration Department called to tell me, as the sponsor, that they had been killed in the crash. We then had to notify their relatives in the United States and then deal with all the items they had shipped from Taiwan. This was a sad time.

Ed Dollase, business manager, '67-'74

Susie and Charlie Robb's father died in 1977 -- my recollection is that he died of a heart attack while jogging with Charlie, but given that I was also in 6th grade at the time, my memory may not be accurate. Who was in 3rd grade, also lost his father that year (in another plane crash, I think). Not a good year...

Eric Linker

The Kotewall Disaster. I remember that vividly. It was typhoon Rose in Aug of '71. The rain from the # 10 signal caused massive landslides throughout the Colony. The first apartment building collapsed when the earth underneath gave way from the massive amount of rainwater. When it toppled over, it hit the second building and clipped the corner of the top three floors. I do not remember how many people died but I still remember a picture on the front page of the local newspapers showing a victim dead sitting up in the corner of a room in his pajamas. He was dubbed as the "sitting corpse" by the local papers when the rescuers couldn't get to him for days.

A friend of my family lived just down the hill from the two buildings. The fire department commandeered their home as the rescue headquarters. I remember seeing the remains of the second building sans the top corner and the massive amount of dirt and debris everywhere with my own eyes. It was very eerie. Because of the landslides, the Government mobilized the British garrisons and used the yet-to-be-opened cross-harbor tunnel to transport the solders and equipment to the Hong Kong side.   *Patrick Pang '80*

•SARS - Severe Acute Respiratory Syndrome
        8 April 03

Dear Friends and Family,
        How I wish I could tell you that all the news about the SARS you're getting in America is exaggerated or biased but it's the same news reports that we are getting from our local stations and newspapers. I feel like we're living two movies: 'Apocalypse Now and The Andromeda Strain or 'Outbreak. We keep thinking that the peak has come, the number of cases each day will go steadily down but they are going back up again. The death count is still low and mostly people that had other major health complications.

        There is no school until April 23. Local schools were all ready scheduled to be out all of Holy Week (we got off Good Friday, Mon, Tues) so the gov't thought it wise to shut everything down and hopefully keep the numbers down as to HOW the virus is spread. There are so many questions - the biggest one being - exactly HOW is it spread? The one theory, given by a Prof at HKU, is the reason that Block E at Amoy Gardens got hit so bad was because of a construction site right outside the

windows and the urine from workers had wafted through the air. Another theory is that people in Guangdong Province (right across the border) have caught the virus from handling and/or eating exotic birds. True? Or comic relief?

        Pictures show people in Central with 75% wearing masks. Doctors do not agree on whether they help or not. Most folks on the public transportation are wearing them. Most taxi drivers are wearing them. I was told that people with asthma have a very difficult time with them, that it makes breathing even harder, so I'm not wearing any. We are staying in Tai Tam, away from crowds, taking care of ourselves as best we can. We have gone to Stanley to eat in open-air restaurants and church Sunday - the first since this all started. We exercise, good healthy eating, drinking lots of water and washing our hands constantly. Good health habits. One report said that there were less people spitting in public so that's a good thing!

        We are doing on-line virtual school at HKIS. We don't want to make up the days in the summer or over the weekends in May. Local schools will be making the days up in the summer. The first week, the whole faculty was expected in each day at 8:30am for an update/gathering. Good community was built, like we've never had before. This is a good thing. This week and next week, each dept. is assigned two days to be on campus and the other days do the work with kids wherever they can get to a computer.

        We have less than 20% of the high school kids gone. Several teachers are gone but I don't know the number. The kids have gone to Australia, China (!!!), India, France, Israel, Sweden, Korea, Japan, USA, Thailand. US Consulate kids have to stay out of the country for 30 days - that's the rule for evacuation.

        And that creates some stress and the up and down feelings we have every day. So it is with a crisis. The Chinese word character means 'danger and opportunity.' A matter of attitude. We're trying to care deeply for each other and not get caught in the panic.

        We met Nury Vittachi recently at a party hosted by Alison Lutz and Todd Wong. We were glad that Todd's dad was there - who happened to be the architect of the original HKIS building so we thoroughly enjoyed getting to know him. Anyway, the Vittacys were there - his wife teaches at Island School and we had wonderful conversations and great laughter. And then we see his article! Ah yes, the fun of Hong Kong, in the midst of the craziness! HUGS and LOVE,

Lois Voeltz ('73-'80; '96-'03)

11 April, 2003

AND NOW THE GOOD NEWS

There is a dangerous virus spreading through Hong Kong.

It is NOT atypical pneumonia.

It is panic.

All outbreaks of any high-profile pathogen or disease (cf the UK's Mad Cow disease) have two major effects. A tiny proportion of people are hit by the disease itself. A large number of people, organizations and entire industry sectors are hit by the panic that accompanies it.

Yes, you should be careful and take all precautions as advised by your medical advisor, but no, you don't have to panic and flee Hong Kong.

•You don't have to stay at home. At the time of writing (first week of April, 2003), more than 99.999% of people in Hong Kong are completely free of the SARS virus.

•An increase in numbers doesn't mean people in every apartment block have it. The virus's growth pattern shows a tendency to remain tightly clustered - for example in the Prince of Wales Hospital and Amoy Gardens.

•Ninety-nine people a day die of flu every day in the United States alone. Of these 99, about 30 die of acute respiratory problems. In Hong Kong, 16 people have died over a month.

•In any large city of this size, there are hundreds of pneumonia sufferers at any time, of which several dozen have some form of atypical pneumonia.

•Yes, the virus does mutate. But this doesn't necessarily mean it continually gets more virulent. Scientists note that as SARS spreads, it is significantly weakening from carrier to carrier.

•The media may call it a killer virus, but the survival rate among those hit in these clusters is 96%. •Yes, we all care about our children, but very few kids get it -careful examination of lists confirms that victims tend to be elderly people with a direct physical link to the clusters.

•Contaminated places get clean by them-

selves. The virus dies without a carrier. Some scientists estimate its life as three hours, others say a little longer, but all agree it cannot hibernate. In other words, you can even check into the Metropole Hotel floor 9 without fear.

•The virus is believed to die when the air temperature reaches 27 degrees C. One hot Hong Kong day could fry all traces of it on exposed surfaces.

•You can keep your air conditioner on in the office. Ward 8B in the Prince of Wales Hospital shares an air conditioning system with the infected Ward 8A. But there was not a single infection in 8B.

•Many people assume the "growth model" of the virus will follow sci-fi movie scenarios. Evidence suggests it is more likely to follow the Guangzhou experience, where it spread for a few weeks and then started to contract.

•The flood of panicky emails from a variety of people, including doctors who should know better, is not helpful. One email doing the rounds is instructing people not to exercise. Panic creates muddle-headedness. Consider the facts above. Hong Kong is our home.

Stay Calm and stay healthy!
Nury Vittachy, in the SCMP

12 April 2003

Dear Students and Parents,

We're finishing week two of "virtual school." Faculty and students, in most part, have responded well to the experience and student learning is moving forward. Communication has been through class forums, e-mails, and occasional phone calls. In general, students who are working in Hong Kong are finding communication and work completion a bit more easily to do than students who are out of Hong Kong.

There's a general sense among faculty that the students who normally perform well in regular school are continuing to perform well, are moving forward with "virtual school" and making it work. It's also fair to say that both teachers and students miss the daily contact, experiences, learning and relationships of "regular school."

Some FAQ's (Frequently Asked Questions) about HKIS, School Opening and Virtual School

•How many students are doing virtual school in and out of Hong Kong? As of April 11, 153 students (20%) are out of Hong Kong and 605 (80%) are in Hong Kong.

•What do I do if I can't keep up with the work? Let your class teacher know when you're behind and why. Copy the e-mail to your homeroom advisor. We've gotten feedback that some students are overwhelmed with the work. Pace yourself, keep communicating. Let your teachers know where you're behind and then keep at it. There will be no new assignments over the Easter break.

•Any evidence of SARS at HKIS? No students, teachers or staff has contracted SARS. Once school resumes, we ask you to keep your child home if he or she is sick and be watchful for symptoms of the illness. HKIS buildings and facilities are disinfected and cleaned daily thanks to our staff. Faculty who are working on campus feel safe. Some good news: both parent medical care workers who were diagnosed with SARS have now recovered and have been discharged from hospital.

•When will we know if school will really reopen on April 23? Dr. Wehrenberg met with Hong Kong Education Department officials yesterday and they will make a decision on that next Thursday, April 17. Dr. Wehrenberg will communicate with everyone about HKIS as soon as we know. We are ready then to publish the next edition of Cross Section with a revised calendar of letter days, upcoming events, and a special schedule for the first day back on April 23. "Virtual school" will not continue once regular classes start. If a student cannot be back on April 23, he or she must take the initiative to e-mail the teachers for any updates on assignments and class activities.

•What if we don't start April 23? If we're out a bit longer, "virtual school" will continue. At this time we are not permitted to use the two public holidays in May (Labour Day and Buddha's Birthday), for make-up of school days. We are considering some make-up days on weekends. Because of the reasonable progress with the curriculum and learning that we are making through "virtual school," at this time we are not considering lengthening the school year beyond June 12.

•Is it true the PFO World's Fair on April 26 is cancelled? Yes, too many questions and organizational challenges faced the PFO if we can only return on campus on April 23. It likely will not be rescheduled for the busy month of May.

Finally, thank you to faculty for their hard work, creativity and amazing ingenuity at launching virtual school and moving learning forward. Congratulations to students for increasing their independence and taking increased responsibility for moving their own learning forward. Life-long learning requires that kind of self-motivation and determination. And thanks to parents, for encouraging both students and teachers with your words and messages.

You'll hear from me again at the end of next week, either with the revised Cross Section as school opens on April 23 or with another e-mail on how we will continue to move forward with virtual school. If you have questions I didn't answer, send me an e-mail or give me a phone call.

Thanks for your continued cooperation.

Jim Handrich, administrator, '83-'07

•Tien An Men

While on assignment for photography class (with good-ole Igor Lau), we actually went to the last candlelight vigil in Victoria Park commemorating the Tiananmen Square incident. While not knowing much of what was said, an amazing experience none-the-less.   *Jason Weber '97*

When I stayed at the Hilton in '89, I remember being able to watch the demonstrators in Status Square from my hotel room window protesting in support for the students in Tiananmen Square. They were there 24/7! On my flight back to US, I met a girl from Philly who was at the Tiananmen Square and had made friends with some of the students.

Several days after I left HK, the massacre happened on the Square. We met up in Philly later and she showed me pictures from the Tiananmen Square and told me that those people in the pictures with her were probably dead.

Patrick Pang '80

•9-11

When I taught high school Math at HKIS ('76-'79) I was part of a very strong community of faculty, students and parents. It is gratifying to see that this sense of community still exists and has been strengthened in the face of the nation's tragedy.

I am thankful for the prayers that have been

posted. I had family in both New York and DC at the time of the attack. My sister in law was returning from the DC airport when she saw the aircraft pass low over the expressway and crash into the Pentagon. She had just put her son-in-law on a flight from DC to LA and it was hours before she learned that he was OK.

My daughter Michelle Pearson Blythe (now living with her family in London) had a Canadian friend who was reporting for his first day on the job at the World Trade Center. He was a few minutes late and was in the massive lobby waiting for the "lift" when the aircraft struck. He was able to dive behind a huge marble reception desk and escape the explosion that went down the elevator shafts and blew out the doors.

The lobby was carnage, but he was unharmed.

My nephew Jason had just arrived in Manhatten when the attack occurred, and took photos from the street as events unfolded

Rich Pearson, math teacher '76-'79

2. In Memorium

• Geoff Ayers ('80)

Geoff Ayers '80 died in the late '80's of AIDS. Our dads worked at the same company and our parents were friends. They were also posted in Japan at the same time we were, right before moving to HK.

Although we only hung out when our families got together, he felt sort of like a brother (since we'd arrived in Japan AND HK at the same times, I guess)... so it was rather comforting to know he was around (and I rather liked it when he'd tease me good-naturedly in class or in the halls... Such a brotherly thing to do, since my real brother was much older and I never really grew up with him around). I remember Geoff as a very vibrant, creative person with such a curiosity and zest for life.

He seemed to have no fear. I always marveled at how self-assured he was, and how easily he could talk to people... especially the first day at a new school!! I really admired that about him. Joan Amy '80.

Geoff was a very good-looking, fairly flamboyant guy who had a lot of issues about who he was vs. who he "should be". He was a lot of fun and he could be a really REALLY good friend, someone you probably wouldn't think you could

depend on, but someone who really cared. I hadn't kept up with him after high school, but one day in October 1996, I went down to the Mall in DC to view the AIDS Memorial quilt because I wanted to see a friend's panel, plus I knew it was going to be last time it would fit the Mall (it covered the whole dang thing!). I was walking around alternating between enjoyment and sorrow, and then came to a panel for "Geoffrey", with Geoff's face beaming out at me. It stopped me in my tracks.

Deborah Smith '80

• Myles Berry ('03)

Myles Berry was in the class of 2003 and in his junior year he sustained a head injury from an accident in his home. They never were able to stem the bleeding and about ten days later he died. The high school community really pulled together with prayers and support.

Jim Handrich, high school principal '83-'07

It was a new decade and most of us were only fifteen or sixteen. We were young, but so much had already happened in our lifetimes. There was the Gulf War, the Handover and, of course, the Millennium. Fall semester started out fabulous - we were juniors, and we were going to rock 2001.

On September 11th of that year, families all over the world sat in front of their televisions watching the Twin Towers. The next morning, we exchanged stories, as well as tears.

While the world watched as New York picked up the pieces, we were thrown another curveball. Gossip circled HKIS faster than Mr. Handrich could even begin to make the announcement. To this day, I still don't know exactly what happened. We knew Myles fell and that it was pretty serious. But it was Myles - he'd be okay. As days passed the rumors got worse, but we knew better. So we did what HKIS'ers do, we hiked "Miles for Myles". We reminisced and we laughed, and when a friend cried, we carved We love you Myles into the chalky hillside to lift his spirits, because we knew we'd hike there again with him and he'd laugh at how silly we were to worry.

We couldn't wait for our big strong Canadian to come back. Drinking it up with him at Beer Castle, partying till the sun came up, and most importantly, returning those polar bear hugs.

I could feel it in my gut, and as our class filed

into the gym, I knew they could feel it too. The tears fell before the news hit. Anger, sadness, disbelief, shock, you name it, we felt it. We couldn't move. But when the tears subsided, what was left was us. We looked to each other for comfort and strength. Some days were worse than others, but through laughter and great memories, we made it through. I can't help but think that he's proud of us.

It's been four years, and if you take a look on the island at the high school entrance, you'll find a young maple tree in the midst of bamboo stalks. Myles will always be in our hearts and in our minds. And how many people can say they've partied with an angel?

Anonymous, Class of 2003 '91–'03

We were there at that time Myles passed away. The way Jim handled the whole thing was absolutely magnificent. In a nutshell, Myles was a Canadian kid who by all accounts everyone liked.

He had a fall in the kitchen of his flat, had a head injury, and soon after died from it. His death really impacted the student body that year.

Fritz Voeltz, high school vice-principal '95–'03

What a difference two weeks has made in the lives of so many of us. First it was the September 11th Tragedy and then it was Myles' death. For high school students at HKIS, most have never experienced before so much sadness and pain. But there were wonderful, soaring moments as well as we remembered Myles. I heard rugby stories about Myles and how the team felt about him. I heard soccer stories and how he helped "grow" last year's soccer team. I heard from teachers what a "presence" Myles was in their classes. You knew right away when Myles was there and when he was absent.

I heard interim stories, Myles was wondering about going to India and building houses for Habitat and then deciding after it was all over, he could definitely do it again. I heard what an ambassador he was at meeting new students and how quickly Myles' friendship became a deeper and more lasting relationship. I heard how Myles was a peacemaker when individuals and groups sometimes didn't get along. I saw first-hand what a spirit Myles was to his homeroom in the "Challenged by Choice" tug of war. There was no way they wouldn't come out on top!

And throughout this week students have lined up to write in the book we have in the office in memory of Myles. I've heard a group of juniors say, let's remember and respect Myles (the way he would have done things) in the way we live our lives. And I took a walk with a group of students raising money for the ICU unit at Adventist; we carried a banner reading "Miles for Myles" and a Canadian flag as we walked through Tai Tam Country Park. I even learned a few more words of "O, Canada . . .." These past two weeks have been an endless, wonderful remembrance to the spirit and impact of Myles Berry.

And then I read in the South China Morning Post, "Myles William Berry – Second of May, 1985 to 25th of September, 2001: Some people come into our lives and quickly go. Some stay for a while and leave footprints on our hearts. And we are never, ever the same." All those stories that we all heard and told this week, they are the footprints of Myles Berry.

So remember Myles, the peacemaker, the friend, the Canadian, the comedian, the teammate, the student, the friend, the brother, and the son; remember Myles and live your life well. May God grant that someday it may be said for each one of us – "We stayed for a while and left our footprints on the hearts of others." Thank you, Myles, for showing us how to do that. Amen.

Jim Handrich. Message at Myles' memorial service, Sept 25, 2001

•Constant Cha ('76)

I didn't really know him, although I sat next to him in choir my junior year. And it was there I heard about him the next year, still remember I was sitting on the right side third row up. We all knew of each other, being such a small school, especially the kids who were there for years. Have any of our Chinese friends written about the family pressures of school and academics as a conflict with the US system along with family expectations? I think the perspectives would have been very different. We all knew we were going to college and would have little trouble fitting in where we ended up (well, sort of). I can't even imagine what that must have been like.
Barb Schwerdtman '77

•Michelle Champeau ('77)

I have to reflect upon Michelle Champeau and her brother Chris, both were classmates of mine. Michelle went to Cotillion, as did I, and I think Chris did too. I don't really know why Michelle was in the class, but it could have been to learn to dance, to socialize, or both. I never asked. I went to learn to dance; I still don't know how. It was really funny to try, as awkward as we were, to be comfortable with each other in a "proper" social situation.

We had to learn to use our etiquette to ask one another to dance, sweaty palms and all. Michelle was such a gracious sweetheart thru and thru in that class and I am sure that she retained those qualities in her adult life. I know I shall miss her charm and grace. *Eric Lee '75*

•Mark Feldman ('75)

I got to know Mark best when he moved to the YMCA in Kowloon our senior year. There were issues at home that disturbed him and it just worked out for the best for him. He used to sneak me into his room and we'd talk for hours, listen to "Stateside" music (how he hated the BBC excuse for "Rock and Roll") and just hang out. When he told the elevator operator I was his sister (sorry Lisa) I often felt that way! Mark wouldn't come over to our house to eat, or take anything that might make his life in that room any easier. He was fiercely independent in that way.

My happiest memory comes after we'd left HK, and returned stateside. Mark and I really didn't keep in touch, mostly because he never answered anything I wrote to him. (And I really didn't expect him to.) Then a letter came back to me, and so I had no way to get in touch. Well one day maybe eight months later, my phone rings. The operator comes on and barely stifling a giggle, says, "I have a collect call from Paul McCartney, will you accept the charges?" I paused for a minute. Uh.ah. (Long distance and COLLECT wasn't cheap for a student then!) when suddenly an absolutely horrible rendition of "I Wanna Hold Your Hand" starts. And I knew then. I accepted the charges, and Mark and I must have talked an hour. He'd just been bumming around south Florida, living the life.

Later, we managed to hook up again after he'd moved to the Tampa area, gotten married, and started showing dogs. Since I'd been showing since 1980, it was like old times. We'd IM and email, mostly talking about how old we'd gotten, how bald he'd gotten (he wasn't), and how much he

loved his wife, Lori. We didn't stay as close as we could through the years, but Mark always had a large and generous heart, a wickedly dry sense of humor, and a shoulder anyone could cry on.
Marcy Brooks '75

Thanks for the experience of having you as a teacher – ceramics, woodshop and Basic Art. Thanks for all the time devoted to the seniors. Someday, we shall all go back to Taroko Gorge and have an "instant replay" How about a game of cribbage? See you in a cosmic galaxy...
Mark Feldman, in Dave Kohl's '75 Orientale

•Kerry Fogarty ('79)

Kathy, Odile and I were at your memorial in PA that beautiful fall day with your Dad and rest of family several years ago. It was a party without a good theme. We stayed up all night and toasted your quirks, (like the time you invited Barry Casler and I down to visit you in Nashville. Just happened to be the day your movers arrived with your family's HK shipment, but you didn't bother to tell us, or your Mom…. boy was she surprised to see us when we showed up), we toasted your demons (can't mention these in print)…most important, we toasted your friendship.

As our HKIS past now hits 40, I can't believe the speed of time. Some of our kids are the now the age (or older) when we first hung out…so annoyed that you can't meet them.

We miss you friend…………
Kevin Kwok '79

•Billy Gavaghen ('82)

Billy Gavaghen used to dig through the band room and turn us on to the greatest music. I remember first hearing Jeff Beck in there, Yes, Genesis – all the great bands. A few years ago, Moira Gavaghen, her parents, Peter Robbins and I got together some resources and funded a new stereo system for the school in Billy's memory. I want to go see it when I am on campus. Moira made a great remark – that she was happy to think of Billy as being the "ghost in the machine." I have always been grateful for his friendship and his musical influence. *Sheila Baker '82*

•Gregg Grimsley ('69)

But he loved people. He loved life. And he loved to tell a good story. Gregg was so admired among his peers in Peoria that they closed the courthouse for the day of his funeral, because they knew no one would be at work anyway. He was a bankruptcy lawyer. Little old farm ladies came up and hugged my mother and told her how they were able to keep their farms, send their kids to college, etc. because of Gregg going to bat for them in the legal system. It was such a tribute to a man who lived well.

Sandy Grimsley '72

•Carolynn Hairabedian ('73)

Carolyn Hairabedian was a very jovial person who took great pride in her Armenian heritage. She was very fond of her younger sister Patty, and quick to introduce her. I remember Patty and hope she is well. Carolyn's favorite joke was "one dollar you buy me drinkee?" which she would recite and then laugh so hard. I heard at our 1973 reunion in 2003 that she had died in an auto accident shortly after high school. I was very sad to hear this as I had often thought of her and wondered how she was.

Wendy Liddiard '73

Carolyn Hairabedian is(was) my cousin. She graduated I think in 73' and was very outgoing, involved in athletics and loved by her friends. Her family moved back to Northern California after she graduated. Unfortunately she had a hard time adjusting to life in the United States after graduating from HKIS. She couldn't seem to find her place and finally ended up joining the Navy, where she was quite happy.

She was killed in a car accident in Maine I believe in 1976 and our whole family was devastated, honestly I don't think my aunt ever recovered from the loss.

The Hairabedians lived around the corner from us growing up in Southern California, we moved to Taiwan in 1968 and they moved to HK 2 years later, we moved to HK in 1971 and I was so happy to have my cousins there (Carolynn and Patty)...tough being the new kid!!!

Stacy Aspaturian '75

•Marie Karr ('76)

Marie (aka Junior, June) quickly became a very important part of my life in 1973 when the O'-Keefe clan moved to 10 Peak Road, Bowen Hill. I was thrilled to learn that the Karrs lived in the next building and even had a yard! Our families quickly became friends. Marie and I were very different, she was worldly, sophisticated, quiet, funny and so

much fun. We were off the boat Americans, loud and looking for trouble.

Everyone that knew Marie had a special place in his or her heart for her, she was so sweet and there was something about her that made you want to be around her. She was not the HKIS student who would be front and center, or be in trouble after every weekend escapade. Actually now that I think about it she was a good influence on me. She was very much into clothes and I would always be jealous of her knack for matching everything she was wearing from jewelry to shoes to sunglasses. How could someone in 10th grade be so put together? Couldn't figure it out and imitating it was a disaster.

We would spend hours laughing in her room, or going out with her mother, Patsy. Her father Ralph was in charge of San Mig (which was another plus in our relationship). She loved her sisters and mother, was very fond of Ricky Gutlan. We had a wonderful high school friendship, exactly what we both needed. We lost touch after high school but Karen tells me that she has 3 beautiful sons. I was so sad to hear of her passing; I would have loved to pick up where we left off. She was a truly special person and my best friend.

Megan O'Keefe '76

•Stephen Ko ('76)

Stephen Ko would've been Class of '76. I used to see him in the high school library a lot with Tommy Oh, Haresh Sakharani, Danny (something...tall lanky Eurasian guy), basically all the varsity soccer guys coached by Mike Fogarty. Stephen and I were on the swim team together coached by Mark Silzer and Bill Driscoll. He's a quiet guy, with a dark complexion and stockily built. He was also involved in Orientale as a photographer. He may have had a brother in HKIS as well.

Ken Koo '79

•Aaron Kohl, infant

When I heard about Aaron I thought of the lifelong sadness that must bring.

Barb Schwerdtmann '77

We lost Aaron, our 2nd son, as a 3-day infant in HK. He was born 8 weeks pre-mature and died of hyline membrane disease. I don't think of him every day, but when I do, I first pause and honor him. Then I spend some time contemplating the gift we still have in Adam. Does not make it any easier, I still wonder what he would have become. Every Christmas, the third verse of *Away in a Manger* still hits me sideways and I lose it. I'm actually glad when that happens. I know I'm a better person and parent because of his short life.

Dave Kohl, art teacher '73-'80

•Connie Laibe ('79)

Connie passed away at the end of 2005 from cancer. She had a wonderful husband and children who live in New York. Connie, a reporter for the NY Times, wrote an amazing book about Coca Cola: "The Real Thing: Truth and Power at the Coca-Cola Company," scrutinizing the history of the soft-drink conglomerate. Her sister Anne lives in Boston with her husband and children. Marc is married with children and lives in Connecticut. Chris married with children and runs a company in Louisiana. Finally, Timmy is in the Northeast as well.

Robert Ketterer '81

•James Langford ('80)

James was like my twin brother growing up, so his death hit me very, very hard. Langfords were part of the same mission group as us – Don Langford was my dad's partner in the Langford and Smith Medical Group, and they were both part of the Southern Baptist mission.

He was the funniest, kindest, silliest guy I've ever known, and I owe him for my love of jazz music and my ability to tell all the old Bill Cosby jokes, among many other things. I have a ton of classic James Langford stories, from "7-12-42" to "Polly Esther Chu, Atlas Chan, and Rachmaninoff Poon", to "Buprengskrul." And then there were the times that he would walk me home from the bus stop... with underwear on his head. I'm sure the people we passed wondered about that crazy gwei lo! Or his ability to fall asleep ANYWHERE! My favorite was in the middle of the back seat on the top deck of a # 7 bus... leaning all the way over into this poor woman's lap!

And of course, he was the best partner to have in a shaving cream fight... heh heh heh. I'm positive that it was 1984 because James's death was a capper on a horrible year for me. He was class of '80 from HKIS, so he would have been a senior at Baylor at the time of his death, I think. He had a huge impact on my life, so I was very pleased and touched to see his award when I went to the Tai Tam campus in 2005 -- it's a perfect tribute.

Deborah Smith '80

Losing James Langford was probably the single most difficult day of my life. I remember it like it was yesterday. My dad had just come back from a business trip to Hong Kong. He called me over to my folk's house. Both my mom and dad were standing in the kitchen with solemn faces. They told me to sit down, that they had some terrible news to tell me. I don't remember much after "James Langford died..."

How could this be? I had talked to him a few weeks before. We were excited because I was going to finally come and visit him in Texas over the spring break. He had called me on my 22nd B-day – I was out with my friends but he ended up talking with my mom for a long time instead. When I crept in late that night, I saw my Mom's light on, so I popped my head in to say 'good night'. She said James had called and insisted I call him back no matter what time I got home. I thought it was too late and didn't want to disturb him. Then I was off to school the next day and forgot all about calling him back. Still to this day, I regret not calling him back. I completely broke down. I went into the deepest depression and had to drop out of college for a semester. I went to counseling for Suicide Survivors. It was painful journey. James had a profound impact on me at a young age. I recall the first time I saw him. It was Orientation day 1976. We were both starting high school. He was transferring from KGV.... There he was this small, shy, lanky kid with crazy hair. We became fast friends. Shared a love of music (Jazz, James Taylor, James Taylor, James Taylor), poetry and general silliness. He was so excited when he sprouted about 5 inches over the summer between junior and senior year.

We grew really close that year - even dated since Theo had gone off to college. I'll never forget how excited he was to show up at my house for the 1980 Prom pre-party. He had the biggest grin on his face when I opened the door - the braces were gone!!! I think he had them on for something like 7 years. What a night. He smiled the whole time. It was a beautiful thing. We also shared beautiful moments during our senior class trip to Cebu. Ahh, the stories we could tell. He was kind, talented, tormented, intense, beautiful, silly, insecure, unique but most of all genuine. The world lost a bright star that day. I, for one, will never forget him. He was a gift. I miss him.

Tracy Birnie '80

I knew James Langford quite well, as teacher, advisor, and friend. I went numb when I got the call about him.... in the days before e-mail that news circled the globe within hours of John finding him. James had a fine spirit, a gift of genuine concern for others, and a laugh that was infectious. He was excited, excitable, a wonderful actor on and off stage, and a blessing to those who knew and worked with him.   *Dave Kohl, teacher '73-'80*

• Barry Laubach ('72)

I first met Barry Laubach when we were 5 or 6 years old and were students at Glenealy Junior School. It was approximately 1960. Barry stood out as the tallest guy in the class. He was a friendly, engaging kid and we all lived in fear of Miss Handyside, the Headmistress of Glenealy. Barry went on to King George V School ("KGV") as we all did since it was the only English medium secondary school in Hong Kong at the time. The opening of HKIS in the late 1960's eventually attracted many American students away from KGV and the newly opened Island School on Borrett Road in the mid-levels. It also attracted non-US kids whose parents ultimately planned to send them to US colleges. Barry's death on New Year's Eve/New Year's Day (1972) was an enormous shock to us all. It was widely covered in the English language press in Hong Kong because it was such a rare occurrence. Drug related deaths at that time were relatively unheard of although there was growing use of heroine and prescription drugs in Hong Kong. Much of it was aimed at the large number of US troops on R and R from Vietnam but it inevitably found its way into the hands of High School students. It was a very difficult moment for all of us and particularly for Earl Westrick who had just finished his first semester as High School Principal. For most of us, it was the first time that we lost someone close to us - "one of us". The second semester was a difficult one for all of us and Barry's absence was very much felt at the graduation of the Class of '72 in June that year.

Barry's younger sister Shari is a very special girl and my brother and I were fortunate to be able to see her occasionally when we were students at the University of Washington and she was at Pacific Lutheran University in nearby Tacoma. Shari attended the HKIS Reunion of the Century in Hong Kong in 1997 and Earl Westrick spoke fondly of Barry and his passing at the Closing Night event. It was a deeply moving moment for all of us present and his loss was still felt some 25 years later.   *Robert Dorfman '72*

I remember taking cotillion dancing at the (I believe it was) Hong Kong Press Club. Barry Laubach was one of the class members and I remember dancing the waltz with him. Dancing with Barry stood out in my mind because he was an excellent cotillion/ballroom dancer. The girls liked to dance with him because he led well, was graceful and light on his feet, wasn't awkward as a dance partner or thought dancing was stupid.
          Diane Reynolds

When Barry Laubach died, there was a shake-up at school over the drug situation. Barry was a shining star, and his death by drug overdose was just completely shocking.
          Jill Liddiard '77

I played in a band with my brother Robert at a place where the main band was the Yellow Railroad and we used their setup. We were pretty bad, but we were having a good time. It was the first time in my life I had ever been behind a drum set. Nobody knew what to make out of us except for Barry Laubach who was going crazy over the music. I always appreciated him for that.
          Eric Mache '68

The shock of Barry Laubachs story opened up a whole different world that was going on around me. I was quite a bit younger, but it brought the reality of drugs, especially with the servicemen, to the forefront.
          Barb Schwerdtmann '77

Barry Laubach was on the school swim team with me, he was a grade ahead of me but I got to know him a little. He was a very sweet guy, a good athlete, and a good person. His death was a tragedy and his involvement with drugs very out of character. He got in with the wrong crowd and paid the ultimate price.   *Wendy Liddiard '73*

I first met Barry when my family moved into Repulse Bay Towers in the early 60s as a 5th grader. We were kids in different schools, Barry at Glenealy and me at Quarry Bay. A new friend at the Towers, Craig Wells (Glenealy School) introduced us the day Barry came home from summer/USA vacation. We were Mutt and Jeff. Barry at 6 feet and me scraping by at 4 feet. Craig in between. They accepted and embraced me in a friendship that is unmatched today. We three friends spent many a day as the 3 Musketeers.... no Typhoon would keep us from the waves at Repulse Bay beach or from trying to get the boat boys at the VRC to let us launch our VJs to sail into the maelstrom: using raincoats as sails on our skateboards to race down the wind tunnel behind the Towers: or riding inner tubes in the raging catchwaters above Tai Tam.... We were wild and crazy kids, hell-bent for adventure. If our parents had ever caught us we would have been grounded BIG TIME!!!

First form at KGV (7th grade), we three families of kids rode a pak pai - 6 Fingers - to the Star Ferry (at 6a.m.) to cross the harbor and then school busses out to KGV. Later that same year thru riots, with armed Gurkahs for protection as the Cultural Revolution put the colony in turmoil. But we three still had our adventures in the mountains above Tai Tam, Big Wave Bay or the outer islands on the Laubach/Well's boat, collecting specimens for Barry and his Mom's salt water aquarium or hiking the islands exploring caves and the coast line. Barry's room was our clubhouse and his amah Ah Choy always had fresh cookies and milk for us upon our returns. They were the best of childhood times, memories and a friendship I will always cherish.

8th grade we started HKIS together and Barry excelled in sports that were previously unavailable to him. The "Gentle Giant" was a natural born sports machine and I (the little midget) was his favorite fan. He was also my protector and kept the bullies at bay when he could that first year. We remained good friends and shared many more friends and adventures in HKIS.

His accidental death on New Years 71/72 devastated me and probably saved my life. I suffered from depression and the shock of losing him snapped me out of it (Thank you also Earl Westerick). Barry had the oyster in his hand and the Pearl was within his ability to grasp. It still pains me too think of it and is so incredibly hard to write of it.

His Mom and Dad live in Kailua close by and are my dearest of friends and surrogate parents as well. We have never talked of Barry and probably never will. I will never fill the void of their loss, but in gratefully accepting their embrace,

love and friendship, I hope I have brightened the shadow he left so long ago.

Barry's sister Shari and husband Parker have 2 wonderful boys, and live on the Big Island of Hawaii. Both kids share Barry's passions: the youngest towers over his older brother and is extremely into sports, while the older is a high academic achiever ... and yes ... I can see my best friend shine in both their eyes.

Our "Gentle Giant" lives on.

Rich Vaughn '72

•Lee Marks ('72)

Lee (Marks) Dixon, class of '72, passed away in September 1998, after a long battle with leukemia. They were living in Sydney Australia. She was survived by her husband, Phil and four children. Lee was a very special person with a great zest for life and the ability to touch all those she came into contact with in her own unique way.

Debbie Smiley '72

•Jim McElroy ('74)

Jim McElroy, brother of Ginger, passed away at home for medical reasons not publicly known. I only knew of Jim thru his sister who I originally knew in my homeroom at (TAS) Taipei American School. She didn't like me then because she didn't know me and thought I was a brat that hung around with the seedy crowd. Our families both relocated to HK in 1971 from Taiwan and we met each other again in class at HKIS. HKIS brought us together again and we became good friends over our high school years. I kept in touch with Ginger after high school and got word from her that her brother was discovered at home by one of her older sisters. I think that was in 1976-1977 not sure exactly when. Ginger was very saddened and missed her brother deeply. I have visited Ginger and her family over the years and we have shared a few tears over our memories of Jim. *Eric Lee, '75*

•Rob McLaren ('75)

Jimmy Hoffman and Charlotte Agell…ah, the memories of Turtle Cove Bay! The incredible water balloon fights with Chip Hoffman and Rob McLaren. I know that he is no longer living, but we had such fun! Since I only had sisters, I enjoyed their company as older brothers… anonymous

Rob knew I liked to play squash, but didn't have a membership at any of the clubs in HK. So he invited me to join him at the Jockey Club for a game or two. He was gracious, witty, poised, and he whupped me good on the courts! No mercy...none expected. One time, my old beater car (Magnolia) got towed while we were playing, because I had not parked in a designated spot for visitors. Rob even helped me negotiate with the HK police and went to the impound yard with me.

He must have been in my advisee group for Interchange, because I knew that he had been born in Umtali, and carried a Rhodesia passport.

When I learned that he had been killed in a mining accident while he was a student, I felt a huge loss. All that potential!   *Dave Kohl '73-'80*

•Monty & Elizabeth McWeeney ('79)

The McWeeney family died when their Pan Am jumbo jet crashed into another jumbo jet on the runway at Papaette in Tahiti It happened in the summer of 1973, while they were vacationing there. The children were twins, Liz and Monty. They were in my sister's fifth grade class at HKIS. I've never forgotten the McWeenies.

Christina Caluori '76

Monty was a great kid.   *Jim Hoffmann '79*

I remember a friend of mine by the name of Monty McWeeney in my 4th or 5th grade class. Monty was a real nice kid. We hung out a lot. Liz was in my class one of those years (4th grade - Mrs. Towery and 5th grade - Mrs. Healey). I remembered hearing his family being involved in a plane crash during that period of time. Monty was a pretty big kid with sandy brown hair.

Ken Koo '79

•Christian Fontaine Myers ('76)

My Dear Friends,

Today I am so grateful that you have been by my side. The last seven months have been HELL. I have gone through a nervous breakdown, DTs, recovery at the VA, found God and AA. I love you all.

I make no claim that I know God in all His fullness. And I certainly don't feel that I understand God to any extent. But that there is a power beyond myself I have felt this healing power which can do wonderful, friendly things for me that I can't do for myself-this I know beyond all question. I have felt this healing power at work in my own

being and I have seen the effects of God's powers in the lives of thousands of recovering alcoholics who are my friends in AA.

For over thirty years I was an agnostic. During that time, I became a helpless alcoholic and a complete failure in all areas of my life, especially in my relationships. All of my horrible suffering was self-induced. During those proud years, I often said, "If God exists, let Him give me a sign". I had quite forgotten I was the one who had broken off communication. At that time, I set out to prove that there was no God, and for over thirty years, the confirmations of my opinion kept pouring in.

So the first thing that I came to understand about God is that He is very cooperative. It took me thirty years of suffering to learn this!

The second thing I leaned is Grace that is God's love. His love and acceptance alone did bring me into the program. I had been offered love and encouragement many times before, but this time His love and acceptance I responded. I was not healed by love alone, but by my response to love. My understanding of God grows through my willing to response to Him.

When I first went to my priest he said, "Pray if you can." Having no faith whatever, thinking that payer must be a kind of play-acting, alone in my apartment I got down on my knees like a little child and prayed to the unknown God. I said, "God take away my compulsion to drink." And my compulsion to drink was removed from that to this. Without knowing how I had done it, I surrendered to God, and God did for me what I could not do of my own will.

For the last four months I went to meetings and prayed and dreamed and procrastinated and I began to feel uncomfortable at times. I began applying myself to Steps Four through Nine and after these months the power of the past to hurt me is largely removed. I came to believe in a God who merciful and forgiving but not forgetful. And I have no desire to forget the past. My memories no longer fill me with shame and remorse, but now fill me with gratitude and joy. I don't know how an intelligent human being ever could have got into this mess and the more established in sanity I become the more amazed I know I will get out of this mess.

I believe I am sober and alive for only one reason, God has a job for me to do. I have also come to believe that I must please God first, myself second, and everybody third. When I can live and feel that way, and it isn't all day every day, things seem to work out.

Love,
Christian

Chris Myers '76, a letter from 2004

Christian Fontaine Myers, born January 26, 1959, passed away on August 20, 2005 at age 46. He passed away due to complications of early onset Parkinson's disease and phenomena. Proud veteran of the US Coast Guard, Christian graduated from Hong Kong International School in 1976. He made his career in food and beverage starting on the Monterey Peninsula as Bar Manager at La Playa Hotel. He spent the most rewarding part of his career with the Pebble Beach Company (1986-1998) starting as a bartender at the Lodge at Pebble Beach, then moved on to become the Beverage Manager, Assistant Banquet Manager, Banquet Manager, and finally rounding out his career as Catering Manager. He left Pebble Beach to live in Oregon where he worked at Sun River Resort. Missing his daughter, Aja, and the city he loved so much, he finishing off his career in San Francisco. Being forced into early retirement due to illness, Christian spent his last years in Sausalito, CA. He is survived by his daughter, Aja Fontaine Cole-Myers

Obituary

It was because of Chris Myers that we were able to hold the San Francisco reunion in '04 so inexpensively. In fact, he was my only link in SF, and I doubt we could have even had the reunion without him and his connections and good will. He got us the rates at the Cathedral Hill Hotel and bargained the food services and when the event happened, even though he was no long employed there, made sure everything went off without a hitch. It was so obvious how much he was admired and respected by his staff.

But more than that, Chris, and his sister Susan, were defacto, my first kids. My wife and I house sat with them several times when their dad went on trips. Ah Kan would have drinks ready for us when we got home, cook great family meals, and hound "Chrissie" to be good. Chris is the only guy I knew who kept a change of clothes at the California bar in WanChai so he could switch out of his school uniform there before meeting up with some of his limey friends. We played lots of squash, too.

We kept in touch, and visited in Texas, California, even Vancouver BC. He joined me on a trip to Italy when I got some bonus travel points. We had such a good time "doing" the Roman Forum and learning ancient history. He was certainly one of my best friends.

Dave Kohl, faculty '73-'80

•Julie Peterson ('75)

She made her way through all of this with the faith and hope that we all know and love her for.

Chris Reaves '75

There is so much to be said about Julie and how she lived life and what she meant to soooo many people. In school she was the true scholar and athlete and always had time for friends and outside activities. CYF on Friday nights and many a Saturday evening at the parent's house playing bumper pool with the gang we hung with. These were the evenings where Cliff Raborn, Ken Westrick and I would run down from the mid levels to catch the last bus to Repulse Bay. It was great times and she and her family could not have been more hospitable. What she accomplished in later life could only be described as phenomenal. Look no further than how many people attended her funeral. She was a great teacher who touched many lives and mine was one and I am the better for having known her.

Gregg Saunders '75

The first one was in drama class with (I want to say Ms. Kwok, but I might be memory deficient) Julie and David Kniseley were to do a vignette of riding the bus and asking for a date. Now picture that they are both standing, facing each other, holding onto the overhead rail and they are both bouncing on their feet like jiggling on the bus. This went on for a minute or so with David totally self conscious about what this looked like and Julie was totally innocent till laughing and snickering started. Poor Julie was upset but she valiantly tried to continue the act without disruption. She hung in there till the end with David leaving the stage totally red faced and Julie bless her heart (I don't know if anyone ever told her).

This next one also involves Julie and David at one of our swim practices. We had just finished swimming practice laps of the pool and David tells Julie there is a bee in the water right in front of her in the shallow end. Julie, tired and exhausted, can't focus on anything close up without her contact lenses in.

David tells her to look closer, and unsuspecting Julie put her face closer to the water surface to see. Of course, ungentlemanly David gives Julie a good dunking and they spend the rest of the practice getting back at each other. *Eric Lee '75*

I met Julie Peterson at HKIS in 1971. Her positive, energetic approach to life and especially to people was immediately visible. Her parents, her sister Pam and brother Rich shared these qualities so their home became a popular place to go to have fun. There would be dancing, enjoyment of the player piano, lots of talking on the balcony with the lights of Hong Kong harbour below and slumber parties for the girls.

However, this was just the beginning of a very special friendship. Julie and I shared two years at the University of Northern Colorado. We were able to gather a small group of HKIS friends (Knisely, Wilson, Templeton, Raborn) together for a memorable camping trip in the Rockies.

Next, Julie moved to the San Diego area. Each visit there was an adventure!!! Julie made sure of it. We sailed during the day and went kayaking under the full moon. We drove to San Francisco, riding horses at Half Moon Bay, bicycling through Golden Gate Park and hiking in the hills above the Golden Gate Bridge. Julie always made sure we had the perfect picnic and discovered unique restaurants for us to try.

Julie remained full of courage and optimism as her husband suffered the effects of cancer. She surrounded their two boys with love, and when she knew her life too would be shortened by cancer, she entrusted them to their aunt and uncle, Pam and Chris Reaves. Her precious sons, Ryan and Casey, bring joy to those around them, as Julie and their father, Glenn, did.

Julie was a person who did everything with extraordinary kindness. She was willing to pour her heart out to others. She showed us all how to maintain faith and a positive attitude through all of life. *Debbie Noren '73*

• Keith Quong ('77)

Keith Quong (Kwan) was a very dear friend of mine for many years. We worked together on many HK film and TV productions, and he became

quite a star on one of the Chinese channels (TVB). Was known all over town as "Kwan San!" He was also closely related to film star Nancy Kwan. He suffered AIDS for over 10 years - privately, tragically - but continued to work and live in the huge family home atop The Peak.

Eventually his illness forced him to return to Canada, where he passed away in the mid '90's. He was a little guy with a HUGE personality, and was extraordinarily talented. His loss was quite a blow to the HK broadcast community, and was one of the first high profile AIDS deaths in the colony. He suffered in silence for so many years - I'm glad he is being remembered now. *Melissa Miller '79*

My old pal Keith and I were pals since 4th grade and went to our senior prom together. We always got together when I came to Hong Kong and I last spoke to him about 2 weeks before he passed away. His dad called me with the sad news. The other sadness was when his Mom was killed by a bus while walking on the sidewalk in HK. It was an awful time. We used to go to Maxiums for lunch with our moms. Many wonderful times as well! *Barbara Schwerdtmann '77*

• Pete Reiner ('78)

I once went to the Sheraton Kowloon with Pete, who said he'd treat for steaks at the fine dining restaurant. This restaurant had semi-circle booths with massively heavy tables that had to be slid out to seat patrons. Two waiters slid the table out and Pete went in first. Then I sat down. The waiters pushed the table back in and Pete screamed in agony. Apparently, the waiters set the table down on his foot!

He kept acting like it was nothing but for the whole meal, agony was written all over his face. Management felt so bad that they comp'd our luxurious dinners. They continued to apologize profusely, as I helped Pete limp out of the restaurant.

We went down to the ferry to come back to HK side, with Pete stepping gingerly with his foot. When the Start Ferry bell started to sing it's "Fi-dee, Fi-dee" bell, imagine my surprise when Pete looked at me and suggested we run for it, and turned and ran full steam ahead. As we crossed the plank onto the ferry I saw the familiar mischievous smile creep onto his face. He had been faking it the whole time! Good meal, though, and definitely good times. Here's to remembering your spirit, Pete! *Kelvin Limm '79*

Pete died in his sleep about 4 years ago from a brain aneurism. My favorite memories of my brother from the HK days are playing baseball - quite an athlete when he wanted. In fact, there was not much he couldn't do once he set his mind to it. His son (Dan) is being raised by my mom here in Orlando. I moved back to Orlando from Michigan 3 years ago, brought my mom down with Dan-they live a half mile from me. *Rob Reiner '75*

•Ellen Sheffer ('77)

Bad week last week - my HKIS classmate Ellen (Sheffer) Barnes, died suddenly and completely unexpectedly of a aneurism in her brain. She was watching TV and just fainted and never came to. I spoke to her husband, and he said he and Ellen's son (from a previous marriage) was doing OK. Ellen's son is 16 and his father was killed in a car accident a few years ago.

Peter Chworowsky '77

•Kathy Smiley ('75)

My sister, Kathy died in April 1974. She was in the class of 1975. We moved back to the States in 1971 where she was on track to graduate in 1974. Her seat sat empty during the graduation ceremony with the exception of her diploma. Kathy lived life to the fullest and loved animals. She had been accepted into the University of Georgia School of Veterinary Medicine.

Debbie Smiley '72

•Diane Steele ('71)

I took Diane to the first senior prom and talked to her on the phone sometime around the 1980s when I found that she lived in my neighborhood in New York City. She sounded like she was doing great and if my memory serves me right she had a new husband and seemed quite happy with life. Soon afterwards I heard a rumor that she had died from cancer or something like that.

Eric Mache '68

•Celia Wood ('75)

I never saw a moor
never saw the sea;
Yet I know how the heather looks,
And what a wave must be.

I never spoke with God,

nor visited in heaven;
Yet certain am I of the spot
As if the chart were given.

Emily Dickinson quoted on Celia's memorial page in the '75 Orientale

•Timothy Paul Von Behren ('77)

My brother Timmy was a precocious young boy, having just been double-promoted after his first year in HK. He was very fond of his HKIS teacher, Mrs. Vasey (and she of him). She lost her husband within a short time, I think, of Timmy's death, which helped forge a strong bond between our family and her.

One of the particularly difficult things for our family when Timmy died right at the beginning of the school year was that my sister, Karen, had graduated from HKIS that June and had recently left to attend Concordia College outside of Chicago. My parents struggled to find the best way to deliver the news to her, finally deciding to ask a professor they knew and trusted to tell her in person, rather than trying to do so by phone from halfway around the world. Because of the expense and the timing, she wasn't able to come home until the next summer. Pivotal life events like this can affect people very differently, but for each of us in our family, this tragedy served to strengthen our ties to Hong Kong. *Jon Von Behren, '73*

Timothy Von Behren was next to me in class when I was 9, and was a really nice kid---for a boy, that is. He didn't have cooties! When he died so suddenly, we all got a lesson on taking care with those bathroom gas water heaters. Death was a very abstract concept at that age. He was such a sweet person, it just seemed that he could come back one day. *Jill Liddiard, '77*

We used to do and make things for the Timothy Paul Study center with church.

Barb Schwerdtman '77

Tim Von Behren's was the first funeral service I ever attended. I remember how worried we all were about the geezers in the bathrooms after he died and so worried we would die too. That is probably what started me keeping the bathroom window cracked all the time. *Debbie Smiley '72*

Chapter 14
Reflections

As one that lived in Hong Kong from 1973-1980 (what Fritz & I call the "teenage years" of Hong Kong) and returned in 1996-present, we see Hong Kong now as the "Sophisticated Lady!" And thinking about that analogy kind of describes some feelings about 'the past' and 'the present.' We often look at our teenage years with rose-colored glasses - which is probably pretty healthy - so those memories do have a glow about them. The fun part for many of you is that you got to spend YOUR teenage years in "teenage" Hong Kong!

It's much more difficult for today's kids to "have fun" in this environment. You should hear what they say when they look at the old yearbooks and wonder why 'those kids seem like they are having so much more fun.' You did! These kids and the environment of HK are much more driven today.

CHANGE is usually difficult to reckon with. We hearken back 'to the good 'ole days' and that's not all bad either but there were some very bumpy times then, too. But the fun part is having this group of people on Dragontrain, of many different ages, and we can share those delightful time and bumpy times. (I was going to say the "highs" but thought better of using that term - remembering HK of the '70s!!!)

Lois Voeltz, teacher '73-'80; '96-'03

To experience this lifelong connection with HKIS is really something that has to be lived. No amount of words or emotion can express what I feel in my heart. I love my school and I'm so proud that I'm still part of its growth. I'm an HKIS product and I continue to write on my memories and experiences. My home still lies deep within the annals of HKIS, and I have my own place in HKIS's "soul", and when I look out through HKIS's eyes, I'm young again, even though I'm (kinda) old.

I embody a bit of the Legacy of HKIS. It is a legacy that is almost 40 years in the making. There have been 40 graduating classes, which span the Beatles to OutKast; from Univac to Compaqs; from Crusaders to Dragons from the Shack to Beachcombers And yet, this HKIS legacy also binds us together with common threads that we can trace through two (sometimes three) generations of alumni as well as faculty!

Ken Koo ' 79 (President, Alumni Assn)

Where is the story? Each chapter in our lives is a shared journey with events and people. And HKIS created many of our vignettes.

Martin Luther's contemporaries used a very specific word that describes our growth and change. They didn't use the word reformed; they used the word reforming. There is a significant difference. They knew the things they wrote and said and decided would need to be revisited, rethought and reworked.

This is the story of HKIS with each student, parent and teacher. We are reforming as we enter and exit the school. We grow, change our thinking and invite others to share their stories.

Thus, the tradition at HKIS is a painting, not to make copies of the same painting over and over. The challenge of the art for us as we move on to other places and events is to take what is great about our previous paintings and incorporate that into new art form.

We embrace the need to keep painting, to keep reforming.

Hong Kong International School.... our home of 20 years that taught us how to learn with passion, embrace diversity and care for all people. Still reforming.

Michael & Kay Lambert, teachers/counselors '86-'06

Hong Kong? Chai, the alleys, or the ferry...the MTR is faster but the tram is tons more fun...that the Jumbo still has the best-steamed shrimp with heads on (and THAT is the good part). The Rice Bowl and Mok Cup are eventsthe place to be...and the American restaurant serves the best Peking Duck pancakes ever (we are NOT talking IHOP) - that dance marathons are taken seriously (BangBang was a sponsor!) - some things only Crusaders know...even those new Dragons don't quite understand...

Amat Tajudin '77

It was truly amazing what access we all had to an island that had 7 million people on it and the things we could do. Travel downtown at night without a worry, jump on the bus to travel to the New Territories, jump on a ferry to go to Macau and so many other things to numerous to mention. It's difficult to explain to someone 30 years later. When I mention I lived in Hong Kong, I get some of the strangest looks. But it's a great icebreaker.

John Morris '76

The five years I spent in Hong Kong (1966-1969, 1973-1975) were a unique time for me. It was rewarding to be part of something new, to watch and help as HKIS worked into its own unique way of contributing to the education of a diverse group of students. The city of Hong Kong was itself in a time of transition, as local culture and tradition were inexorably changed because of changes in transportation and technology. While Hong Kong of the late 1960's was vibrant and up to date, it was still possible to find sites and events that were part of a long and rich local history.

Those five years were also personally highly formative because, alongside the charm and excitement of Hong Kong, I developed important relationships that continue to the present. In most cases, those relationships have been interrupted by long periods of absence … but in all cases, when I am with someone who shared those HK years with me, we take up as if we'd been together throughout, and for that, I am particularly thankful.

Dave Christian '69, Jr Hi teacher '73-'75

I will never forget those days. Those days in fact defined who I was for years to come. Truthfully, to a degree they continue to affect everything I do today. Mention to anyone that you "grew up" in Hong Kong and you automatically stand a head above the crowd. It must be true because you can talk to someone that spent as little as year or two in Hong Kong and they will tell you that they "grew up" there.

Certainly we would all agree that we grew a lot in our time there despite the fact that we may have spent more years in other places. The Law of Attraction could never be more applicable. Everyone wants to know what it was like. They want to know what happened that was different than what they experienced.

It's really not what happened in the time spent in Hong Kong that is important but more importantly it is what we all became. We became self reliant, flexible, tolerant and independent people in a world that teaches compliance, judgment and rigidity but demands the prior. We gained a worldview along with compassion for the individual. We had the opportunity to "see" free enterprise, capitalism and democracy from the perspective of an outsider.

We certainly experienced first hand the Third World Kid Culture of being an American growing up on a foreign soil. Imagine what would happen if all world citizens had to spend several years living in a foreign country? The world would be a more understanding and acceptable place. More people would embrace our cultural differences as desirable and interesting. Hong Kong certainly had that affect on me.

Brad Doyle '76

The unique up bringing we had in Hong Kong can't help but give us a wider perspective on life. Some can use that to enrich contacts with people; some will benefit from it; and fewer may not. All the more to cherish are those contacts with people who can relate to the November feel and smell the Harbor breeze on the bottom deck of the Star Ferry. How to get the best of both worlds?

David Vaughn '69

A friend of mine, who attended elementary school at HKIS has been working in a specific office of his company's for about 1 year now. Recently, he started talking on a personal level to a female coworker he's working with all this time. The "where are you from" topic comes up during a conversation, and he says he grew up in HK and Japan. She responds by saying she went to HKIS at the same time he did. It turns out she's Tracey McAllister, only with a married name!

Isn't that a trip?

Ok, it gets better. The other people present during this conversation are tripping on this revelation. One guy goes back to his home office in Arizona, and relates the story to someone over lunch. The person he's telling the story to says, "Wait a minute, I went to HKIS, too!" Now, this guy is really blown away. He calls Andy, and Andy freaks out, cause he's supposed to do a teleconference call with this person (female) the very next day. He calls me up, asks me to pull out a yearbook from elementary school and scan a picture of her and e-mail it to him. The next day, during the conference call, he e-mails her 2nd grade picture to her and says, "OK, check out the file I just e-mailed you. We need to go over it." She opens the file and sees her second grade picture and freaks out!

Isn't that a trip???!!

Kelvin Limm '79

In 1996, I had very deep troubled feeling about the eminent Handover, so I wrote them down as follows:

Is Hong Kong home?
If it's where I live now.... no.
If it's where my parents are now...no.
If it's where I was born....no
If its where I go on furlough....no
If it's where my mind goes when homesick, escaping, or simply daydreaming...a great big YES   *Diane Anderson '69*

•Our Epilogue

I feel tremendous awe and recognition of God's love and grace, as I write this, a 75 year old who humbly shares some thoughts 25 years after leaving Hong Kong. I look back to 1966 when we were considering the call from the LCMS Board for Missions to serve as an educational missionary to open the International School in Hong Kong. I had dreams and visions of a school that could truly be of service to residents and the broader community of Hong Kong, and could share the message of God's redeeming love with many students, with their families, and beyond. I also had a feeling that perhaps in the future, through Hong Kong, the doors to China might reopen to the message of the Gospel, and perhaps in some way, HKIS might even play a small role in this.

It did not take long to recognize that HKIS students were basically intelligent, knowledgeable, and privileged individuals who would someday live in all parts of the US and of the world. Many would become leaders in community, in business, and even in the church. If they could experience God's saving love in their lives, they could pass this on in many places and in many circumstances.

I had no idea that the school would experience such tremendous growth. Today HKIS has four excellent facilities, valued in the tens of millions of dollars, with a student enrollment of 2600,

more international than ever. I did not dream that some day the school would be located in China proper, and be one of the few places where Chinese citizens could attend not only an American type school, but one, which functioned from a Christian perspective and shared the good news of Jesus. I did not envision that under the leadership of visionary and competent leaders and teachers, the school would develop the quality creative educational approaches and the prominence that it enjoys. I did not see that part of my long time dream of reaching into China, could be attained through the opening of an HKIS sister school, namely Concordia International School in Shanghai.

May God continue to smile upon the mission and ministry of Hong International School, granting His special blessings to all who serve there, attend there, and are touched by the school. May HKIS continue in its successful endeavors, in its service to many people of all ages, and in its Christian ministry to all who partake of its program.

Bob Christian, Founding Headmaster, '66-'77

I feel we need a partnership to preserve the HKIS Legacy. To achieve this critical step, it is necessary that the past, the present and the future of HKIS be viewed as one continuous unbroken chain. A synergy must be created from this chain which harnesses the strengths of each link past, present and future so that we can take the emotion and energy we feel for HKIS in different epochs of the school's history and bring it into new situations ...and then we (the alumni and HKIS) let those new situations incorporate and homogenize and produce a newly unique entity. And that entity will be the basis of some future nostalgia. It won't be ours, but just like raising kids, we give our best input as parents and then celebrate who these new entities become: unique combinations of what we give them and what they glean from the rest of their own environment. Hopefully, the product incorporates the best of these influences, which in turn will serve as a springboard for the new generation of HKIS alums to grow into new situations and challenges.

Just like art and architecture HKIS is continually evolving based on influences from philosophy, technology and talent, a place like HKIS is always going to be the unique product of the best efforts of its people in a physical setting with a stated goal using the latest technology.

And I've been a part of this HKIS Legacy, year-in and year-out. I have so much to share, so many stories to tell, stories of the growth and maturation of a small all-white building perched on top of a hilly knoll overlooking Repulse Bay.

Ken Koo '79

The San Francisco reunion was a lot of fun. I haven't been to HK since my family left in '78 or '79. I have many wonderful memories of HK, the family is now all deceased except for me, so I've thought it best to just leave my vivid memories intact without complicating things by going back to HK & seeing how much it has changed (we lived in a very nice apartment complex at 31 Perkins Rd, Jardine's Lookout, and I understand the apartment complex is long gone, etc.).

Tim Tyler '84 One of a Kind

The everlasting image of HKIS in my mind and heart is children of all sizes, shapes, and colors playing, working, and learning together in a demanding but loving environment. HKIS is truly a one of a kind institution. The years 2000-2003 were stressful times in the leadership of the school, and yet the mission and student learning results stayed in the forefront. HKIS was and remains a beacon of excellence for all of Hong Kong and the international school community. I give thanks for having the opportunity to play a small part in the incredible 40-year journey of HKIS, and pray for God's continued bless ings on its faculty, staff, and students.
Stephen Goldmann, '00-'03

I need to mention Jesus!

Faith is what I got in those tumultuous '70's at that Lutheran international school in the capitalist paradise that was the British colony of Hong Kong. Those songs we sang come back to me still sometimes out of the blue. "I am the lord of the dance said He and I'll lead you on wherever you may be and I'll lead you on in the dance said He"...I am in possession of Shannon Stringer's old songbook from Junior High with her doodles all over it. Thievery aside, the education was outstanding at HKIS. We made fun of you teachers and resisted your best efforts, but we'll never forget you. I'm a teacher at Hunters Woods Magnet School for the Arts & Sciences, a public elementary school in the Reston, Virginia a suburb of Washington, D.C. My husband works for the government--ours. Don't

know if we'll ever be assigned to Hong Kong, but if we are...there's no finer school in the entire world than HKIS. With eternal gratitude,

Moira Gavaghen '80

My parents who always have been caring but not in the way of giving me money to substitute food for ice cream or sweets, now and then gave me the 10 HK cents needed for that green ice cream bar that was in the colour of green 'pistage' (French) covering vanilla or something like it. Anyway, being this young lad of 7-8 years of age, I felt the need to show off (sad story) for some reason and then having money to by sweets and ice cream off the ice cream man in the stand down the hill from HKIS. In the morning my father had his jacket hanging over a chair, and I had that period when I 'fished' small monies out of pockets - never much, but occasionally–fear of being caught. Next to it or on the table was a sum laid out - most likely part of my mother's food shopping money for the month – and it was most likely some four or more ten-dollar-bills and not understanding that they would notice if one was gone, I pinched one and pocketed it.

At school end-of the-day I remember offering to everyone in sight that I would buy ice cream and especially one boy that I very much wanted as friend, Chico Dains who was dressed in his blue Scout uniform with yellow scarf. To impress, I suppose, I offered him an ice cream and he took one off me but I think was smart enough to ask where I had got the money. I remember lying quickly and feeling a twinge of embarrassment.

And that I think was the first and last time until I relapsed back in Sweden some 3-4 years later. I owe Chico... he was a good friend and it took me off the road of crime.

Henrik Mjoman, '78, Latvia

I'm glad there are quite a few HKIS Alumni who are in the teaching profession. Whether it is academics, music, or whatever have you, I'm confident that you teachers have much to offer your students based upon your worldly experiences. Now that I am older, I can appreciate what opportunities a good, diverse, education has to offer. Too bad there aren't more of you out there. God knows we need you! Hats of to you teachers!

Kelvin Limm '79

It was the luck of the class of '75 to pretty

well stay intact from 7th thru 12th grade. There were many families that stayed the entire time, which was quite unusual, such as we Birnies, the Trepaniers, McCoys, Garveys and Reaves etc. I always felt this contributed to a very strong sense of unity in an ever-changing landscape of faces at HKIS.

Most of all I, to this day, am still amazed at how strong memories of 35 to 40 years ago are. Some feel like they happened just yesterday others not so far behind. Even more amazing and gratifying is the strength of the bond we all feel towards each other whether we were close friends or not. When ever we meet at mini reunions or on the 'train' it is palpable how bonded we all feel with the shared memories of our lives in that 7 story building at 6 South Bay Close.

Gavin Birnie '75

Our hangouts were mostly the mountains behind the 23 South Bay campus. Took me until later on in my senior year to really grasp what an opportunity to connect with people I had in front of me. In general we were a pretty close-knit class all things considered but there were people I wish I had had a better connection with during my time there. Most of my regrets are in not being outgoing enough to make those connections back then.

In some ways I didn't realize how important those connections would be to who I am today. Had such opportunities that I was oblivious to at the time. Not to be silly but a quote from 'Meet the Robinsons' seems apropos, 'Keep moving forward'. Missed some of those opportunities and makes me want to keep my eyes open that much more to those connections around me and try to reconnect at the events such as The 40th Reunion.

Jason Weber '97

•9/11

Dear Alumni – I hope that all alumni and their families are well and safe. From Canada, I can say that everyone I've spoken to here is horrified and dismayed. Something like this touches us all because of the implications for where we may be heading. After living in the Philippines and Hong Kong during the years of the Vietnam War, I had hoped that humanity would over come its aggressive tendency – after all it's a no win proposition – every side loses in the end.

Someone said to me today that religion has

been the cause of all wars and strife and that without religious factions we would not have had wars. Wasn't Hitler an atheist and yet he managed wholesale slaughter? As a Christian I feel that God's message is one of peace and love for all people, regardless of race, religion, etc. The religion classes we took at HKIS not only taught us about Christianity but other religions as well and most importantly they taught us that the other religions were also about peace and love and tolerance.

I believe that people who commit acts of terrorism in the name of God would find something else to twist and distort in order to pursue their violent paths. I feel that God, by whichever name one chooses to call him/her, would also be horrified and dismayed by these terrorist acts.

Lynn Barratt Frau '73 written 9/11/'01

We are trying to make sense of an insane action. That's really what *community* is all about! You folks created a community because of your attendance at a school in Hong Kong. That personal experience has helped you to view the world in a different way. When Lynn Barrett ('73) said that "what we learned in our religion classes at HKIS" helped her to see things differently than those who have not had those opportunities – I just cried. You see, that's "my job/role" now at HKIS, (as well as teaching religion in the high school) to help teachers and students to really learn to understand and respect PEOPLE who see the world differently than myself. And then to help them try to find a way of living that affirms and encourages that respect – that's a religion.

You've also created a community of care and support via the Dragontrain! By talking to each other, comparing your unique understandings of the world (because of your experience at an international school) we try to make sense of what has happened. What a wonderful community to be a part of!

HKIS is having school today. Jan Westrick, the deputy head, is now over in Repulse Bay at the upper and lower primary schools, to support and help were needed. Bill Wehrenberg, head of school, has cancelled all meetings and is spending time in the middle school and high school. The high school is having an assembly right now & I've asked Fritz to read your letter, Lynn. (I don't have class on F-days and am supposed to be doing all my work for the Religious Education Facilitator job!)

The Consulate is closed, security is heightened (whatever that means) and we in HK are trying to do what you folks in America are doing - watching TV. The cable TV is great - CNN, BBC, CNBC - so we have the news. And TVB Pearl is even continuing all the ABC coverage from the States, too, this morning. So we are informed. It's also interesting to me that as we could not reach our kids last night (as the tragedy was unfolding - all the lines to America were busy) our son was reading the up-to-date news on the South China Morning Post website. So he's in Arizona getting the news of what's going on America via Hong Kong. It has become such a small world with technology.

Thanks again for your wonderful words. I, too, believe that our God is bigger than all this terrorism and is grieving at this time, with all the people of the world. Why this God didn't intervene and stop the tragedy is the question that all religions try to answer! I still trust this God, in the midst of chaos.

Lois & Fritz Voeltz, faculty '96-'03, 9/12/'01

I am a Humanities teacher at HKIS and just had a conversation with a colleague that helped me make sense of some of this. Our appreciation of drawing upon the resource of prayer reflects an unmet need in our modern/post-modern culture for transcendence - for something much larger than ourselves to give us a sense of fulfillment. Now that we've met a tragedy that is far larger than our individual lives - a tragedy that has painfully reminded us that we are actually far more inter-connected than we knew – we are searching for a positive interconnection that can make us whole in the face of such a tragedy.

The search for meaning has been an individual search for most of us in the post-modern world, but now we see that it is a collective need. We keep hearing that the world has changed; I hope that is changed in making public what we as humans – both individually and collectively – really need. Of course those things are well known love, community, hope, purpose – but those values have retreated to our homes and generally only given lip-service in the power structures of our world. Pray without ceasing, as the good book says!

Marty Schmidt, hs teacher, written 9/12/'01

• Reunions

(Recent all-school reunions happened in Hong Kong '96; Denver '98, Washington DC '00, Portland '02, San Francisco '04, and Hong Kong '07) Ed.

My sister (Cathy Smith '75) and I were complaining to each other about not being able to attend all the cool reunions on the West Coast or in Colorado, so we decided to throw our own! It was in Washington, DC in 2000, and in my humble opinion, it was a blast! It was an all-classes reunion and I think we had a range of people from the 1968 to 1986 graduating classes. It was so much fun, even the spouses enjoyed it! *Debbie Smith, '80*

• Portland '02

I have not recovered from the Portland experience but at least I am now able to talk about it. Since leaving HKIS in '71 I have continued to travel not for fun but for work. My point? I am used to getting to a place and having defined objectives, and a very detailed briefing.

Portland's airport is OK. Getting a rental car was slightly stressful as I could not remember with whom I had made a reservation-turned out to be Budget. Portland had extolled its virtues as a "pedestrian friendly" city. Little did I know that the other side of that coin most assuredly reads "motorist beware". After two attempts I was able to get on the Highway.

I still have difficulty talking about the nightmare of finding my hotel in the labyrinths of one-way streets. Finally through sheer accident I spotted it. Parking was "difficult". The hotel manager was on the downhill side of a 24-hour shift. When I told him I would only be staying three nights he said "good". He then went on to say that too many people come to Portland for a visit and then stay.

I told him that as a Texan I understood exactly what He meant. In Texas we have two groups of Yankees - "Yankees" and "damn Yankees." The first group simply passes through and we are grateful, the second group stays. In retrospect my interpretation of his comment was naive - people don't stay in Portland for a long time because they like it - they stay because they can't find their way out !!!

Checked in and moved in to my room. Fortunately the desk clerk had given me not only a remote for the TV but an ashtray as well. There was a towel in the bathroom. I poured over my reference material, HQ for the reunion was the Marriott - no problem there it was on my map approximately 8 blocks away. Fortunately it was all down hill- an omen. I had already learned that driving in Portland is a frigging nightmare - so I walked. You have to understand that where I live one drives across the road to visit a neighbor. A pedestrian in Texas is assumed to be either destitute or having car trouble. No problem - I can adapt. I got to the Marriott and the place was full of "barber shop quartet" members. I broke down and asked the Bellman for directions to the HKIS reunion - he had no clue - so he called the other Marriott-they had no clue. My anxiety level was high. No problem! I thought I would walk back to the hotel-take a nap and find the Chinese Garden tonight. Which I did.

Got to the Garden early, as people who have nothing going on are apt to do. Parking was available. I have been to the original Suzhou Gardens many times, I made the mistake of opining to the docent that Portland's was much nicer than the original - her reply was "it is newer" The place started to fill up with beefy beer swilling Lutherans--former faculty. I didn't recognize any of them.

My real objective in this trip was to see an old friend whom I knew would be one of a cluster of three sisters. All of the groupings I saw I had to eliminate, for one reason or another, and I was very uncomfortable trying to read name tags - I have to squint (need to update the bifocals.) As I walked around the Gardens for the umpteenth time, I discovered a small group of women...smoking in a corner, finally some one to talk to. We were joined by other people and I was finally able to establish some links.

Feeling somewhat better I left. I got back to my hotel-no parking-desk clerk is now deep into a 48 hour shift-he told me to park in the driveway and leave the keys with him-which I did. I reviewed my materials again and decided there must be a third Marriott - one that was not on the freaking map!!!

The next morning (Friday), I went out in search of the Marriott Residence Inn. The only glitch was waking up the desk clerk for my keys. After many attempts I found the place-went to the hospitality room-no body there. Logged myself in got my shirt, bag, and name tag. Feeling much better, I went to the desk and located my friend. Of course we hadn't seen each other in 30 years - so I made a point of telling her exactly where I was sitting and what color shirt I was wearing. Things were much better now.

Walked to the Willamette River and got on the boat-cruise which was nice. Developed more and more contacts. Greg Harvey is a couple of years younger than me, his brother Tim, and I were pretty good friends; our parents were missionaries-from competing sects but we were all Texan's, so during the summer when we all went to Laan Tau mountain camp, religious differences were put aside in order for the parents to play dominoes. Greg comes up to me we chat-he apologies-thirty plus years ago he had complained to my dad and his that his brother and me were being mean to him. He knew we had both gotten into trouble over this-frankly I had no recollection. I told him no hard feelings. But...for the rest of the trip whenever I saw someone I knew, I thought "what horrible thing did I do to them all those years ago?"

The rest of the stay was great – the animosity I was feeling for academics in general, and for the poor quality of the map – not mentioning THREE Marriotts – disappeared. Fortunately in one of Dave's letters he had mentioned that reunions can be stressful for people coming alone this was a comfort to me. The dinner at the Fong Chong was great- I won a prize for being the first one present to arrive in HK by boat – the APL President Wilson-1962. Fellowship was great! MY class – 1973 - was heavily represented (5). Left the next day feeling very positive about the whole thing. Of course getting to the Airport and finding the correct exit was a challenge. Bottom line: It was a great experience

Mark B McIntosh '73

•Imperfections---

An elderly Chinese woman had two large pots, each hung on the ends of a pole, which she carried across her neck.

One of the pots had a crack in it while the other pot was perfect and always delivered a full portion of water.

At the end of the long walks from the stream to the house, the cracked pot arrived only half full.

For a full two years this went on daily, with the woman bringing home only one and a half pots of water.

Of course, the perfect pot was proud of its accomplishments.

But the poor cracked pot was ashamed of its own imperfection, and miserable that it could only do half of what it had been made to do.

After two years of what it perceived to be bitter failure, it spoke to the woman one day by the stream

"I am ashamed of myself, because this crack in my side causes water to leak out all the way back to your house."

The old woman smiled, "Did you notice that there are flowers on your side of the path, but not on the other pot's side?"

"That's because I have always known about your flaw, so I planted flower seeds on your side of the path, and every day while we walk back, you water them."

"For two years I have been able to pick these beautiful flowers to decorate the table.

Without you being just the way you are, there would not be this beauty to grace the house."

Each of us has our own unique flaw. But it's the cracks and flaws we each have that make our lives together so very interesting and rewarding.

You've just got to take each person for what they are and look for the good in them.

SO, to all of my crackpot friends, have a great day and remember to smell the flowers on your side of the path!

anonymous, submitted by Eric Lee '75

206

Epilogue

Random Hong Kong Memories

Here is a poem about Hong Kong
A place I moved to when I was eleven
Wearing a scratchy wool kilt and white gloves
Dressed up for the airplane ride from Sweden to Hong Kong

It was 1971, and people still believed in proper attire
The sixties hadn't reached us yet.
In steamy Bangkok, my father left his hat,
A gentleman's fedora,
On the transit bus, and for all I know, it's still riding around on that sticky seat.
Men don't wear those hats anymore, that was the last one I ever saw

It was the end of an era
Everything changed
And never stopped changing….
When we descended to Kai Tak
I thought we might crash into people hanging their laundry on the rooftops
Just a few feet below
But we landed and
We rode the ferry over choppy grey water
My ears adjusting to the loud radios and people arguing
And Cantonese opera,
And to that flowers and garbage smell
Of Fragrant Harbor

We were all beyond tired when we wound our way
On that sick-makingly steep
green hillside road
to the Repulse Bay Hotel, set back on its colonial lawn
a 150 year old tortoise in its little pool
good luck (except for the tortoise)

A place out of Somerset Maugham novel,
Although I did not know that yet -
The way the ceiling fans rotated on the verandah
And the white-suited waiters brought drinks
While we lived a life of total privilege and boredom,
My sister Anna and I hid Karl, then 3,
Under a rattan table in the bar
Where he played Loud Scary Tiger until the patrons protested
I saw the waiters laughing behind their hands.

We stayed there for four months
What were we, rich?

Yes/No- just expats on a company card.
Even room service – ice cream in silver dishes - got old
The tall-ceilinged room I shared with Anna
Became a badminton court

I took the bus to the Island School,
That former military hospital halfway up the peak
Where I was in Da Vinci house, and the girl selected
to show me around on my first day
grinned and asked, "Do ya want to smoke in the loo?" And
Left me standing, an innocent fool

I felt so much younger than everyone; because I was.
It was there I whispered in French class and was made to stand
With my nose pressed against the chalkboard, trying not to sneeze
And my first friend, Marie, invited me to sleep over at her house
On an island – Hei Ling Chau? - where her father was the minister
Of the leper colony, and Marie pressed wildflowers and tolerated marmite,
That revolting brown stuff I would not eat on sandwiches.

Just when I got used to Island School
I transferred to HKIS: grade 7 with Mr. Anchor
Who had a soft voice and read us Flowers for Algernon
By then we lived way out in Tai Tam,
In Turtle Cove, where there is now a campus
But at the time, not much
Beyond our connected villas and the tall apartments

On the top of lonely Red Hill Rd.,
The next mountain over had the profile
Of a sleeping lady
I remember when the gardener slit open the snake he caught
And ate a steaming little bladder as we kids watched
Making sure we knew it was for men only
And that he would become very virile
All this we understood by sign language
Since my Chinese friends spoke English, and
I didn't know much Cantonese
Except for counting and swearing
And how to pay the pak pai.

Wild dogs were a problem, I walked my own dog with a baseball bat
She was a crazy half chow
Whom I saved from being dinner on the beach
while my parents were in
Peking, as it was called,
Which reminds me of the day when Chairman Mao died.
I was watching television. I think there was a typhoon.
It was 1976.

By then I was in high school and had one foot out the door
that revolving door of home leave and new postings:

everyone always coming and going
And sometimes coming back again.
But mostly not.

That was over thirty years ago,
Still, everything from back then is so vivid-
How it was such freedom to hike those hills,
With my dog Krissie
and Kim and Kelly and their Lucky and Kasey
That yin/yang pair: one an old stray with a mean streak,
The other a pedigreed miniature collie

We would stumble upon ancient graves,
Fresh hell money blowing in the breeze,
Then never find them again. Ever
Even though we tried.

All the colors come back to me-
The way the pale blue HKIS girls' summer uniforms were so perfect
For swimming (during a bomb scare, or when we just decided that
Lunch at the Drift Inn would be better than in the cafeteria)
The thin material was starched with salt as we sang in chorus,
But we were dry and cold in the air-conditioning,
Having just been so very hot on our run up the hill
Back to campus

And the strange places I ate lunch, like, for example
Under the stairs by the old kindergarten (works best with boyfriend)
Or up the hill, where old ladies would sweep the mountain,
And there were snakes;
Linda and I could see her dad (some kind of herpetologist)
Trying to catch them, but we hid from him

Since we were 17 and drinking Mateuse from a bottle
Celebrating our recent trip to Macao, with its black sands
And good Portuguese bread.
We would talk about everything, our futures, mostly
Although I, rather shy, probably left out my recent adventures
Making out at the Stanley Prison Club with my true love,
Where the searchlight caught us, two gweilo kids kissing,
Then swept away again
We weren't what they were looking for,

And, somehow, thinking back on all this,
The entirety of years becomes illuminated,
And I am now the prison guard,
Stopping at each memory, for a long look,

Then moving on.

Charlotte Agell, '77
Brunswick, Maine/March 2007

Acknowledgments

This book came together in a very short period of time - 12 weeks from inception to binding. It's been a fun and crazy ride, and it would not have reached completion without the help of some very significant people.

In the first instance, this work is the writings of nearly 200 contributors. Alumni have been writing to each other with stories old and new through the Dragontrain e-group since 1999. When I got the idea for this book, I contacted them, and tried to use the network of former teachers and students to reach as many as possible. Scores of people that I wish could have been contacted are "lost." Many wrote a time or two, several have been generous in their time and observations; many have been patient with my prodding to develop their tales. You know who they are by glancing at the Index...the majority of page numbers refer to authorship.

This work is produced independently of Hong Kong International School, its current administration, staff, or students. For any errors in concept or detail, I accept full accountability.

I have taken the liberty to dissect and categorize many writings. Hopefully I have not done them a disservice in hacking their work up like a Stanley chicken. I also have tried to walk a thin line between "fixing" others' writings without taking away their "voice." The only modifications I have made have been to keep similar tenses, correct spelling of names if possible, and combine similar or related writings.

What a pleasure it is for a one-time classroom teacher to hear from so many alumni, and to see not only their appreciation for HKIS, but to realize what fine writers some of these people are. I expect to see some of them putting out their own books...they have stories to tell and a gift of wordsmithery. If you will check in the appendix of suggested readings, you will see a few of them have indeed authored their own works.

Over the past two months, interviews with historically significant people in the history of HKIS have been "moments of discovery" for me. Mel Kieschnick, Bob Christian, Len Galster, and Earl Westrick have given generously of their time, memorabilia, and memories. They are treasure chests of HKIS trivia.

My grateful thanks to Lois Voeltz, who plodded through about 4000 archived Dragontrain messages to select the bulk from which I selected the final entries. She also gave four days of her time to help edit and arrange and generally advise on the book. My other long-time pang yau is Bruce Richards, who worked in Hong Kong for the "other" Lutheran ten years before I arrived. His editing and counsel, and shared laughter, has been essential. And for the patience and guidance of Suzanne Deakins, the publisher, I am grateful. She, too, has lived In China, and brought several other perspectives into the work. Fang has been ever faithful.

E-support has meant encouragement when I wasn't sure this whole thing was a good idea. Inspired writing by Charlotte Agell, Brad Doyle, Ken Koo, Eric Lee, Jill Liddiard, and Mark McIntosh, and Bar Schwerdtmann not to mention a lot of banter with Kelvin Limm, energized me at the right times.

Regarding the photographs.... shortage of production time has meant a couple omissions regarding the pictures. Hopefully the lack of captions has been more of a stimulation than a frustration. This writer knew HKIS people for just 7 of the years covered. Rather than mistakenly identify faces, I/we have chosen to leave them blank, the same with historical events, and geographic locations.

Secondly, photo credits are not given for individual photographs. However, the great bulk of the photos were taken and provided by Bob Christian, Dave Christian, John Morris, Patrick Pang, Jason Weber, Earl Westrick, and myself. Additional significant donors include Joan Amy, Sue Arneson, Julia and Sheila Baker, Tracy Birnie, Jerry Cashman, Nand Harjani, Kathy Isaacs, Margaret and Elizabeth Keenan, Jill and Wendy Liddiard, Kelvin Limm, Eric Mache', Chris and Megan O'Keefe, Amat Tajudin, and Tim Tyler. I cannot thank these people enough. Not only did their donations provide the visual material to enhance in the book, the images have helped solve several historical mysteries.

Archival material was generously loaned to me by Eric Mache' and Bob Christian, who must have a file and diary for every project he has ever launched (which are legion). However, the treasure trove was provided by Barbara Schwerdtmann, whose sainted mom, Betty, threw nothing away.... thankfully... providing student directories, school newsletters, memorabilia, photos, and artifacts.

This type of activity is a work in progress. Would you like to participate in a Volume Two of this project? If you are an alumni of HKIS, or lived and worked in Hong Kong during the later third of the 20th century, I would welcome your contact, and input. There are so many more stories to tell, and so many pieces to put together; that I know another volume could be produced.

Contact me and send me your stories at chinadave@comcast.com or through the publisher at publisher@spiritpress.org

Copies of this book are available thru HKIS Alumni Director, 1 Red Hill Road, Tai Tam Hong Kong SAR or from the publisher Wisdom Hall, PO 12346, Portland, Oregon 97068 USA. Inquiries and donations of historical material may be made to the same addresses.

The story goes on...

In humble appreciation,
Dave Kohl

Appendix: Suggested Reading

If you haven't read enough, or this book has energized your interest in Hong Kong, there are several books that alumni have recommended, or in some cases, written, that may be of interest. * Marks authors with HKIS in their past

Agell, Charolotte, *The Sailor's Book*, Firefly Press, 1991
This was my first book. It begins "The sun is a dragon's eye" and was directly inspired by sailing in Hong Kong (as well as in Sweden). The mountains in this picture book pitch right into the sea, just as they do in the South China Sea. The_book is now out of print, although apparently available here and there on the web.   Charlotte Agell '77

Alcorn, Randy, *Safely Home,*Tyndale, 2001
Set in modern Shanghai, this novel is a gripping tale of the lives of Christians and home churches in recent China. It is an unabashed statement of sincere Christian faith and determination in the face of official discrimination. Very graphic in its revelation of persecution techniques. And the description of living conditions of the disaffected are haunting.   Dave Kohl, '73 - '80

Allen, W. H., *This is Hong Kong*, Miroslav Sasek, 1965
If you can find this book and/or have kids/grandkids, grab it. We read it to Adam from age 1 to 3. Definately dated and very Colonial, but ohhh so full of memories. Illustrated with watercolour paintings of Tiger Balm Gardens, Queens Road East, school kids carrying Pan Am and BOAC flight bags, and still has the Tai Pak floating restaurant in Castle Peak!   *Dave Kohl '73 - '80*

Berkeley, Jon, *Chopsticks*, Oxford University Press, 2005
If you don't fall in love with this little paperback kids book, you have no heart. "Chopsticks" is a mouse who lives on the Jumbo, and befriends one of the carved dragons at the main entrance after hours. Their adventures are tied in with an old wood-carver who lives among the sampans of Ap Lei Chau. The illustrations are BEAUTIFULL   Dave Kohl '73 - '80

Blonder, Ellen, & Low, Annabel, *Every Grain of Rice*, Potter 1998
This is a cookbook, an account of the author's growing up Chinese in America, with 120 recipes and charming illustrations. My daughter recently gave me this book, and each recipe is laced with memories and accompanied with a small story   Liz Jackson '72

Booth, Martin, *Golden Boy, St Martin's Press* published in HK as Gweilo Bantam, 2004
This is a first hand account by a 7-year old Brit who sails to HK with his parents on Government service in 1952. He lives in a Kowloon Hotel on Waterloo road and sneaks off to explore Kowloon Tong, Tsim Sha Tsui, Mongkok and Kowloon walled city and has adventures similiar to what some on you found yet in the '60s and '70s in the back alleys and ladder streets. I recommend the book....its a good read.   Dave Kohl, art teacher '73-'80

Chan, Nien, *Life and Death in Shanghai*
Life and Death in Shanghai" This book takes The Joy Luck Club and Wild
Swans to an even deeper, more emotional place. Nien chronicles her life in
Shanghai during the Cultural Revolution, which is the exact years that I lived in HK (1965-1974).
As I read about the destruction, imprisonment, torture and death taking place in Shanghai, I recollected how I had playfully collected Mao posters, wore Mao buttons on the inside of my blazer and coveted a Mao hat with red star that I got for Xmas. I had no "idea" what was happening in China, even though dead bodies washed down rivers in the New Territories, I interviewed a 16 year old girl hired at my father's GE plant in Kowloon who had swam for three days from China and curfews kept us off the streets after 8pm. Mao shattered millions of lives. I am honestly ashamed.
    Read the book and see what you think.   Carolyn Cole '73

Carew, Tim, *The Fall of Hong Kong*, Anthony Blond Ltd, 1960

This is a full account of the fall of Hong Kong to the invading Japanese forces from Dec 8 to Christmas Day, 1941. For once, you can read a detailed history of an important event, and recognize just about every landmark, road, and locale. And, the final engagements were in Repulse Bay

Dave Kohl '73 - '80

*Carroll, John M, *Edge of Empires: Chinese Elites and British Colonials in Hong Kong* (Harvard University Press, 2005; Hong Kong University Press, 2007)

In an engaging, revisionist study, John (HKIS '80) argues that in the century after the Opium War, Hong Kong's colonial nature helped create a local Chinese business elite. By the end of the nineteenth century, the colonial government saw Chinese businessmen as allies in establishing Hong Kong as a commercial center. The idea of a commercially vibrant China united them. Chinese and British leaders cooperated on issues of mutual concern, such as the expansion of capitalism and political and economic directions for an ailing China. At the same time, by contributing to Imperial war funds, organizing ceremonies for visiting British royalty, and attending Imperial trade exhibitions, the Chinese helped make Hong Kong an active member of the global British Empire. Hong Kong sits squarely within the framework of both Chinese and British colonial history, while exploring larger questions about the meaning and implications of colonialism in modern history. abridged by Dave Kohl '73 - '80

*Carroll, John M, *A Concise History of Hong Kong* (Rowman and Littlefield/Hong Kong University Press, 2007).

Cheng, Irene, Clara Ho Tung: *A Hong Kong Lady, Her Family and Her Times*, Chinese University Press 1976; re-issued by University of Hong Kong

The title speaks for itself. Find out about the great-grandmother of your Hotung and Ketterer classmates. Explains the clan all the way back to Clara's husband, Sir Robert, the noteworthy philanthropist. Patrick Hotung also recommends Dynasty, by Robert Elegant, which is the most true-to-facts telling of his family history. Dave Kohl '73 - '80

Choy, Rita Mei-Wah, *Read and Write Chinese*, China West Books, 1990

Choy, Rita Mei-Wah, Understanding Chinese, China West Books, 1989

These are two good books, which cover both Mandarin and Cantonese, plus she devotes eight pages to food terms, which should go over well with anyone from HKIS.

Mark Shostrom '74

Clavell, James, *Noble House*, 1981

As many of us did it seems, I read "Noble House" too, shortly after moving to California. Even reading about the typhoons made me homesick. It happens in 1963. Mark Shostrom '74

Clavell, James, *Tai-Pan*, 1966

Set in 1841, this is Clavell's detailed telling of the founding of Hong Kong, with historical figures thinly disguised as his main characters. This is such an important read for anyone wanting to understand historic Hong Kong, and the traditions that have been handed down for generations: Local Chinese families; Compradors acting as go-betweens and agents; European colonialists from several home countries; Eurasian generations; even a funny old painter. So many historic locations are explained, including Tai Tam, the pirate's lair. I know this to be true, as I found several clay opium cooking vials while exploring the beach across from the new school in 1997, thanks to Jerry Marken and Lois Voeltz.

Dave Kohl '73 - '80

Fritz, Jean, *Homesick*, Yearling Books, 1984

Children's author Jean Fritz came from parents who were YMCA missionaries in Shanghai earlier this century. Homesick - My Own Story tells about her first 11 years in Shanghai in the British school, longing to be in America where she could be 100% American, and her dismay at getting to America finding she wasn't 100% American. It's an excellent book. My copy is in the Philippines, so I can't give you detailed information on publisher, etc.   Diane Anderson '69

Gaan, Margaret, *Last Moments of a World*, Norton, 1978

This is the true story of a Eurasian family living thru the turmoil in Colonial China from 1927 to 1950. I found myself fascinated with the story and details, especially since there were several families at HKIS who had a similar experience - living the good life in pre-war China; watching their world crumble with Japanese, Nationalist, and Communist turmoil; spending the war years under house arrest, in a POW camp, or abroad; and returning to pick up the pieces.

*Galster, Lenard, *Good News About Jesus*, www.goodnewsaboutjesus.com

This work is Rev/. Galster's condensation and presentation in understandable language about Christ and what His message is and means to everyone. Galster was the pastor instrumental in organizing what became HKIS and Church of All Nations. This work has been translated into some 30 languages and is easily available singly or in quantity.   Dave Kohl '73 - '80

Gittins, Jean, *Eastern Windows - Western Skies*, South China Morning Post, 1969

This is an account of the descendants of Sir Robert Hotung, written by the aunt of several HKIS students. This is one of those books you read because you've been there and want to know more about the little details of life in old Hong Kong, in this case before, during, and after the Japanese occupation.

And the photo on the dust jacket is the house (now demolished) at 8 Seymour Road where several HKIS students grew up.   Dave Kohl '73 - '80

Greenway, Alice, *White Ghost Girls*, Grove Press, Black Cat, 2006

I read the book this summer and it's wonderful. But the world the author describes wasn't quite as familiar as I expected. I'm not sure if this was because it focused so intensely on what was going on in the head of the main character or because I'm getting old and can't remember things as well as I used to! White Ghost girls is definitely fiction but filled with memories very real to me. A review in the HK Standard talked more about Alice Greenway but mostly she is hard to trace. She was in HK at HKIS only two years, and described herself as withdrawn and uninvolved. Anyway, happy reading....   Linda Lierheimer '77

Han Suyin, *A Many Splendored Thing*, Penguin 1961_Upon my return to HK in search of a job in 1978-I read the classic novel set there: Han Suyin's "A Many Splendored Thing." For those of you who haven't read this well known love story yet, it's brilliant -- full of depth and insight into the meshing of Asian and Western thought and culture -- set against the backdrop of HK's flood of refugees in the early 1950s. The neat part about reading it in HK was that sometimes I could read a chapter set in a certain locale, then get on a bus and finish reading the chapter in the place it was set in!   Mark Shostrom '74

*Hayes, Constance, *The Real Thing - Truth and Power at the Coca-Cola Company*, Random House 2004

This book is written by HKIS' own Connie Laibe, '79, who wrote for the New York Times. She starts: "Coca-Cola began simply, as so many things do. Filled with sparkle and democratically priced, it was as American as baseball, as accessible as jazz. It cost a nickel, which almost anyone could afford. Before long, it was everywhere...   Dave Kohl '73 - '80

Holdsworth, May, *Foreign Devils - Expatriates in Hong Kong,* Oxford, 2002

This work focuses primarily on the British community of Hong Kong, with all of their uniqueness. She minces few words honestly discussing topics such as early discrimination against Chinese and Eurasian families, using the Hotung clan as an example. Imagine my surprise on page 243...there's a drawing of the Tai Tam campus, and a good two-page write-up on the school. "If one wants one's child to slot back into the US Curriculum on return, there is the Hong Kong International School (HKIS). Arguably no school in Hong Kong is as well appointed and equipped. HKIS's 2500 pupils, ranging from the very youngest in reception class to the pre-university 12th graders taught on two campuses tucked between the hills and the sea on the southern shore of Hong Kong island." There is also reference to David Pollack's Third Culture Kid. Dave Kohl '73 - '80

Keay, John, *Last Post - The End of Empire in the Far East*, Murray, 1997

Last Post is the British equivalent of "Taps," sounding the end of a life or era. Keay traces an academic but emotional narrative of the final years of British rule in Asia - from 1940 when half of the world's population was under British flag to 1997 and the lowering of the Union Jack on June 30. So much familiar material to anyone who lived or traveled anywhere in the "Raj" - India, Australia, Malaya, and the Fragrant Harbour. Dave Kohl '73 - '80

*Kohl, David, *Overseas Chinese Architecture*, Wisdom Hall, 2008
 A reissue of Chinese Architecture in the Straits Settlements, Heinemann, KL 1984

OK, so I have to toot my own horn a bit. This was my master's thesis at HKU in 1978. A rep from Heinemann was also one of the people in this first MA in Asian Studies course at HKU. They ran 3000 copies, and it got me enough recognition that I was invited to speak at a Preservation conference in Malaysia in 1986. Now out of print, we are re-issuing it with a new introduction and title. My own travels since I wrote the book, plus my work ion Portland at the Chinese Classical Garden have convinced me that I have identified patterns that apply to the overseas Chinese built environment, whether in California, Australia, or Southeast Asia. Dave Kohl '73 - '80

Lawrence, Anthony, *The Fragrant Chinese*, Chinese University Press, 1993

You'll be nodding your head in agreement with Lawrence's observations, and the color photos are definitely early '90s Hong Kong, in full color. Worth buying on remainder.

Dave Kohl '73 - '80

*Mache', Eric, and Clark, Bill. *The Paper Ark*, Everest House, 1979

You should recognize the Mache' name. Eric ('68) has illustrated several books, this is the finest, I think. It is a thorough look at the wild life of the Holy Land, with a detailed text. Illustrations are line drawings in the style of etching. Beautiful work, in the tradition of Albrecht Durer and Leonardo. I suspect it is out of print, but I found a beautiful copy second hand. Eric has also produced several cover designs for books, some by Nancy Zi (mother of Vincent and Violette Li) on the art of breathing, for singers and others. Dave Kohl '73 - '80

Lindsay, Oliver, *The Lasting Honor - The Fall of Hong Kong 1941*, Hamish Hamilton, 1978

In this work on the Fall, the author looks at factors beyond just the Colony itself. Written while many of us were in Hong Kong, the author was able to interview several survivors and defenders, both Chinese and European. He also brings into the work a great deal of research from Britain and Canada, whose troops had been in Hong Kong less than a month when the Japanese Invasion began. Gives another perspective on a traumatic time. Dave Kohl '73 - '80

Mitchell, David, *A Boy's War*, OMF Publishers.

 This book tells about David's experience as a young boy at the Chefoo School just before and during the Japanese internment. It includes the time at the Weihsien Internment Camp in Shantung where Eric Liddell of "Chariots of Fire" was also interned and died, and tells quite a bit about him. I really enjoyed the book because it included pictures of the Chefoo School where my grandfather attended until around 1912. The last part of the book tells about David's months in HK waiting for transportation to Australia to rejoin his parents. In HK he was at the Army Camp on Argyle St., right across from King George V School. David Michell survived the war, and on Christmas Eve 1997 was killed by a drunk driver in Toronto.   Diane Anderson '69

Morris, Jan (James), *Hong Kong*, Vintage Books/Random House, 1985The descriptions are quite vivid and rang true. There's a blurb by Paul Theroux on the front -- "A wonderfully enlightened portrait -- intelligent, insightful, lucid, up to the minute, and elegantly written."   Sheila Baker '82

Mason, Richard, *The World of Suzie Wong, 1959*. Not to be missed either is **Richard Mason's** *The World of Suzie Won*g. Don't be put off by your preconceived notions -- this book is really well done with characters you'll love, and it captures the true flavours of HK and the people.   Mark Shostrom '74

Parker, Dave *A Brush with Hong Kong*, Odyssey, 1990This is just one beautifully painted and fun book, with lots of familiar scenes, illustrated with pen, ink, and watercolor in a large format book. Delightful subtle local humor most understood by someone who has lived ion Hong Kong. A fun book for kids and adults. Really good.   Dave Kohl '73 - '80

A Brush with Hong Kong by Dave Parker is rather lovely and on my shelf...all drawings and they really do capture it!   C h a r l o t t e Agell '79

Pollock, David, and VanReken, Ruth, *Third Culture Kids*, Intercultural Press, 1999This is THE book that explains who you are, and why...at least in connection with your overseas living experience. So many people have found this book an eye-opener...anyone who has read it will recommend it.
                                                                                                        Dave Kohl, '73 - '80

Proulx, Ben, *Underground from Hongkong*, Dutton, 1943
    If you can find a copy of this wartime account of the battle for the Repulse Bay Hotel, snap it up. This British fellow gives a moment-by-moment first person account from his first sighting of Japanese planes over Happy Valley to his internment at Stanley Fort. Written during the war, amazing. So many familiar places and scenes, and we were there 25 years later.
                                                                                                        Dave Kohl '73 - '80

Snow, Philip *The Fall of Hong Kong: Britain, China, and the Japanese Occupation* (Yale University Press, 2003).   John Carroll, '80

Tan, Amy, *The Joy Luck Club*"
    Joy Luck Club and The Kitchen God's Wife are the only books by Amy Tan that I've read, but I really enjoyed them. Joy Luck was also made into a pretty decent movie, the first American movie to have an entirely Asian starring cast. Generally, they are about White Swans.   Deborah Smith '80

Thoreaux, Paul, *Kowloon Tong*, Houghton Mifflin, 1997
    I've been a fan of Paul Thoreaux's railway books, but this is a novel, based on fictitious but very real circumstances during the Chinese "Take-away" of Hong Kong. Big money, influences from across the Shum Chun, disappearing working girls from sweatshops, and a lot of insight into our lives and times on the edge of China. A good quick read.   Dave Kohl '73 - '80
    When I read his *Kowloon Tong* I found mistakes/inaccuracies and I was very annoyed at both him and his editor.   Sheila Baker '82

Steve Tsang, *A Modern History of Hong Kong* (Tauris/Hong Kong University Press, 2004)   r e c -
ommended by   John Carroll '80

Woodcock, George, *The British in the Far East* - A Social History, Atheneum, 1969
I love this book, because it traces more of the life and times in the British Empire, rather than military
conquests and governmental decrees. The author talks about what life was like for expats and local
Asians, domestic issues, explorers, merchants, householders, missionaries, and the like. And the photographs alone are worth the price of acquisition.   Dave Kohl '73 - '80

Wright-Nooth, George, *Prisoner of the Turnip Heads*, Casell, 1994
Read this book after you have digested the works of Proulx and Carew, because this is not about the fall
of Hong Kong, but about life in Stanley prison from Feb 1942 to August 30, 1945. The author kept a
secret diary while interred by the conquering Turnip Heads (Law Pak Tau) that is the translation of the
Cantonese name for the occupation forces. Would be very instructive to compare Clavell's King Rat,
written about the similar situation in Singapore.   Dave Kohl '73 - '80

DRAGON TAELS

Index

To the best of our knowledge, the graduating years for alumni are in ('), even if they did not finish at HKIS. Teachers have their years of service given, however, records are incomplete, so there are several empty (-), which indicate this person was staff, but we have incomplete information. Corrections and compliments can be addressed to Dave Kohl, PO Box 12346, Portland, OR 97212 USA

INDEX

colophon

This Book is set in Palatino 11 Pt
Headlines are set in Inburrow, 24, 30 and 36 Pt
Composed in QuarkXpress 7.1
Printed on 80# Matte Text
Printed by Bang Printing
Book Layout by Suzanne Deakins
Picture Layout by David Kohl
Cover Design by Ethan A. Firpo

Cover Photographs by Kevin Kwok and David Kohl